THE SEARCH FOR
THE NORTH WEST PASSAGE

The Search for the
North West Passage

Ann Savours

St. Martin's Press
New York

FRONTISPIECE: Vessels sent to search for the *Erebus* and *Terror* (commanded by Sir John Franklin) from the Atlantic end of the North West Passage, anchored in what was then called Union Bay, near Beechey Island, 1850 (NMM, PY 0070)

St. Martin's Press, Scholarly and Reference Division,
175 Fifth Avenue, New York, N.Y. 10010

First published in the United States of America in 1999

Printed in Great Britain

ISBN: 0-312-22372-2

Library of Congress Cataloging-in-Publication Data

Savours, Ann.
    The search for the North West Passage / Ann Savours.
        p.   cm.
    Includes bibliographical references and index.
    ISBN 0-312-22372-2
    1. Northwest Passage.   I. Title.
  G640.S38   1999
  910'.0916326—dc21   99–22261
                                                                         CIP

Contents

Prelude

What is the North West Passage?

It is the name for the sea route linking the North Atlantic Ocean with the North Pacific Ocean. It extends from Baffin Bay (between West Greenland and Baffin Island) to Bering Strait (between Alaska and Siberia), through the Canadian Arctic archipelago. In the sixteenth and seventeenth centuries it was sought as a way to get round America to reach the riches of China and the Far East. By the beginning of the nineteenth century the search had become in part a geographical challenge, to understand and map the wide blank spaces in the Arctic regions of North America; a commercial route was no longer of great significance. At the end of the Napoleonic Wars in 1815, the Admiralty had a huge navy on its hands and, until the outbreak of the Crimean War in 1853, no major wars to fight. Sir John Barrow, its Second Secretary, persuaded that body to dispatch a series of British naval expeditions, culminating in Franklin's tragic voyage which sailed from England in 1845. With his belief in the open polar sea, Barrow was confident that a northern sea route to the Pacific could be found. By then, national ambition, itself a reflection of British imperial pride, was a significant motivator. At the end of the century we see more personal, or individual, ambition inspiring expeditions to both the Arctic and the Antarctic. Scott, Shackleton, Nansen, Mawson, Peary and Amundsen were central figures and it was the latter who first navigated the North West Passage in 1906.

Why did it take centuries to discover?

The short answer is the presence of ice, as well as the intricate geography of the archipelago. It has often been said that 'Ice is where you find it', meaning that changes of wind direction and tides can bring the floes flooding round a ship, or can pack the ice off the coast or can make a channel impassable. The Arctic sea freezes in winter, first of all becoming like a very thick grey soup, from which elegant 'pancakes', looking more like waterlillies, are formed. The pancakes coalesce to form young ice which is sometimes thickened by 'rafting' – the layers being piled on top of each other by pressure. Compression of first-year or older sea ice leads to the formation of hummocks and ridges, which in extreme cases may reach forty feet in height. They can be very menacing to a vessel, which is 'beset' or 'nipped' in the sea ice, unable to move, sometimes carried by winds and currents in any direction. Much of the sea ice formed in this way melts and breaks up in July, August and September, thus creating the short navigation season. However, what is or was called 'multi-year ice', 'polar ice', or even 'palaeocrystic ice' is formed in the central polar basin of the Arctic Ocean. It is far more formidable than the year-old ice. Often blue in colour it can be encountered along the north coast of Alaska and the western Canadian Arctic, off the west coasts of Banks Island and Prince Patrick Island, in M'Clure Strait, M'Clintock Channel and Victoria Strait.

Explorers' ships

It is obvious that a powerful modern icebreaker can work in icy seas that were impenetrable to the wooden sailing vessels of Frobisher, Parry and Franklin from the time of Queen Elizabeth I to Queen Victoria's reign. The addition of steam engines in the mid-nineteenth century was a step in the right direction. It is surprising at first sight that two small vessels, *Gjøa* and *St Roch*, made the first successful transits in the twentieth century. However, smaller ships are able to take advantage of what are known as 'shore leads', narrow stretches of open water between the pack ice and the shore. Both had effective motor engines running on diesel rather than the cumbersome combination of coal and steam. It has also been observed that the climate in the late 1500s and in the 1840s and 1850s was colder than at other periods.

Names and place-names

I have on the whole referred to the Inuit, the people of the polar north, as Eskimos, partly because to many readers this name will be more familiar and partly because the Inuit were largely known to the outside world in the nineteenth century as Esquimaux, and earlier in the twentieth as Eskimos. I hope that it will be obvious to any Inuk reading this history, that in so doing, no offence is intended. 'Polar pundits' may feel that I have been rather cavalier in my treatment of place-names; generally speaking, where a name is still recognisable today, I have kept to its older form, as being more sympathetic to the narrative.

Acknowledgements

Working first at the Scott Polar Research Institute, Cambridge, and later at the National Maritime Museum, Greenwich, I could not fail to become interested in the centuries-long search for the North West Passage. In fact, Dr Basil Greenhill, Director of the NMM during many of my years there in the 1970s and 1980s' encouraged me to write a book based on the museum's collections. However, other research intervened, and I was also daunted at the prospect of covering so many centuries, not being at all familiar with the earlier voyages. This was to be remedied by close association during the past few years with Professor David Beers Quinn and other members of 'ARTAF', the Archival Research Task Force (UK) of the Meta Incognita Project in Canada, which was concerned with Frobisher's Arctic voyages of the 1570s. The main stimulus for the present book came from the late Barry Ranford, a Canadian schoolteacher and photographer. He had become enthralled with the story of Franklin's lost expedition of 1845 to 1848 and had told me of his visits to King William Island and the discovery of skulls and bones on a small island in Erebus Bay. Seated with a map at the kitchen table, he showed me where he had been and what he intended to do next, in co-operation with Canadian colleagues. After his third expedition, he was signed up by McClelland and Stewart, of Toronto, to write a book for which I agreed to write the historical introduction. I had nearly completed those chapters, when news came of his death in tragic circumstances. Sadly, Barry's own writing had not progressed far enough for the publication to continue, so that McClelland and Stewart abandoned it. Having spent time and effort on my contribution, I was reluctant to follow suit. My former colleague at the National Maritime Museum, Dr Pieter van der Merwe, came to the rescue and contacted Chatham Publishing with the present happy result. My regret is naturally that only so much can be squeezed into a book of this size and deciding what to omit has caused me some anguish.

I am most grateful to two colleagues in Kent, Professor Glyndwr Williams and Dr G Hattersley-Smith for reading the whole draft; likewise to Professor Quinn for commenting on the earlier chapters. Dr Charles Swithinbank supplied the photograph of the Manhattan and has cast an eagle eye over certain sections, while Mrs Shirlee-Anne Smith did the same for Dease and Simpson. Needless to say, any errors of omission or commission rest on my shoulders alone.

It has been a pleasure to work in the library of the Royal Geographical Society, in the British Library, the Scott Polar Research Institute and at the National Maritime Museum, whose staffs I thank warmly. I must thank in particular Mrs Karen MacLellan, who has typed and amended the whole draft over many months, indeed years. Thanks are due to John Maggs, Mrs Audrey Roche and Miss Ann Parry, also to Mr George Hobson for information on fossil forests and to Anne Keenleyside and Margaret Bertulli for copies of their papers relating to the Ranford site on King William Island. Spencer Scott and other staff of the Templeman Library, University of Kent at Canterbury, have always been helpful, as have the staff of Priors Bridge. Encouragement has come from a number of individuals, among whom are my long-suffering husband and my grandson Sam.

Envoi

Perhaps these few last lines can send this book on its way:

> Ah, for just one time I would take the North West Passage
> To find the hand of Franklin reaching for the Beaufort Sea
> Tracing one warm line through a land so wide and savage
> And make a north west passage to the sea
> *Seafarer's song, provenance unknown to me*

ANN SAVOURS
Little Bridge Place, Kent, May 1999

The Polar Seas

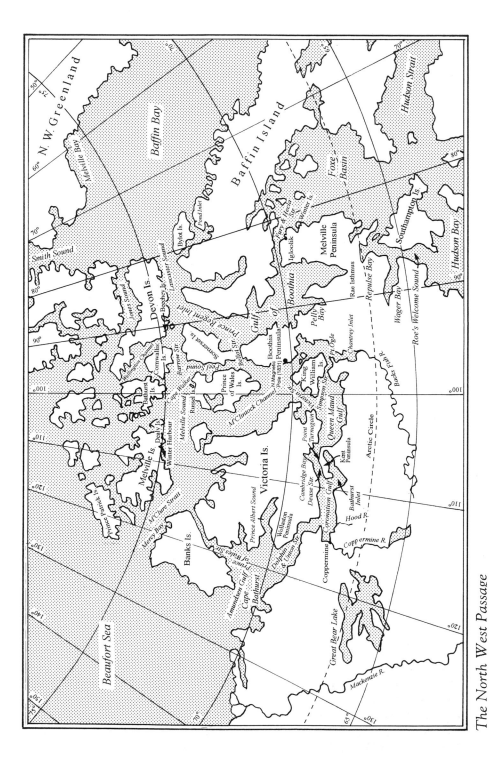

The North West Passage

CHAPTER 1

The Elizabethan Voyages

A seafarer who travels to the desolate Arctic regions of North America cannot fail to know the names of the early navigators who, during the reigns of Queen Elizabeth and the early Stuart Kings, first explored those unknown regions. To reach northern Canada he might sail through the Davis Strait, along Hudson Strait and across Hudson Bay, stretches of water named after their discoverers, John Davis and the luckless Henry Hudson. On sailing further north a vessel might find herself pushing through the ice of that vast bay, named after the intrepid old navigator William Baffin. Most of us have heard of Frobisher, whose quest for a North West Passage in the 1570s turned into a fruitless search for gold; and in even the most cursory perusal of an atlas we find the names of Bylot, James or 'North West Foxe' – which conjure up visions of voyages long ago.

Who were they all? What led them to leave Shakespeare's 'sceptred isle' to penetrate the fogs, storms and ice of the Arctic in their small wooden sailing ships? What accounts have come down to us of their voyages? How did they deal with the native peoples? Can we make sense of their charts?

Still earlier, the intrepid Norsemen had crossed the North Atlantic to found colonies on the west coast of Greenland. The ruins of their churches can still be seen, but effective contact was lost in the early fifteenth century, even if the Vatican continued to appoint non-resident bishops. Many reasons have been given for the failure of the colony after some three hundred years of settlement, not very long before a long series of voyages began, mainly from England, in search of the North West Passage to the riches of Cathay, as China was then called, and of which Sir John Franklin's voyage of 1845-48 may be considered the last. It has been said that the officers and men of that expedition 'forged the last link with their lives', although by then the Passage was no longer thought of as a short-cut to the Far East, because the nature of its icy seas and channels was largely known and understood.

However, it was the idea of the short-cut, away from the influence of Portugal and Spain, which first stimulated the quest for Cathay across the Arctic. Christopher Columbus had been bound for Cathay when he sailed westward across the Atlantic from Spain in 1492. Instead of reaching China and Japan, he discovered the islands of Cuba and Haiti, in the West Indies. It took a surprisingly short time for South America to be circumnavigated, first by Magellan in 1520 and then by Sir Francis Drake. A southwestern sea route was thus found into the Great South Sea, or Pacific Ocean, although the land route across Central America was more often traversed to and from the Far East. Meanwhile, Vasco da Gama had rounded the tip of Africa – the Cape of Good Hope – and had discovered a southeast sea passage to India and China which did away with the dangers of crossing by land. By the Treaty of Tordesillas in 1494, Spain and Portugal accepted the Pope's line of demarcation between their spheres of influence, Portugal's to the east and Spain's towards the west. The Dutch and the English searched for shorter sea routes in the north – the North East Passage north of Eurasia, and the North West Passage north of what came to be realised was the great land mass of North America – when no channel could be found in lower latitudes.

The story of the pioneering navigators of the sixteenth and seventeenth centuries is not an easy one to tell. Time has dealt kindly with some and much less so with others. For instance, we can read vivid, first-hand accounts of Sir Martin Frobisher's Arctic voyages of 1576, 1577 and 1578, because these have been preserved to the present day. On the other hand, the earlier voyages of John Cabot and his son Sebastian from Bristol have had to be pieced together by historians from scattered evidence, because their original charts and manuscripts are largely lost.

It is interesting, and perhaps a little sad, to see how the charts showing Baffin's remarkable voyage of 1616, northwards through Davis Strait to the bay named after him (Baffin Bay), were so altered over the decades and even the centuries as to become quite distorted, casting doubts on the voyage itself. Similarly the 'straits' discovered by Frobisher in the 1570s (later proved to be, in fact, Frobisher Bay on the east coast of Baffin Island) were moved by the cartographers to bisect southern Greenland until the mid nineteenth century. Both Hudson Strait, the westward waterway from Davis Strait, and Hudson Bay are named after Henry Hudson, the seventeenth-century navigator who also discovered the Hudson River in the United States. However, it seems that a century earlier Sebastian Cabot may have made the same voyage into the great bay. Likewise, Martin Frobisher's ships were blown westwards in 1578 along the 'Mistaken Straits', which must have been the later named Hudson Strait.

The wooden ships in which the navigators sailed were small – some were even tiny. It was the development of the three-masted ship that enabled mariners from the British and European ports to set forth with the prospect of coming back again, even when winds were likely to be adverse. A ship of 200 tons was considered a large one, while some were 60 tons or less. It was usually possible to ascertain latitude (distance north or south of the Equator), but longitude (distance to the east or west) had to be roughly calculated by what is called 'dead-reckoning', using a wooden log on a line to find the speed of the ship and hour glasses to tell the time. William Baffin tried to discover a method of finding longitude at sea by mathematical means, but it was not until the late eighteenth century that longitude could be found with reasonable certainty. The early voyagers also had virtually no reliable charts. Many were the fictions of a geographer's imagination, while others were faulty for technical reasons. We can learn a great deal about the early voyages from Richard Hakluyt (1552-1616) who assembled, edited and published in three bulky volumes between 1598 and 1600 a great work entitled, *The Principal Navigations, Voiages, Traffiques and Discoveries of the English Nation, made by Sea or over-land, to the remote and farthest distant quarters of the Earth, at any time within the compasse of these 1500 yeeres.*

As might be expected from the comprehensive title, the voyages, either narrated or edited by Hakluyt range far and near. Many are concerned with trade and colonisation, others with pure adventure or privateering, while those of most interest to us are the explorations of Sebastian Cabot, Martin Frobisher and John Davis. There is even an Eskimo vocabulary. The new world which he described opened the eyes of the English people to real lands almost more amazing than the legends of mediaeval times. Hakluyt had earlier compiled his *Principall Navigations* (1589) in the dedication of which he described how his interest began while a schoolboy at Westminster when he visited a cousin in his legal chambers in London, finding open on the table 'certeine bookes of Cosmographie, with an universall Mappe'. Young Hakluyt was curious to know more, so his cousin showed him the various divisions of the Earth and pointed out their geography and trade. His instructor then opened the Bible and directed Hakluyt to Psalm 107, which says that 'they that go down to the sea in ships and occupy their business in the great waters . . . see the works of the Lord, and his wonders in the deepe'. Hakluyt resolved to study these matters and when at Oxford University, he 'read over whatsoever printed or written discoveries and voyages' he found existed in Greek, Latin, Italian, Spanish, Portuguese and English. He also gave public lectures and compared the old maps, globes and spheres with the new. In time, he got to know 'the chiefest Captaines at sea, the greatest Merchants, and the best Mariners of our nation'. He did not find the task an easy one. After 'great changes and infinite cares', and after 'many watchings, toiles, and travels', which wore him out, he at length 'collected three several volumes of the English Navigations, Traffiques, and Discoveries, to strange, remote, and farre distant countreys'.

The first of the Tudor monarchs, Henry VII, had granted in 1496 what were called 'Letters patent' to John Cabot and his three sons to make voyages of discovery in northern, eastern or western seas. These were printed in Hakluyt's *Divers voyages* (1582). Hakluyt's *magnum opus* appeared in the final years of the last of the Tudors, Queen Elizabeth I. Although much has been pieced together from the records about the Cabots' voyages, it is for those of Frobisher and Davis that we first find substantial sources. These two Arctic navigators therefore stand four square among the predecessors of Parry, Franklin and the Rosses during the nineteenth century in the search for the North West Passage. In both his *Principall Navigations* (1589) and in the later three volumes of his *Principal Navigations* (1598-1600), Hakluyt gave full coverage to Martin Frobisher's three voyages of 1576, 1577 and 1578 and to those of John Davis of 1585, 1586 and 1587, including some published and some unpublished narratives.[1]

Martin Frobisher's Voyages, 1576-78

Martin Frobisher was a quick-tempered Yorkshireman who was orphaned as a child and who first went to sea under his uncle's protection. He was captured by the Portuguese during a voyage to the Guinea coast of west Africa and spent some time in a Lisbon gaol; it may have been there that he first heard of the three Corte Real brothers and their ill-fated voyages from Portugal towards the North West earlier in the sixteenth century. The Muscovy Company of London, chartered in 1555 to sail the northern seas and reach Cathay, first concentrated its efforts on the North East Passage, north of Russia. A voyage through the North East Passage was attempted in 1556 by Stephen Borough in the *Serchethrift* and this was the first of a number of unsuccessful English, and later Dutch voyages to that region. Failing to navigate this ice-bound sea route, the mariners of the Muscovy Company turned south into the White Sea and trade with the subjects of the Tsar resulted. However, some Muscovy merchants thought that not enough exploration had been attempted to the North West and as a result the 'Company of Cathay' was set up in 1577, but not chartered. The Secretary of both was the Merchant Adventurer Michael Lok, who was responsible personally for the finances of Frobisher's voyages.

The aim of Frobisher's first voyage of 1576 was to reach Cathay through a passage to the North West. As Frobisher's two small barks the *Michael* and the *Gabriel* (both little over 20 tons), with a pinnace of seven tons, sailed down the Thames in the early summer of 1576, Queen Elizabeth waved from her window in the red brick Tudor palace of Placentia on the waterfront at Greenwich (where the buildings of Greenwich Hospital now stand).

The little pinnace was to be lost in a storm in the North Atlantic while the *Michael*, after several days amid fog and ice off Greenland, turned for home, leaving Frobisher in the *Gabriel* to cross what is now called Davis Strait, between Greenland and Baffin Island (not then so named.) They entered what Frobisher called Frobisher's Straits (now Bay), which he considered to be a northern passage, like Magellan's Strait in the South. The country proved to be barren, with snow on the mountain tops, and swept by bitter winds. It was nevertheless inhabited by 'Men, Women Children, and sundrie kind of Beastes in great plentie as Beares, Dere, Hares, Foxes and Dogges', as well as numerous birds.[2] Nineteen people came out to the *Gabriel* in their boats, but their language was incomprehensible and they were described as being 'like to Tartars, with long blacke haire, broad faces and flatte noses and tawnie in colour, wearing Seale skinnes, and so doe the women, not differing in the fashion, but the women are marked in the face with blewe streekes downe the cheekes, and round about the eyes'.[3] Their boats were also made of seal-skin, being 'flat in the bottome and sharpe at both ends', and 'with a keele of wood within the skin'.[4] Frobisher's only boat and the five men in it were taken by the Inuit when they disembarked an Inuk who had just visited the ship and been given a knife and a bell as presents. Though Frobisher tried to contact his men by firing a gun and sounding a trumpet, they were never seen again. He named the stretch of water where they were taken 'Five Men's Sound'. In retaliation one of the 'countrey people' in his kayak was enticed by a bell on board the *Gabriel*. Next morning (21 August 1576) the snow lay a foot deep on the hatches. With a depleted crew, no boat, and with winter approaching, Frobisher could do little more and the *Gabriel* set sail for England. As 'tokens of possession', he had the 'strange man' and his kayak and also a piece of black rock 'as great as a halfe pennye loaf'.[5]

That piece of black rock was to have major consequences for Frobisher and his backers and indeed, for the Queen. It was thought to contain gold. A second expedition to Frobisher's Straits was despatched in 1577, under the auspices of the 'Company of Cathay', with instructions to mine for ore, to rescue the five missing sailors, to bring back to England a number of the people of the country (the Inuit) without causing offence and after winning their friendship, and to seek the North West Passage should there be time. The venture thus changed in character from exploring to prospecting. Efforts to find the lost men brought about hostility, either side wounding the other with arrows. Rather than be taken captive, ('being ignorant what mercy meaneth') a number of the wounded Inuit having 'manfullye' resisted the Englishmen, jumped headlong off the rocks and drowned themselves.[6] One of those present, remarked in his published book that if they had 'submitted them selves,' or if they had by some means been taken alive, 'we would both have saved them, and also have sought remedie to cure their woundes received at our handes'.[7] However, a young woman and child were made captive and an old shirt, shoes and other clothing, presumed to belong to the five lost sailors, were found in a tent. In his account of the voyages, George Best, who served as Frobisher's Lieutenant in the *Ayde* in 1577 and as Captain of the *Anne Frances* in 1578, remarks on signs that the inhabitants had previous contact with foreigners. The fact that some of them would rather drown than be taken alive suggests that they had been cruelly treated by earlier visitors. His description of the 'countrey people', as he called them, must be one of the earliest, and is worth quoting at some length, especially since the Inuit, or Esquimaux as they became known to later explorers, feature so prominently in all the subsequent voyages. Best found their way of life similar to that of the Samoyedes of Muscovy (Russia). Their colour was that of a 'ripe olive', despite being born in such a cold climate.

> They are men, very active and nimble. They are a strong people, and very warlike . . . [who can] mannage their bowes and dartes with greate dexteritie. They goe clad in coates made of the skinnes of beastes as of Ceales, Dere, Beares, Foxes, and Hares. They have also some garments of feathers . . . finely sowed and compact togither . . . In Sommer, they use to weare the hearie side of their coates outwarde, and sometime go naked for too much heate. And in winter (as by signes they have declared) they weare foure or five fold upon their bodies withe ye heare (for warmth) turned inward . . .
>
> These people are in nature verye subtil, and sharpe witted, readie to conceive our meaning by signes, and to make answere, well to be understoode againe . . . They will

A skirmish between Frobisher's men and the 'Country People' of Frobisher Bay at 'Bloody Point' during one of the expeditions of 1576, 1577 and 1578. (Drawing by John White, British Museum, NMM, B7665)

teache us the names of eache thing in their language, which we desire to learne, and are apt to learne any thing of us. They delight in Musicke above measure, and will kepe time and stroke to any tune which you shal sing, both with their voyce, heade, hande and feete, and wyll sing the same tune aptlye after you. They will rowe with our Ores in our boates, and keep a true stroke with oure Mariners, and seeme to take great delight therein. They live in Caves of the Earth, and hunt for their dinners or praye, even as the Beare, or other wilde Beastes do. They eate rawe fleshe and fishe, and refuse no meate, howsoever it be stincking. They are desperate in their fighte, sullen of nature, and ravenous in their manner of feeding . . .

For their weapons, to offende their enimies, or kill their pray withal, they have Dartes, slings, bowes, and arrows headed with sharp stones, bones, and some with yron. They are exceeding friendly and kinde harted, one to the other, and mourne greatly at the losse or harme of their fellowes, and expresse their griefe of minde, when they part one from an other, with a mournefull song, and Dirges. They are very shamefast in betraying the secretes of nature, and very chaste in ye manner of their living . . .

They have boates made of leather, and covered cleane over, saving one place in the middle to sit in, plancked within with timber, and they use to rowe therein with one Ore, more swiftly a great deale, than we in our boates can doe with twentie. They have one sort of greater boates, wherin they can carrie above twentie persons, and have a Mast with a Sayle thereon, whiche Sayle is made of thinne Skinnes or bladders, sowed togither with the sinewes of fishes. They are good fishermen, and in their small Boates, being disguised with their coates of Ceales skinnes, they deceyve the Fishe, who take them rather for their fellowe ceales, than for deceyving men. They are good marke men. With their dart or arrowe they will commonly kill Ducke, or any other foule, in the head, and commonly in the eye. When they shoote at a great fishe with any of theyr Dartes, they use to tye a bladder thereunto, whereby they may the better finde them agayne, and the fishe not able to carrie it so easily away, for that the bladder dothe boy the darte, will at length be weerie, and dye therewith.

They use to traffike and exchange their commodities with some other people, of whome they have such things . . . as barres of iron, heads of iron for their dartes, needles . . . , certayne buttons of copper, whiche they use to weare uppon theyr forheads for ornament, as our Ladyes in the Court of England do use great pearle . . . We found also in their tents a Guinney Beane . . . the which doth usually grow in the hote Countreys; whereby it appeereth they trade with other Nations which dwell farre off, or else themselves are greate travellers.

They have nothing in use among them to make fyre withall, saving a kind of Heath and Mosse which groweth there. And they kindle their fyre with continuall rubbing and fretting one sticke againste an other, as we do with flints. They drawe with dogges in sleads upon the Ise, and remove their tents therwithal, wherein they dwel, in somer, when they goe a hunting for their praye and provision againste winter. They do sometime parboyle their meate a little and seeth the same in kettles made of beasts skins; they have also pannes cutte and made of stone very artificially; they use preaty ginnes wherewith they take foule. The women carry their sucking children at their backes and do feed them with raw flesh, which first they do a little chawe in their owne mouthes. The women have their faces marked or painted over with small blewe spottes; they have blacke and long haire on their heades, and trimme the same in a decent order. The men have but little haire on their faces, and very thinne beardes.

George Best surmised that the timber used to plank and strengthen the people's boats and to make darts, bows and arrows must have drifted from far to the southward, from Canada 'or some other part of newe founde land.' No poisonous snakes were found, but the Englishmen were sorely tried by a small stinging fly or gnat. Snow and hail occurred even at the height of summer, when the ground was frozen three fathoms deep.

Best considered the 'countrey people' to be 'greate inchanters' and provides a description of their ceremonial weight lifting. He also lists the numerous animals and birds, of which two hawks were taken to England.[8]

A narrator of Frobisher's second voyage of 1577, Dionyse Settle, also provides a description of the 'countrie people', which parallels and supplements Best's. Settle's was the first published account of the voyages (1577). Here is a short extract from it:

They . . . keep certeine doggs, not much unlike Wolves, whiche they yoke together, as we do oxen and horses, to a sled or traile: and so carrie their necessaries over the ice and snowe, from place to place . . . They make their apparell with hoods and tailes . . . Those beastes, flesh, fishes, and fowles which they kil, they are both meate, drinke, apparel, houses, bedding, hose, shooes, thred, saile for their boates, with many other necessaries, whereof they stande in neede, and almost all their riches. Their houses are tentes made of Seale skinns, pitched with foure Firre quarters, foure square, meeting at the toppe . . . , so pitched . . . that the entraunce into them, is alwayes South or against the Sunne. They have other sortes of houses, which wee found not to be inhabited, which are raised with stones and Whal bones, and a skinne layd over them, to withstand the raine or other weather; the entraunce of them being not much unlike an Ovens mouth.

These would have in fact been inhabited during the winter. Settle goes into some detail in describing the bows and arrows, also mentioning the people's use of dogs, their two types of boat and their possession of a small amount of iron. He notes their probable trade with another people and their delight in anything bright or able to make a sound.[9]

In late August 1577 the three vessels of the voyage – the *Ayde* (the Queen's tall ship of 200 tons) with the *Michael* and the *Gabriel* – departed from Frobisher Bay, after examining both shores and loading nearly 160 tons of the hard black ore. One of the principal mines was on a small island, which they called 'Countess of Warwick Island' and which is known today as Kodlunarn (White men's) Island, since designated an historic site. All three ships returned safely and the ore was locked away while furnaces to refine it were built on the lower Thames at Dartford. The man, woman and child were made much of and drawings of them still exist, although their portraits in oil seem to have perished.[10] Despite careful medical attention, the adults sickened and died and were buried in Bristol, the child later died in London where he was buried in the same churchyard as the Inuk of 1576.[11]

Though not an ounce of gold was refined from the black ore, a third voyage to 'Frobisher Straightes' was made, again with Frobisher in command in the *Ayde*, the flagship of a huge fleet of fifteen vessels. Because the search for the North West Passage had become a secondary aim, aboard these were not only the usual complement of sailors and soldiers, but over one hundred miners from Cornwall and the Forest of Dean, who were to form a wintering party on the small island (Kodlunarn), under the leadership of Captain Edward Fenton and accompanied by Master William Wolfall, a brave and learned man, as their minister and preacher. He had been appointed by the Queen's Council and he was later to celebrate the first Anglican communion in North America. Because of rough weather and fog, the fleet was unable to keep together, while ice blocked the entrance to Frobisher Bay. It was at this time that Frobisher in the *Ayde* with several other vessels sailed up what he called the 'Mistaken Straightes' – the Hudson Strait of today. Their experiences in a storm were described in his *True report of the third and last voyage* by Thomas Ellis, 'sailer and one of the companie', published in 1578:

The storme still increased, and the yce inclosed us, so that we were faine to take downe toppe and toppe-mastes; for the yce had so environed us that we could see neither land nor Sea, as far as we could kenne; so that we were faine to cutte our gables, to hang over-

> boorde for fenders, somewhat to ease the shippes sides, from the great and drierie strokes of the yce: some Capstan barres, some fending off with Oares, some with planckes of 2 ynches thicke, which were broken immediatly with the force of the yce, some going out uppon the yce to beare it off with their shoulders from the shippes.[12]

At length that 'dismall and lamentable night' came to an end. The gale subsided, the fog lifted and with God's mercy they reached the more open sea.

Most of the fleet were eventually reunited at the end of July in Countess of Warwick's Sound, in the region of which some 1200 tons of 'black ore' were hacked from the hard rock and loaded into the ships. Kodlunarn ('Countess of Warwick') Island had been mined the previous year and it is still possible to see the so-called 'ship's trench' and the 'reservoir trench' on its surface. The foundations of a small house, built of stone, can also be seen. This was erected to see how it stood up to the Arctic winter and the attentions of the local people, for whom gifts were left inside. A quantity of peas and a miner's basket have recently been excavated there. Other relics of Frobisher's expeditions were shown by the Inuit to the American explorer Charles Francis Hall in the 1860s. He was searching for traces of the lost Franklin expedition of 1845-48 and he gradually tumbled to the fact that the 'white men', whose visits had been remembered in oral tradition over the generations, were Elizabethans, not early Victorians.[13]

Because half the pre-fabricated hut, the beer and other necessaries had been lost in the storms at sea no colony was established and the remaining ships returned home. The story of repercussions in England when the huge quantity of 'black ore' was found to be worthless cannot be told here, but anyone interested can visit Dartford on the lower Thames where blocks of the ore can be seen in an old wall along Priory Road and in the museum.

Recently a letter written by an agent of King Philip II of Spain, who accompanied the third voyage has been deciphered, and there exist a number of small contemporary books translated into Latin, French, Italian and German, which demonstrate that these voyages from England attracted the attention of Europe, so that the way of life of the 'countrey people' became quite widely known. The man who had assumed financial responsibility for the three voyages, Michael Lok, was unable to persuade all the 'venturers' to pay their share. He therefore found himself personally liable and was subsequently thrown into a debtors' prison. A map showing part of western Europe, and Africa and America from the Tropic of Cancer to the North Pole appeared under Lok's name in 1582. It shows Frobisher's discoveries quite clearly. The understanding of the geography of the world was, then, tenuous and Frobisher's discoveries loom large in a poorly-defined map. A more detailed one was drawn by James Beare, Master and principal surveyor, as well as an important world map, incorporating Frobisher's explorations.[14]

John Davis and his First Voyage of 1585

John Davis (c 1550–1605) had a very different character from the heroic but barely literate Frobisher. Born and bred in Devonshire he not only practised navigation but wrote about the art as well. He also devised a simple instrument called the Davis back-staff, which made easier the taking of sights of the sun. In the words of the editor of his *Voyages and Works*, 'as a seaman combining scientific knowledge and skilled pilotage with the qualities of a fearless and determined explorer, John Davis stands foremost among the navigators of the great Queen'. Among the qualities that made him 'a perfect sea captain' was his ability to gain the love and confidence of his men. 'He was as genial and considerate, as he was conscientious and honest'.[15] As a child, Davis's neighbours at Sandridge were the three Gilbert brothers and their half brother Walter Raleigh, of the later Virginia voyages. Humphrey Gilbert was to publish a *Discourse for a discovery for a new passage to Cataia* in 1576 and to claim Newfoundland for Queen Elizabeth in 1583, while the youngest brother, Adrian Gilbert was also a keen promoter of voyages of exploration. Davis was known to John Dee, the polymath, cosmographer and authority on the art of navigation, who had earlier advised Frobisher and his captains. Davis is believed to have spent some time in Dee's home at Mortlake in the 1580s, when he would have had access to his host's library.

Davis's first voyage to find the North West Passage seems to have been conceived in that very library on 23 January 1584 when Dr John Dee and Adrian Gilbert were joined by Sir Francis Walsingham, the Secretary of State, who expressed a desire to know more about Arctic discoveries. A meeting was arranged elsewhere next day, in which John Davis took part. Dee recorded that 'only we four were secret, and we made Mr Secretary privie of the North-West Passage, and all charts and rutters were agreed upon in general'.[16] Sir Francis Walsingham gave his approval, a matter which no doubt helped to influence William Sanderson, a merchant adventurer, who subscribed liberally to the enterprise and whose relative John Janes sailed as supercargo to represent him. Other merchants from the City of London and Exeter also subscribed.

Two small vessels, the *Sunshine* of London (50 tons) and the *Moonshine* (35 tons) were fitted out at Dartmouth, where the smaller had been built. Owing to a misunderstanding of Frobisher's discoveries, as well as the errors on the maps of the North Atlantic which Frobisher took with him and the inability of mariners to calculate longitude, Davis believed Frobisher's Strait cut across southern Greenland. He did little, therefore, to build on his predecessor's discoveries.

The *Sunshine* and *Moonshine* seem to have made their first northern landfall on the east coast of Greenland, (which Davis called 'Land of Desolation') where sea-ice and driftwood were abundant. The *Moonshine* came across a tree sixty feet long, with a thick trunk, still with its roots. A little later they met the 'people of the country' on the west coast, the English musicians in the party playing and both groups dancing. Next morning (30 July), thirty seven 'canoas' came to the ships, beckoning the strangers to come ashore. One of the Greenlanders 'went up to the top of the rocke, and leapt and danced as they had done the day before, showing us a seales skinne and another thing made like a timbrel, which he did

Left: An Eskimo man (Kalicho), woman (Arnaq) and child (Nutaaq) were brought to Bristol in 1577 by Martin Frobisher, where the man and woman died and were buried at St Stephen's church. The child died in London and was buried at St Olaves, Hart Street. (Drawing by John White, British Museum, NMM B7667CN) *Right:* 'Arnaq and Nutaaq' (in hood). (John White, British Museum, NMM, B7666CN)

beate upon with a sticke, making a noyse like a small drumme.'[17] Five 'canoas' and bird and seal skin clothing were bought. John Janes, Sanderson's representative, thought the people to be 'very tractable' and 'voyde of craft or double dealing, and easier to be brought to any civilitie or good order.'[18] Many ships were to follow in the wake of the *Sunshine* and *Moonshine* up the west coast of Greenland in later centuries, and sailors and the native people would dance together, as they had done on Davis's first northern voyage. Along this desolate coastline, there was a great abundance of seals and berry bushes, while willows and birch grew close to the ground. The cliffs consisted of the same rock 'as M Frobisher brought from Meta Incognita'.[19]

A fair wind took the vessels across what became known as Davis Strait. They found land in 66 °40′N and anchored below 'a very brave mount' which was named Mount Raleigh.[20] 'Cape Walsingham' on an eastern point of what is now Baffin Island was also named. Four 'white beares of monstrous bignesse' were seen, two of which were killed for 'fresh victual and the sport.'[21] In what is now Cumberland Sound, a pack of twenty dogs met the boat as it came ashore, and thinking they were wolves, the men shot two of them, only to find a leather collar on one of them. Janes described them as like mastiffs 'with prickt eares and long bush tayles'. A little further on, two sledges were discovered 'made like ours in Englande', one being made of 'firre, spruse and oken boards', while the other was made entirely of whalebone. Signs were found of the inhabitants, but none was seen. The Englishmen found the coast 'very barbarous, without wood or grasse', while the rocks were 'very faire, like marble full of vaynes of diverse coulors'.[22] They departed homewards on 24 August, reaching the 'Land of Desolation' on 10 September, but were unable to land because of rough weather. The *Sunshine* and *Moonshine* were separated in another gale, but both reached Dartmouth on 30 September within two hours of each other. So ended the account of John Janes, Merchant, 'servant to the worshipful Mr William Sanderson'. It is a very detailed one and gives, for example the men's names and their victualling ration.

Having sailed in an open ice season, Davis returned full of optimism for the imminent discovery of the passage and wrote accordingly to Walsingham. Several towns in the west of England demonstrated their support for a second voyage by supplying cloth and other goods for eventual sale in China.[23]

Davis's Second Voyage, 1586

The narrative of this second voyage was written by Davis himself. He departed again from Dartmouth, on 1 May, this time with the *Mermaid* (a ship of 120 tons), the barks *Sunshine* and *Moonshine*, and a pinnace named the *Northstar*, 'our scout for this discoverie' of ten tons, which was carried on board the *Mermaid*. Land was sighted 'mightily pestered with yce and snow', probably Cape Farewell (Kap Farvel), on the southern tip of Greenland, on 15 June. Being unable to land, the vessels sailed northwards along the west coast of Greenland towards the inlet which Davis had called Gilbert Sound, later named Godthaab Fiord by the Danes where the settlement is now known as Nuuk. Here he intended to assemble the pinnace, carried in frame, on one of the 'mightie companie' of islands, 'full of fayre soundes and harboroughs', there being little snow on the land and the sea free of ice.

When they spied the ships' boats, the 'people of the country' welcomed the crews with real pleasure, especially those who had been there the year before, and when Davis went ashore with 'the merchaunts and others of the company', the natives 'lept out of their Canoas, and came running to mee and the rest, and imbraced us with many signes of hartie welcome'. Davis gave a knife each to all eighteen of the party as a present. While the pinnace was being assembled next day on an island, some one hundred 'canoas' arrived at a time, bringing with them the skins of seal, deer and Arctic hare, as well as fish and birds. Curious to know more of the country, Davis sent away one of the ships' boats with strict orders 'that there should be no injurie offered to any of the people, neither any gunne shot'. Some fascinating descriptions of the land and its inhabitants, both human and animal, occur in Davis's account, including the

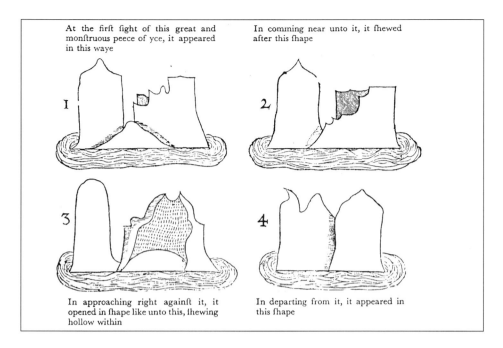

At the firſt ſight of this great and monſtruous peece of yce, it appeared in this waye

In comming near unto it, it ſhewed after this ſhape

In approaching right againſt it, it opened in ſhape like unto this, ſhewing hollow within

In departing from it, it appeared in this ſhape

Four views of a single iceberg by Thomas Ellis from *A true report of the third and last voyage*. Ellis calls himself a 'sailer and one of the companie' of Frobisher's 1578 voyage.

discovery on an island of a grave with a cross laid over the sealskin which covered the bodies.

Before long, however, oars, a gun, spear, sword and other armaments were found missing and the ships' masters wished Davis 'to dissolve this new friendship, and to leave the company of these theevish miscreants'. Davis, nevertheless, found cause for laughter when he realised the people just could not help stealing iron 'and willed that in no case they should be any more hardly used, but that our owne company should be the more vigilant to keepe theyr thinges, supposing it to be very hard in so short time to make them know theyr evils'. He wrote down a vocabulary of forty words, of which twenty resembled those in use in the late nineteenth century. Another, smaller vocabulary of seventeen words had earlier been compiled by Christopher Hall during Frobisher's first voyage.[24]

Davis went off in the pinnace to see more of the country for himself for three days (7-9 July 1586). On his return, the sailors 'complained heavily against the people and said that my lenity and friendly using of them gave them stomacke to mischiefe: for they have stollen an anker from us, they have cut our cable very dangerously, they have cut our boats from our sterne, and now since your departure, with slings they spare us not with stones of halfe a pound weight and will you still indure these injuries . . .' Davis went ashore, to give bracelets as gifts and welcome a number of the people on board. However, the stone-throwing was resumed at dusk and even Davis's patience was tested when the boatswain was knocked down. The next day the ring-leader was taken as hostage in order to recover the anchor, but the wind turned fair and the ships set sail with the man still aboard, who 'at length became a pleasant companion among us'. Davis gave him 'a new sute of frize, after the English fashion, because I saw he could not indure the colde, of which he was very joyfull'. He helped to make oakum and sometimes lent a hand to haul a rope. He lived on dried fish, but died during the voyage.

During the second half of July, they met what must have been a huge iceberg. Interestingly four thumb-nail sketches of views of an 'Island of yce' met during Frobisher's third voyage had been published in Thomas Ellis' *true report* of 1578.[25] The weather turned foggy and cold, and froze the shrouds, ropes and sails. The men began to sicken and despair of a successful outcome to the voyage and respectfully entreated Davis to have regard for his own safety and the preservation of their lives 'and not through my over boldnesse leave their widows and fatherlesse children to give me bitter cursses'. Not wishing to abandon the search Davis hit on a solution, whereby he would provision the *Moonshine* and proceed in her, while allowing the less handy but valuable *Mermaid* to return home. The little squadron therefore sailed back to southern Greenland, where a good anchorage was found and where it was hot and they were 'much troubled with a flie which is called Musketa'.

Having revictualled and prepared the *Moonshine* again for sea, Davis sailed westwards from the Greenland coast on 12 August 1586 finding land again two days later in the latitude of 66 °19′N, probably in the vicinity of Cape Walsingham, southeast Baffin Island. In warmer waters further south they entered on 28 August 'a very fayre harbor' from which Davis walked inland for some miles through woods of pine, apple, alder, fir, yew, willow and birch where there were pheasants, wild geese, ducks, partridges, blackbirds, jays and thrushes. Pheasants and partridges were shot with bows and arrows, while a great store of cod was caught at the harbour mouth. Further south still, two of the ship's company were surprised and killed by the 'Savages' ashore. A 'mighty tempestuous storme' added to their troubles but the *Moonshine* was able to set sail with a fair wind for England on 11 September and arrived in the West Country in early October.

Meanwhile the *Sunshine* had visited Iceland, Greenland and Newfoundland, and returned to Dartmouth on 4 October with a cargo of seal skins, but without the pinnace which had foundered in a storm. In a letter to William Sanderson of 14 October, Davis said that his experience of the North West led him to believe that the passage must exist in one of four places or else not at all. He assured his employer that a further voyage could be undertaken at no cost and even with profit to the adventurers (presumably through the sale of furs and fish.) 'Surely, it shall cost me all my hope of welfare, and my portion of Sandridge' (his Devonshire home), he declared, 'but I will, by God's mercy, see an end of these businesses.'

Davis's Third Voyage 1587

John Janes, Sanderson's representative, sailed again with Davis towards the North West in May of 1587 and again wrote an account of the voyage. The title of this reminds us of the purpose of these attempts, this one being financed mainly in London.

> The third voyage Northwestward, made by John Davis, Gentleman, as chiefe Captaine and Pilot generall, for the discoverie of a passage to the Isles of the Molucca or the coast of China . . .

The Moluccas were the spice islands of the Far East, where Drake had called during his circumnavigation of 1577-1580.

The barks Sunshine of London, Elizabeth of Dartmouth and a clinker-built pinnace, the Ellen of London, set sail from Dartmouth on 19 May 1587. The Ellen showed few good qualities – 'at Sea she was like to a cart drawen with oxen', wrote Janes. On the fourteenth day at sea, they were off the west Greenland coast, where they anchored two days later and began to assemble a smaller pinnace which had been brought in frame from England. The 'country people' showed them seal skins for trade, shouting 'Il y a oute' (I mean no harm), as before. However, just when the new pinnace was ready to be launched, they tore off the two upper strakes and carried them away for the sake of the nails in the boards. This ruined the little vessel and she was consequently given to the Elizabeth as a fishing boat. To help towards the cost of the voyage, it was agreed that she and the Sunshine would keep company and fish, while Davis was to explore to the north in the small and leaky Ellen, which could only be kept free of water by constant pumping. Nevertheless, Davis (in Janes' words) 'determined rather to end his life with credite then to returne with infamie and disgrace' and the crew agreed and 'purposed to live and die together', carrying all their things on board and departing northwards from the islands at 64 ° latitude, trading with the Greenlanders as they went. On 25 July

> . . . we descried 30 Savages rowing after us, being by judgement 10 leagues off from the shore: they brought us Salmon Peales, Birds, and Caplin, and we gave them pinnes, needles, bracelets, nailes, knives, bels, looking glasses, and other small trifles, and for a knife, a naile or a bracelet, which they call Ponigmah, they would sell their boat, coates, or anything they had, although they were farre from the shore.

The Englishmen obtained about twenty skins as part of this exchange, having followed what they named the 'London coast' of Greenland for over a week. They reached the relatively high latitude of 72 °12′N (possibly in fact 72 °49′N) on 30 July, a hot, calm day. This was their furthest north, where they turned westwards, naming the spot 'Hope Sanderson', a great cliff, whose ledges give nesting space to thousands of seabirds and whose name 'Sanderson's Hope' occurs in most subsequent Arctic narratives. The sea was clear to north and west and a north wind enabled the Ellen to run for forty leagues (120 miles) without sight of land.

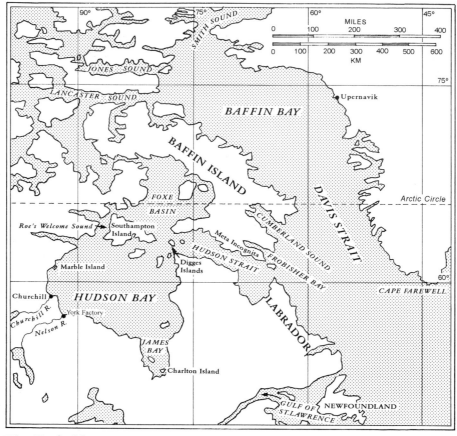

The Early Voyages

She soon encountered what later became known as the 'middle pack' of Baffin Bay, escaping from it with some effort, Davis hoping that the hot sun and the continual beating of the waves would soon despatch the ice. On 19 July they again sighted 'Mount Raleigh' (Baffin Island) and the entrance to Cumberland Sound, discovered on the first voyage. This they coasted for sixty leagues (180 miles), naming the islands at the 'bottome of the gulfe' after the Earl of Cumberland. A whale was seen travelling westward between the islands, but on 24 July, finding no passage, they turned southeast towards the sea. The next day, a hot, calm one, the master of the *Ellen* landed with some of the seamen to course their dogs, but these had become 'so fat that they were scant able to run', presumably through lack of exercise on board ship. Graves were found ashore, with some spilt train oil (oil made from whale or seal blubber).

Having coasted the south shore of Cumberland Sound, they re-entered Davis Strait in latitude 64 °N. A little further south they 'passed by a great banke or inlet, which lay betweene 63 and 62 degrees of latitude, which we called Lumleys Inlet', doubtless the 'straits' previously discovered and named after himself by

Frobisher in 1576. Sailing south along the western coast, they often came across 'great rootes, the water, as it were, whirling and overfalling, as if it were the fall of some great water through a bridge.' On 31 July they passed a promontory, which they called 'Warwikes Foreland', little knowing that the name of the Countess of Warwick had been given by Frobisher to a small sound within his 'straits' and that the headland was Queen Elizabeth's 'Meta Incognita', which name still appears on the charts of Baffin Island as the Meta Incognita Peninsula.

Under full sail in a gale of wind the *Ellen* was carried rapidly south by what we now call the Labrador current, passing 'a very great gulfe'. (No doubt Frobisher's 'Mistaken Straights', subsequently called Hudson Strait), where the water was 'whirling and roring, as it were the meeting of tides'. There is, indeed, a meeting of currents here, which became known as Davis's 'furious overfall', where an easterly current along the south shore of Hudson Strait meets the southward flowing Labrador current. Davis named the 'Southern most Cape of the gulfe' after John Chudleigh, or Chidley, a Devonshire friend of his, by which latter name it is still known. An attempt to kill some of the twelve deer (caribou) seen on an island off the coast of Labrador, named after Lord Darcy, was foiled by their swimming away to another island, 'because our boat was so small that it could not carie us and rowe after them, they swamme so fast'. Janes described one of the deer 'as big as a good pretie cowe and very fat'. He only managed to shoot a grey hare. On 13 August, three or four polar bears were sighted, but there was no hope of going ashore for them, for lack of a good boat. Davis had instructed the two fishing vessels to erect 'any kind of marke, token or beacon . . . upon every head land, Island or Cape' in the vicinity of their fishing ground, which he had assigned to between 54 °N and 55 °N. None was sighted and, on 15 August 1587, the *Ellen* set a course to cross the Atlantic for England, despite having on board only a little wood and fresh water. On 17 August, they met a ship at sea, which they judged to be a 'Biskaine' (from the Basque country) fishing for whales in latitude 52 °N. This encounter is confirmed by insurance policies and other records concerning the vessels of the Basque whale fishery which provide a well documented history of this little known enterprise, which lasted from 1517 to 1713.[26]

After 'much variable weather and change of windes' the little *Ellen*, ill-made as she was for ocean voyaging, reached Dartmouth on 15 September. Captain John Davis and his company, not surprisingly, gave thanks to God for their safe arrival.

Although Davis wrote no narrative of this third and notable voyage, his log or 'Traverse book', as he called it, can be studied in a special plate in Hakluyt's *Principal navigations* (1598-1600). It reveals what a careful and accurate navigator he was and in the section headed 'Discourse' ('Remarks' in more modern logs), there is some of his own writing.[27] The publication of this plate was a serious attempt by Hakluyt to set out a standard form of log – a compliment to Davis. The day after his arrival in Dartmouth, Davis sent a letter to his employer which read as follows:

Good Mr Sanderson, with God's great mercy I have made my safe returne in health, with all my companie, and have sailed threescore leagues further than my determination at my departure. I have bene in 73 degrees, finding the sea all open, and forty leagues betweene land and land. The passage is most probable, the execution easie, as at my comming you shall fully know. Yesterday, the 15 of September, I landed all wearie, therefore I pray yon pardon my shortnesse. Sandridge, this 16 of September, anno 1587. Yours equall as mine owne, which by triall you shall best know,

JOHN DAVIS

However, despite his conviction, this was to be Davis's last Arctic voyage, owing to the threat of Spanish invasion in 1588 and the death of Sir Francis Walsingham, the Secretary of State who had favoured the search for the North West Passage. His discoveries were shown on the famous Molyneux globe of 1592, paid for by Mr Sanderson, and also on the 'New Map' of 1600, drawn by Edward Wright, the mathematician, both almost certainly with Davis's help.[28] In 1595, Davis published *The Worldes hydrographical discription* in which he endeavoured to prove that all lands were habitable and all seas navigable, and that therefore it 'appeares that from England there is a short and speedie passage into the South Seas, to China, Molucca, Philippina, and India, by northerly navigation, to the renowne, honour, and benifit of Her Majesties state and community'. The previous year he had published a book of practical navigation, entitled *The seamans secrets*, which is illustrated with drawings, one of which shows the use of the back staff, which he invented. The book went into eight editions between 1594 and 1657.

The achievements of this great seaman and scientific navigator in the search for the North West Passage were summarised with some hyperbole by his biographer, Clements Markham, in 1889 as follows:

Davis converted the Arctic regions from a confused myth into a defined area, the physical aspects and conditions of which were understood as far as they were known. He not only described and mapped the extensive tract explored by himself, but he clearly pointed out the work cut out for his successors. He lighted Hudson into his strait. He lighted Baffin into his bay. He lighted Hans Egede to the scene of his Greenland labours. But he did more. His true-hearted devotion to the cause of Arctic discovery, his patient scientific research, his loyalty to his employers, his dauntless gallantry and enthusiasm, form an example which will be a beacon-light to maritime explorers for all time to come.

The same author provides an interesting and longer assessment of Davis's Arctic explorations. Writing a century later, the historian David Beers Quinn has concluded: 'His careful charting of his route was his great achievement, and he was able to return satisfied that he had done his best and had placed the great entry, shortly to be known as Davis Strait [between west Greenland and Baffin Island], indelibly on the map (even if he still believed that southern Greenland was a separate island.)'[29] His determination to find the passage led him to try from the Pacific end in 1591-93, as Drake had done earlier, but he never even reached the Pacific, unable to pass through the Straits of Magellan against the westerlies. His crew barely survived the return passage across the Atlantic to England.

CHAPTER 2

Henry Hudson and William Baffin

A new monarch and a new century witnessed two notable attempts by English seamen to find a North West Passage. They were Henry Hudson and William Baffin, who proved worthy successors to John Davis. The story of the experienced navigator and explorer, Henry Hudson is a tragic one. In 1610, his ship *Discovery* (55 tons) sailed beyond Davis's 'furious overfall' and westward for 450 miles through the long strait and into the great bay, both of which bear Hudson's name. Hudson did not keep on to the west, but turned south, and the vessel was obliged to winter at the southern end of Hudson Bay. She escaped from the ice in June 1611, but soon afterwards a mutiny took place and Hudson, his son, the sick and the loyal were cast adrift in a boat and never seen again. Two of the mutineers were killed by the Eskimos at the western end of Hudson Strait while others died during the homeward voyage. Plausible stories were told by the survivors and no-one was punished. It was Hudson's achievement to have navigated the ice-encumbered westward passage of Hudson Strait, although George Waymouth, sent by the East India Company, may have proceeded along it for a good distance in 1602. The little *Discovery* (one of the earliest of a line of exploring ships bearing that name) had braved the shallow and shoaling waters of that vast inland sea. A passage leading further westward, however, needed to be found.

A voyage to follow up Hudson's discoveries (but with no instructions to search for him) sailed in 1612, commanded by Thomas Button in the *Resolution* with the *Discovery* in company. Two of the unconvicted mutineers, Prickett and Bylot were among the ship's company. Part of the west coast of Hudson Bay was charted and Port Nelson, their wintering place, was named after one of the mates who was buried there. As with Hudson, supplies ran low and scurvy attacked them, while the *Resolution* was nipped in the ice and sank. However, with the return of spring, enough game was shot to enable the *Discovery* to proceed northwards to 65 °N into what was called Sir Thomas Roe's Welcome between Southampton Island and the east coast of America. She then returned safely to England, having charted a considerable length of coastline and made one important discovery: the voyage had shown that there was no westward passage from Hudson Bay, but that there might be one further to the north west. As a Welshman and a native of Glamorgan, Button named the newly discovered land 'New Wales'.

Meanwhile, the excitement in England resulting from the discovery of Hudson Strait and Bay led to an abortive expedition by William Gibbons sent by the 'Merchants of London, Discoverers of the Northwest Passage', under royal charter with grantees. The ship was beset for about ten weeks off the coast of Labrador in 'Gibbons, His Hole'.[1] Next year, in 1615, Robert Bylot and William Baffin in the *Discovery* again sailed through Hudson Strait, but found no passage to the northward through what became known as Frozen Strait. However, many of the discoveries of Hudson and Button were precisely located in the ship's log and on the fine chart of this voyage which is reproduced in facsimile in Clements Markham's edition of Baffin's voyages.[2] Like Davis, Baffin was a scientific navigator, even able to calculate longitude by lunar distances, a method of navigation not understood until the following century. Two further voyages through Hudson Strait and into Hudson Bay were made independently twenty years later in 1631–32, by the *Henrietta Maria* (Captain Thomas James) from Bristol and by the *Charles* (Captain Luke Foxe) from London. James Bay (at the head of Hudson Bay), where the *Henrietta Maria* wintered, and Foxe's Channel, which the *Charles* entered, were named after the two captains. But still no North West Passage via Hudson Strait and Bay had been found.

We have seen that John Davis had tried to persuade Queen Elizabeth's Privy Council in May 1595 to renew the search beyond his farthest north in an appeal entitled 'The Worlde's Hydrographical Description'. This fell upon deaf ears and it was not until Bylot and Baffin's voyage of 1616 through Davis Strait and past Sanderson's Hope that the quest was resumed in that direction. Baffin had returned from the voyage to Hudson Bay the previous year disillusioned as to finding a westward passage via that route, since the Bay was blocked by ice in its northern reaches. Baffin's sixth Arctic voyage of 1616, was financed by the merchant venturers Sir Thomas Smith, Sir Francis Jones, Sir Dudley Digges and Sir John Wolstenholme, who anticipated in their instructions that the *Discovery* (presumably on her sixth and last Arctic voyage) would reach Japan. Robert Bylot was master of the *Discovery* and William Baffin the navigator. It was a remarkable voyage, coasting west Greenland beyond Sanderson's Hope into what was later called Melville Bay. They sighted and named Wolstenholme Sound, Cape Dudley Digges, Hakluyt Island, the Cary Islands and Smith Sound (the entrance to what is now called Nares Channel between Greenland and Ellesmere Island), and then sailed south westward past Jones Sound and Lancaster Sound, the one named after one of the venturers of the voyage and the other after Sir James Lancaster of the East India Company.

Although Baffin thought that these three great waterways of the Canadian Arctic were merely bays, he retains the credit for their discovery, and that of Baffin Bay, as well as, what the whalers of the nineteenth century called, the North Water, an area of open sea in northern Baffin Bay. Only a partial narrative was ever published in *Hakluytus Posthumus or Purchas his Pilgrimes* by the Reverend Samuel Purchas, Hakluyt's less illustrious successor as collector of the English voyages. 'It is an irreparable misfortune', lamented the later editor of all

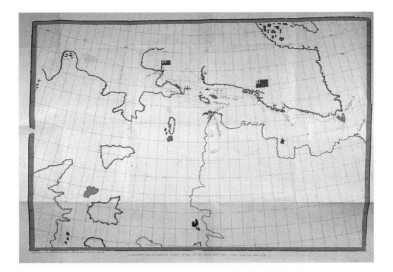

Chart by William Baffin, after whom Baffin Bay and Baffin Island were named. This chart is of Hudson Strait. (From Clement Markham's edition of *Baffin's voyages*)

Baffin's voyages, 'that Baffin's papers and maps should have fallen into the hands of old Purchas. It was upwards of two centuries before the mischief done by his suppression of the journal and maps was repaired'.[3] Purchas explained the omission in a marginal note, which read, 'This map of the author, with the tables of his journal and sayling, were somewhat troublesome and too costly to insert'.[4]

However, in defence of Purchas, the editor of *The Purchas handbook*[5] points out that he had another reason, cited without comments by Markham, for not printing the chart and journals: 'His [Baffin's] mappes and tables would have illustrated his voyages, if trouble, and cost, and his own despaire of a passage that way, had not made us willing to content our selves with the map following of that thrice learned mathematician, Master Brigges.' 'In short', writes Professor Pennington, 'the Baffin map did not indicate the possibility of a north-west passage and the Briggs map did'.

We have here a direct link with the British Arctic expeditions of the nineteenth century. By the time the first of these came to be despatched in 1818 even the very existence of Baffin's Bay was doubted. Of the two Arctic maps published in 1818, one showed 'Baffin's Bay. According to the relation of W. Baffin in 1616 but not now believed' and the other deleted the bay altogether.[6] That very year, 1818, was in fact to see Baffin vindicated by the expedition of Captain John Ross, who identified all Baffin's place-names and who paid tribute to the accuracy of his observations in his narrative of the voyage. He also expressed pleasure that by re-discovering Baffin Bay, he had 'placed in a fair light before the public the merits of a worthy man and able navigator . . .'[7]

The Elizabethan and Jacobean navigators towards the North had shown that even if a North West Passage existed it would be encumbered by ice and far from easy to traverse. 'The hopes of 1612 were at an end', writes David B Quinn regarding the *Discovery*'s voyage of 1616, 'if a pilot as skilled as Baffin could not find a passage then who could?'[8] Nevertheless, backed by the King of Denmark, the experienced seaman Jens Munk tried unsuccessfully in 1619–20. His two ships wintered near the site of the later Hudson's Bay Company post, Fort Prince of Wales, on the Churchill River. Only Munk and two others survived the winter, to accomplish a remarkable homeward voyage.[9]

These sixteenth and seventeenth-century voyages had results not anticipated by their sponsors. Instead of trade with the Far East, furs from Hudson Bay, whale products from Davis Strait and cod from the coast of Labrador eventually resulted, and their geographical discoveries were considerable. However, as David B. Quinn has remarked, for Europeans in subsequent decades, there were 'grander and more world-shaking events to write and think about' than the North West Passage, which thus 'faded into the icy mists in which it still lay undiscovered'.[10]

CHAPTER 3

The Hudson's Bay Company, James Cook and the Eighteenth Century

The founding of the Hudson's Bay Company and the slow opening up of what we now call Canada was the most significant development in the wake of the discoveries of Hudson, Foxe and earlier navigators. Though the Company was not primarily concerned with finding a route to the Pacific, the exploration with which it was associated inevitably extended the knowledge of the Arctic seas.

The Hudson's Bay Company

In 1668 a small vessel from London, the *Nonsuch,* sailed through Hudson Strait and into Hudson Bay. Her successful voyage opened up a sea route for trade in furs with the North American Indians and led to the incorporation of the Hudson's Bay Company in 1670 by royal charter. This body had what Sir Winston Churchill, who was its Grand Seigneur in the 1950s, called a 'resounding title': *The Governor and Company of Adventurers of England Trading into Hudson's Bay.* Under the Great Seal of England, King Charles II made his nephew, Prince Rupert, their Governor, and granted the 'sole trade and commerce of all those Seas Streightes Bayes Rivers Lakes Creekes and Soundes in whatsoever latitude they shall bee that lye within the entrance of the Streightes commonly called Hudson's Streightes, together with all the Landes and Territorys upon the Countryes Coasts and confynes of the Seas Bayes Lakes Rivers Creekes and Soundes aforesaid that are not actually possessed by or granted to any of our subjectes or possessed by the Subjectes of any other Christian Prince or State'. They were to be the 'true and absolute Lordes and Proprietors' of this vast territory, to be known as Rupert's Land, which comprised nearly forty per cent of modern Canada.[1]

The fur trade proved profitable in the early years of the company. Three wooden forts were built on James Bay, the southern arm of Hudson Bay, in 1685, and during the next century long inland journeys were undertaken with the aim of stimulating peaceful trade with the Indians. However, by 1776, the North West Company, based in Montreal, had also become a power in the land. The rivalry which ensued was based on the competition of two routes – Hudson Bay versus the St Lawrence River. Each side established posts in the interior and endeavoured to wrest the fur trade from the other. There followed years of 'violence, bloodshed, and a bewildering flood of seizures, warrants, arrests and court actions'.[2] The Hudson's Bay Company was at times reproached for its 'sleep beside the frozen sea' during the mid-eighteenth century, but its charter in fact laid no obligation upon it to search 'for a new Passage into the South Sea', which was merely mentioned in the preamble to the charter of 1670.[3] Nevertheless, it was involved in three episodes which proved significant in the search for the North West Passage during the eighteenth century.

James Knight's Expedition 1719

The first was the tragic expedition of 1719 led by the elderly Captain James Knight, to seek for minerals and to traverse the 'Strait of Anian'. These mythical straits became synonymous with the idea of the North West Passage and were yet another example of the unreliable nature of the charts and globes of the time. The expedition consisted of forty men, in two vessels which were well found and provisioned by the Hudson's Bay Company. They departed from Gravesend on the lower Thames in June 1719 and were never seen again. Knight had been in the company's service off and on since he landed in August 1676, as carpenter and shipwright, to spend his first five years at the 'Bottom of the Bay'. The first paragraph of his draft instructions of June 1719 read as follows:

> Upon the Experience wee have had of yr. Ability and Conduct in the Management of our Affairs wee have Upon your Aplication to us fitted out the Albany Frigg[tt] [Frigate] Capt[t] Geo Berley Commander, the Discovery Cap[t] David Vaughan Commander, Upon a Discovery to the Northward & to y[t] End have Given you Power and Authority to act and do all things Relating to the Said Voyage (the Navigation of the Said Shipp and Sloop Only Excepted) and have Given our Said two Commandrs Orders and Instructions to that Purpose.[4]

Sealed instructions gave further orders as to the conduct of the venture, should Knight die. During the following two years, there were reports about white men from the Indians and Inuit to the north of the company forts on the west coast of Hudson Bay. In 1722, Captain John Scroggs, master of the company's sloop *Whalebone*, found the remains of a substantial house, large enough to accommodate forty men and other signs that Knight's party had wintered on Marble Island, some 25 miles off the northwest coast of the Bay, a place where it is said time stands still.

What little was known of the disaster can be found in the narrative of that remarkable traveller and servant of the Hudson's Bay Company, Samuel Hearne. In the introduction to his book, *A journey from Prince of Wales's Fort in Hudson's Bay to the Northern Ocean . . . in the years 1769, 1770, 1771 and 1722*, published some twenty-five years afterwards, Hearne provides a description of the scene on Marble Island in the 1760s, when he was mate of a company vessel employed in the whale fishery. At a small harbour on what is now called Quartzite Island, attached to the east end of Marble Island proper, were found guns, anchors, cables, bricks, a smith's anvil and many other articles, which the hand of time had not defaced, and which being of no use to the natives, or too heavy to be removed by them, had not been taken from the place in which they were originally laid. The remains of the house, though pulled to pieces by the Esquimaux for the wood and iron, are yet very plain to be seen, as also the hulls, or more properly speaking, the bottoms of the ship and sloop, which lie sunk in about five fathoms water, towards the head of the harbour.[5]

The guns and the *Albany*'s figurehead were transported to the company in London, as proof of the expedition's fate. An interview with a couple of Inuit who were 'greatly advanced in years' provided an account of the building of the house and the subsequent deaths of the party from 'sickness and famine' until by the summer of 1721, only five were left, three of whom were so upset from eating raw seal meat and whale blubber, bought from the natives, that they died. The last days of the remaining two men were poignantly described. They did their best to bury their three shipmates, despite great weakness. Hearne wrote:

> Those two survived many days after the rest, and frequently went to the top of an adjacent rock, and earnestly looked to the South and East, as if in expectation of some vessels coming to their relief. After continuing there a considerable time together, and nothing appearing in sight, they sat down close together and wept bitterly. At length one of the two died, and the other's strength was so far exhausted, that he fell down and died also, in attempting to dig a grave for his companion. The sculls [*sic*] and other large bones of those two men are now lying above ground close to the house.[6]

Coat of arms of the Hudson's Bay Company, chartered in London 1670. The latin motto 'Pro pelle cutem' is thought to mean, 'it wanted the skin, *cutem*, for the sake of the fleece, *pro pelle*'. (NMM, C5529)

Archaeological, underwater and archival research by Dr Owen Beattie and John Geiger in 1989-91 have led them to question the validity of Hearne's account. However, as Professor Williams remarks in his Preface to *Dead Silence*, the book by Geiger and Beattie, 'Much has been found at that ominous site and a sounder interpretation of many aspects of the expedition is now possible, but the central issue of what happened to the forty men of the expedition remains as much a puzzle as ever. In a sense, the mystery has deepened . . . Marble Island is not giving up its secrets easily'.[7]

Captain Middleton 1741–42

No mystery, only bitter controversy, surrounds the voyages which took place during the middle of the eighteenth century commanded by Christopher Middleton in 1741-42 and William Moor and Francis Smith in 1746-47, both by way of Hudson Strait and Hudson Bay. As with Frobisher's Arctic voyages, much documentary and published material resulted from the arguments, accusations and counter-blasts, for which one Arthur Dobbs a member of the Irish House of Commons was largely responsible. It was he who wrote a lengthy *Memorial on the Northwest Passage* in 1731, with the intention of reviving the search for a shorter sea route to the 'great Southern and Western Ocean of America'[8] which would increase British overseas trade and menace Spanish America. He addressed copies of the memorial to those in high office, who he thought might support his proposal for an expedition. Among these were the First Lord of the Admiralty and the Deputy Governor of the Hudson's Bay Company. 'It was an appeal,' write the modern editors of these voyages, 'to national pride, to commercial acquisitiveness, to old fantasies of the wealth of the South Seas'.[9] Dobbs had examined the narratives of the Elizabethan and Jacobean seamen and had concluded, mainly because of references by some of Foxe's mariners in 1631 to tides coming from the west in the northern reaches of Hudson Bay, that the best route would be via Hudson Strait and Bay.

Partly because of the dismal failure of Knight's attempt and partly because of fears for its monopoly, the Hudson's Bay Company was by no means enthusiastic at the prospect. This coolness and the lack of support by other merchants led eventually to Dobbs' attacking the very foundations of the Honourable, yet secretive, Company – its charter. However, he was able to interest one of its ship masters, Captain Christopher Middleton, in finding out more about the prospects for a passage and meanwhile a rather feeble attempt was made in 1737 by two company sloops. Eventually, late in 1740, Sir Charles Wager, the First Lord of the Admiralty, was induced to speak to King George II, who gave his approval. Middleton received a naval commission and became chiefly responsible for advising the Navy Board in fitting out the appointed ships, the *Furnace* and the *Discovery*, for navigation in icy seas. Like a number of her successors in the nineteenth century, the *Furnace* (265 tons) was a bomb vessel, strongly built to withstand the recoil of heavy mortars. The *Discovery* (150 tons) was a 'pink' pur-

Carvings on the stone slab at Sloop Cove, near Churchill, Manitoba, made during the voyage of the *Furnace* and *Discovery* in 1741-42, commanded by Captain Christopher Middleton (Provincial Archives of Manitoba).

chased on Middleton's advice and renamed. William Moor, Middleton's former chief mate, became her master and they sailed from the Nore off the north Kent coast on 8 June 1741.

The vessels wintered at Sloop Cove, between the Hudson's Bay Company's massive stone fort named after the Prince of Wales, where Middleton stayed, and the recently vacated Old Factory on the Churchill River where the men were housed. On the smooth, sloping slabs of rock at Sloop Cove can still be seen the inscription giving the names of the *Furnace* and *Discovery* and the date, 1741. The expedition eventually set sail the following year northwards and during the brief summer accomplished 'a very competent piece of seamanship and exploration effected under very difficult and frustrating conditions'.[10] The ships navigated the uncharted and ice-infested waters of Sir Thomas Roe's Welcome (now Roe's Welcome Sound), between the west coast of Southampton Island and the east coast of North America. Three days after escaping from the ice-bound Wager River (now Wager Bay) into the Welcome they 'saw a fair Cape or Headland on the West or North Shore . . . the Land trending away from the EbN to the NbW making 8 Points of the Compass. This gave us Great Joy and Hopes of its being the Extream Part of America, and thereupon nam'd it Cape Hope.'[11] They then reached a deep bay whose upper reaches touched the Arctic Circle. In his disappointment, Middleton named it Repulse Bay, there being no hope of a

Fort Prince of Wales, Hudson Bay, near Churchill, Manitoba. Its ruins can still be seen. (From Samuel Hearne's *A Journey from Prince of Wales Fort . . . to the Northern Ocean*)

passage there. The ships entered what Middleton called the 'Frozen Straits', which he viewed from a 'very high mountain' overlooking the 'Frozen Straits and the East Bay on the Other Side'.[12] With a scurvy-ridden and dispirited crew, Captain Middleton turned his vessels about and headed south along the Welcome Sound. The expedition reached Stromness in Orkney on 15 September and the Thames in October 1742.

The failure to find a passage and the bitter row which resulted between Middleton and Arthur Dobbs, the instigator of the voyage ruined the former's reputation. A second attempt to find the elusive Passage was privately organised by Dobbs, with the support of a number of merchants who formed the 'North West Committee'. This took place in 1746-47, and was commanded by William Moor in the *Dobbs* and Francis Smith in the *California*. The expedition 'carried out some useful exploration in difficult conditions, but . . . every move, it seemed was dogged by disagreement, ineptitude and controversy'.[13] One turns with relief to the more straightforward doings of Samuel Hearne.

Samuel Hearne's Journey to the Northern Ocean, 1770–72

To read Samuel Hearne's *Journey from Prince of Wales Fort in Hudson's Bay to the Northern Ocean* is to accompany him in one's imagination almost every step of the way, so observant was his eye and reflective his mind. Inured to hardship and danger from service in the Royal Navy from boyhood, and familiar with Hudson Bay as a sailor and Company servant, he set off, after two false starts, to find and trace the Coppermine River and to ascertain whether or not a passage existed from Hudson Bay into the Western Ocean, cutting through the American continent. The river was said by the Indians 'to abound with copper ore and animals of the furr kind etc. and which is said to be so far to the Northward, that in the middle of the Summer the sun does not set, and is supposed by the Indians to empty itself into some ocean.' So ran part of Hearne's *Orders and Instructions* from Moses Norton, Governor of Fort Prince of Wales, on behalf of the Hudson's Bay Company in November 1769. 'This river', continued the *Orders and Instructions*, 'which is called by the Northern Indians Neetha-fan-fan-dazey, or the Far Off Metal River, you are if possible, to trace to the mouth, and there determine the latitude and longitude as near as you can; but more particularly so, if you find it navigable, and that a settlement can be made there with any degree of safety, or benefit to the Company'.

Hearne was to accompany the Northern (or Chipewyan) Indians, led by a remarkable chief named Matonabbee, of whom Hearne wrote after his death:

> It is impossible for any man to have been more punctual in the performance of a promise than he was; his scrupulous adherence to truth and honesty would have done honour to the most enlightened and devout Christian, while his benevolence and universal humanity to all the human race, according to his abilities and manner of life could not be exceeded by the most illustrious personage now on record; and to add to his other good qualities, he was the only Indian that I ever saw, except one, who was not guilty of backbiting and slandering his neighbours.[14]

Nearly six feet high, his 'features were regular and agreeable', and expressive of his thoughts, while his conversation was pleasant and lively, yet modest too. His aristocratic and elegant manners at table 'might have been admired by the first personages in the world', for they combined 'the vivacity of a Frenchman', the 'sincerity of an Englishman' with the 'nobleness of a Turk'. Born about 1736 the son of a Northern Indian and a slave woman, Matonabbee was adopted as a boy by Richard Norton, Governor of Prince of Wales Fort, when his father died. He acquired a fluency in both Northern and Southern Indian languages, and a knowledge of English. As a young man, he had been appointed mediator between the Northern Indians and the 'Athapuscow Tribe' of Southern Indians, who were always at war with each other. He was subsequently persuaded to visit the Coppermine River in company with a celebrated chief. This journey resulted in the one made by Samuel Hearne. After hearing of the destruction of Fort Prince of Wales and the abduction of the Company's servants by the French in 1782, he 'never afterwards reared his head', but hanged himself. His six wives and four children died of starvation during the following winter.

Matonabbee was to lead Hearne to the Coppermine, a river which was followed to its mouth some fifty years later by John Franklin. Besides his journal, chart, quadrant and watch for use in recording his travels, Hearne took little else with him 'as the nature of travelling long journies' in those northern lands, 'will never admit of carrying even the most common article of clothing; so that

'A winter view of the Athapuscow lake' (Lake Athabasca). (From Samuel Hearne's *A Journey from Prince Of Wales Fort . . . to the Northern Ocean*)

the traveller is obliged to depend on the country he passes through, for that article, as well as for provisions'. He took only the clothes he stood up in, plus a pocket telescope, 'one spare coat, a pair of drawers, and as much cloth as would make me two or three pair of Indian stockings'. A blanket for his bedding as well as 'ammunition, useful iron-work, some tobacco, a few knives, and other indispensable articles' made up the rest of his load for a journey intended to last some eighteen months to two years. Snowshoes and sledges for winter travel, tents and tent poles, canoes and paddles provided transport and shelter for the party of some two hundred individuals.

Hearne and the Indians set out on his third and successful journey on 7 December 1770. The women not only carried heavy loads and infants, but sewed and cooked, while the men hunted and sometimes ate while the women went hungry. Matonabee then had eight wives, all tall and strong. The large folded map at the beginning of Hearne's book, his folded Plan of the Copper-mine River, his 'winter view in the Athapuscow Lake' and the drawings of Indian canoes, a sledge, a snowshoe, kettle, bow and arrow, plus the engraving of Fort Prince of Wales all enhance the volume, as do his descriptions of the Indians, the countryside, the beaver, the musk-ox, and many other creatures. Feasting where there was plenty of game, starving when there was none, the party reached the Coppermine River on 14 July 1771, but it proved full of shoals and rapids and unnavigable. On 17 July at what became known as Bloody Fall, Hearne's Indians surprised and massacred a party of Inuit fishing there, showing no mercy and

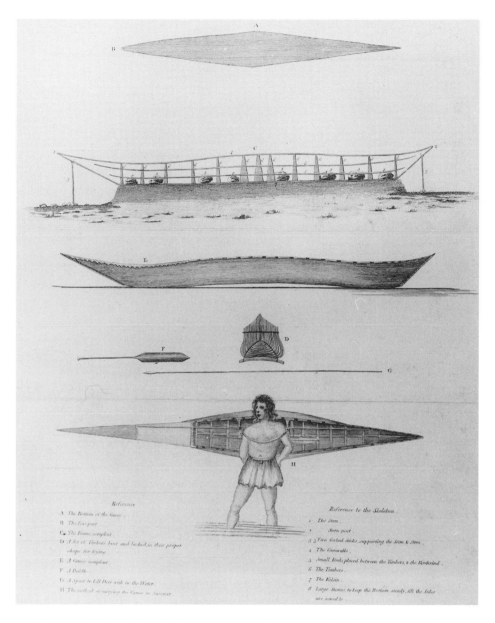

The canoe of the Northern Indians about twelve feet long, made with a hatchet, a knife, a file and an awl, generally used for crossing rivers. (From Samuel Hearne's *A Journey from Prince of Wales Fort . . . to the Northern Ocean*)

wantonly destroying their tents, stone kettles, provisions and other items necessary for life in a hard land. Not only Hearne's Northern Indians, but the Copper Indians took part in this episode, which Hearne described vividly and with great feeling. He was the first Englishman that the Copper Indians had ever seen.

It was curious to see how they flocked about me, and expressed as much desire to examine me from top to toe, as an European Naturalist would a non-descript

A portrait of Captain James Cook
by Nathaniel Dance (1776).
(NMM, B1355)

[unclassified] animal. They, however, found and pronounced me to be a perfect
human being, except in the colour of my hair and eyes; the former, they said,
was like the stained hair of a buffaloe's tail, and the latter, being light, were like those
of a gull. The whiteness of my skin also was, in their opinion, no ornament, as
they said it resembled meat which had been sodden in water till all the blood
was extracted.

They reached the sea some hours after the massacre, Hearne completing
his survey in the early hours of 18 July. He found the estuary 'full of islands and
shoals', with unbroken sea ice three quarters of a mile off shore. The tide was
out so that the river water tasted fresh, but the whalebone and sealskins at the
Eskimo encampment and the seals on the ice helped to convince him
that he had reached the 'Northern Ocean', the first European to do so.
However, although it was light all night, he was unable to obtain an observation
for latitude, owing to fog and drizzle. He did not stay to do so, having found that
'neither the river nor sea were likely to be any use' (for trade and settlement).
The latitude given on the map in his published journal proved to be over one
hundred miles too far to the north when Franklin reached the same spot fifty
years later. The importance of Hearne's journey was to demonstrate that no passage existed through the American continent south of the Arctic Circle.

'Natives in their Canoes off the Island of Oonalaska, on the North West Coast of
America', Aleutian Islands, June 1778, during Captain Cook's third voyage of 1776-80.
One of his ships can be seen anchored inshore. (Author's Collection)

Captain Cook's voyage in the Resolution and Discovery, 1776-80

The most famous of a number of circumnavigations in the 'Age of
Enlightenment' were the three commanded by Captain James Cook, a
Yorkshireman of humble origins, who had first attracted notice for his admirable
charting of Newfoundland and the Saint Lawrence River at the time of the siege
of Quebec in 1759. His voyages of 1768-71 in HMS *Endeavour*, and during 1772-
75 commanding HM Ships *Resolution* and *Adventure* in the southern hemisphere
were succeeded by his third voyage of 1776-80, when he commanded HM Ships
Resolution and *Discovery*, with the object of finding the North West Passage via
the Pacific Ocean or 'Great South Sea', as it was sometimes called.

Dr Andrew Kippis, Cook's first biographer, relates how the Captain (supposedly retired to a shore post) was invited one evening in February 1776 to dine
with Lord Sandwich, the First Lord of the Admiralty, where plans for a voyage
to search for the Passage were discussed. No-one, wrote Kippis, had presumed
to solicit Cook upon the command of the service, being well aware of what he had
already undergone and achieved during his two great circumnavigations, from
the second of which he had returned only six months earlier. Kippis continued,
saying how on that fateful evening

'The Resolution beating through the ice, with the Discovery in the most eminent danger
in the distance', probably off Icy Cape, Alaska, in August 1778. (Drawing by John
Webber, NMM, A130)

many things were said concerning the nature of the design. Its grandeur and dignity,
the consequences of it to navigation and science and the completion it would give to
the whole system of discoveries were enlarged upon in the course of conversation.
Captain Cook was so fired with the contemplation and representation of the object that
he started up and declared that he himself would undertake the direction of the enterprise.[15]

To his great honour, Cook did take command and, of course, met his end on the
Sandwich Islands (now Hawaii), but the charts brought home by Cook's officers
and published in 1784 'showed the reality of his achievement. In outline at least,
the shape and position of the northwest coast of America were known; for the
first time the region takes recognizable shape on the map, but it was not the shape
that Cook had anticipated when he sailed from England in the summer of 1776.'[16]
He had been misled by the men whom we would call today 'armchair cartographers', who drew their maps or charts from theory and not from surveys, and
caused growing frustration to Cook and his officers while coasting southern
Alaska. Their difficulties were increased by the state of the seas to the north of
Bering Strait, separating Asia from America, which they found ice covered, not
free of ice, as they had been led to believe. The culprit in this case was the
Honourable Daines Barrington, a Fellow of the Royal Society of London (founded in 1662), who believed that beyond the ice – which fringes the Arctic coasts
and the mouths of great rivers – an open polar sea existed, because the tumult of

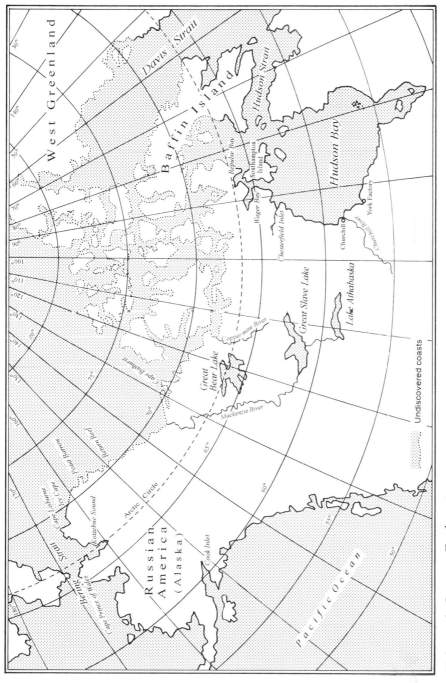

Eighteenth-Century Exploration

the waves in mid-ocean and the continuous sunlight would prevent the sea from freezing. Not the least extraordinary aspect of this theory was that it was the brain-child of one Samuel Engel, citizen of a completely land-locked country, Switzerland. It was Barrington who influenced the Royal Society, which then applied to Lord Sandwich for a naval expedition to be organised. A voyage towards the North Pole in 1773, made by Captain Constantine John Phipps, originated in the same way.

Cook's ships penetrated as far as Icy Cape, on the coast of what is now Alaska. This westerly route via the Pacific Ocean into the North American Arctic was taken later, as we shall see, by ships of the Royal Navy, sailing in the wake of the *Resolution* and *Discovery*.

Alexander Mackenzie's Journey to the Northern Ocean 1789

Born on the Isle of Lewis, one of the Western Isles of Scotland, Alexander Mackenzie was a young partner in the North West Company of Montreal, fur traders, his original firm having been displaced from the country round Detroit by the American Revolution of 1776. Driven by the need for a trading route to the Pacific, he departed from Fort Chipewyan on the southern shore of Lake Athabasca on 3 June 1789, accompanied by four French-Canadian voyageurs, the Chipewyan Indian known as the English Chief (who had been one of Matonabbee's followers, 1770-72), a number of the Indian's wives and followers and a young German, John Steinbruck . They reached the great northward flowing river which bears his name by way of Great Slave Lake. Once embarked on it Mackenzie followed it downstream all the way to the Arctic Ocean, which they reached on 14 July 1789, the same day as the outbreak of the French Revolution. He realised by accident that it was the sea because the rise of the tide wet their baggage. With the help of the current they were able to travel 75 miles a day down river, and covered a distance of 1,075 miles. The return journey upstream was slower, of course, but the expedition returned to Fort Chipewyan on 12 September. Mackenzie was described as 'blond, strong and well-built', and having a remarkable stamina himself, he drove his men hard, though he retained their trust and loyalty.[17] It is interesting that years later, when Lieutenant John Franklin was preparing for his first overland expedition of 1819-21 to the northern ocean, Mackenzie advised him in various practical matters and suggested contacting his 'old Friend if alive Nestabeck commonly called the English chief'.[18] Two of his voyageurs accompanied him on the lengthier and more arduous westward journey, across the Rocky Mountains to the Pacific Ocean in 1792-93. He thus became the first European to cross the breadth of North America.

His journey to the 'frozen ocean' of 1789 was of great significance in Arctic exploration. Mackenzie wrote later:

> I went [on] this expedition in hopes of getting in to Cook's River [presumably Cook Inlet, southern Alaska]; tho' I was disappointed in this, it proved without a doubt, that there is not a North West passage below this latitude [69 °15′N] and I believe it will

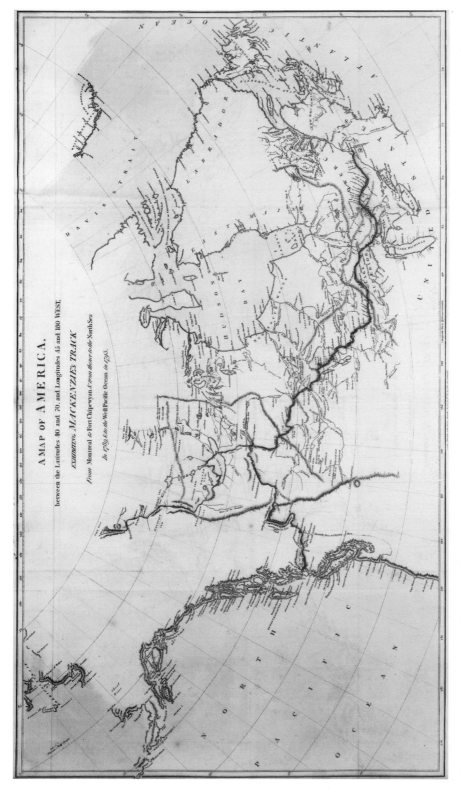

Map of North America showing Alexander Mackenzie's track down the great river named after him to the Arctic Ocean and west across the Rocky Mountains to the Pacific in 1789 and 1793 respectively. (NMM, D930).

generally be allowed that no passage is practicable in a higher latitude, the Sea being eternally covered with Ice.[19]

Vancouver

We bid farewell to the eighteenth century with Captain George Vancouver's great survey of the North west coast of America in 1792, 1793 and 1794 which showed conclusively that no waterway navigable by ships existed in temperate latitudes between the Pacific and Atlantic Oceans, thus silencing for ever the speculative geographers of Europe.[20] As Williams remarks about Vancouver:

> His explorations left no hope that a strait might be found along some inadequately explored stretch of coast. They marked the end of an era; it was at last evident that for sailing ships the Northwest Passage would never provide a route of commercial or strategic value. If a passage existed, it must lie among the ice of the polar sea. Here lay both the failure and the achievement of the eighteenth-century explorers. They had not found a passage, because there was none to find where they had searched, but at the same time as they had explored and opened for development the long Pacific coast-line from California to Bering Strait, they had defined one of the most baffling of geographical problems. Their explorations pointed the way north for the more dispas-sionate scientific navigators of another generation. Where there had been uncertainty and ill-founded optimism there was finally knowledge and a realization of the task ahead.[21]

CHAPTER 4

Sir John Barrow and the Renewal of Arctic Exploration in 1818

The French Revolution in 1789 was followed by twenty-six years of war, which at one time engulfed all Europe from London to Moscow and which had repercussions in India, South Africa, Egypt, the West Indies and North America. The French Emperor, Napoleon, was exiled to St Helena after his defeat at Waterloo by Wellington and there followed, for Britain, a century of peace, only broken by the Crimean War. Sea power had had a great influence on the course of the French wars, especially at the Battle of Trafalgar in 1805, when Nelson defeated the French and Spanish fleets leading to the Royal Navy's domination of the seas. After 1815, the Navy's rule became one mainly of deterrence and many of its ships found themselves employed in more peaceful pursuits such as the suppression of the Slave Trade, charting the coasts and oceans of the world, and diplomatic activity in every corner of the globe.

The Second Secretary of the Admiralty at this time was Mr (later Sir) John Barrow. Appointed in 1804 at the height of the French wars, he did not retire until 1845. Point Barrow on the north coast of Alaska and Barrow Strait in the eastern Canadian Arctic were named after him. They symbolise the breadth of his interest in polar exploration, and that of his son John, also an Admiralty official. Born the son of a small farmer near Ulverston in north Lancashire in 1764, the elder Barrow made a voyage to Spitsbergen aboard a whaler as a deck hand, in his youth. Partly because of his abilities and partly because of his patrons, he rose from humble beginnings to become a Fellow of the Royal Society, a well-known author, a founder of the Royal Geographical Society and in particular Second (or Permanent) Secretary of the Admiralty from 1804 to 1845 (apart from a brief intermission from 1806 to 1807.) He made great improvements in the running of the Royal Navy, while his son later took charge of the Admiralty records. On his death in 1848, a tower was erected at Ulverston, overlooking Morecambe Bay, modelled on the Eddystone lighthouse. Eight thousand people attended its inauguration.[1] As a geographer he was responsible to a large extent for promoting the dispatch of naval vessels to seek the North West Passage and to navigate towards the North Pole. As an old man, Barrow described in his autobiography how these voyages came to be made after the cessation of hostilities.

Sir John Barrow, Second
Secretary of the Admiralty from
1804 to 1845. He was the chief
instigator of the North West
Passage voyages in the first half
of the nineteenth century.
(NMM, 8855)

During all this period of tranquillity, there was but little demand on the services of the
royal navy: it had since the year 1817 afforded a fitting opportunity of employing a few
small ships in voyages of discovery [to West Africa] for the advancement of geography,
navigation, and commerce. In this year I wrote, and caused to be published in a popular journal, a curious and interesting account of the disruption of large fields and
masses of ice and huge icebergs from different parts of the Arctic regions, and their
transport far down into the Atlantic. The authenticity of this event was unquestionable, being corroborated by numerous eye-witnesses; it was deemed a fair occasion to
explore these northern seas, and to renew the attempts to discover a north-west passage from the Atlantic to the Pacific, which has engaged the attention of the learned
and ingenious, as well as the mercantile interests of this kingdom, at various periods;
and I proposed a plan of two voyages for Lord Melville's consideration, which, after
consultation with his colleagues, supported by the recommendation of the Royal
Society, was adopted.[2]

Lord Melville was at that time First Lord of the Admiralty, after whom Melville
Island, Melville Sound and Melville Peninsula were later named. The 'popular
journal' was the *Quarterly Review* for October 1817. The key 'eye-witness' was
William Scoresby, junior, a young whaling captain and a native of the Yorkshire
port of Whitby, where Captain Cook had been apprenticed and where his ships
had started life as colliers.

Son of Captain William Scoresby, senior, inventor of the crow's nest, the
younger Scoresby had a scientific bent and is remembered for his authoritative
book *The Arctic regions* (1820), the result of many northern voyages made with

Map of the central polar basin, 1817, illustrating John Barrow's theories.
From the *Quarterly Review*. (NMM, 9080)

his father to the seas between Spitsbergen and Greenland. During the winters, he studied at Edinburgh University and, by 1815, a learned society had published his treatise 'On the Greenland or polar ice'. The aged Sir Joseph Banks, who had sailed with Cook and who was President of the Royal Society for almost a lifetime, wrote to him in 1817 to draw attention to a newspaper report describing how the coast of East Greenland had proved ice free for a considerable distance that summer. Scoresby replied enclosing a copy of the treatise with a letter which said:

> I found on my last voyage about 2000 square leagues of the surface of the Greenland sea, between the parallels of 74° and 80° north, perfectly void of ice which is usually covered with it . . . Had I been so fortunate as to have the command of an expedition for discovery instead of fishing, I have little doubt but that the mystery attached to the existence of a north west passage might have been resolved . . . I do conceive there is sufficient interest attached to these remote regions to induce Government to fit out an expedition . . . In case of any whales being taken – and the fishery might be prosecuted without detriment to the other objects of the voyage – the expenses would be proportionally reduced and might possibly be altogether defrayed.[3]

Frontispiece and title page from William Scoresby's *Account of the Arctic regions*, Volume 1. Scoresby's reports of ice-free seas encouraged the Arctic expeditions sent by the Admiralty.

However, this was not to be. Having previously suffered from entrusting the command of naval vessels on scientific or exploring voyages to non-naval captains, the Admiralty would not appoint Scoresby, eminently well qualified though he might have been. He declined to sail as pilot with one of the Arctic expeditions of 1818, which was sanctioned by Lord Melville after receiving a letter from Banks on behalf of the Royal Society. Four ships were to be sent – two towards the North Pole and two to seek the North West Passage. Although not as experienced as Scoresby, both commanders had navigated in northern waters: Captain John Ross in the Baltic and Captain David Buchan surveying off Newfoundland. While the expeditions were in progress, Barrow's *Chronological history of voyages into the Arctic regions* was published. His last paragraph outlined the scientific results to be expected, and stated that should a passage be found, it would benefit all the maritime nations of Europe 'without having incurred either the expense or the risk of exploring it'.[4]

Dorothea and Trent 1818

The expedition towards the North Pole was commanded by Captain Buchan in the *Dorothea*, with Lieutenant John Franklin appointed second-in-command in

Trent. There was a precedent for this voyage set by Captain Constantine John Phipps, who in 1773 was despatched by the Admiralty at the behest of the Royal Society to find the North Pole. Phipps was instructed to turn back at the Pole (90 °N), but in fact the *Racehorse* and *Carcass* were able only to reach just beyond 80 °N and spent some weeks skirting the sea ice to the north of Spitsbergen. Both Phipps' expedition and that on which Buchan and Franklin sailed in 1818 were influenced in their objectives by Daines Barrington's theory of the open polar sea said to be found away from the land, where the waves could roam at will. (A new edition of his book had been published in 1818.) However, the *Dorothea* and *Trent* could again get little further than 80 °N in the same seas as Phipps. Both expeditions were accompanied by experienced whalers as ice pilots, as became usual with all such naval vessels. Buchan's instructions told him to proceed to Bering Strait, supposing he were fortunate enough to reach the North Pole. Failing that, he was to 'endeavour to pass between Greenland and the east coast of America, into the sea called Baffin's Bay, for the northern limits of which, as it appears in the charts, there is little or no authority, and thence by Davis' Strait to England.'[5] These instructions, could only be carried out today by powerful icebreakers, never by small sailing ships, and they reflect the depth of ignorance at the time. No narrative of the voyage was published until 1843, when one was written by Franklin's lieutenant in the *Trent*, Frederick William Beechey.

Since John Franklin features prominently in this book it seems fitting to introduce him here, on taking up his first command. Born in the Lincolnshire market town of Spilsby on 16 April 1786, Franklin was educated briefly at Louth Grammar School until he joined the Navy as a First Class volunteer (cadet) in HMS *Polyphemus* at Chatham, Kent, on 9 March 1800, in the midst of the French wars. Franklin was at the battle of Copenhagen in 1801 and on returning to England he joined HMS *Investigator*, commanded by his kinsman Captain Matthew Flinders, whose orders were to survey the whole seaboard of Australia. An astronomer, naturalist, landscape artist, gardener, miner and natural history painter all accompanied the expedition. Flinders had already spent five years surveying in Australian waters. He was able, energetic, resourceful, strict yet kindly, a fine officer, sailor and surveyor for Franklin to emulate. Franklin returned to England in August 1804 after three adventurous years in Australia, which included being shipwrecked on a reef off the east coast, followed by weeks surviving with the ship's company on a sand bank awaiting rescue. He was at the battle of Trafalgar on 21 October 1805, as signal-midshipman of the *Bellerophon* and later took part in the attack on New Orleans. Like many other naval officers, he was put on half pay after the peace of 1815.[6]

The floes of sea ice in what is called the central polar basin (the heart of the Arctic Ocean), vary both in their solidity and their southern extent, the loose floes at the edges tending to move into warmer waters with the Labrador and other currents. There is usually a huge extent of sea ice from the North Pole to about 80 °N. It was this barrier which defeated Phipps' attempt to reach the North Pole by ship in 1773 and which was also to defeat Buchan and Franklin in

1818. The ice is broken by 'leads' and 'polynyas' (pools) of open water in the summer and crossed by huge hummocks or ridges of ice, caused by the pressure of wind or current, which make the edges of the ice floes rise up and form ridges sometimes thirty to forty feet high. It was not until two centuries after Phipps that a ship was able to navigate these floes and reach the North Pole. The importance of this voyage for Franklin, second-in-command and captain of *Trent*, was to give him ample experience of ice navigation and an awareness of the rapidity with which the floes could come together or separate with a change of wind. The ships could make progress either by sailing with a fair wind along a lead, or by towing with the boats, or by hauling on ice anchors. Giant ice saws, hung from a cast iron tripod, were used when practicable and a set of these survives at the National Maritime Museum, Greenwich.

The vessels made their passage to Spitsbergen, whose waters had long been familiar to English, Dutch and other whalers. The freezing weather caused several tons of ice to stick to their sides, which had to be chopped away with axes, while the icy ropes were freed by beating them with heavy sticks. The vessels entered the main pack and were beset there, as were a number of distant whalers, for some two weeks. However, they were diverted from 'the monotony of the daily duties of the ship' by wandering polar bears which sometimes came near enough 'to sniff at the linen drying upon the ice', or by 'the gambols of seals and walruses', likewise whales or narwhals in nearby pools of open water. The pressure round the ships became intense and the *Trent* was 'suddenly lifted four feet by an enormous mass of ice getting under her keel.' A northerly wind enabled them to escape.

The chance was taken to enter the pack again through a narrow channel, which was navigated with the help of a few men on the ice floes. The channels became narrow, and laborious efforts were made to drag the ships through the ice 'by fixing large ropes to iron hooks [ice anchors] driven into the ice, and by heaving upon them with the windlass, a party removing obstructions in the channels with saws'. A few miles were gained to the north by a relatively clear passage to reach a furthest north latitude of 80 °34′ N. However, the pressure of the ice caused the vessels to rise. The *Trent* 'was so twisted that the doors of all the cabins flew open, . . . while timbers cracked to a most serious extent'. After three weeks beset in ice extending to the horizon in all directions, open water was reached. 'The pleasure we felt', wrote Beechey, 'at again having our vessels under command cannot be equalled . . . They at first appeared to bound through the water, and every passing wave brought with it a peculiar gratification.'

Their pleasure was short-lived. In steering westwards towards Greenland, the ships were caught out in bad weather and blown towards the edge of the pack, where they ground against the heavy floes. The *Dorothea* and the *Trent* were obliged to take refuge in the body of the ice, but before entering the breakers and braving the tumbling floes, Franklin ordered a cable to be cut into thirty-foot lengths and hung round the *Trent*, together with some walrus hides and the square iron plates supplied as fenders, with which they were already equipped.

'The masts . . . were secured with additional ropes, and the hatches were bat-tened and nailed down'. Beechey's account of this dangerous course continues:

> While we were yet a few fathoms from the ice, we searched with much anxiety for a place that was more open than the general line of the pack, but in vain; all parts appeared to be equally impenetrable, and to present one unbroken line of furious breakers, in which immense pieces of ice were heaving and subsiding with the waves and clashing together . . . occasioning such a noise that it was with the greatest diffi-culty we could make our orders heard by the crew.

As the little *Trent* flew before the gale towards the ice edge, in Beechey's words:

> Each person instinctively secured his own hold, and with his eye fixed upon the masts, awaited in breathless anxiety the moment of concussion. It soon arrived – the brig, cut-ting her way through the light ice, came in violent contact with the main body. In an instant we all lost our footing, the masts bent with the impetus, and the cracking tim-bers from below bespoke a pressure which was calculated to awaken our serious apprehensions. The vessel staggered under the shock, and for a moment seemed to recoil; but the next wave, curling up under her counter, drove her about her own length within the margin of the ice.

However, she did not penetrate far enough into the relative calm of the main pack. Thrown broadside to the wind, she was caught between the moving floes, which assaulted her like battering rams. Unable hardly to keep their feet, the crew could do little for the *Trent*. 'The motion indeed', wrote Beechey, 'was so great, that the ship's bell, which in the heaviest gale of wind had never struck of itself, now tolled so continually that it was ordered to be muffled, for the purpose of escaping the unpleasant association it was calculated to produce'. By the des-perate measure of setting more sail, the *Trent* split a floe fourteen feet thick and passed far enough into the pack to escape from danger.

When the storm abated, both vessels emerged disabled from their ordeal, the *Dorothea* almost ready to founder. Franklin was eager to proceed on his own in the *Trent*, but prudence and concern for his crew decided Buchan to return home.

Sir John Ross' Voyage to Baffin Bay 1818

In his anonymous article justifying the decision of the Admiralty to dispatch the expeditions of 1818[7] John Barrow had written of the need to correct the 'defec-tive geography' of the western Arctic and to ascertain 'the existence of a north-west passage from the Atlantic to the Pacific'. Barrow felt this to have been 'a peculiarly British object', since the 'earliest period of British navigation' and earlier in George III's reign. He argued that a trans-polar current must exist moving from Bering Strait to Davis Strait. Interestingly, he cited the recovery of harpoons lodged in the flesh of whales killed off the northwest coast of America, which had first been struck off Spitsbergen, as an 'additional argument for a free communication between the Atlantic and Pacific'. He reminded readers of the far shorter 'polar route' to China from London, compared with that round the Cape

'Portraits of the Vessels on the Polar Expedition of 1818'. The four ships of the 1818 voyages towards the North Pole (*Dorothea* and *Trent*), and to find the North West Passage (*Isabella* and *Alexander*). (Author's collection)

of Good Hope. He too thought it likely that open water (not ice) would be found in the absence of land in the polar basin.

The little map published with the article demonstrated his ideas. It also illustrated the contrast between the clearly drawn northern coast of Eurasia (effectively surveyed by the Russians in the eighteenth century) and the barely delineated northern coast of America. It depicts the mouths of the Coppermine and Mackenzie rivers, marked respectively 'The sea according to Hearne' and 'The sea according to M'Kenzie'. Davis Strait is also shown, though there is no sign of Baffin Bay, Smith Sound, Lancaster Sound and Jones Sound, all the discoveries of William Baffin. A further reason given by Barrow for resuming the search for the North West Passage was the fact that Russian ships were seeking a northern sea route from the North Pacific, and he felt it would be 'somewhat mortifying, if a naval power but of yesterday should complete a discovery in the nineteenth century, which was happily commenced by Englishmen in the sixteenth'. The voyage of Captain John Ross in the *Isabella* with the *Alexander* (Lieutenant William Edward Parry) in company was intended to counter this threat to national pride.

As we have seen, Captain David Buchan, seeking the polar passage in the *Dorothea* and *Alexander* in 1818, never published an account of that voyage. Captain John Ross, searching for the North West Passage the same year, did so in style. His weighty narrative of *A voyage of discovery . . . in His Majesty's Ships Isabella and Alexander for the purpose of exploring Baffin's Bay and inquiring into the probability of a North-west Passage* was published by John Murray in 1819. It was the first of a number of well-produced and beautifully-illustrated quarto volumes recounting the explorations, achievements, encounters and results of the nineteenth-century Arctic voyages. John Ross himself executed numerous watercolour sketches during the 1818 expedition and some of them were engraved in colour for the book. There are also three fine folding charts. Unfortunately for Ross's reputation, one of these charts, that of Lancaster Sound, Baffin's old discovery, later shown to be the entrance to the principal channel between the Arctic islands, is shown blocked to the west by a range of mountains, which Ross named after the First Secretary of the Admiralty, J W Croker. The following year, 1819, Ross's lieutenant, William Edward Parry, sailed right through and it is for this considerable error and the controversy that followed Ross's return that the expedition tends to be known. However, a reading of the narrative shows that there was much more to it than that.

His book provides many interesting details, for instance about the way all four of the 1818 ships were strengthened for ice navigation. Attention had also been given to preparations for a winter in the ice by the supply of a roof to cover the deck. In case of a shipwreck, the 'bed-places of the officers and crew' were fitted in such a way that they could 'be taken on shore with ease, and formed into a dwelling'. The books in the fine ship's library aboard the *Isabella* are listed while thirty Bibles and sixty New Testaments were distributed among the four ships, the gift of the Naval and Military Bible Society. There is a list of presents for the natives of the coasts of Greenland and America which included brass kettles, axes, knives, red flannel, awls, mirrors, needles and thread, scarlet caps, swords, pistols, rifles, scissors, handkerchiefs, crockery, soap, gin, brandy, beads and cowrie shells, and forty umbrellas. Ross also provides a glossary of 'sea terms used in icy seas', which differs in some respects from those in use today, and there is a table showing the 'Articles of warm clothing' supplied *gratis* to each man, a listing of the monthly rates of pay for officers and men, as well as lists of the scientific and other instruments.

The 'Official Instructions' to Captain John Ross from the Admiralty ordered him to proceed to the northward through Davis Strait, and 'In this passage', it was written, 'you may expect to meet with frequent obstructions from fields and islands of ice; to get clear of which, and to ensure the safety of the ships and people committed to your charge, will require from you, and all who are under your orders, the greatest precaution and vigilance'. Because ice navigation 'may be considered as an art to be acquired only by practice', the Instructions continued, 'we have directed that there be appointed to each of the ships . . . a master and a mate of whale-fishing vessels, well experienced in those seas, from whose knowledge and skill you may derive material assistance'.[8] Reliance was placed on his 'skill and zeal', tempered with the prudence needed to avoid accidents, and he was reminded to be friendly with the 'Eskimaux or Indians' in case the ships were to winter in the Arctic and to give them such presents 'as may be useful or agreeable to them'. Various other eventualities were covered, for example the need to fix a rendezvous with Captain Buchan in the Pacific. Then came a special paragraph:

> Although the first, and most important, object of this voyage, is the discovery of a passage from Davis' Strait, along the northern coast of America, and through Behring's Strait, into the Pacific; it is hoped at the same time, that it may likewise be the means of improving the geography and hydrography of the Arctic Regions, of which so little is hitherto known, and contribute to the advancement of science and natural knowledge.

Mention was made of the 'great variety of valuable instruments' to be placed in his care and also of Captain (later General Sir) Edward Sabine, of the Royal Artillery, who had been recommended by the Royal Society as a 'gentleman well skilled in astronomy, natural history, and various branches of knowledge'. Sabine later accompanied other expeditions and became well known for his work in terrestrial magnetism. He was to assist Ross in 1818 'in making such observations as may tend to the improvement of geography and navigation'. Lieutenant H P Hoppner, son of the portrait painter, was to help in the drawing of coastal views, whenever the vessels were impeded by ice.

Every means in Ross's power should be used 'to collect and preserve such specimens of the animal, mineral, and vegetable kingdoms', as could be conveniently stowed on board the ships, while drawings should be made of the larger ones. Once north of 65 °N, Ross and Parry were to throw overboard at intervals a sealed bottle containing a paper in several foreign languages, dated, and with the ship's position shown, which might be sent to the Admiralty by the finder, not only as evidence of the direction of currents, but to give news of the expedition's progress. (It was on one of these forms that the last record of the Franklin expedition was written in 1848.)

Finally, on the return of the *Isabella* and *Alexander* to England, Ross was to 'immediately repair to this office, in order to lay before us a full account' of his proceedings, 'taking care to demand from the officers and petty officers, the logs and journals they may have kept' before leaving the ship. Captain Sabine's 'journals and memoranda' were to be similarly collected and sealed up; Lieutenant Parry was to be ordered to act likewise. The authorities in Kamchatka (on the

Sir John Ross as a young man.
Portrait in oils by an unknown
artist. His mild expression belies
his later peppery disposition.
(NMM, BHC2982)

Pacific coast of Siberia) should have been directed by the Court of Russia to provide 'for the safe conveyance of any despatches you may intrust to them' (as they
had done some forty years earlier with those from Captain Cook's third voyage).
These instructions give a good sense of how the nineteenth-century voyages were
prepared and what the priorities were.

On 18 April 1818, His Majesty's Discovery Ships *Isabella* and *Alexander*
departed for the Shetland Islands and the northwest. At Lerwick, they met
Captain Buchan and Lieutenant Franklin in the *Dorothea* and *Trent* and doubtless the two captains fixed their Pacific rendezvous. At Lerwick, the Ross
expedition acquired 'an excellent violin player', who volunteered to join them
from the *Prince of Wales* revenue cruiser. His 'tuneful art' would 'charm away
the weariness of many an hour, among those cheerless scenes which so often
presented little variety or amusement'. We meet him later in Ross's narrative
valiantly leading the marching crews, who were hauling the ships along leads in
the ice. He occasionally disappeared into the icy melt pools, violin and all,
because (unlike the sailors), he had no hawser to hold on to. This greatly
amused the men and, says Ross, 'they never failed to exercise their wit on the
occasion'.

Being towed by the boats northwards along the shore lead off the west coast of
Greenland, the *Isabella* and *Alexander* found themselves sometimes in the company of the whalers of Hull, helping each other when in difficulty[9]. Ross was

anxious to make contact with the natives of Greenland. On board *Isabella*, was an Inuk, called in the narrative John Sackheuse, Sackheouse or Sacheuse, one of the members of the ship's company, signed on as interpreter. He came from West Greenland and had stowed away in May 1816 aboard the *Thomas and Ann*, Captain Newton, a whaler from Leith. He had remained in this vessel during the 1816 and 1817 seasons but then returned to Leith. During the 1818 voyage, Ross listened to Sackheuse's 'many adventures and narrow escapes in his canoe'. Converted by the missionaries to Christianity, the Inuk intended to return eventually to his own country, once he had learnt the scriptures and had been taught how to draw. In 1817 he was painted by Nasmyth, the artist, and his desire to accompany the expedition was conveyed to the Admiralty, who appointed him as interpreter. He proved extremely useful, as Ross relates in the narrative, and on his return the Admiralty 'treated him with the utmost liberality'. Thinking to employ him again on future expeditions, their lordships sent him to Edinburgh to be 'properly instructed'. Although he had been 'like the rest of the crew, in perfect health, during the passage home,' he contracted typhus in Scotland and died on 14 February 1819, greatly lamented by his shipmates.

John Sackheuse was first sent ashore about half way up the coast of west Greenland, in the region of Disco, his homeland. He returned 'with seven natives in their canoes, or kajacks'. The little party was given coffee and biscuits aboard the *Isabella*, while their portraits were made. Scottish reels were danced on the deck by the Greenlanders and the sailors 'to the animating strains of our musician'. Ross tells us that 'Sackheuse's mirth and joy exceeded all bounds' as he 'performed the office of master of ceremonies', with 'good-humoured officiousness', justified by his 'superior knowledge'.

In early July, the ships passed Sanderson's Hope and began to come up with the 'Women's Islands', the 'Three Islands' and other features named so long ago by William Baffin. A passage to the north was made with difficulty through icebergs. Interestingly, Ross remarks that while 'laying to' waiting for the sea ice to open on 15 July, he used some of his spare time to construct 'an instrument for bringing up substances from the bottom of the sea 'to replace an ineffective one which they had found wanting. This was his 'Deep Sea Clamm', well known to historians of oceanography.

Once the sea ice had opened up they got under way again but the difficulties involved in sea ice navigation are vividly described by Ross:

> Next morning at six, the ice opening to the North, we endeavoured by every exertion to work towards the entrance of the channel, but had no sooner attained our object, than the ice closed in upon us, and nothing was to be done unless by setting the crews to saw through the floes; but one of them continuing in motion, every effort was, for a long while, rendered fruitless, as it closed again as fast as it was sawed. In the evening a narrow passage was effected, and both the ships were warped through with great difficulty. In passing along another narrow lane, as it were, further on, the Alexander was suddenly closed in; three boats were sent to her assistance; and after two hours' hard work, she was extricated.

The plate facing this paragraph is entitled 'Crews of the Isabella and Alexander, sawing a passage through the Ice'. It is from a drawing by Captain Ross and illustrates two sets of ice saws being employed. By late July they had left all the whalers far to the south, except the *Dexterity* of Leith, aboard which vessel despatches were sent from the 'spacious bay' at 76 °N which Ross named Melville's Bay 'from respect to the present First Lord of the Admiralty', Viscount Melville. In early August, owing to heavy ice pressure, there occurred 'a trial of strength between the ship and the ice', after which peril the Greenland masters, mates and men 'declared, that a common whaler must have been crushed to atoms'. Ross attributed their safety 'to the perfect and admirable manner in which the vessels had been strengthened when fitting for service'.

There next took place a meeting with an isolated group of Eskimos, whom Ross called the 'Arctic Highlanders' in the far north west of Greenland. They were first seen on the sea ice on 9 August driving dog sledges and ingenious ways to tempt them to come nearer the ships were tried in vain. It was not until John Sackheuse volunteered to meet them, unarmed and alone, that they became more confident and less fearful of the strangers' intentions. Sackheuse could not converse with them until he realised that they spoke the drawling 'Humooke' dialect, which he at once adopted. They stood at one edge of the 'canal' and Sackheuse at the other. He threw across an English knife, a check shirt, and some beads, but not before one individual had drawn a knife from his boot and threatened to kill him. They then began to ask many questions.

> They first pointed to the ships, eagerly asking, 'What great creatures those were?' 'Do they come from the sun or the moon?' 'Do they give us light by night or by day?' . . . They again asked, 'What creatures these were?' pointing to the ships; to which Sacheuse replied, that 'they were houses made of wood'. This they seemed to discredit, answering, 'No, they are alive, we have seen them move their wings'.

Captain Ross watched the encounter through his telescope, noting the natives' hesitant retreat and advance, their trembling limbs and their faces which displayed 'extreme terror and amazement'. Sackheuse crossed the channel on a plank and convinced them that he was flesh and blood with parents like them. More presents (mirrors, knives, caps and shirts) were distributed by Ross and Parry, on their joining the party. 'It now consisted', wrote Ross, 'of eight natives, with all their sledges, about fifty dogs, two sailors, Sacheuse, Lieutenant Parry and myself'. The novelty of this meeting on the ice floes struck Ross. 'The noise and clamour', he wrote, 'may easily be conceived, the whole talking and shouting together, and the dogs howling, while the natives were flogging them with their long whips, to preserve order'. To this was added general laughter when Ross, Parry and the sailors joined in the merriment of their 'new acquaintances' on seeing themselves in the looking-glasses. Sackheuse later drew this 'ludicrous scene', which was reproduced in Ross's narrative.

Gaining confidence, the party was persuaded to approach the *Isabella*, but stopped within a hundred yards of the ship, examining the masts and every part of it with great fear and amazement. They cried out to the vessel, as if she were

a living being, 'Who are you? what are you? where do you come from? Is it from
the sun or the moon?' Once on board ship, the visitors were shown many new
wonders and initial astonishment was always followed by 'loud and hearty laughter'. Never had they seen wood in such quantity and they were tempted to
remove articles of both wood and iron, as John Davis had earlier found. 'The
only thing they looked on with contempt', wrote Ross, 'was a little terrier dog,
judging, no doubt, that it was too small for drawing a sledge'. However, in contrast, 'they shrunk back, as if in terror, from a pig, whose pricked ears, and
ferocious aspect, being of the Shetland breed, presented a somewhat formidable
appearance'. The pig's grunt frightened them even more. Portraits were taken in
Ross's cabin of the last three remaining visitors, Errick and his nephews,
Marshuick and Otooniah. After being loaded with some clothes, biscuit and
wood, they drove off in their sledges, 'hallooing, apparently in great glee'.

On 11 August, the day after this encounter, a southerly breeze allowed the ships
to sail westwards. Sackheuse was asked what additional information he had learned
from the visitors and he related among other things, that the women and children
had been sent to the mountains and that iron was obtained 'from a mountain near
the shore', that there was a rock of it, and that pieces from it were cut off with a
sharp stone, and fashioned into knife blades. By the time this information was
obtained, it was too late to turn back. We have here almost certainly a reference to
iron of meteoric origin. In 1895 and 1897 the American explorer, Robert Peary,
who made northwest Greenland the base for his attempts on the North Pole,
removed to the United States the three meteors, named by the Eskimos the
Woman, the Dog and the Tent, which had been worked by many generations of
the native people. A modern scholar has observed that 'the identification of one of
the Inughuit's main sources of iron by Ross and his officers was a noteworthy
achievement'.[10]

Another group of 'Arctic Highlanders', as Ross called them, visited the ships
two days later. He described how fast their dogs were driven. A bone sledge was
presented in return for gifts, which is presumably the one now in the British
Museum, London.[11] With difficulty, he persuaded them to sell him a dog, which
unfortunately was later washed overboard in a gale. More information was
obtained about their source of iron and Ross offered to give a reward for any
specimens brought from that spot, a place called Sowallick, as he suspected that
the rocks were 'masses of meteoric iron'. Though he acquired another sledge he
failed to obtain the sought-after specimens of iron.

Ross named this northwest area of Greenland the Arctic Highlands, of which
a 'plan of the part of Baffin's Bay which was found to be inhabited' appears in his
narrative. Wolstenholme Sound, Cape Dudley Digges and Whale Sound are all
indicated there as being places-names given by Baffin and Ross is to be commended for his anxiety to do justice to Baffin. In the introduction he wrote:

> In re-discovering Baffin's Bay, I have derived great additional pleasure from the
> reflection that I have placed in a fair light before the Public, the merits of a worthy and
> able Navigator; whose fate, like that of many others, it has not only been, to have lost,

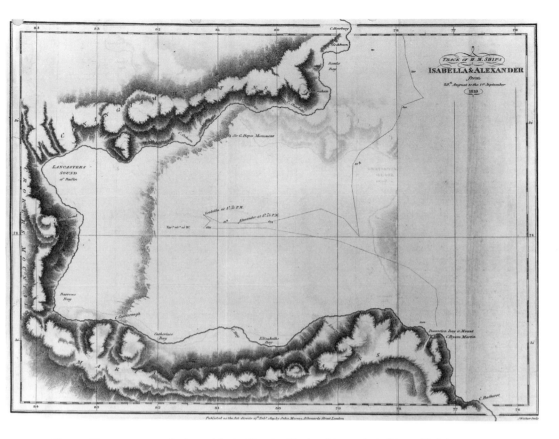

Chart of Lancaster sound, shown blocked by the 'Croker Mountains'. (From Sir John Ross' *A Voyage of Discovery . . .*)

by a combination of untoward circumstances, the opportunity of acquiring during his life-time the fame he deserved; but could he have lived to this period, to have seen his discoveries expunged from the records of geography, and the bay, with which his name is so fairly associated, treated as a phantom of the imagination.

On 16 August a prominent headland was named Cape York, which again became one of the landmarks mentioned by later seafarers. It was near here that the 'crimson cliffs' pictured in the narrative were discovered. Beyond Cape Dudley Digges, the ships encountered a considerable swell and open water was spotted from the mast-head to the northwest; this was what the whalers, who came after Ross, were to call the 'North Water' and which, like him, they crossed to reach the entrance to Lancaster Sound. On 18 August, the 'Carey's Islands' of Baffin were sighted, likewise his 'Hackluit's Island' and his 'Smith's Sound', the latter now known to form the entrance to Nares Channel between Greenland and Ellesmere Island, named after Sir George Nares, who sailed up it in HMS *Alert* during the Arctic expedition of 1875–76.

Further westward, Baffin's 'Alderman Jones's Sound' was confirmed, though fogs and heavy ice prevented access to the shore and made navigation difficult. Soon after midnight on 19 August, it was estimated that the *Isabella* had been beyond the high latitude of 77 °N. On nearer approach, Jones Sound appeared to be very nearly blocked by mountains, as was its narrow entrance by sea ice and icebergs. There were also many extensive glaciers in this northwest corner of Baffin's Bay.

Ross continued southwards along the mountainous and icebound coast, naming capes and other features. On the last day of August, the *Isabella*, with the *Alexander* several miles astern (being a poorer sailer), entered Baffin's Lancaster Sound. As Parry's ship, the *Alexander,* sailed westwards along Lancaster Sound, her Purser, William Harvey Hooper, expressed their hopes in his diary for that day:

> The long sought and much wished-for passage seemed to be before us, and it is difficult to describe the feelings of delight with which the bearings of land were taken at 7 a.m. when the atmosphere was remarkable clear, the strait still fourteen leagues wide, we had passed to the westward of the 80th meridian, and no appearance of any land to the westward.[12]

During the afternoon, Ross records that he was called from his dinner, because the bottom of the bay could be seen. 'Immediately therefore went on deck, and soon after it completely cleared for about ten minutes, and I distinctly saw the land, round the bottom of the bay, forming a connected chain of mountains with those which extended along the north and south sides.'

He ordered bearings of the land to be taken and inserted in the log. He observed ice stretching right across the so-called bay and named the mountains which appeared to obstruct his passage 'Croker's Mountains' after the Secretary of the Admiralty and the southwest corner, 'Barrow's Bay' after the Second Secretary. The views of this imaginary landscape and the corresponding chart appear in Ross's narrative, where he again paid tribute to 'the accuracy of that able navigator', William Baffin. The weather deteriorated soon afterwards and the *Isabella* returned to join the *Alexander,* because Ross was 'perfectly satisfied' that there was no passage in this direction' . . . As his biographer, M J Ross, has pointed out, he was 'very unwise not to seek the confirmation of his officers.'[13] He also discusses the reasons for Ross's decision and quotes the reactions of one of the *Alexander*'s officers on having to leave Lancaster Sound. 'Thus vanished our golden dreams, our brilliant hopes, our high expectations: and without the satisfaction of proving these dreams to be visionary, these *hopes* to be fallacies, these *expectations* to be *delusive*'.

Next day, 1 September 1818, this same officer (the Purser, William Harvey Hooper) continued in his diary:

> Sun shining upon the Southern land gave to the pointed conical spires . . . a noble and magnificent appearance . . . It was impossible not to gaze in admiration of these grandeurs, altho' we were labouring under painful feelings of disappointment and as they lessened from our sight we continued our gaze with a last, lingering look, as if with them expired all our hopes and all our prospects.

As they neared the British Isles, Hooper expressed his 'mortification and disappointment': when the 'eyes of all Europe' had been watching to see if a North West Passage existed, the *Isabella* and *Alexandra* had returned 'without adding one iota to the discoveries of Baffin', two hundred years before![14]

The subsequent public controversy surrounding the voyage was considerable, and it was lampooned in a cartoon by George Cruickshank. Another expedition was soon decided upon, to be commanded by the captain of the *Alexander*, Lieutenant William Edward Parry. Barrow and John Ross had become bitter opponents by them. This new seaborne expedition was to be complemented by an overland one down the Coppermine River, led by Lieutenant John Franklin.

CHAPTER 5

The First Expeditions of Parry and Franklin

Significant to the expeditions in the second half of the eighteenth century and in the following century were the official incentives for attaining a high latitude and for discovering the North West Passage. A number of Parliamentary Acts were introduced and the first was passed in 1745. It offered:

> to any subject, or subjects of His Majesty, a reward of twenty thousand pounds for discovering a North-West Passage through Hudson Strait. A subsequent Act, passed in 1776, offered a similar reward for the discovery of a North-West Passage; it imposed as a condition . . . that the passage should be discovered to the north of the 52nd. parallel of north latitude, but abolished the stipulation, contained in the Act of 1745, that the passage should be discovered by way of Hudson Strait. The Act of 1776 offered a further reward of five thousand pounds, for reaching, by sea, the latitude of 89 ° north. Yet another Act, passed in 1818 greatly extended these provisions. It not only offered the same rewards as the Act of 1776 . . . but also authorized the [payment of] smaller rewards for partial success . . . five thousand pounds to the officers and men of the first ship to cross the 110th meridian of west longitude to the north of America by sailing within the Arctic Circle; ten thousand pounds to those crossing the 130th meridian, under similar conditions; and so on.[1]

Parry was to benefit from these incentives on returning from his first and most successful voyage.

Parry's First Voyage 1819-20

We have seen that Parry's voyage in the *Hecla* (a bomb vessel of 375 tons) and *Griper* (a former gun-brig of 180 tons), Lieutenant Matthew Liddon, was approved by the Admiralty not long after John Ross's return. It was to be an extraordinarily successful one. The vessels entered Lancaster Sound, sailed through the imaginary 'Croker Mountains', and proceeded westwards along what is now called Parry Channel. In September 1819, they passed longitude 110 °W, thus qualifying for the first of the rewards. 'It was a proud moment for us', wrote the Purser, 'it at once compensated for all the *misery* and *mortification* of the last voyage', while the 'fond hope' of reaching the mouth of the Mackenzie before winter closed in 'had no little effect in exhilarating our spirits and producing happy countenances'.[2] They reached and named Melville Island, one of the outermost of the Canadian Arctic islands. Here they wintered in Winter Harbour. This was the first winter spent in the Arctic by a seaborne naval expedition of the nineteenth century and it set a pattern for others to follow. There were schools for the seamen, amateur theatricals and musical entertainments. Scientific observations (including meteorology and magnetism) were made and there was a good health record. The ships were roofed with padded cloth as insulation. Game, including reindeer (caribou) and musk oxen was shot when possible, amounting to 3,766lbs during nearly twelve months on Melville Island. A prominent sandstone rock near winter quarters was carved with the names of the *Hecla* and *Griper*. It was to play an important role years later as a letterbox during the Franklin Search. An overland journey, with a hand-cart and tents, preserved meat and blanket bags, was made in June 1820, when Liddon's Gulf was named.

As far as wintering was concerned, progress was often made by trial and error. For example, the hard leather boots supplied to the men caused frostbite. Parry therefore 'directed a pair of canvass boots, lined with blanketing, or some other woollen stuff, to be made for each man, using raw hide as soles.'[3] Similarly, keeping the bedding and the atmosphere below deck dry, despite the steam from cooking and laundry, was not easy. At the end of the winter, one hundred buckets of ice had to be chipped away. A wolfskin blanket per man kept the ships' companies warm in their beds at night.

It is interesting to note how food for the expedition had been prepared in England. Parry tells us in the Introduction to his narrative that:

> The ships were completely furnished with provisions and stores for a period of two years; in addition to which, a large supply of fresh meats and soups, preserved in tin cases, by Messrs Donkin and Gamble, of Burkitt's essence of malt and hops, and of the essence of Spruce, was also put on board, besides a number of other extra stores adapted to cold climates and a long voyage. The anti-scorbutics consisted of lemon-juice (which forms a part of the daily rations on board His Majesty's ships), vinegar, sourkrout, pickles and herbs, and the whole of the provisions, which were of the very best quality, were stowed in tight casks, to preserve them from moisture or other injury. As a matter of experiment, a small quantity of vinegar, in a highly concentrated state, recommended and prepared by Doctor Bollman, was also put on board, and was found of essential service, the greater part of the common kind being destroyed by the severity of the frost. In order to save storage, only a small proportion of biscuit was received; flour, which had been previously kiln-dried with great care, being substituted in its place.

The invention of canned food earlier in the nineteenth century was a significant factor in enabling vessels to winter in the Arctic. Scurvy was a danger on long voyages, but it was understood before the days of Captain Cook that fresh food and lemon juice were antidotes, though its cause (lack of Vitamin C) was not scientifically ascertained until the twentieth century. There were a few cases of scurvy during this 1819-20 expedition, perhaps due to the relative abundance of game, but Parry did his utmost to prevent or cure its outbreak. After the long winter,

A portrait of William Edward Parry, who led four Arctic expeditions between 1819 and 1827, painted by Samuel Drummond. (National Portrait Gallery, London)

sorrel leaves could easily be gathered on Melville Island and used as an anti-scor-butic in the diet, making the crews healthy in anticipation of the summer's operations at sea.

Parry's first voyage proved to be not only one of geographical exploration, but of understanding about living and working in the Arctic. For example, by 29 October 1819, the temperature had dropped to −24 °F and 'it now became rather a painful experiment to touch any metallic substance in the open air, with the naked hand ... We found it necessary, therefore, to use great caution in handling our sextants, and other instruments, particularly the eye-pieces of the telescopes.' Soft leather coverings were found to be the remedy. Parry remarks on the adaptation of their bodies to the cold, so that 'the scale of our feelings ... was soon reduced to a lower standard than ordinary; so that, after living for some days in a temperature of −15 °F or −20 °F, it felt quite mild and comfortable when the temperature rose to zero, and *vice versa*'. They were wintering at nearly 75 °N.

The shortest day (22 December 1819) came upon them remarkably soon, so well occupied had everyone been and the men even complained of a lack of time

'Situation of HMS *Hecla* & *Griper*, July 4th, 1819', during Parry's first voyage. (From William Edward Parry's *Journal of a Voyage . . .*)

to mend their clothes. Parry was pleased to hear such a complaint and aside one afternoon a week for that purpose.

Parry writes of the 'death-like stillness of the most dreary desolation' and of the 'total absence of animated existence', for most creatures had migrated further south for the winter months. Foxes and wolves did visit them occasionally, and three of the officers' pet dogs joined the wolves from time to time, although the encounters were not always friendly. With the return of the sun, ptarmigan and 'caribou' returned to Melville Island. Parry then saw fit to remind members of shooting parties 'that every animal killed was to be considered as public property; and, as such, to be issued like any other kind of provision, without the slightest distinction between the messes of the officers and those of the ships' companies.' It was such fairness that must have helped him to maintain discipline with little corporal punishment, though, on 14 February 1820, after the *Hecla* had been in commision for thirteen months, he found it necessary to inflict thirty -six lashes each on two of the marines for drunkenness the previous night.

After nine days' cold and tedious digging and sawing of the ice round the ships, they were afloat again by mid–May, when a survey of the provisions was

The crews of *Hecla* and *Griper* cutting into Winter Harbour, Melville Island. (From William Edward Parry's *Journal of a Voyage . . .*)

made and found to amount to supplies for another year. Mustard and cress had been grown below decks during the winter and used to combat scurvy, but attempts to grow radishes, onions, mustard and cress outdoors in the warmer weather proved a failure. However ships' peas, sown for amusement by the crew, were a success. The last number of the ship's newspaper, the *North Georgia Gazette,* was penned and the 'North Georgia Theatre' had given its last performance with the approach of spring, when more active work could be done by the men and the vessels were prepared for sea. The winter frost had opened the seams, so that the upper works and decks needed caulking.

The *Hecla* and *Griper* were at last able to depart, and on leaving Winter Harbour on 1 August 1820, they set a course westwards to attempt a passage from Melville Island to Bering Strait, through which they hoped to enter the Pacific. However, they were stopped by closely-packed and heavier ice (40 to 50ft thick) than they had previously encountered, and resembling that met by the *Dorothea* and *Trent* north of Spitsbergen. This was, of course, the multi-year ice of the central Arctic Ocean, which was later called 'palaeocrystic ice' by members of the British Arctic (Nares) Expedition of 1875-76, who sledged across it

Hecla and *Griper* housed in for the winter of 1819-20, with their yards and topmasts sent down. (From William Edward Parry's *Journal of a Voyage . . .*)

towards the North Pole. The 'loose pieces being most of them of infinitely greater bulk and weight in the water than either of our ships', wrote Parry, 'the latter could no longer turn them out of the way . . . but were invariably stopped . . . with a violent concussion, which nothing but their extraordinary strength could have enabled them to withstand'. The expedition's furthest point west (looking towards Cape Dundas on the south coast of Melville Island) was reached on 16 August (113 °46'43''.5W) and finding no passage to the southward either, Parry determined to return to England. This was after land seen to the south of Melville Island, across what was subsequently called M'Clure Strait, was named Banks Land.

After surveying to the eastward on their return passage to Davis Strait, naming the coasts, headlands, capes and islands (including one feature, Cape Franklin, 'after my friend, Captain John Franklin, of the Royal Navy, now employed in investigating the northern shore of North America'), Parry, Liddon and the crews of the *Hecla* and *Griper* sailed for home. On reaching England, Parry 'had the hap piness of seeing every officer and man on board both ships (with only one exception out of ninety-four persons), return to their native country in as robust

Parry's sandstone rock on Melville Island inscribed to commemorate the wintering there of *Hecla* and *Griper*, 1819-20. (From Clement Markham's *Life of McClintock*)

health as when they left it, after an absence of nearly eighteen months, during which time we had been living entirely on our own resources'. At the end of his narrative Parry affirmed his belief in the probable existence and likely accomplishment of a North West Passage into the Pacific Ocean. He also favoured the extension of the British whale fishery, as a result of Captain Ross's voyage of 1818, not only as 'one of the most lucrative branches of our commerce', but almost as importantly as 'one of the most valuable nurseries for seamen which Great Britain possesses'. Parry's first voyage was undoubtedly a successful one and to examine the large folding chart in his *Voyage* is to see the first stage in the unveiling of the intricate waterways of what is now the Canadian Arctic archipelago.

Franklin's First Overland Expedition, 1819-22

Complementary to Parry's seaborne attempts to find the North West Passage were Franklin's much smaller overland expeditions of 1819-22 and 1825-27. As we have seen, the northern coast of America had been reached, first by Hearne and then by Mackenzie, in the late eighteenth century at the mouths of the Coppermine and the Mackenzie rivers respectively. Franklin's overland expeditions, promoted by the Admiralty, were sent to chart the north coast of America to east and west of the known points at the mouth of these two rivers.

The personnel consisted of small parties of officers and men of the Royal Navy. However, Lieutenant Franklin received his instructions from Earl Bathurst, the Colonial Secretary, by whom he was appointed and after whom Bathurst Inlet, off Coronation Gulf, was later named. The expedition narratives were published in beautifully illustrated quarto editions, with large folding maps, showing the routes of the exploring parties and the results of their surveys.

On both expeditions, Franklin was accompanied by Dr (later Sir) John Richardson, the distinguished naturalist and naval surgeon, and by Midshipman (later Admiral Sir) George Back, a gifted artist, whose knowledge of French (from his time as a prisoner-of-war) proved useful in company with the French-Canadian voyageurs. On his return to England, after the privations of the first, down the Coppermine River, Franklin became known as 'the man who ate his boots': the circumstances of the second, down the Mackenzie River, were more propitious and Franklin returned from it with his boots no doubt worn out but his reputation enhanced.

His instructions[4] for the first 'journey to the shores of the Polar Sea' informed him that 'the main object of the Expedition was that of determining the latitudes and longitudes of the Northern Coast of North America, and the trending of that Coast from the Mouth of the Copper-Mine River to the eastern extremity of that Continent,' (ie as far as the western shore of Hudson Bay.) Another objective was 'to amend the very defective geography of the northern part of North America'. He was instructed to 'erect conspicuous marks' along the coast, where information about it could be deposited for Lieutenant Parry's use. Helped by Midshipmen Back and Hood, he was to record regular observations of the temperature, wind and weather, the aurora borealis and geomagnetism, this last important for navigation. The midshipmen, noted for their sketching abilities, were also to 'make drawings of the land, of the natives, and of the various objects of natual history', especially those considered by Dr Richardson (responsible for this subject) 'to be most curious and interesting'. At the mouth of the Coppermine River, Franklin was to ascertain the whereabouts of the source of copper brought down to Hudson Bay by the Indians. Dr Richardson was to examine this, from both a commercial and a mineralogical point of view.

Before leaving England in May 1819, having been appointed to the command only during the previous February, Franklin consulted the Governor and London Committee of the Hudson's Bay Company and such Gentlemen of the North West Company as were in England. No doubt with their help he drew up a scale of provisions, with guns and ammunition, to be carried from England in packages not exceeding the Hudson's Bay Company's customary 90lbs in weight. He also gave Sir John Barrow a list of instruments and books required (including both Hearne and Mackenzie) and forwarded to him Dr Richardson's list of collecting and preserving materials and his list of books on Natural History.[5] The two companies in turn ordered their agents and servants in North America to do their utmost to help the expedition and the offer by the Hudson's Bay Company to transport the expedition was accepted. The instructions allowed Franklin to determine which northward route to follow to the coast and to the mouth of the Coppermine River. Shortly before leaving Gravesend in the company ship *Prince of Wales* on 23 May 1819, Franklin had the pleasure of meeting Sir Alexander Mackenzie of the North West Company, who had reached the coast of the Polar

Sir John Franklin as a young naval officer at the time of his two overland expeditions in the 1820s. Watercolour by W. Derby (NMM, 3548)

Sea on 14 July 1789. 'He afforded me', wrote Franklin, 'in the most open and kind manner, much valuable information and advice.' Mackenzie's letter to Franklin, of 21 May 1819, recommended the composition of the overland party and suggested that once on the sea coast, the Esquimaux should be persuaded to accompany them and perhaps transport them in an umiak. The 'wintering servants' of the Hudson's Bay Company were to be instructed to advise Franklin as to his route, once arrived in North America and they were also to provide him 'with the necessary escort of Indians to act as guides, interpreters, game-killers etc.; and also with such articles of clothing, ammunition, snow-shoes, presents, etc., as should be deemed expedient for me to take'.[6]

The expedition was to enter Rupert's Land (still by right of their royal charter the exclusive province at that time of the Honourable Company) by way of Churchill or York Factory, on the western shore of Hudson Bay. For the previous 150 years, the fur trading posts on this great inland sea had been supplied every year from England and the 'returns' – furs, oil and goose feathers, plus any passengers – taken on board for the homeward voyage. Probably the last of these 'ships from England' to make the voyage largely under sail was Captain R F Scott's *Discovery*, now berthed in Dundee.[7] One of the most fascinating documents in the archives of the venerable company (in Winnipeg) is the large, vellum-bound book of ships' movements, which covers the years 1719-1929 – an epitome of its maritime history.

As was usual, the *Prince of Wales*, with her consorts the *Eddystone* and the *Wear*, put into the Orkney town of Stromness before making the Atlantic passage. Here Franklin hoped to engage boatmen for the overland journey, though all he obtained were four cautious Orkneymen, who agreed to accompany the expedition as far as Fort Chipewyan. The Moravian Missionary brig *Harmony* happened to be in Stromness too, *en route* for Labrador, and Dr Richardson and Franklin went aboard to learn about the 'manners and habits' and vocabulary of the Esquimaux. The missionaries were eager to communicate, 'but as they only spoke the German and Esquimaux languages, of which we were ignorant, our conversation was necessarily much confined'; but the brig's captain gave Franklin (who was deeply religious) a translation into Inuktitut of the Gospel according to St John, published in London by the Moravian Society.

The *Prince of Wales* made a slow passage across the Atlantic, through Hudson Strait (at the entrance to which the vessel was nearly wrecked), then south west to York Factory across the shallow, shoaling, uncharted inland sea. The anchorage at York Flats came into view on 30 August 1819 and the Governor of the Hudson's Bay Company's posts, William Williams, came aboard that afternoon. Richardson, Franklin and Hood accompanied the governor to York Factory the same evening and conferred with him about the routes and conditions which might be anticipated. Franklin drew up a questionnaire, which the governor and three 'masters of districts' answered in writing. These make interesting reading. The route via Churchill, for instance, (where Hearne had begun his long and deviating journey) was pronounced 'perfectly impracticable at this season of the year'. On the basis of the information they received Richardson and Back opted for the Cumberland House route, while Hood suggested proceeding in the summer from Churchill, after wintering there and gaining the confidence of Esquimaux who might accompany them to the northern ocean. This proposed route would have the advantage of passing through country unvisited since Hearne's journey of fifty years before.

Built since Franklin's time, the main wooden clapboarded building of York Factory still stands today on the edge of the wilderness, above the Hayes River, whose soft banks are eroding and bringing York Factory ever closer to its edge. Part of the cemetery seems already to have been lost. York Factory was a Company post for 275 years until 1957, being acquired by the Canadian Government in 1968 and designated an historic site. Although many of the subsidiary buildings have gone, the modern visitor has little difficulty in imagining life as it was when York Factory was the main distribution centre, inward and outward, of an ingenious network of rivers and portages over most of the lands to the northwest. It was also the administrative and commercial capital of the fur trade in the earlier nineteenth century.[8] Franklin described its situation.

> The surrounding country is flat and swampy, and covered with willows, poplars, larch, spruce and birch trees; but the requisition for fuel has expended all the wood in the vicinity of the fort and the residents have now to send for it to a considerable distance

. . . Though the bank of the river is elevated about twenty feet, it is frequently over-flown by the spring-floods, and large portions are annually carried away by the disruption of the ice . . .

After remarking on the hazards for shipping of the Hayes River, he went on to observe that vessels of 200 tons could navigate certain channels as far as the Factory.

During the fifty years since Samuel Hearne's journey, both the Hudson's Bay Company and the rival North West Company (based in Montreal) had greatly extended their operations by building fur trading posts (often adjacent to each other) to the north and northwest of Hudson Bay and the St Lawrence River. These were linked by canoe or York boat in the summer and by dog sledge and carriole in winter. The conflict between the two companies was unfortuately at its height during the years of the first overland expedition (1819-21). This ceased after their amalgamation in 1821 under the name of the Hudson's Bay Company, though it was too late to help Franklin. In the decades before that, peace had been largely established not only between warring Indian tribes, but between Indians and the Esquimaux (Inuit) and there were few massacres like that of the Bloody Fall, as witnessed by Hearne. Franklin found a number of North West Company partners 'under detention' at York Factory to whom he showed letters of intro-duction from their London agent. He was assured that the company's wintering partners would 'promote the interests of the Expedition' and, having become aware of the 'violent commercial opposition existing in the country', Franklin was pleased to receive this assurance, as well as advice as to the interior. He wisely drew up a memorandum for his officers forbidding them to interfere in the quarrels between the two companies. This he showed to both parties, to their satisfaction.

York Factory offered relatively easy access to the interior of the country. The route lay up the Hayes River, and via Norway House (on the northeast corner of Lake Winnipeg), Cumberland House (on the Saskatchewan River), Fort Chipewyan on Lake Athabasca, Fort Providence on Great Slave Lake and thence further north to the Yellowknife and Coppermine rivers. The party was to travel by York boat (the river freighter used by the Hudson's Bay Company), for which only a helmsman (but no crew) could be found by the governor. The party there-fore consisted of Franklin, Dr Richardson, the two midshipmen, the four Orkney boatmen, the helmsman and John Hepburn, who was to play a crucial part in the privations to follow. He has been described as 'a splendid specimen of a British sailor, steady, faithful, willing, always cheerful, and possessing bulldog tenacity of purpose.'[9] On the day of departure (9 September 1819), it was discovered that the boat could not carry all the provisions and on the governor's advice and assurance that tobacco, ammunition and spirits could be purchased inland, these were left behind. In addition, the bacon, some of the flour and the rice were also relinquished on the understanding that Governor Williams would forward all but the bulky bacon the following season.

The York boat in which they sailed and tracked the 700 miles westward to

'Manner of making a resting place on a winter's night'. (From John Franklin's *Narrative of a journey to the shores of the Polar Sea*)

Cumberland House was one of the Company's transport boats for goods on the lakes and rivers of Rupert's Land. Lightly constructed and of very light draft, the York boats were about 40ft long, with fine ends, and a broad beam. They required a crew of some nine to twelve men. They were of course more cumbersome than the birch-bark canoes used for faster and lighter travel, and when the rapids were impassable, not only the cargo, but the craft had to be carried or 'portaged' overland, which was a laborious task. Oars were used on the lakes and going down stream, but when travelling upstream (as on the way up the Hayes River), the York boats had to be 'tracked' or dragged along, by the crew from the bank. Rudders could be fitted, but the boats were generally steered with an oar astern.[10] The midshipmen took compass bearings of every turn in the rivers, and young Hood showed 'extraordinary talent', wrote Franklin, for the survey work. Franklin's *Narrative* describes the winding and beautiful Steel River in its narrow wooded valley where, on 13 September 1819, the leaves were ready to fall.

> The light yellow of the fading poplars formed a fine contrast to the dark evergreen of the spruce, whilst the willows of an intermediate hue, served to shade the two principal masses of colour into each other. The scene was occasionally enlivened by the bright purple tints of the dogwood, blended with the browner shades of the dwarf birch, and frequently intermixed with the gay yellow flowers of the shrubby cinquefoil.

However, he found the scene a desolate one 'from the want of the human species', and noted that 'The stillness was so great, that even the twittering of the *whiskey-johneesh*, or cinereous crow, caused us to start'. The rivers being low, more of the cargo had to be left behind *en route*, to be forwarded the following season. The expedition obtained scant help from those in charge of the Hudson's Bay Company's boats, travelling the same way, despite the Governor's circular enjoining them to assist.

The winter freeze-up made further travel by water out of the question, and the boat party remained at Cumberland House, which they reached on 23 October 1819 at the end of a laborious journey of some 700 miles. The few Indians whom they had met *en route* were suffering badly from whooping cough and measles or else mourning those relatives who had died and were therefore unable to hunt. Fearing that his earlier letters to the partners of the North West Company in the Athabasca department might not have arrived, Franklin decided to proceed there in person to obtain guides, hunters and interpreters, having procured none at Cumberland House. He left in the depths of the winter, on 19 January 1820, with Back and Hepburn, while Dr Richardson and Hood stayed on at Cumberland House. The Orkneymen were to return home, not wishing to go any further.

Franklin's account of the long winter journey to Fort Chipewyan on Lake Athabaska to the north is an interesting one. They travelled 857 miles, mainly along the rivers – the frozen highways at that season – and over portages including the Methye portage of 13 miles, between the Churchill and Athabasca river systems. They slept beside a camp fire under the stars on pine branches laid on ground cleared of snow, wrapped in blankets and coats which were sometimes covered by a snowfall in the night. They were kindly received by the largely Scottish gentlemen of both companies on their unexpected arrival at their posts, some of whom accompanied them onwards for part of the journey. Franklin, Back and Hepburn arrived at Fort Chipewyan at the western end of Lake Athabasca on 26 March 1820 and were hospitably welcomed by the partners of the North West Company and then at the rival establishment, Fort Wedderburn.

In reflecting upon the long winter journey, Franklin considered that on balance, the disagreeable outweighed the agreeable, one of the worst aspects being the need to walk on snow shoes, 'with a weight of between two and three pounds constantly attached to galled feet and swelled ankles'. This pain could only be surmounted with 'perseverance and practice' by the novice. Too kind-hearted to kill a mosquito, Franklin hated 'being constantly exposed to witness the wanton and unnecessary cruelty of the men to their dogs, especially those of the Canadians, who beat them unmercifully, and habitually vent on them the most dreadful and disgusting imprecations'. All other 'inconveniences' would be quickly forgotten at the end of the day 'when stretched out in the encampment before a large fire, you enjoy the social mirth of your companions, who usually pass the evening in recounting their former feats in travelling'. Then the Canadians would be 'cheerful and merry', despite frequent interruptions from the dogs, which prowled round the circle snatching at food. Best of all were the welcomes at the fur trading posts when the 'trappings of a voyager' could be shed for a short time and cleanliness restored again.

Down the Coppermine River to the 'Hyperborean Sea'

Dr Richardson and Hood joined Franklin at Fort Chipewyan, once the rivers were running and such supplies as were obtained could be brought up from Cumberland House. Meanwhile, Franklin had made further arrangements and had learnt something of the route to the Coppermine and down to the sea. On 18 July 1820, they all left Fort Chipewyan, where there was again a shortage of supplies, in canoes paddled by Canadian voyageurs, and proceeded (accompanied by clouds of biting flies) to Fort Providence, on the north shore of Great Slave Lake, where they arrived on 29 July after traversing several portages.

The post belonged to the North West Company, whose clerk, Willard-Ferdinand Wentzel, awaited them, together with Jean Baptiste Adam, one of the interpreters and an Indian guide. Wentzel prepared Franklin for a conference with the Indian chief Akaitcho, which in the end turned out satisfactorily. Wentzel agreed to join the expedition with the duties of managing the Indians, superintending the voyageurs, obtaining and distributing the provisions and issuing other stores. Having carried out similar duties during a residence of twenty years, he was considered a great acquisition to the party, being able to check on the interpreters from his fluency in the language of the northern Indians. The chief agreed to accompany Franklin's party and also that his tribe should hunt for them *en route*. Although they had made war in the past on the Esquimaux, he said that now they were anxious for peace, but warned Franklin against their treachery, about which he had already been warned at York Factory. Franklin was impressed by Akaitcho's 'penetration and intelligence' during the conversation. Gifts were presented to the chief, the two guides and seven hunters who were to accompany them on the journey, but more were promised on their return when their debts to the North West Company would be made good.

The Indians set off from Fort Providence on 1 August and Franklin's party the next day. This last consisted of twenty-eight persons – six Europeans, seventeen voyageurs, two half-breed interpreters (Adam and Pierre St Germain), plus three wives (and three children) of the voyageurs, who were to make clothes and shoes for the men during the winter. On 20 August, a Sunday, they arrived at the Winter River, the place chosen by the Indians for winter quarters. There were numerous tall pine trees and a pleasing view of the hills and lakes from the top of the well-clothed river bank, where it was decided to build 'Fort Enterprise'. That afternoon, prayers were read and thanksgiving offered 'to the Almighty for his goodness in having brought us thus far on our journey'. Franklin had hoped at once to make a reconnaissance down the Coppermine River to its mouth, but had to be satisfied with sending the two midshipmen, St Germain, eight Canadians and one Indian in a light canoe on a shorter journey cross-country to the river, to include, at Back's discretion, a few days' descent. This was because Akaitcho considered that a full descent would be 'rash and dangerous', mainly owing to the lateness of the season, and he told Franklin he would forbid his men to go.

Guided by old Keskarrah, one of the Coppermine Indians, Franklin, Dr Richardson, Hepburn and a voyageur walked to the river over hills and barren land in chilly, sometimes foggy weather, returning on 15 September to find Hood and Back already at winter quarters after their journey. The house was well advanced in its construction and, on 6 October, the tents were taken down and Fort Enterprise became the party's home. It was, wrote Franklin, 'merely a log-building, fifty feet long, and twenty-four wide, divided into a hall, three bedrooms and a kitchen. The walls and roof were plastered with clay, the floors laid with planks rudely squared with the hatchet, and the windows closed with parchment of deer-skin'. After building up a good fire in the large, clay-built chimney, they 'spent a cheerful evening before the invigorating blaze', in far greater comfort than in the tents. Dr Richardson remarked that 'the clay froze as it was daubed on, and has since cracked in such a manner that the wind rushes in from every quarter'. However, 'with the aid of warm clothing, and good fires, we expect to get comfortably over the winter'.[11]

The same hatchets and 'crooked knives' as had constructed the dwelling were soon put to use in making chairs, tables and bedsteads. Franklin explained to the readers of his *Narrative* that:

> The crooked knife, generally made of an old file, bent and tempered by heat, serves an Indian or Canadian voyager for plane, chisel and auger. With it the snow-shoe and canoe-timbers are fashioned, the deals of their sledges reduced to the requisite thinness and polish, and their wooden bowls and spoons hollowed out. Indeed, though not quite so requisite for existence as the hatchet, yet without its aid there would be little comfort in these wilds.

Two canoes were made at Fort Enterprise, where the expedition and a number of Indians remained for ten months altogether. Supplies grew short, partly because, as before, the Indians were often mourning the loss of loved ones, rather than hunting, and partly because the ammunition and other items, which had to be left behind *en route* for the north, had not been forwarded. Midshipman George Back and a small party made a record-breaking midwinter journey of some 1,100 miles on snow-shoes to Fort Chipewyan to see what had gone wrong. He was away from November till March, returning with some supplies and the promise of more. One small family of Copper Indians stayed on at Fort Enterprise after the rest had returned in December to their winter camp. They were the guide, Keskarrah, his wife (being treated by Dr. Richardson), and their beautiful young daughter, Green-stockings. Father and daughter were drawn by Robert Hood, who is believed to have fathered Green-stockings' child. During one of the Franklin Search expeditions, thirty years later, old Hepburn revealed that the two midshipmen nearly fought a duel over her, so that sending Back on this long journey may have relieved the situation.[12]

Franklin's party left Fort Enterprise for the Coppermine and the Polar Sea on 14 June 1821, accompanied by French-Canadian voyageurs, among whom

'View of the Arctic sea from the mouth of the Copper Mine river, midnight'. (From John Franklin's *Narrative of a journey to the shores of the Polar Sea*)

was an Iroquois Indian named Michel and an Italian named Fontano. By this time the two Inuit interpreters had arrived from Churchill on Hudson Bay, where they had been given the names Augustus and Junius commemorating the months of their arrival. Franklin gives their real names as 'Tattannoeuck and Hoeootoerock, the belly and the ear'. Because of the shortage of supplies and gifts, Franklin still had difficulty in persuading Akaitcho ('Gros Pied' – Big Foot) and the other Copper Indians to accompany the party to the sea. Before the expedition's departure, Wentzel translated Franklin's request, in the presence of the other Indians, to Akaitcho that provisions should be deposited at Fort Enterprise by September, against the party's return from the Arctic Sea. Wentzel was to travel as far as the mouth of the Coppermine River and then return to Fort Enterprise on his way south, picking up a box of journals, drawings and charts secured in one of the rooms for transmission to London. He was also to leave a letter for Franklin about the Indians' whereabouts before leaving.

To reach the Coppermine, the party had to travel across the ice of numerous lakes, pulling the canoes on sledges. The flesh of deer caught by the hunters was pounded into pemmican, after being dried in the sun, when not required for immediate use. Fish were caught through holes in the ice. On reaching the river, Franklin issued orders about the descent of rapids. These should be inspected by the bowmen first and, in case of danger, the ammunition, guns and instruments should be taken out of the canoes and carried along the banks, to provide a means of subsistence in case of an accident. Repairs to the canoes could be quickly made with gum or resin from the bark of the spruce. The course of the Coppermine was surveyed and the scenery sketched by the officers.[13]

The position of the mouth of the Coppermine was found to be much further south than Samuel Hearne had calculated. In his honour, Franklin named the most prominent cape 'Cape Hearne'. The party had travelled some 334 miles from Fort Enterprise, reckoned Franklin, and the canoes and baggage had been dragged over snow and ice for 117 miles of this. A few of the voyageurs had been sent back with Wentzel to reduce the size of the party, which amounted to twenty when the voyage eastwards along the sea coast was begun. The sailors were pleased to return to their usual element after the 'difficulties and impediments' of inland navigation, though the Canadians, on the contrary, had never seen the ocean; Franklin paid tribute to their courage 'in encountering the dangers of the sea, magnified to them by their novelty'. On 21 June 1821, the party embarked upon its voyage on the 'Hyperborean Sea', soon afterwards finding an Inuit cache of skins, sledges and fishing gear on an island. Having taken four seal skins to mend their shoes, they left a copper kettle, some awls and beads in exchange.

To proceed eastward for over 500 miles along an unknown and often rocky and ice-infested coast, as did Franklin's party in two birch-bark canoes, exploring Coronation Gulf and the intricacies of Bathurst Inlet and other bays and sounds, was extraordinarily risky and bold. Gales and foul weather in mid-August presaged the coming end of the summer, their pemmican supply was low and no Inuit had been seen, with whom the winter might have been passed. There was no hope of reaching Repulse Bay (on the west coast of Hudson Bay), as had been hoped, so on 22 August at Point Turnagain at 110 °5` W, they set off on what was to prove one of the most terrible of journeys, up the newly discovered river named after young Hood (rather than the Coppermine) and across the barren grounds to an empty Fort Enterprise. Since the Hood River turned out difficult to navigate and led in a contrary direction, the party struck out across barren, treeless country not knowing what obstacles in the way of rivers and lakes there might be.

Two smaller canoes had been fashioned from the big ones, because of the uncertainty and in case it proved necessary to divide the party; and even these were difficult to carry in a gale across hilly and stony ground covered in snow or ice. One was damaged beyond repair and the other abandoned, despite Franklin's pleas. The Canadians also threw away or burnt the fishing nets and floats. Food was short and the cold was severe; sometimes the party starved and at other times ate *tripe de roche*, a lichen gathered off the rocks. Occasionally a partridge, musk ox or deer was killed and various berries were gathered. At other times the skin and bones and putrid flesh of a deer's carcase, perhaps left by the wolves, plus leather from old shoes or pieces of their buffalo robes, were eaten. Because there were few if any clumps of pine, and infrequent dwarf willows, fuel was rarely procured. Franklin had a lucky escape from drowning in a torrent, but lost a portfolio containing observations and his precious journal.

(Part of his book, therefore, was written with the help of the other officers' diaries). One morning he had a fainting fit as a result of exhaustion and a bitter wind.

By the end of September 1821 even George Back, who seems to have been the strongest of the naval party, was feeling 'excessive weakness', and found it necessary to use a stick to support himself, despite which he 'was driven twice backwards by the wind'. He and the two interpreters (St Germain and Adam) had been sent ahead of the main party to hunt. This was on 23 September. Next day, walking round lakes and large hills, eating a few berries and a partridge, Back received a note from Franklin saying 'that the men were in a state of mutiny and had started throwing away their loads to follow me – that the canoe was broken to pieces and left the day before . . . '.[14]

Dr Richardson made a heroic attempt on 29 September to swim across the icy Coppermine River with a cord tied round his middle, so that his companions could be pulled across on a raft of green willow. Although he had cut his foot by stepping on a dagger at the outset, he got a good way over, but had to be hauled out more dead than alive and hardly able to speak. The men too suffered from standing in the icy water and when the surgeon's clothes were removed to wrap him in blankets beside a fire, they looked at his gaunt frame and exclaimed, 'Ah! Que nous sommes maigres!' In the end St Germain constructed a canoe out of the painted canvas used to keep the officers' bedding dry on a willow frame, so that the whole party was drawn across to the other bank on 4 October, once St Germain had paddled it over, much to everyone's joy and to Franklin's relief. Probably the strongest, ablest and most resourceful of the interpreters and voyageurs, it was he who shared a last morsel of meat he had saved, bringing tears to everyone's eyes.[15]

However, by the time they came to cross the Coppermine, all the officers were very weak, and the voyageurs perhaps slightly less so, but so despondent as to be disinclined to any exertion. They were cheered by the find of a cap dropped by one of the Indians on the outward journey, which assured them (more than the officers' words) that the river really was the Coppermine. After the crossing had been made, their spirits rose and they shook the officers by the hand, thinking to reach Fort Enterprise, even in their feeble state, within a few days. The only cause for regret was the absence of the faithful Junius 'whose good Nature and mild disposition' had 'gained him the friendship of the whole party.' He was well equipped with ammunition, blanket, knives, nets and other necessaries and Augustus thought he would join some of the Eskimos in the region, but he was never seen again. Franklin sent Back ahead with St Germain and three other Canadians to search for the Indians, after first visiting Fort Enterprise. In case the Indians were not there, a note left by Wentzel (as agreed) should indicate their whereabouts.

The frozen tents and bedding were difficult to bend into bundles, and walking in the snow was both exhausting and slow. On 6 October, Franklin tells us that before setting out, 'the whole party ate the remains of their old shoes, (moccasins of untanned leather) 'and whatever scraps of leather they had, to strengthen their stomachs for the fatigue of the day's journey'.[16] The voyageurs, Crédit and Vaillant fell down in the snow and were unable to rise; the others wanted to throw down their burdens and go on to Fort Enterprise. As a compromise, Hood, Dr Richardson and Hepburn stayed behind, in a clump of willows near some *tripe de roche*, while Franklin reluctantly proceeded with the men. He considered Hood's decision to stay behind both prudent in view of his exhaustion, and also generous and unselfish in his wish not to impede his companions. Dr Richardson and Hepburn could have kept up with the men but volunteered to remain, in Richardson's case, according to Franklin, because of 'the desire which had distinguished his character, throughout the expedition, of devoting himself to the succour of the weak' and in Hepburn's 'by the zealous attachment he had ever shown towards his officers'. Three of the voyageurs with Franklin were soon worn out after struggling through the heavy snow, so that he permitted them to return on their tracks to find Richardson, Hood and Hepburn.

Franklin's party then consisted of four voyageurs – Adam, Peltier, Benoit, Samandré and himself. They struggled on with little to eat but moccasin leather and country (herb) tea, but were cheered by the familiar landscape. They walked at last one morning in silence towards Fort Enterprise not knowing whether to hope or fear. To their 'infinite disappointment and grief', Fort Enterprise was empty, desolate and deserted. In Franklin's words, 'There was no deposit of provision, no trace of the Indians, no letter from Mr Wentzel to point out where the Indians might be found'. The whole party wept 'not so much for our own fate, as for that of our friends in the rear, whose lives depended entirely on our sending immediate relief from this place.' George Back had passed the house two days earlier and had left in search of the Indians with St Germain and Bélanger. He would try to walk south to Fort Providence, if Akaitcho and his band were not to be found. Franklin's party were relieved to find some discarded deerskins and, in the ashes of the fire, some bones. The house gave them little protection from the bitter winds, since the parchment had been torn from the windows. However, floorboards provided wood for the fire. As they sat round singeing the deerskin for supper, in walked Augustus, who had followed an entirely different route to Fort Enterprise, across country unknown to him – 'a remarkable proof of sagacity', thought Franklin. He reflected regretfully on the 'vast herds of reindeer' in the vicinity, at the same time the previous year, when there was little snow on the ground, whereas now it lay thick. Then the Winter River was open: 'now it was frozen two feet deep'.

The party at Fort Enterprise survived on their pitiful diet, growing weaker and weaker but still hopeful of relief. It was while they sat round the fire on the evening of 29 October, that Peltier interrupted the conversation by exclaiming joyfully 'Ah! le monde!' But to his disappointment no crowd of Indians stood there. Each carrying a bundle, only Dr Richardson and Hepburn entered the

'Expedition doubling Cape Barrow , July 25, 1821'. (From John Franklin's *Narrative of a journey to the shores of the Polar Sea*)

room, and Franklin's fears for 'my friend Hood, and our other companions' were confirmed when Dr Richardson said that Hood and Michel were dead and that there had been no sign of Perrault and Fontano. He left the details until later, since Franklin's party was not only plunged into gloom at the news, but shocked to see the 'emaciated countenances' of the new arrivals. They in turn were distressed to see that their companions were 'little more than skin and bone'. Hepburn had managed to shoot a partridge which was divided, slightly cooked, into six portions. 'I and my three companions ravenously devoured our shares,' wrote Franklin, 'as it was the first morsel of flesh any of us had tasted for thirty-one days, unless, indeed the small grisly particles which we found occasionally adhering to the pounded bones may be termed flesh.' Dr Richardson read prayers, psalms and passages from the Bible before they all went to bed. He and Hepburn missed killing a deer next day, being unable, through weakness, to hold their guns steady. Franklin's task was to find skins under the snow for food, but he had little strength to drag them inside. Several were putrid and hardly edible, even by starving men.

After their 'usual supper of singed skin and bone soup', Dr Richardson told Franklin about the 'afflicting circumstances attending the death of Mr Hood and Michel'. He, Hepburn and Hood had moved slowly and painfully from the willow thicket to a clump of pines, as advised in Franklin's note, brought by Michel. Only *tripe de roche*, which was hard to collect when frozen, 'country tea', singed

'Expedition encamped at Point Turnagain'. The furthest east of Franklin's first overland expedition of 1819-21. (From John Franklin's *Narrative of a journey to the shores of the Polar Sea*)

buffalo hide and the very occasional partridge kept them alive. They read some religious books given to the expedition 'through the extreme kindness and fore-thought of a lady', which provided some solace. Their minds decayed with the weakening of their bodies, observed the doctor, but Hood was particularly debilitated because he could not stomach the *tripe de roche*.

They had welcomed Michel on his return, but became annoyed with him when he refused to hunt. It was when Hood, feeble as he was, tried to argue with him in the tent, that Hepburn heard a shot and found the young midshipman shot through the back of the head. The doctor thought at first that he had put an end to his life, but decided that Michel must have killed him, though the latter protested his innocence. After reading the burial service, Dr Richardson, Hepburn and Michel set off for Fort Enterprise. Convinced by now that Michel had probably murdered Bélanger and that they had unknowingly fed off him, both the doctor and Hepburn concluded from his threatening behaviour that he was prepared to kill them too once he knew the way to the fort. Dr Richardson took on himself the responsibility of putting an end to Michel's life with a pistol. In his official report, Dr Richardson went into some detail concerning Michel's conduct in order to set down the reasons that influenced him 'in depriving a fel-low-creature of life'.

Dr Richardson and Hepburn then made their painful way towards Fort Enterprise, through deep snow, unable to kill any of the deer that they encoun-tered, but cheered at last to see smoke coming from the chimneys, although they were concerned at the lack of footprints. On entering, they found Franklin and his companions in the wretched state already described. 'Our own misery had stolen upon us by degrees', wrote Richardson, 'but the ghastly countenances, dilated eye-balls and sepulchral voices of Captain Franklin and those with him were more than we could at first bear'.[17]

Two of the voyageurs, Peltier and Semandré, died on 1 November (All Saints Day), the date when one of them had forecast his death – a severe shock to the others, causing great despondency, especially in Adam, the remaining Canadian. The doctor and Hepburn had just strength enough to tear down and bring in some of the timbers making up the store house, but even they became weaker and weaker. They all became fretful and dreamt of feasting whenever they slept for a few hours.

On 7 November a musket shot was heard and three Indians arrived from Akaitcho's encampment, sent by Back with dried deer's meat, some fat and a few tongues. The three Britons fell upon the food while Adam, who was almost on the point of dying, was fed by the Indians. They brought in dry firewood and kept up a cheerful blaze, and 'set about everything with an activity that amazed us', wrote Franklin in his narrative. In contrast to the others' weakness, the new arrivals seemed like giants with supernatural strength. 'These kind creatures,' (Crooked Foot and the Rat) made the four survivors shave and wash while the

Pair of moccasins made of untreated hide of the kind eaten by Franklin's starving party during the first overland expedition 1819-21. (NMM, D9477)

third and youngest Indian, Boudel-Kell, left with a note for Back, requesting more supplies. After prayers of thanksgiving, Fort Enterprise was at length deserted on 16 November. The Indians lent the travellers their snow shoes for the journey and did without themselves; they set up camp, did the cooking 'and fed us as if we had been children'.

On arrival at Chief Akaitcho's encampment, he and the main body of Indians expressed great sympathy for the party's sufferings and gave them food. Their relief was due to George Back, who had made a heroic journey of great privation. By degrees, and delighting in a change of linen, the four officers and Hepburn (the surviving Canadians having departed for Montreal) together with Augustus, arrived at York Factory on 14 July 1822 and were kindly received by Governor George Simpson and all the officers of the newly united companies. 'And thus terminated,' wrote Franklin, 'our long, fatiguing, and disastrous travels in North America, having journeyed by water and by land (including our navigation of the Polar Sea) five thousand five hundred and fifty miles'.

What then were the achievements and failures of this first overland expedition across what is now northern Canada to the shores of the Polar Sea? The disasters have already been described, but need to be explained. Why, for instance, did Wentzel fail to leave a message at Fort Enterprise for the party's return? Why did chief Akaitcho also fail to leave supplies, or to be at hand? The rivalry, indeed warfare, between the North West Company and the Hudson's Bay Company was one of the biggest factors, for the expedition's being inadequately supplied. This meant that supplies in general were hard to come by, so that Franklin's promissory notes given to the Indians to be drawn on the North West Company were not honoured and were one of the factors resulting in Akaitcho's loss of faith in the enterprise. Wentzel's explanations regarding himself and the Indians are printed in the penultimate pages of Franklin's *Narrative*. Neatby observes that the 'best excuse for Wentzel is that he allowed himself to be persuaded by the assurances of the Indians' (who had suffered great privations, with him, on their return up the Coppermine) 'that none of the expedition would return from the coast alive'.[18] Although Franklin had a fair grasp of the circumstances and the environment in which he had to operate, he and the rest of the naval personnel were strangers in a strange land, having to deal not only with the climate, but the Indians, the voyageurs, the mode of transport (by canoe and on foot) and the food supply, in order to fulfil their scientific and geographical objectives. The published narratives of Hearne and Mackenzie and the few other books that they were able to obtain would have given them much food for thought during the outward voyage to Hudson Bay, but Hearne and Mackenzie only touched the northern coast and returned, whereas Franklin's party charted some 350 miles of it to the east of the Coppermine, including the great indentation of Bathurst Inlet, which took up much time and effort and prevented their navigating any further east than Point Turnagain on the curiously shaped Kent Peninsula. A further handicap was the birch-bark canoes, which, although easily and quickly mended, were only river craft and unsuitable for use at sea, especially when that sea is encumbered with ice floes. Stouter boats, built in England, were to prove a great advantage during Franklin's second overland expedition of 1825-27. With hindsight, it would have been wiser for Franklin to have left the coast earlier in August 1821, because winter then came on so much sooner than in the previous year, but he must have felt obliged to carry on as long as he dared.

The tragedy of the return journey from the coast, across unknown country, was the death of eleven out of the original party of twenty: ten of the interpreters and voyageurs and Midshipman Hood. The editor of the Champlain Society's recent edition of Franklin's journal and correspondence for the 1819-21 expedition sees the core of his failure as an inability to adapt to the ways of Indians and voyageurs who knew the country so well, something perhaps easier said than done. He sees the explorer as 'a solid representative of imperial culture, not only in its many positive aspects, but in its less generous dimensions as well'.[19] However, the fact that four out of five of the naval personnel survived and that so many of the voyageurs did not, could perhaps be ascribed to a faith in the aims of the expedition, though the latter, carrying the heavy burdens, must have felt the lack of food even more than the others, since 8lbs of fresh meat per day (2lbs of pemmican) was their usual ration. Franklin learnt from his terrible experience in 1819 21 and his second overland expedition turned out to be in great contrast to his first. Perhaps (rather than 'ethnocentric') he should be viewed as a naval officer carrying out, in adverse circumstances, an unusual, arduous and difficult assignment, largely overland, which began the survey of the north coast of America, and which had many important scientific results. Would any of his critics, transported in time nearly two centuries ago, have done any better, were they in his shoes?

CHAPTER 6

Franklin's Second Journey to the Polar Sea 1825-27

It is interesting to note from John Franklin's introductory chapter to his *Narrative of a Second Expedition to the Shores of the Polar Sea*, published in 1828, that it was he who suggested this venture to the British Government, after hearing of the decision made towards the end of 1823 to despatch Captain Parry on a third voyage in search of 'a northern passage by sea between the Atlantic and Pacific Oceans'. Franklin considered that since 'the object was one for which Great Britain had thought to contend for upwards of three centuries . . . it might be desirable to pursue it by more ways than one'. He therefore proposed that an expedition should be sent 'overland to the mouth of the Mackenzie River, and thence, by sea, to the northwestern extremity of America, with the combined object, also, of surveying the coast between the Mackenzie and Coppermine Rivers'. Well aware of public sympathy for the sufferings of members of his first overland expedition and of the 'humane repugnance' of the Government 'to expose others to a like fate', he was nevertheless able satisfactorily to show that 'similar dangers' need not be feared on a second venture, 'while the objects to be attained were important at once to the naval character, scientific reputation and commercial interests of Great Britain'. Franklin's proposal was approved, and he was appointed commander of the expedition, presumably early in 1824, and authorised by the Colonial Secretary to equip it. The official instructions were dated 31 January 1825.

Meanwhile Franklin's only child, Eleanor, was born in June 1824. In the spring of that year (while still pregnant) Eleanor Franklin had told her sister-in-law, Betsy, how the newspapers reported her brother being 'pulled to pieces' at Captain Parry's ball.

> He was in such request that I wonder they left a bit of him for me. I do not quite know what to say to his flirting in such a manner with half of the Belles of London, but I threaten to take my revenge in kind as soon as I get my wings.[1]

Dr John Richardson offered not only to serve as Naturalist and Surgeon of the second overland expedition, but to undertake the eastern coastal survey between the mouths of the Mackenzie and Coppermine rivers, while Franklin himself would travel westwards with the aim of reaching Captain Cook's Icy Cape, in what was then Russian America (now Alaska). Lieutenant George Back was offered an appointment (from among numerous other naval officers who applied) and 'accepted with his wonted zeal'; it was a tribute to Franklin that these two officers of his first overland expedition should wish to serve again E N Kendall, Admiralty Mate, who had been an Assistant Surveyor with Captain Lyon, was to accompany Dr Richardson on his eastward voyage, while acting as Assistant Surveyor before the party was divided. Thomas Drummond, a Scotsman of Forfar, Angus, was appointed Assistant Naturalist on the recommendation of a number of eminent scientists. Mr Peter Warren Dease, a Chief Trader of the Hudson's Bay Company joined the expedition to manage its food supply by making arrangements with the Canadian voyageurs and the Indians, as well as obtaining a daily supply of fish.

The first overland expedition had met with many difficulties, some of them, particularly as regards supplies and relations with the Indians, caused by the emnity between the North West Company and the Hudson's Bay Company. The coalition of the rival concerns in 1821 came too late to help Franklin then, but by 1825, when he set out again, the enlarged Hudson's Bay Company virtually ruled the northern lands of British North America from the shores of Hudson Bay to the Rocky Mountains. This it continued to do until 1870 when its charter was annulled and the Dominion of Canada created.

Soon after his appointment, Franklin wrote to the Governor and Directors of the Hudson's Bay Company in London, who wrote in turn to 'their officers in the Fur Countries', enjoining them to provide provision depots where Franklin indicated and to give other help when required. He took the prudent precaution of writing himself to the Chief Factors and Chief Traders along his proposed route, setting out the aims of the expedition and seeking their co-operation. He also ensured that a supply of pemmican made in spring and winter was ordered. One of the chief traders took charge of stores sent out in March 1824, via New York, which were taken to Mr Dease at Lake Athabasca in three north canoes (the smaller of two types of canoe in use by the Company). Dease's instructions requested him to fish in Great Slave Lake during the winter of 1824-25 in order to support his party, and to begin building the expedition's winter residence at Great Bear Lake in the spring of 1825. Franklin had chosen Great Bear Lake on the advice of the traders, who told him that it was the nearest place to the mouth of the Mackenzie River, which could provide fish for a large party.

In June 1824, three specially designed light boats were sent in the Company ship to York Factory, with more stores, two carpenters and a party of men. This advance party was intended to reach Cumberland House that season and to travel in the spring of 1825 towards Great Bear Lake, before being overtaken by the officers of the expedition, who would come out via New York. Franklin also ordered two *canôts de maître* (the larger freight canoes) to be ready, equipped and provisioned at the naval depot on Lake Huron for the officers' arrival in the spring of 1825. The wisdom and foresight shown in the above preparations made in 1824 indicate the way in which Franklin profited not only from his previous experience on the north, but also from the greater ease, in

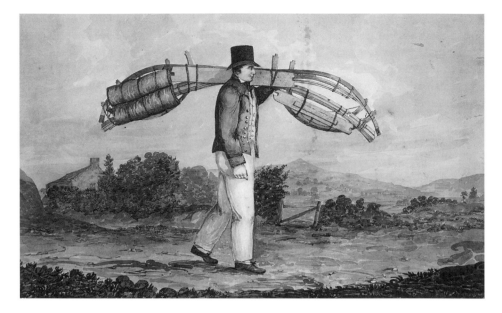

Watercolour of the 'Walnut Shell Boat' built for crossing rivers and lakes during Franklin's second overland expedition. (NMM, D3332)

more settled times there, with which orders and requests could be carried out.

The three specially designed boats were particularly interesting. These were intended for the coastal survey of the Arctic Sea and were constructed under Franklin's and Captain David Buchan's superintendence at Woolwich Dockyard. While recognising that birch-bark canoes, 'uniting lightness and facility of repair with speed', were well suited for navigating the rivers of North America, Franklin had found them 'much too slight to bear the concussion of waves in a rough sea' and even more so when 'coming into contact with ice'. The boats he designed had to be small and light enough to ascend and descend the numerous rapids between York Factory and the Mackenzie River and to be carried over the portages – 'in fact, as much like a north canoe as was consistent with the stability and capacity required for their voyage at sea'. They were built partly of mahogany on frames of ash and were double-ended; they could be steered with either a rudder or oar. Eleanor, Franklin's wife, described the boats as 'varnished and adorned with blue and gold, and painted with all sorts of mythological devices'.[2] The largest boat was 26 ft long and the two smaller 24 feet long, all capable of carrying an officer, crew and two to three tons of cargo. They were tried out on the Thames at Woolwich 'and found to answer fully the expectations that had been formed of them'. On the same occasion, another, smaller boat was tried out. This was the 'Walnut-Shell', designed and built by Lieut-Colonel Pasley of the Royal Engineers. Nine feet long, its frames were of ash and it was covered with 'Mr Mackintosh's prepared canvas, and shaped like one valve of a walnut shell'. Weighing only 85lbs, this portable boat could be assembled in less than twenty minutes. The 'Walnut-Shell' was mainly intended for the crossing of rivers, which had so materially delayed the first expedition. 'So secure was this little vessel', wrote Franklin in his Introduction, 'that several ladies, who had honoured the trial of the boats with their presence, fearlessly embarked in it, and were paddled across the Thames in a fresh breeze'.[3]

Clothing and stores included two waterproof suits for each person, made by Mr Mackintosh of Glasgow, while waterproof canvas, in three layers, also covered each 85lb package of cargo in the boats. Two years' supply of 'wheaten-flour, arrow-root, macaroni, portable soup, chocolate, essence of coffee, sugar and tea' was provided, while the expedition's guns were adapted to use in the north, and the ammunition was of the best quality.

> There was likewise an ample stock of tobacco, a small quantity of wine and spirits, marquees and tents for the men and officers, some books, writing and drawing paper, a considerable quantity of cartridge-paper, to be used in preserving specimens of plants; nets, twine, fishing-lines and hooks, together with many articles to be used at winter-quarters, for the service of the post, and for the supply of our Indian hunters, such as cloth, blankets, shirts, coloured belts, chiefs' dresses, combs, looking-glasses, beads, tapes, gartering, knives, guns and daggers, hatchets, awls, gun-worms, flints, fire-steels, files; whip and hand saws, ice-chisels and trenching-irons, the latter to break open the beaver lodges.[4]

In these matters Franklin had profited from the advice of Mr William M'Gillivray of Montreal.

Travelling via Liverpool and New York to Canada in the spring of 1825, Franklin and his party (Lieutenant Back, Dr Richardson, Mr Kendall, Mr Drummond and four marines), waited eight days for the voyageurs to arrive from Montreal at Penetanguishene, the naval depot on Lake Huron. (It was here that Franklin learnt by letter of the death at the end of February 1825 of his brave and beloved wife from tuberculosis. One of his sisters would look after baby Eleanor.) Enlarged to thirty-three, the party travelled in two *canôts de maître* to Fort William, the North West Company's former main depot, where the large canoes were exchanged for four small north canoes. In one of these, more lightly laden, Franklin and Dr Richardson went on as swiftly as possible to organise the supplies of food at the fur trading posts. They arrived at Cumberland House on 15 June, where they learnt that their boats (sent via York Factory) had started for the north on 2 June. Franklin and Richardson caught them up on Methye River in late June.

The Official Instructions (in which he no doubt had a hand himself) ordered Franklin to set up his winter quarters on Great Bear Lake, where he should 'endeavour to open a friendly communication with the Esquimaux'. In the early spring of 1826, he should proceed down the Mackenzie River and on the opening of the ice on the polar sea travel in the boats to Icy Cape and on to 'Kotzebue's Inlet' where HMS *Blossom* would be awaiting him, ready to take the party to the south. At the mouth of the Mackenzie, Dr Richardson and Mr

Kendall and party should depart (in the other direction) to examine the coast as far as the Coppermine River. Dr Richardson's principal task was to complete 'as far as can be done, our knowledge of the Natural History of North America'. Lieutenant Back would take command of the expedition in the event of Franklin's death.

When Franklin and Richardson caught up the boats and men from England, in late June 1825, they received a warm welcome both from the men and 'from our excellent friend and former interpreter Augustus the Esquimaux, and Ouligbuck, whom he had brought from Churchill as his companion'. They reached Methye portage on 4 July, across which well over one hundred packages of between 70 and 90lbs were transported, plus the men's personal baggage. The smaller, yet still heavy, boats were carried or dragged, but a truck was constructed on the spot for the largest boat; Franklin expressed the hope in his narrative that the fur traders would adopt this device to alleviate the 'fatigue and suffering' of the voyageurs. At Fort Resolution, on Great Slave Lake, the Canadians celebrated the crossing of the last portage on the way to Great Bear Lake with dancing, despite having paddled for thirty-six out of the previous thirty-nine hours and they continued until dawn, dancing to the sound of the bagpipes and, now and again, the Jews' harp. The officers were delighted to meet again at Fort Resolution 'our worthy old Copper-Indian friends, Keskarrah and Humpy' (Akaitcho's brother), who had been waiting to see them for two months. Akaitcho was out hunting for the expedition, but he had apparently shown and expressed his esteem for Franklin by making peace with the Dog-rib Indians to the north, through whose grounds the expedition would pass. They were said to have had murdered most of the Copper Indians, who had taken part in the previous expedition.

On branching out westward towards the Mackenzie River, Franklin and party met a band of Chipewyan Indians whose chief was persistent in his requests for rum, but these Franklin resisted and gave him instead some of their supper and tea, and tobacco, which he accepted with a bad grace. Franklin had decided on returning to the Fur Country never to give spirits to the Indians and he noted in his book that the following season, the Hudson's Bay Company itself stopped sending rum there.

The party travelled the three hundred odd miles from Fort Resolution to Fort Simpson, the principal depot of the Mackenzie district at the confluence of the Mackenzie and the River of the Mountains. At Fort Norman, over 200 miles downstream on the broad Mackenzie River and only four further days' journey from Great Bear Lake, Franklin arranged that he should continue down river in the *Lion*, the largest of the boats, to the mouth of the Mackenzie on reconnaisance, with Mr Kendall, Augustus and a chosen crew of six Englishmen. Dr Richardson would meanwhile coast the northern shore of Great Bear Lake and decide on a spot nearest the Coppermine River to which to bring his party the following year, on their return from the polar sea. A third party under Lieutenant Back would take the winter's supplies, in three canoes, to set up winter quarters on Great Bear Lake and superintend the Indians' hunting and fishing, with Mr Dease's advice.

The *Lion*, Franklin was pleased to find, kept the lead on the river, much to the surprise of the voyageurs in the canoes. He observed that the canoes of the Dog-ribs were 'made of the bark of the pine-tree, sewn at the ends and top with the fibrous parts of the root of that tree, leaving only a space sufficient for the legs of the sitter'. Lower down the broad, muddy river, he also noted the admirable canoes of the Hare Indians – larger than the Chipewyans', with 'the fore part covered with bark', to fit them for the navigating the wide Mackenzie, which could become rough. Helped by a swift current, they rapidly descended the river reaching Fort Good Hope, the lowest fur trading post over 300 miles from Fort Norman, on 10 August, where the master of the post was amazed to see the party arrive a good two months before the Company's boats from York Factory. They learnt that peace was in force between the Loucheux Indians and the Eskimos.

On nearing the estuary where the Eskimos might be found, a guard was kept, since a party of traders had been massacred by them some thirty years before. On 16 August 1825, the party reached the sea and landed on a low island which Franklin called Garry Island, in fact almost certainly Mackenzie's Whale Island. 'The Rocky Mountains were seen from S.W. to W.½N.; and from the latter point, round by the north, the sea appeared in all its majesty, entirely free from ice, and without any visible obstruction', recorded Franklin. 'Many seals, and black and white whales were sporting on its waves; and the whole scene was calculated to excite in our minds the most flattering expectations as to our own success, and that of our friends in the Hecla and Fury' (Parry's ships during his third Arctic voyage). The men pitched the tent on the beach and, with suppressed emotion, Franklin ordered a silk union-flag to be hoisted. This had been made by his late wife, Eleanor, as a parting gift, on condition that it should only be flown when the expedition reached the polar sea.

The event was celebrated with three cheers and a toast to King George IV. Unfortunately, the small quantity of brandy reserved for the occasion by Kendall and Franklin was mixed with salt water by Baptiste, the voyageur, so that it had to be used, as in Ancient times, as a libation poured on the shore. This same Baptiste, finding that he had actually reached the sea, 'stuck his feathers in his hat, and exultingly exclaimed, 'Now that I am one of the Gens de la mer, you shall see how active I will be, and how I will crow over the Gens du nord', the name, by which the Athabasca voyagers are designated'. Letters for Captain Parry (who never navigated that far) were deposited under the flag pole and a waterproof box containing an account of their journey was consigned to the waves north of Garry Island. They then turned back to the great river. Franklin was startled to find his pocket, in which was a powder-horn, on fire from the spontaneous ignition on a piece of 'wood-coal' from Garry's Island.

At the end of his account of their descent of the Mackenzie River, Franklin paid a tribute to 'our enterprising precursor, Sir Alexander Mackenzie', asserting that it would have been far too dangerous for the latter to venture his frail canoe on the ocean 'against such winds and seas as we experienced in advancing beyond the volume of fresh water poured out by the Mackenzie' far enough to taste salt water, though the sight of white whales and the rise and fall of the tide had confirmed Mackenzie's opinion that he had reached the sea.[5] Franklin remarks that their survey differed in outline only slightly from that of Mackenzie, 'whose general correctness we had often occasion to admire'. He hoped that 'the custom of calling this the Great River', a name in common use 'among the traders and voyagers, will be discontinued and that the name of its eminent discoverer may be universally adopted'. Presents of kettles, knives, hatchets, files, ice-chisels, beads and pieces of cloth dyed red and blue were left beside the 'winter habitations' of the Eskimos, none of whom they had encountered.

On 5 September 1825, Franklin's boat party reached winter quarters on Great Bear Lake, where they found Dr Richardson, Lieutenant Back, Mr Dease and the other members of the expedition, happy to be 'snugly settled' before the severe winter weather set in. In honour of their commander, the officers had named their winter residence Fort Franklin. The site chosen by Mr Dease was that of an abandoned and derelict post of the old North West Company, but their small building proved to be of little use in the construction of Fort Franklin. Timber had been rafted from some distance, causing delay, but the new building only lacked finishing touches to make it comfortable during the winter. There were fifty persons in the expedition – 'five officers, including Mr Dease; nineteen British seamen, marines and voyagers; nine Canadians; two Eskimos; Beaulieu the interpreter, and four Chipewyan hunters; three women, six children, and one Indian lad; beside a few infirm Indians, who required temporary support'.

Fish from Great Bear Lake was to be the main diet, so that two additional houses were built, four and seven miles from the Fort where twenty people could live and fish, leaving thirty at Fort Franklin. Under the superintendence of an experienced old fisherman, the nets yielded in the autumn from 300 to 800 fish daily. During the winter months, most of the British crew learnt to read and write in evening classes taught by the officers. Divine service was held twice on Sundays and during the week, apart from school days, the hall was used for games at the wish of the men. The officers usually joined in and Franklin remarked that, 'by thus participating in their amusements, the men became more attached to us, at the same time we contributed to their health and cheerfulness'.

Meanwhile the officers were also occupied on a rota, making and recording hourly observations of the temperature, magnetism and the atmosphere, from 8am till midnight. Each had in addition a special duty. Lieutenant Back superintended the men and he also made finished drawings from the sketches done during the outward voyage. Dr Richardson, as medical officer, was kept busy with patients among the Indians, in addition to studying natural history and observing the radiation of the sun. Mr Kendall drew charts using data re-calcu-

Homme sauuage amené des païs Septentrionaux par   M. Furbisher L'an 1576

Inuk (Eskimo) brought by Frobisher in 1576 to London. He was probably buried at St Olave's Church, Hart Street, London (Watercolour in Lucas De Heere's *Théâtre de Tous les Peuples . . . de la Terre.* Ghent University Library, Belgium)

Ross and Parry meeting the 'Arctic Highlanders' of Northwest Greenland in 1818, by the interpreter, John Sackheuse, whose passion was drawing. (Reproduced in Sir John Ross' book, *A Voyage of Discovery*)

'A bear plunging into the sea' in Davis Strait, September 1818, during the voyage of the *Isabella* (Captain Ross) and *Alexander* (Lieutenant Parry). (Drawn by Ross and engraved for his book, *A Voyage of Discovery*)

Right: A portrait of John Sackheuse by Nasmyth, 1817. He had stowed away in a Scottish whaler in 1816. Living in Leith, he volunteered to join Ross' expedition of 1818. (Scottish National Portrait Gallery, Edinburgh)

Below: Portrait of Akaitcho, Chief of the Copper Indians. Drawn by Lieutenant Hood during Franklin's first overland journey to the Polar Sea, 1819-22. (Frontispiece to Franklin's *Narrative,* 1823)

'Vale of the Clear Water River from the Methye Portage'. (from John Franklin's
Narrative of a Second Journey to the shores of the Polar Sea)

lated by Franklin but also made drawings and carried out experiments on the
speed of sound. Mr Dease was responsible for obtaining and issuing provisions,
while at the same time directing the Canadian voyageurs and the Indians.

Franklin vividly described their life during the winter at Fort Franklin in a
long and affectionate letter to his niece, Miss Kay, written on 8 November 1825.
After mentioning his late wife and little daughter, he continued:

> The building forms three sides of a square . . . the whole being surrounded by stock-
> ades, which are of ancient standing (there having been a house here before) and as they
> lean in all ways, they add little to the ornament of the building – but we expect them
> to prove useful in keeping the drift snow from burying us. Our dwelling is 44 feet by
> 24 – having a large hall in the centre, and two rooms on each side – one of which is
> inhabited by Dr R., myself – another by Mr Back, another by Mr Kendall, and the
> fourth by Mr Dease and his family which adjoins to that of Dr R's and mine, and we
> are constantly reminded of the rising generation by the squalling of a young boy – a
> little older than my dear Eleanor's – but this inconvenience is amply repaid by the
> amusement we derive in playing with him and his little sister 2½ years old – when they
> are in good humour. The Hall has been ornamented by flags – deers head – and the
> appropriate device of a Crown and Anchor painted on the white washed walls by Mr
> Back. Each of the private apartments have been arranged accordingly to the taste of its
> occupants. During my absence at the Sea – I found that Wilson had exercised his skill
> as an reupholsterer in furnishing my bed in a tent shape using the lining of the mar-
> quee – the Dr's is somewhat plainer fitted but very neat. The shelves at the sides are
> fitted with books, Astronomical and Atmospherical instruments and though the total
> ensemble would to your eyes appear an odd collection yet we fancy that everything is
> well placed and comfortable.[6]

With the advance of ice on the lakes and snow on the ground, the first dog-sledges were despatched, being used from October onwards to carry wood for the fires, as well as letters to Fort Norman and timber for the construction of a new boat. Thomas Matthews, the carpenter who had broken his leg at Cumberland House, arrived by dog sledge, his leg still weak. The magnetic observatory was completed on 1 October. Fish were netted where possible, providing an allowance of seven 'herring salmon' per man and two for each dog. Christmas and New Year's Day were happily celebrated and on Boxing Day the hall accommodated a party of sixty, including the Indian hunters' wives and children, who were spectators at these festivities, having been entertained on Christmas Day to a game of snapdragon. 'Seldom', wrote Franklin, had come together such a variety of individuals and of tongues. 'The party consisted of Englishmen, Highlanders (who mostly conversed with each other in Gaelic,) Canadians, Eskimos, Chipewyans, Dog-Ribs, Hare Indians, Cree women and children, mingled together in perfect harmony.' English, Gaelic and French songs provided part of the entertainment. On 16 January 1826, a packet of letters was received, which had been posted the previous June in England, as well as newspapers, magazines and journals, which were spread out on the table, stimulating much discussion and many topics of conversation.

In February, the supply of fish almost dried up, but a moose was shot and additional supplies of pemmican, arrowroot and portable soup, as well as iron for nailing the new boat, were obtained from Fort Norman. A requisition for the 1827 supplies was sent by Franklin to Governor Simpson at York Factory. The rest of the winter passed uneventfully and writing to his brother and sister-in-law in February 1826, after elaborating upon the 'recent domestic afflictions' of the Franklin family and his own 'entire submission' to God's will, Franklin told them that the past five months had passed rapidly and comfortably away, and that as the days lengthened they were looking forward to the 'enhancing season of Spring', more to be 'enjoyed in this country than many other':

> Imagine to yourselves a solitary dwelling in a snow-covered wilderness – birds and animals fled from the dreary scene and universal stillness reigns sovereign mistress over this waste – then conceive the way you would feel at the return of the birds, the disappearance of snow, the opening of leaves, and all the works of nature breaking from their long slumber and bursting into freshness respecting the return of spring.[7]

In April, Dr Richardson, Kendall, and an Indian guide with a sledge and dog driver left on snow shoes to continue the survey of Great Bear Lake. The first swallow arrived on 16 May as swans and geese flew northwards. Mosquitoes appeared towards the end of May, while white anemones flowered at its end. The new boat, named the *Reliance*, was finished by the carpenters. It was very similar to the *Lion* and made of fir with birch timbers. The other boats were then repaired for the coming summer season. Once the four boats were fully equipped, the men were issued with uniforms of sky-blue waterproof cloth, feathers and warm clothing. Fourteen men, including Augustus were to accompany Franklin and Back in the *Lion* and *Reliance*, while the *Dolphin* and *Union* (the smaller boats) were to carry Dr Richardson, Kendall, Ouligbuck and nine men. When Franklin called for two volunteers from among the Canadian voyageurs to make up the complement of fourteen to accompany him, every man stepped forward, out of whom François Felix and Alexis Vivier were picked. Prayers were said on the Sunday before their departure, imploring the protection of Providence upon their undertaking. The officers packed the charts and drawings to be stored at the fort and by 20 June, Fort Franklin was left to the care of Coté, the worthy old fisherman.

The river ran high with the spring melt, so there was no difficulty with obstructions. On approaching the lands inhabited by the Eskimos, weapons were issued in case of a hostile reception. On 3 July came the parting of the ways for the eastern and western parties, after reaching the channels in the delta of the great river. The warm clothing, shoes, and gifts for the Eskimos had already been packed into separate bundles, but the provisions still had to be divided; twenty-six bags of pemmican were provided for the *Dolphin* and *Union*, and thirty-two for the *Lion* and *Reliance*. Each party received two bags of grease, plus supplies of arrowroot, flour, macaroni and portable soup. The whole summer, barring untoward occurrences, was provided for and it was hoped also to shoot the odd deer.

On the evening of 3 July, Franklin gave Dr Richardson his instructions, the substance of which was that he should survey the coast between the Mackenzie and Coppermine rivers. Beaulieu would await him on the northeast arm of Great Bear Lake with a boat to take the party to Fort Franklin on his return. Other contingencies were provided for in the Instructions. Unfortunately, only a watch, lent by Mr Dease, could be given to the eastern party, since two out of three chronometers provided had broken. However, E N Kendall (Mate and Assistant Surveyor) would be able to ascertain longitude by the elaborate calculation known as 'lunar distances', and they were also given 'that excellent instrument Massey's log' (which measured distances travelled by boat). Since Kendall had an 'intimate acquaintance with marine surveying', Franklin had 'no doubt of his being able to make a correct survey of the coast'. At 'Point Separation', the evening 'was spent in the most cordial and cheerful manner', both parties looking forward to meeting again and exchanging their news. A good supper was followed by a bowl of punch and by 6am, 4 July 1826, the boats were fully laden and ready to depart.

Franklin and Back could not help being struck by the difference between their present well equipped state and 'that on which we had embarked on our former disastrous voyage. Instead of a frail bark canoe, and a scanty supply of food we were now about to commence the sea voyage in excellent boats, stored with three months' provision'. Franklin lists his boats' crews as follows:

'Hill by the River Side, Mackenzie River'. Two of Franklin's four boats descending the Mackenzie River. (From John Franklin's *Narrative of a Second Journey to the Shores of the Polar Sea*)

Lion	*Reliance*
John Franklin, Captain, R N	George Back, Lieutenant R.N.
William Duncan, Cockswain	Robert Spinks, Cockswain
Thomas Matthews, Carpenter	Robert Hallom, Corpl. of Marines
Gustavus Aird, Bowman	Charles Mackenzie, Bowman
George Wilson, Marine	Alexander Currie, Middle Man
Archibald Stewart, Soldier	Robert Spence, Ditto
Neil MacDonald, Voyager	Alexis Vivier, Canadian
Augustus, Eskimo	Francois Felix, Ditto

The *Lion* and the *Reliance* proceeded northwestwards, sometimes glimpsing the Rocky Mountains, whose peaks provided a striking contrast to the dull and 'muddy islands' immediately in view. Proceeding with some difficulty along the shallow channel towards the sea, past what was named Halkett Island, a 'crowd of tents' was seen on an island, 'with many Esquimaux strolling amongst them'. Franklin immediately prepared to approach them, as ordered by his Instructions, and presents and trade goods were selected, with the remainder kept out of sight. The men were directed to keep their guns at the ready while Franklin landed, accompanied only by Augustus. He forbade the men to fire unless he himself did, or Lieutenant Back ordered them to do so. About 300 Eskimos gathered in kayaks and umiaks (the much larger boats, carrying usually women and children). When one of the kayaks was accidentally upset, by an oar, its owner was taken aboard one of the expedition's boats and lent his great coat by Augustus. He spied the remaining goods and alerted the rest of the crowd, who began to pillage the boats, even trying to cut the anchor buttons from Lieutenant Back's waistcoat and remove the men's clothes. By this time the tide had fallen and left the boats grounded in the mud, preventing any escape. The crews were overwhelmed by numbers and various articles were carried away, but not the 'arms, oars or masts, or anything on which the continuance of the voyage, or our personal safety depended'. Attempts to steal the box which contained the astronomical instruments were frustrated by Duncan, who rescued it three times and then secured it to his leg, 'determined that they should drag him away also if they took it'. The Eskimos were finally deterred from their marauding when Augustus translated into Inuktitut Franklin's threat 'to shoot the first man who came within range of our muskets'. Franklin named the spot 'Pillage Point'.

A few important items had been carried away including 'the mess canteen and kettles, a tent, a bale containing blankets and shoes, one of the men's bags, and the jib sails', and Augustus persuaded Franklin to allow him ashore to negotiate with his countrymen. Franklin watched anxiously while Augustus spoke to the forty-or-so armed men explaining to them the benefits which had come from the white men at Churchill and which they were jeopardising by the unseemly treatment of Franklin's party. They excused themselves by saying they had never met white men before and that everything they had seen was so new and desirable that they had been unable to resist stealing, but they returned the tent, a large kettle and some shoes and then Augustus was permitted to join in a dance 'and he was, for upwards of an hour, engaged in dancing and singing with all his might in the midst of a company who were all armed with knives or bows and arrows'. He was delighted to find that the words of the song, and the dance, were the same as a welcome to strangers in his homeland, hundreds of miles away. Franklin was later led to believe that a plot was subsequently hatched to kill the whole expedition, including Augustus, but this was frustrated when the boats pulled into deep water and Franklin persuaded the kayakers to turn back by firing a shot across the bows of the leading one.

The sight of a frozen sea (in contrast to the open water of the year before) met their eyes when at last the boats reached the coast on 9 July 1826. A small group of Eskimos arrived and to gain their confidence in the whole party, Franklin thoughtfully got each man to present beads to them. Augustus put on his medals and his most colourful rig-out which so intrigued the newcomers that it was only after some time that they could be induced to give their minds to the subject of sea ice along the coast to the west. According to Augustus, who could understand them well, the group had a low opinion of their countrymen, who had earlier attacked the expedition, and offered to provide reinforcements on the homeward track.

The boats were able to approach what was named Herschel Island by taking advantage of an intermittent shore lead (a passage between the shore and the sea ice). Another party of Eskimos was met near the island on 17 July. Franklin remarks that Augustus thought it beneath his dignity to enter into serious conversation with three 'old wives'. A larger party assembled, when the expedition tents were pitched, bringing dried meat and fish, to whom presents were given in return. Some interesting information was obtained about trade between these people and the Indians of the interior (to the south) and the Inuit to the west, who were said to speak a very different dialect. Iron, knives and beads were traded for oil, furs and sealskins but the knives and other articles were not British-made and were unlike those traded by the Hudson's Bay Company and since the visitors said that they emanated from some white people ('Kabloonacht') living a long way to the west, Franklin concluded that they must be the fur traders from Russian America (now Alaska) further along the sea coast. He was also told that Herschel Island abounded with deer, and its waters with fish in the summer, thus attracting many native hunters and fishers and he observed that the channel between the island and the shore provided the only possible anchorage for a ship so far encountered, but even that was shoal in parts. Herschel Island was to be the scene of great activity in the American whaling industry later in the nineteenth century.

The boats proceeded in fits and starts along the shore westwards, being frequently stopped by sea ice blocking their way. Of July. Franklin remarked that they 'had to draw largely on our nearly exhausted stock of patience', waiting for the ice to clear. They were then in longitude 139 °42′W. Excursions to climb 'Mount Conybeare' (800 ft) to reconnoitre the state of the ice along the coast were always plagued by hordes of mosquitoes and tedium and anxiety left the party with little inclination to read 'even if there had been a greater choice of books in our travelling library and still less composure to invent amusement'.

The river nearest to the border between the British dominions (what is now Canada) and Russian America was named the Clarence River after HRH the Lord High Admiral (later King William IV) and this was reached on 27 July. A pile of driftwood was erected near its mouth in which was deposited a tin box containing a royal silver medal and an account of the expedition's progress. An unwelcome reminder of the summer season coming to an end occurred on 30 July when they saw the sun set at 11pm. Up till then the daylight had been continuous. On 3 August, the boats were able to make 28 miles – the longest day's run since leaving the Mackenzie River. That evening the party passed what Franklin called the 'British chain of Mountains' and neared another range, which he named after 'the late Count Romanzoff, Chancellor of the Russian Empire, as a tribute of respect to the memory of that distinguished patron and promoter of discovery and science'. Nikolay Rumyantsev had privately financed the voyage of

Kotzebue in the *Rurik*, 1815-18. Like Captain Cook before him, Kotzebue was seeking a North West Passage eastward beyond Bering Strait.

The coast continued shallow and usually fringed by reefs on which 'icebergs' and masses of drift ice were grounded. Gales and fog were intermittent while an occasional meeting with the Eskimos enlivened what must have seemed a never-ending struggle to the west. Flaxman Island, named after the sculptor, was reached and then Foggy Island. Here the carpenter, presumably Thomas Matthews, who had earlier broken his leg, repaired damage done to the *Lion* by the ice while gales and fog further delayed the expedition's progress. Franklin remarked on the havoc which the weather made among the flowers. 'Many that had been blooming on our arrival, were now lying prostrate and withered', a poignant reminder that 'the term of our operations was fast approaching'. They all wished they could embark in a decked vessel, where the food could be kept dry and the crew could be given shelter and rest. Then they might have left the shallow coast to 'steer at once towards Icy Cape'. The men's legs were 'swollen and inflamed' from dragging the boats across the mud flats, while the water temperature was 40 °F and the air 41 °F. Because of the return of the fog, the party had to go back again to seemingly enchanted Foggy Island to camp there and Franklin remarked on the dangers of trying to navigate in fog along a shoaling and icy shore.

The frequent presence of fog along this coast was in contrast to the generally clear conditions east of the Coppermine in 1821. The tents became sodden in the murky atmosphere and driftwood became scarce. A clear day on 16 August enabled them to escape from this 'detestable island' and round the reef projecting from 'Point Anxiety' at last. Keeping away from the shallow shore, they attempted to navigate across the mouths of Yarborough Inlet and Prudhoe Bay, the latter name to become well known in the late twentieth century for its oil installations. A combination of fog, a violent gale and surf over the mud flats forced them to seek shelter away from the land in the lee of a large piece of ice but before reaching it they found themselves in calm water among low gravel banks, on one of which they landed and erected their tents.

Franklin's thoughts were by then dwelling on their return journey. On the evening of 6 August, as a result of his deliberations, he decided that it would be rash to proceed further west towards Icy Cape, having only come to a half-way mark between the Mackenzie and the cape, with the so-called summer nearly at an end and the crews' legs in a poor state. In any case, his Instructions told him to turn back by 20 August. Were the boats to be wrecked further along the coast, which he understood from the Eskimos was still bordered by shallow water, reefs and ice, it would be fatal, he considered, to attempt to travel inland to the south when the deer would have left and when any Eskimos would be either unwilling or unable to provide food for them. A clear spell enabled astronomical observations to be made for the first time in a week and these determined their longitude to be 149 °37′W, their latitude 70 °24′N. Here their explorations came to an end and they left their gravel patch, which Franklin named Return Reef, on 18 August to make for the Mackenzie River and 'home' to Fort Franklin.

Another gale detained them for a further three days on Foggy Island, a spot which even Franklin then called 'ill-omened'. However, more driftwood must have been blown on shore by the storm and this provided a good fire and a hot meal, the first for a couple of days in the cold clammy fog. Much of the timber was piled up to make a landmark on which a flag was flown. Here a tin box was buried, containing a letter for Captain Parry, a silver medal and a halfpenny. (Parry's ships in fact never reached this far.) 'An unsealed letter, wrapped in bark, addressed to the Russian Fur Traders', giving a summary of the expedition's activities, was also left in the hopes that the Eskimos would take it to the Russians and that the British Government would eventually hear its news, supposing the expedition should fail to return. A number of implements were hung up for the Eskimos.

Progress to the east was made more difficult with adverse winds and the formation of young sea ice, so that the oarsmen became exhausted after long hours in the boats. The stranded floes were mostly 10 to 15ft high, but some up to 20 or 30ft, while their length ranged from 20 to 100yds. It was clear to Franklin that 'unless a strong wind blew from the land, that the new ice would soon unite the pack with the shore, and preclude the possibility of making the passage in boats', except by navigating to seaward, beyond the ice, a dangerous venture in open boats because of the lack of shelter in a gale. They had no sledges.

Approaching Herschel Island in dense fog and 'being assailed the whole way with continued shouting from persons to us invisible' (the Eskimos) they landed briefly and learnt that the people were busy killing whales, seals and deer for the winter. A violent squall on 26 August made the sea 'white with foam' in ten minutes and raised waves to which Franklin 'had never before been exposed to in a boat'. The *Lion* and *Reliance* sped swiftly along under close-reefed sail but, despite their buoyancy, were in danger of foundering. Fortunately, the party was able to land in a 'favourable spot' where the boats were unloaded and safely dragged up the beach. Next day, the bedding, clothes, pemmican and guns were dried. A party of Eskimos with whom Augustus later spent the night watched their arrival in astonishment. The women kindly sewed sealskin soles onto the men's moccasins in anticipation of the labour of tracking up the rivers, and it was through a timely warning from these people that the party escaped an ambush at the mouth of the Mackenzie by 'Mountain Indians' armed with guns at the end of August. Franklin here remarked in his *Narrative* that they had followed the coast westward from that river for 374 miles, yet discovered no safe harbour for a ship. (There is in fact one at Herschel Island later frequented by American whalers.)

On 2 September they mistook what Franklin named the Peel River for a branch of the Mackenzie, but finally ascended the great river and calling *en route* at Fort Good Hope, reached Fort Franklin on Great Bear Lake on 21

'Winter View of Fort Franklin' on Great Bear Lake. (From John Franklin's *Narrative of a Second Journey to the Polar Sea*)

September, where all was well. Dr Richardson and party had returned on 1 September and Franklin sent off a report on the proceedings of both parties to the Government in London. During their absence of three months from Fort Franklin, his party had travelled 2,048 statute miles 'of which six hundred and ten were through parts not previously discovered'. He paid tribute in his book to Lieutenant Back 'for his cordial co-operation, and for his zealous and unwearied assiduity' during the journey. Back had delineated the coast daily in his field notebook, besides drawing the landscape and its people and making a collection of plants. Franklin also expressed his 'warmest thanks' to the men of his party, 'who met every obstacle with an ardent desire to surmount it'. Most of them were new to sea voyages and the two Canadians had never even seen the ocean before. He also took the opportunity to thank Dr Richardson, in whom a combination of 'caution, talent and enterprise . . . enabled him to conduct, with singular success, an arduous service of a kind so foreign from his profession and ordinary pursuits.'

*   *   *

Dr Richardson's own account of the proceedings of the 'Eastern Detachment' of the expedition from 4 July to 1 September 1826 was published between pages 187 and 283 of Franklin's *Narrative*. The party was as follows:

Dolphin	*Union*
Dr Richardson	Mr Kendall
Thomas Gillet, Coxswain	John M'Leay, *Coxswain*
John M'Lellan, Bowman	George Munroe, *Bowman*
Shadrach Tysoe, Marine	William Money, *Marine*
Thomas Fuller, Carpenter	John M'Duffey
Ooligbuck, Eskimo	George Harkness

Richardson's Instructions were to trace the coast between the Mackenzie and Coppermine rivers (some 500 miles), returning overland to Great Bear Lake. The boats were provisioned for eighty days. Their voyage among the marshy islands in the delta of the Mackenzie was 'enlivened by the busy flight and cheerful twittering of the sand-martins, which had scooped out thousands of nests in the banks of the river, and we witnessed with pleasure their activity in thinning the ranks of our most tormenting foes the musquitoes'. The party breakfasted each day before noon, since it was at that time that Kendall (as surveyor) needed to land to take an observation for latitude.

Gifts were left at an empty Eskimo encampment, with a letter written in hieroglyphics by Kendall which pictured the party, the boats, the gifts and their joyful recipients. Although Franklin writes in an interesting way, Dr Richardson appears to have a rather more observant eye for detail and he must have had at least some knowledge of Inuktitut, because he frequently gives words in that language. He remarks of Ouligbuck that because he knew no English he was not of great use as an interpreter 'but his presence answered the important purpose of showing that the white people were on terms of friendship with the distant tribes of Esquimaux'. As one of the boat's crew, 'he was of the greatest service, being strongly attached to us, possessing an excellent temper, and labouring cheerfully at his oar'. A large party of Eskimos was encountered on 7 July, with whom some trade was done, Richardson always purchasing their fine bows (in case of a quarrel) which he thought the archers of Sherwood Forest would greatly have prized. Anxious to establish good relations with these people, it was not until they attacked one of the boats that Richardson allowed muskets to be produced from the arms chest, where they had been out of sight till then, and Kendall given discretion to fire. Fortunately, this proved unnecessary, as the Eskimos knew the power of guns from the Indians.

A stream of heavy ice about nine miles off-shore was seen on 9 July and on 10 July a glass of grog each was issued to the men to celebrate their arrival at the sea. On 13 July on Atkinson Island they came across seventeen winter houses and a large 'assembly hall', carefully constructed of wood. Dwarf willow, thrift and eight other plants common to the Scottish hills (Richardson was a native of Dumfries) were found here. Fog had driven the party to land. As with Franklin's party, progress was often slow and tedious in the shallow water and among low islands and shoals. From another island, on 15 July, a view was obtained of ice-covered sea to the east. They camped on a beach in the longitude of 127 °45′W, latitude of 70 °7′N. At breakfast ashore on 18 July, the air was scented by a 'beautiful phlox' and an even more handsome and 'fragrant cruciform flower, of a genus hitherto undescribed'. Later that day twelve tents were seen. The inhabitants proved threatening, until Richardson bawled 'noowoerlawgo' (I wish to barter), and they came off in kayaks and three umiaks.

> A bundle of strings of beads being thrown into an oomiak, it was caught by an old woman, who hugged the treasure to her breast with the strongest expression of rapture, while another elderly dame, who had stretched out her arms in vain, became the very picture of despair. On my explaining, however, that the present was for the whole, an amicable division instantly took place; and to show their gratitude, they sang a song to a pleasing air keeping time with their oars.

The Eskimos had heard of white people, but this was their first encounter.

The cape which they reached later proved the most northerly point of the mainland met during the whole expedition in the latitude of 70 °36′N. It was called Cape Bathurst, a name that would feature in later exploring voyages. From this point cliffs, rather than shoals and islands, were the feature of the eastward trending coast. Richardson named what he called a 'remarkable and extensive bay' after Franklin and, in recording this in his account of the coastal voyage, Richardson paid a generous and touching tribute of 'respect and regard' to Franklin.

Beyond Cape Bathurst a second cape, enclosing Franklin Bay, was named Cape Parry on 23 July 'after the distinguished navigator whose skill and perseverance have created an era in the progress of northern discovery'. A letter for Parry was deposited in a cairn at the top of a hill on his promontory and Richardson observed that although numerous coves near Cape Parry appeared to offer shelter, the bottom was rocky and the reefs made navigation unsafe for a ship. In the vicinity of Clapperton Island next day (24 July), various species of seal were seen and the last of the black whales, none being seen any further east. Another cairn was erected and a letter deposited for Captain Parry on Cape Lyon, 'named after the distinguished traveller, Captain G F Lyon, RN'. A rocky headland was named Point De Witt Clinton, after the Governor of the State of New York, 'as a testimony of our sense of the urbanity and love of science which had prompted [him] . . . to show so much attention to the members of the Expedition, in their passage through his government'. A ridge of hills, parallel to the coast, was called the Melville Range after Viscount Melville, First Lord of the Admiralty.

Heavy ice hindered the party's progress from time to time, occasionally endangering the boats through the erratic and sudden motion of the floes. Deer were shot and cooked when possible, and a shore lead facilitated the party's voyage ever eastward, while closely packed ice, apparently impenetrable to a ship, could be seen stretching to the horizon. Five miles beyond a river named after a friend of Kendall's, the Harding River, some store houses were discovered made of drift timber by the Eskimos. These were filled with dried deers' meat and seal blubber 'along with which, cooking kettles, and lamps made of potstone, copper-headed spears, and various other articles were carefully laid up'. Recently extinguished fires showed that the owners had left only a few days before. Richardson recorded his party's pleasure 'in figuring to ourselves the surprise and joy with which they would behold, on their return, the iron utensils that we deposited in the store houses for their use'.

The sea ice continued closely packed against the flat coastal limestone rocks on 2 August, so that there was no shore lead and progress was made 'only by the constant use of the hatchet and ice-chisel'. The hunters were too tired after the voyage of 32 miles achieved in this way to pursue the deer grazing on the beach. Next day, 3 August, the labour of making a passage for the boats continued, and they were sometimes in danger of being upset by the calving of large pieces of ice from the base of the floes. The *Dolphin* just escaped being crushed between two floes. Sometimes, the boats were able to progress by sailing *over* the ice in the fresh water lakes, formed of melt water. On 3 August, Kendall reckoned that they were nearly in the longitude of the Coppermine River, with its mouth lying some 70 miles to the south of where they were encamped. Though new ice had been forming during several nights, in the early morning of 4 August the boats easily broke through it, as did a few eider ducks which were using their wings to make a passage for their young. Only the yellow poppy was in flower.

Fears that land sighted to the north might form part of the mainland were proved groundless, much to the party's relief. This island, much the largest seen on either of the Arctic land expeditions, was named Wollaston Land, after Dr Hyde Wollaston, the 'most distinguished philosopher'. This is now known as the Wollaston Peninsula, the south-western part of what was later called Victoria Land (now Island), one of the largest in the Canadian Arctic archipelago. Richardson named the strait between mainland and island Dolphin and Union Straits, after the party's 'excellent little boats'. It was between 12 and 20 miles across. Always conscious of the need to be able to navigate these seas in ships, as opposed to boats, Richardson remarked that despite closely packed ice in the bays, a ship might find a passage by keeping along Wollaston Land. He noted later that the navigation of the straits would be dangerous to ships because of numerous sunken rocks near the southern shore. He also remarked, interestingly, in view of the relative infancy of steam navigation, that a steam ship would find plenty of drift wood along the shores to fill its boilers.

Proceeding on their voyage towards the mouth of the Coppermine, they found themselves steering between whirling and colliding ice floes, and the *Dolphin* suffered a broken frame and several broken planks, when caught between a moving floe and a piece of grounded ice. Walking along the coast for some miles after landing to camp on 6 August, Richardson and Kendall were happy to find it trending southwards, 'although no doubt now existed' wrote

Richardson, 'as to our accomplishing the voyage sufficiently early to allow us to cross the barren grounds to the eastward of Great Bear Lake, before the cold weather set in'. Although most of the plants on the coast had come to the end of their flowering season, in travelling southwards the summer would be prolonged, giving some comfort to Richardson who must have always had in mind the spectre of that terrible and tragic journey from the coast of the first overland expedition. A 'conspicuous hill', seen during this walk, was called 'Mount Barrow, in honour of John Barrow, Esq., Secretary to the Admiralty'.

The next morning (7 August) a 'deeply indented bay was crossed and named after Lieutenant-Colonel Pasley of the Royal Engineers, to whose invention we owe the portable boat, named the Walnut-shell, which we carried with us'. A promontory nearby was named Cape Krusenstern 'in honour of the distinguished Russian hydrographer'. Here the *Dolphin* and *Union* entered King George the Fourth's Coronation Gulf (now Coronation Gulf), thus connecting their own survey with that of the first overland expedition. One wonders whether expectations were raised at this juncture, subsequently to be dashed. Richardson records that they 'had the honour of completing a portion of the northwest passage, for which the reward of five thousand pounds was established by his Majesty's Order in Council, but as it was not contemplated, in framing the Order, the the discovery should be made from west to east, and in vessels so small as the *Dolphin* and *Union*, we could not lay claim to the pecuniary reward'. The passage had to be navigated in ships, not boats.

On 8 August, a prominent point near the mouth of the Coppermine was named Cape Kendall by Richardson, after his 'highly esteemed friend and companion'. The men had been kept in ignorance of the coming end to their voyage for fear that an unexpected prolongation of it would cause them to despond and so the news that they were about to enter the Coppermine was therefore 'totally unexpected' and resulted in 'heartfelt expressions of gratitude to the Divine Being, for his protection on the voyage'. Richardson and Kendall were delighted that the men were 'still fresh and vigorous, and ready to commence the laborious march across the barren grounds, with the same spirit that they had shown in overcoming the obstacles which presented themselves to their progress by sea'. Acknowledging that the 'comfort and ease' of the voyage owed much to the 'judicious and plentiful provision of stores and food which Captain Franklin had made for us', the thoughts and good wishes of the party were united in hoping for the success of the *Lion* and *Reliance*.

Another reason for pleasure, remarked Richardson, was 'the correctness of Mr Kendall's reckoning'. Since the two chronometers ear marked for the eastern party had been broken by the winter frost, Kendall had to rely on lunar observations to correct the dead reckoning, whenever these could be made. Yet on approaching the Coppermine, his reckoning only differed by 'twenty seconds of time, or about two miles and a half of distance, which is a very triffling difference when the length of the voyage and the other circumstances are taken into consideration'. Their voyage from Point Separation (where the two parties of the

'Esquimaux Encampment on Richard's Island'. (From John Franklin's *Narrative of a Second Journey to the Polar Sea*)

overland expedition divided in the Mackenzie Delta), to the mouth of the Coppermine River had amounted to 902 statute miles. In coming to the end of his account of the boat journey, Dr Richardson referred to the small rise and fall of the tides observed en route, to the variation of the magnetic needle, to ice conditions, and to the botany and geography of the area.

Bearing in mind the extremely heavy ice met by Parry southwest of Melville Island in 1819-20 (in what was later called M'Clure Strait), Richardson expressed the opinion, with regard to the North West Passage, that Dolphin and Union Straits held out 'greater prospects of success for a similar attempt, not only from their more southern position, but from the strong current of flood and ebb, which flows through them and keeps the ice in motion'. As we shall see, the strait was later navigated under sail by Captain Richard Collinson in HMS *Enterprise* (a large ship by the standards of the time) eastward in September 1852 and westward in August 1853. Roald Amundsen in the small *Gjøa* sailed westward through it in August 1905, and likewise the Hudson's Bay Company's SS *Bay Chimo* passed in both directions during the summer of 1929, followed by Henry Larsen in the *St Roch* in the 1940s. With what was probably some sadness, the *Dolphin* and *Union* were deposited at Bloody Fall, before the ascent of the Coppermine, with gifts for the Eskimos inside the tents, which had been firmly pitched with flags flying. The portable boat was taken along, but discarded later, as tracking proved difficult and it was known that there were no more broad rivers to cross.

Beaulieu was late in arriving at the *rendezvous* on Great Bear Lake, causing Richardson some anxiety and inconvenience, but he did come in the end and the whole of the Eastern Detachment eventually travelled across the lake to Fort Franklin, where they were heartily welcomed by Dease (and no doubt his family) on 1 September. They had been absent for seventy-one days during which they had travelled 1980 statute miles. In ending his account of their journey, Dr Richardson paid a glowing tribute to the crews 'for their cheerful and obedient conduct', and added that 'not a murmur of discontent was heard throughout the voyage, but every individual engaged with alacrity in the laborious tasks he was called upon to perform'. He praised Ouligbuck's part in the expedition, referring to his loyalty and to the party's affection and regard for him. Kendall was promoted to Lieutenant, RN (he was later to marry Franklin's niece). Richardson recorded his 'deep sense of the good fortune and happiness in being associated with a gentleman of such pleasing manners, and one upon whose friendly support and sound judgment I could with confidence rely, on occasions of difficulty and doubt inseparable from such a voyage'. Richardson was to visit the Arctic coast again in August 1848, when with Dr John Rae of the Hudson's Bay Company, he went in search of his old commander and friend, Sir John Franklin.

*   *   *

During the winter of 1826-27, which was passed in part by the whole company at Fort Franklin, Franklin set down an account of the beliefs and traditions of the Dog-rib Indians, obtained from the old men of the tribe in answer to his questionnaire translated by Dease. He later expressed pleasure that the Chipewyan and Copper Indians were using dogs (not women) to pull their sledges, having abandoned their belief that women originated from dogs. Franklin and five men left in February 1827, with the charts, drawings and journals, and reached Cumberland House on 18 June. Here he had the great pleasure of meeting Dr Richardson again, after nearly a year since they parted on the Arctic coast. Richardson had left Fort Franklin before Franklin's return from his coastal voyage to travel south, circumnavigating the Great Slave Lake, when the trees were in their autumn livery and there were no mosquitoes to plague him, in order to study the geography, geology, flora and fauna of the area. He spent the rest of the winter at Carlton House on the Saskatchewan River, where he was joined in April by the assistant naturalist, Thomas Drummond, who had travelled alone for an astonishing distance into what is now British Columbia, making extensive collections of flora and fauna.[8] George Back had received news of his promotion to Commander, RN and he took charge of the party at Fort Franklin, with instructions to leave once the ice had broken up and proceed to England via York Factory. At Norway House, the

The two Eskimo interpreters, Junius (left) and Augustus, drawn by Lieutenant Back. (From John Franklin's *Narrative of a Journey to the Shores of the Polar Sea*.)

Company post on Lake Winnipeg, Augustus shed tears at parting with Franklin and Richardson. His affection for them was mutual. Franklin and Richardson travelled on via Montreal and New York and arrived home in late September 1827, Back and party a month after.

The geographical and scientific work of the expedition (a part of it appearing in the 150-page Appendix to Franklin's *Narrative* and in the fine maps in its end pocket) was recognised in London, Oxford and Paris; Franklin was knighted in April 1829 and he also received the gold medal of the French geographical society and an honorary doctorate from Oxford University. At the end of his introduction to the published *Narrative*, he acknowledged the expedition's debt to Earl Bathurst, Lord Melville and other officials, as well as to the Hudson's Bay Company in London and in the 'Fur Country'; he also paid tribute to all the members of the expedition. From the collections made on both overland expeditions resulted Richardson's monumental *Fauna Boreali – Americana* (1829-37) and W J Hooker's *Flora Boreali – Americana* (1840).

In a letter written to his old senior officer, Captain William Pryce Cumby of Darlington, Franklin expressed himself as gratified at their reception by the Lord High Admiral and his Council. He thought however that 'the leading men are beginning to suppose enough has been expended on the Northen Regions', so that it might prove difficult 'in these economical times' to get their sanction for further enquiry, 'though I shall certainly press them to let me finish the undiscovered bit of the western end, if Beechey does not complete it'.[9] One touching object he brought home was an attractive Indian doll made from a corn husk and its leaves, with deerskin legs, and clothes decorated with beads, for his little daughter, Eleanor Isabella, probably bought from the Iroquois in 1827. Two

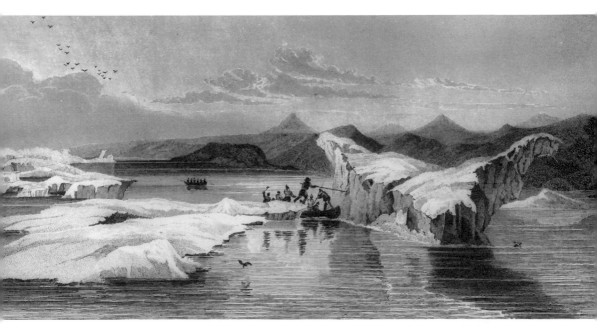

'The Dolphin squeezed by Ice'. (From John Franklin's *Narrative of a Second Journey to the Polar Sea*)

years earlier he had written from Great Bear Lake to his niece saying that he often thought of his 'little darling . . . kicking with all her might and pointing at her dear Mama's picture'. The doll and the letter are in the National Maritime Museum, Greenwich.[10]

CHAPTER 7

The Seaborne Voyages of Parry, Beechey and Lyon

We return now to the seaborne voyages of the 1820s in search of the North West Passage, two of which were sent in the stout well-strengthened bomb vessels, HMS *Fury* (374 tons) and HMS *Hecla* (375 tons) under the command of Captain William Edward Parry. G F Lyon and H P Hoppner commanded the *Hecla* and the *Fury* respectively during both these voyages. Hoppner had served as Lieutenant in the *Griper* with Parry during his first voyage, 1819-20. Both these men were competent artists and their sketches were later engraved for publication in Parry's narratives of the two voyages. Lyon had previous experience of an expedition in that he travelled in North Africa in 1818-20 and in the Sudan. He published lively, well written books not only about his African travels and his Arctic voyages, but subsequently about his tour of Mexico, made in 1826. Parry tells us that those officers and many of the seamen of the former expeditions, who volunteered for his second expedition were appointed. The Reverend George Fisher, who had accompanied Buchan's 1818 expedition, was appointed both Astronomer and Chaplain.

By degrees, a body of experienced 'Arctic officers' and men was being built up and one sees many of the same names in the lists of expedition members right through the nineteenth century. An interesting *Arctic Navy List, 1773-1873* was compiled by Clements R Markham and published in 1875 (reprinted 1992) and it contains notes on all those about whom he could find information.

Parry's Second Voyage 1821-23

The two vessels of Parry's first expedition had been barque-rigged (the foremast and the mainmast having square sails on the yards, and the mizzen only a fore-and-aft spanker) making them easier to handle than full-rigged ships. A smaller number of men were needed to work the vessels – 'a consideration of no little importance', wrote Parry, 'where it was a material object to sail with as few persons as possible, in order to extend our resources to the utmost'. With fewer sails to handle the ships' companies could be divided into three watches, giving each watch a longer period of rest off-duty than was possible when there were only two watches.[1]

The *Fury* and *Hecla*, the ships for Parry's second voyage, were also barque-rigged. Their hulls were given six inches of extra planking on the outside, while the rudder cases were made larger, so that there was more room for the rudders to be shipped and unshipped, if necessary, when in the ice. The *Fury* and *Hecla* were both the same size and identical in all respects, and even the fore and main-masts were 'equalized' in each vessel, so that the gear was interchangeable. But each vessel was intended to be independent of the other for provisions, spare equipment and stores. In the event of one vessel having to be abandoned, the crew could be accommodated without tremendous difficulty. Condensation and the resulting layers of ice accumulated below deck had been the bane of Parry's first expedition and so a coal burning stove, invented and fitted by one Mr Sylvester, was to circulate warm air into the living and sleeping quarters. Thick linings of cork were fitted round the ships' sides, on the underside of the upper decks and over the windows and skylights.

Victualling was based on the experience of the previous voyage. A much larg-er number of Messrs Gamble's tins of preserved meat were stowed which would give each man 2lbs of meat a week, plus a quart of vegetable or concentrated meat soup, enough to last for three years. Space was saved by taking spirits of 35 per cent proof, and best quality kiln-dried flour was substituted for half the biscuit supply, taking up only a third of the stowage space, and thus providing freshly baked bread during the winter instead of the traditionally hard ship's biscuit – 'hard tack' – proverbially full of weevils. As before, vinegar was taken in concen-trated form to save space and to avoid its freezing. Considerable loss of that essential anti-scorbutic, lemon juice, during the previous voyage had occurred because the glass bottles froze and burst: this time, the juice, squeezed from fresh lemons, was stored in strong, five-gallon kegs and a little rum was added to each keg to hinder freezing.

For his second voyage,

> a number of valuable anti-scorbutics were liberally supplied, consisting of carrots pre-served in tin cases by Messrs. Gamble and Co., crystallized lemon acid, cranberries, lemon marmalade, tamarinds, pickled walnuts and cabbage, essence of malt and hops, essence of spruce with molasses, dried herbs for tea, and a quantity of the seed of mus-tard and cress to be grown as circumstances required.

Salt beef had been found less digestible than salt pork, so that only casks of the pork were taken, apart from some corned beef. A large quantity of fresh potatoes and beetroot lasted fairly well for two or three months during the outward voy-age from England. The provisioning was for three years.

The *Fury* and *Hecla* were found to be too deep in the water when fully loaded, so that a transport, the *Nautilus* (405 tons), was requisitioned by the Navy Board to accompany them across the Atlantic as far as the edge of the ice. She took a good proportion of their stores and carried some extra, including twenty live bul-locks and a load of coal. Besides these necessities, a considerable number of 'valuable chronometers and instruments . . . were embarked on board each ship', some of them to be used by Mr Fisher in experiments suggested by the Royal

Society. Parry lists the instruments in his Introduction to the second *Voyage*. He also referred to the collections of animals and plants, to the meteorology, and to the views and charts, including several reproduced in his book compiled from sketches by the Eskimos of 'such parts of the coast as those people are acquainted with, but to which our own efforts have not hitherto enabled us to obtain access'.

In this last sentence, there is a hint of Parry's disappointment at the outcome of his second voyage of 1821-23. He expressed this quite plainly toward the end of his Introduction, saying: 'That our efforts have not hitherto been crowned with greater success, cannot fail to be a matter of extreme disappointment, as well as sincere though unavailing regret . . .'

This was, of course, in contrast to his first voyage, which had been remarkably successful. His third voyage to find the North West Passage of 1824-25, however, was to be a failure, mainly because of poor ice conditions which led to the wreck of the *Fury*. The first and second voyages, however, contributed pieces which enabled the geographical jigsaw of Arctic Canada eventually to be completed, while the scientific work of both was of considerable importance. After the brilliance of his first voyage, he and his crews must indeed have been disappointed, but, Christian as he was, Parry would have done his best to bow to the will of Providence. Nevertheless, even before a second voyage was ordered, he stressed in a conversation with Sir John Barrow how much the success of the first voyage owed to a 'concurrence of many very favourable circumstances' and that the next attempt would have to be made in a lower latitude, where there was no guarantee of, say, Hudson or Cumberland Straits, leading into the polar sea. 'I am confident', he wrote, 'another Expedition will end in disappointment to all concerned and interested in it, *because* so great has been our late success, that nothing short of the entire accomplishment of the North-West Passage in to the Pacific will satisfy the Public'.[2]

The navigators of earlier times, as we have seen, found no passage leading to the west from Hudson Bay. Parry's ships were to try again by this route through Hudson Strait, across the north of Hudson Bay and into Middleton's Frozen Strait. The official Instructions from the Admiralty for his second voyage of 1821-23 highlighted the two main aims: the finding of a passage to the Pacific and the delineation of the northern limits of the American Continent. Scientific research was important but secondary. The Instructions also reminded him of Franklin's first overland expedition, which would be in progress at the same time, and ordered him to erect flagstaffs along the northern coast of North America, with bottles containing messages buried at their feet. These same Instructions, incidentally left a certain amount to Parry's own discretion as far as the expedition's route was concerned, once Hudson Strait had been navigated and the ships had entered Hudson Bay.

Parry read carefully the accounts of Captain Middleton's voyage and the subsequent one of Captains Moor and Smith in the 1740s. He took the decision to sail directly via the *north* of Southampton Island to the Frozen Strait through

The *Hecla* and *Fury* cutting into Winter Island during Parry's second voyage of 1821-23. (From William Edward Parry's *Journal of a Second Voyage*)

which he was the first to navigate. He vindicated the much maligned Captain Middleton's discovery of Repulse Bay, off which no westward passage could be found, thus setting to rest the 'doubts and conjectures' which had for so long been entertained. He also called the 'great opening leading to Fox's Furthest', Fox's (now Foxe) Channel and gave Baffin Island its name, having proved the accuracy of many of the old navigator's observations.

By 8 October 1821, having explored the indented coast of the continent to the north of Southampton Island by ship and boat, young ice and dark nights gave some urgency to searching for winter quarters. These they found at a small island – Winter Island – by cutting a canal through the undulating newly-formed sea ice. Parry's remarks about the effect of the formation of young ice on a ship's progress is illuminating.

When the sheet has acquired a thickness of about half an inch, and is of considerable extent, a ship is liable to be stopped by it unless favoured by a strong and free wind; and even then when still retaining her way through the water, at the rate of a mile an hour, her course is not always under the control of the helmsman, though assisted by the nicest attention to the action of the sails, but depends on some accidental increase or decrease in the thickness of the sheet of ice, with which one bow or the other comes into contact. Nor is it possible in this situation for the boats to render their usual assistance, by running out lines or otherwise; for having once entered the young ice, they

can only be propelled slowly through it by digging the oars and boat-hooks into it, at
the same time breaking it across the bows, and by rolling the boat from side to side . . .
A ship in this helpless state, her sails in vain expanded to a favourable breeze, her ordinary resources failing, and suddenly arrested in her course upon the element through
which she has been accustomed to move without restraint, has often reminded me of
Gulliver tied down by the feeble hands of Lilliputians . . .

Parry was satisfied with the work accomplished during this first navigation season. Despite their 'constant exposure' to the risks of 'intricate, shoal, and
unknown channels, a sea loaded with ice, and a rapid tide', no injury to either
ships or men had been sustained, and they had 'discovered and minutely
explored' in pursuit of their object more than 200 leagues (about 600 miles) of the
coastline.

   Mr Sylvester's apparatus worked wonderfully well in keeping the living quarters of the ships warm, dry and comfortable throughout the winter: it was
adopted in future naval voyages to the polar regions. Clothes were easily dried
and bedding aired. Captain Lyon became manager of the fortnightly theatrical
entertainments aboard the *Fury*, where a larger and warmer theatre than during
the previous voyage benefited both actors and audience. Further amusement was
provided by what Parry called 'a large and handsome phantasmagoria, or magic
lantern' presented by an anonymous lady. Those officers with a musical bent got
together on certain evenings in Parry's or Captain Lyon's cabins for 'musical parties'. Besides the pleasure of the music itself, those present were sometimes
transported in imagination 'into the social circle of our friends at home, in spite
of the oceans that roll between us'. Schools for the seamen operated most
evenings on a voluntary basis, some twenty individuals in each ship sitting at
tables learning to read and write. That Christmas, Captain Lyon 'received six-
teen copies from those who, two months before, scarcely knew their letters'.
These well written offerings were 'sent with as much pride, as if the writers had
been good little school-boys, instead of stout and excellent seamen.'[3] That every
pupil could read his Bible by the end of the expedition gave Parry great satisfaction. The whole expedition formed a congregation on Sundays aboard the *Fury*.
Nor was science neglected; a portable observatory was built for Mr Fisher on
shore. Myriads of 'insects' – small shrimps – were found beneath the sea ice. One
day they completely cleaned a goose belonging to the officers of the *Hecla*, which
had been hung overboard to keep fresh. 'We took advantage, however', wrote
Parry, 'of the hunger of these depredators to procure complete skeletons of small
animals, for preservation as anatomical specimens, enclosing them in a net or bag
with holes, to which the shrimps could have access, but which prevented the loss
of any of the limbs, should the cartilage of the joints be eaten'. This system was
adopted in the Antarctic early in the following century near the *Discovery*, during the National Antarctic Expedition, 1901-04.

   Improvements had been made to the clothing and especially the footwear
issued to each individual, leather boots having been found constricting and liable
to cause frostbite. The 'snow boots' of the second expedition were made of

'Group of Esquimaux' from Winter Island, 1822, met during Parry's second voyage.
(From William Edward Parry's *Journal of a Second Voyage*)

'strong drab cloth with thick soles of cork, the slowly conducting property of which substance, together with their large size, allowing a free circulation of the blood, afforded the utmost comfort that could be desired'. Those officers with a musical bent got together on certain evenings in Parry's or Captain Lyon's cabins for 'musical parties'. Besides the pleasure of the music itself, those present were sometimes transported in imagination 'into the social circle of our friends at home, in spite of the oceans that roll between us'.

The unseen arrival of a 'little village' of 'snow-huts' and their Eskimo inhabitants, as if by magic, greatly enlarged the expedition's own 'social circle'. Parry endeavoured to give what he was at pains to stress was 'a faithful and impartial sketch' of the 'manners, disposition and general character of these people'. He was well aware of the 'misapprehensions' that could arise from their 'imperfect knowledge of their language', and as there was no interpreter, the first encounter took place on 1 February 1822 under a slight cloud of apprehension. Parry, Lyon, two officers and two men set out to meet the twenty-five Eskimos, who were walking towards the ships. The party was unarmed and particularly quiet and orderly and they exchanged some blades of whalebone for nails and beads. Some of the women wore 'handsome clothes' of deerskin, which looked 'both clean and comfortable'. On the way back to their igloos,

the Esquimaux were much amused by our dogs, especially by a large one of the Newfoundland breed, that had been taught to fetch and carry ... and the children could scarce contain themselves for joy, when Captain Lyon gave them a stick to throw for the dog to bring back to them.

Parry and his little party were astonished to find a previously undetected 'establishment of five huts, with canoes, sledges, dogs, and above sixty men, women, and children, as regularly and, to all appearance as permanently fixed, as if they had occupied the same spot for the whole winter'. They were invited to enter 'these extraordinary houses', which consisted of low passages leading to three 'inhabited apartments', each with a perfectly arched dome. Light came in through a circle of ice let into the roof. Inside each:

> The women were seated on the beds at the sides of the huts, each having her little fire-place or lamp, with all her domestic utensils about her; the children crept behind their mothers, and the dogs, except the female ones, which were indulged with a part of the beds, slunk out past us in dismay.

Parry remarked on their hosts' extraordinary 'orderly, respectful and good-humoured' behaviour. They eagerly received presents, but did not beg for anything, 'nor did the well-known sound of 'pilletay' ['give me'] once escape them'. In addition, they were found to be extremely honest, always returning gloves, or other items dropped by mistake, and on one occasion a couple of dogs which had gone back to the igloos to their new masters. They had a few possessions of European manufacture, no doubt acquired through trading channels, and, on coming on board ships were less surprised than might have been expected. Some of them were invited by Parry to what turned out to be a joint concert. The officers listened to their singing, while Parry and Henderson took down the notes, 'for which', wrote Parry in his journal, 'they gave us all the opportunity we desired, for I thought they would never leave off'. Then it was the turn of the flutes and violins, followed by some songs. 'I thought', wrote Parry, 'that some of them . . . would have gone into fits of delight, when I introduced our names mingled with theirs, into a song we were singing'.[4]

The Eskimos became generally fond and familiar visitors to the ships, while Captain Lyon and others were often welcomed to their huts. Efforts were made by the officers both to learn their language and to compile a vocabulary at Winter Island and at Igloolik, where the expedition wintered a year later. 'Bread dust' (crumbs of ship's biscuit), sometimes mixed with seal or whale oil helped the natives in times of hunger, when the hunters met with no success, as happened when some of the naval people joined them one day. 'I was completely fagged', wrote Parry 'and am now quite certain I should make a very bad Esquimaux'. Parry published the vocabulary, as well a factual appendix about the people (which includes the music of two songs) at the end of his *Narrative*. In reading his book, and in particular the *Private journal* of Captain Lyon, published in 1824, one gets to know the Eskimos as individuals, and as a group, almost as well as the officers must have done. The person who stands out for her intellect, her love of music and her ability to draw maps was Iligliuk.

Captain Lyon was struck with the children, 'whose first appearance', he wrote, 'gave me a most favourable idea of their quiet and unobtrusive manners, and I never afterwards had occasion to alter my opinion of them', any comparison being to the disadvantage of 'many sweet little spoiled children in England'. He resolved that if ever he had a family of his own, he would tell them about the Eskimo children, 'whose orderly behaviour might be an example to them'. He continued:

> Of the outward garb of my young friends I cannot say much, for they were as dirty as human creatures could possible be; their large dresses . . . giving them when their faces were hidden, the appearance of young bears, wolves, seals and puppy dogs: they were, however, the picture of health, rosy, fat, and strong, with the finest black eyes imaginable, and a profusion of long jetty hair.[5]

William Harvey Hooper, on his third Arctic voyage, also praised the children. He found that they hardly ever cried, even when accidentally receiving a blow 'that would set an English child roaring for an hour'. He was astonished at the little notice even the youngsters took at the 'numerous blows they are constantly receiving, when stowed in the hood of the mother's jacket, and the mother bustling about in some active employment'.[6]

Captain Lyon's little black cat greatly entertained any Esquimaux visitors to his cabin. As noted previously, the Sunday service was held for the whole ships' companies in the *Fury*. The visitors were therefore not allowed aboard the *Hecla*. When Lyon, his officers and men left in uniform to attend church, the Esquimaux' 'astonishment was unbounded; never having seen us in regular uniform, but generally in thick great coats, they could scarcely recognise even their particular friends'. Indeed, Lyon continued, 'The gay appearance of the marines [sea soldiers], such, even in this climate, is the attractive influence of a red coat, so delighted the ladies, that they all danced and shouted in an ecstasy of pleasure as each soldier passed before them'.[7]

The Eskimos did not only lighten the dreariness of the winter. From conversations with them, and taking other evidence into account, the officers became hopeful of the existence of a western sea. One of Iligliuk's charts, wrote Lyon, 'connected the land, from our winter quarters to the N.W. sea, rounding and terminating the northern extremity of this part of America, by a large island, and a strait of sufficient magnitude to afford a safe passage for the ships'. This information about a 'little North-West Passage' set the officers building castles in the air, fancying that the worst of the voyage was over and that before the summer's end, the ships would arrive at Akkoolee, the natives' 'settlement' on the western shore.[8] Parry described how Iligliuk was first persuaded to draw the coast on a large scale, covering a dozen sheets. A smaller scale was then tried, and having just learnt the Eskimo words for north, south, east and west, the officers persuaded Iligliuk to 'box the compass', with the idea of making her familiar with the lands already drawn. She was then asked to complete the rest. She began and

> with a countenance of the most grave attention and peculiar intelligence, she drew the coast of the continent beyond her own country, as lying nearly north . . . from Winter Island. The most important part still remained, and it would have amused an unconcerned looker-on to have observed the anxiety and suspense depicted on the countenances of *our* part of the group, till this was accomplished, for never were the

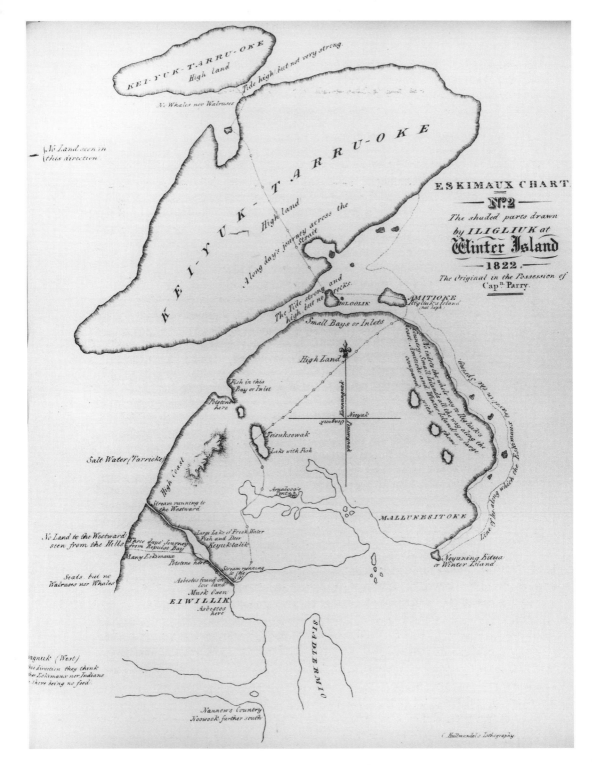

Iligiuk's chart drawn at Winter Island, 1822, during Parry's second voyage, 1821-23. (From William Edward Parry's *Journal of a Second Voyage*)

tracings of a pencil watched with more eager solicitude. Our surprise and satisfaction may therefore . . . be imagined when, without taking it from the paper, Iligliuk brought the continental coast short round to the westward, and afterwards to the S.S.W. so as to come within three or four days' journey of Repulse Bay. The country thus situated upon the shores of the Western or Polar Sea is called Akkoolee, and is inhabited by numerous Esquimaux.

Years later, Sir John Barrow wrote of Iligliuk as an 'Esquimaux female', who 'would have distinguished herself in any society, not merely by her musical cravings, for her whole soul appears to have been music, but more by her untaught intellectual powers'. Of her map making, Barrow wrote that the 'new information, thus unexpectedly opened to him' provided Parry with the 'satisfactory prospect of his soon rounding the northeastern point of America which . . . he subsequently discovered to be as, and where, represented by this intelligent woman'. Barrow finished by pronouncing that 'to her alone, therefore, is the merit due of the discovery of the extreme northern boundary of America'.[9]

Leaving three of the crew buried in two handsome stone tombs, the *Fury* and *Hecla* left Winter Island on 2 July 1822, exploring northwards along the east coast of what Parry named the Melville Peninsula. Next day the ships caught up with the party of Eskimos who had left for the northward forty days earlier. On being invited on board they halted in a line under the bows and gave three cheers, which were returned by those on the forecastle. They were overjoyed at the unexpected meeting, earnestly repeating the names of the officers and men.

> Ewerat being now mounted on the plank which goes across the gunwales of our ships for conning them conveniently among the ice, explained in a very clear and pilot-like manner, that the island which we observed to lie off Cape Wilson was that marked by Iligliuk in one of her charts (No. 1) and there called *Awlikteewik*, pronounced by Ewerat *Ow-littee-week*.

Parry was anxious to know where the ships were according to the Eskimos' geography and all the party agreed that ten more days' journeys were needed to get to Amitioke, another island drawn on their charts, off the coast to the northward. Iligliuk drew a line of sleeping places on her first chart. About these, Parry remarked on the caution needed when assessing the distance from one place to another, when given 'in the number of *seeniks* (sleeps) or day's journeys, to which in other countries a definite value is affixed'.

He went on to say that since individuals would differ from each other in their charts, with the same individual sometimes differing from himself at various times the approximate truth could only be found by carefully comparing all these accounts and by making allowances for the different circumstances. Parry, nonetheless, acknowledged the value of the information.[10]

The ice prevented the ships from nearing the strait – 'stopped at the very threshold of the North-West Passage for nearly four weeks . . . suspense at such a crisis was scarcely the less painful because we knew it to be inevitable'. It is easy to write these words, yet they cloak the seamanship involved in attempting to pass through the strait named after the ships as Fury and Hecla Strait. One of the fine folding charts at the end of Parry's second *Voyage* shows the strait and the three islands towards its middle – Ormond, Liddon and Amhurst, the strait being two miles wide and some 110 miles long and inclining roughly east and west. A large floe at the eastern approaches was helped to break away by the ships being 'made fast to it by several hawsers, and all their sails set aback, the wind blowing fresh from the westward'.

Being unable to reach the entrance to the strait by ship, Parry travelled across rotten sea ice, with a small party and a plank to bridge the gaps. At 'Cape North-East', they got a good view of the strait and gave three cheers. After a twelve-hour journey and much 'jumping and wading' across the moving ice, they reached the ships again. This was on 20 August and six days later the ships were steering 'under all possible sail up the Strait'. After passing through the narrow waters between an island and the southern shore and hoping to make rapid progress to compensate for earlier delays and frustrations, 'it was suddenly announced from the crow's nest that another barrier of fixed ice stretched completely across the Strait, a little beyond us, in one continuous and impenetrable field, still occupying its winter-station'. The heavy, hummocky ice and an eastward flowing current confirmed the belief that they must be in a wide channel leading to a western sea. Heavy snow fell towards the end of August, making a 'comfortless prospect' for three parties sent by Parry to reconnoitre on the 30th. Lieutenant Reid and Bushnan (who drew a plan of the strait) made a journey along its north shore between 10 and 15 September. They reached the junction of Fury and Hecla Strait, with the 'Polar Sea', as marked on Parry's chart. It was entered a few years later by Sir John Ross in the *Victory*, who called it the Gulf of Boothia. Parry's *Voyage* narrates the delays, the obstacles and the painfully gradual steps by which this information had been obtained – 'not without considerable mental solicitude, as well as physical exertion'. With only the prospect of old multi-year ice ahead and with young ice forming, having consulted the senior officers, Parry ordered their return. The Fury and Hecla Strait was eventually navigated from west to east in 1948 by a United States icebreaker and from east to west by the Canadian icebreaker HMCS *Labrador* in 1956.[11]

The expedition wintered at Igloolik from October 1822 till August 1823, again with the Eskimos to enliven the dark days. Parry and Lyon had tried their hands in the summer at managing an Eskimo kayak – not an easy matter – and during the second winter they bought dogs from the Eskimos and learnt to drive them with enjoyment of the exhilarating experience. Lyon's attempt to sledge westwards overland achieved little, through starting late in the season. A further unsuccessful effort to sail through the strait was made before the ships returned home, having discovered, however, what might (if ever navigable) prove to be a shorter route to the west than through Lancaster Sound.

Parry's Third Voyage 1824–25

Having found that Fury and Hecla Strait was so blocked with old ice (kept in place by an easterly current), as not to provide a navigable link in the North West

Passage, Parry, undaunted, proposed another possible route to the Admiralty. This was via Lancaster Sound and south down Prince Regent Inlet, which he had partially explored in 1819, during his first voyage. He had come to the conclusion (contrary to Sir John Barrow's belief that ships in polar seas were best served by keeping away from the land) that 'continuous land' provided the best way to navigate, by proceeding along the coast in the shore lead between it and the moving sea ice off shore. He ended the narrative of his second *Voyage* on an optimistic note:

> For my own part, I never felt more sanguine of ultimate success in the enterprise . . . than at the present moment; and I cannot but entertain a confident hope that England may yet be destined to succeed in an attempt which has for centuries past engaged her attention, and interested the whole civilized world.

Lord Melville, First Lord of the Admiralty, had sent for Parry on his return and had asked for his views on the Passage in writing. Shortly afterwards, he was offered (to his astonishment) the post of Hydrographer of the Navy, with the assurance that its acceptance would not prevent his taking up more active employment. In his long letter to his brother Charles, reporting what he had written to Melville, Parry reiterated that he considered another attempt well worth while – 'that we had now narrowed the ground of enquiry, by having proved, at least where the thing was *not* to be done   and that, to give it up now, would be, in my opinion, to lose the benefit of our experience ourselves. . . . while it must point out to other nations the best mode of accomplishing this long-sought object'.[12]

He was to be sadly disappointed by his third expedition of 1824–25, which was again carried in the *Hecla* and *Fury* (Captain Hoppner). The events of the voyage were to prove the wisdom of employing two almost identical vessels, and a 'transport', the *William Harris*, again accompanied the *Hecla* and *Fury* as far as the west coast of Greenland. Parry's third voyage was dogged by ill-luck from the start by difficult ice conditions and bad weather, while attempting the passage between Greenland and Lancaster Sound, which took eight weeks and involved the securing of ice anchors on a floe ahead of each ship and then heaving on the hawsers to force them through the ice. This was a dangerous operation because of the frequent breaking of the hawsers and Parry recounts how on 'one occasion three of the *Hecla*'s seamen were knocked down as instantaneously as by a gunshot, by the sudden flying out of an anchor'. The ships were warped or towed by boats for between 300 and 400 miles through ice which was often thick and sometimes rising to more than 20 feet above the sea. There were numerous icebergs, some between 100 to 200 feet high, over one hundred of these 'immense bodies' being counted from the deck at one time.[13]

As a result of this lengthy passage, they did not sight the lofty entrance to Lancaster Sound until 10 September, towards the end of the navigation season. Once inside the sound, ice and winds continued to hinder progress, but eventually the ships reached a winter harbour in October at Port Bowen, on the east side of Prince Regent Inlet, and by then young ice covered the sea. Snow too

The *Fury* beached on the coast of
North Somerset during Parry's
third voyage, 1824–25. (From
Willian Edward Parry's *Journal
of a Third Voyage*)

blanketed the land, creating 'a dreary, monotonous whiteness' lasting more than
half the year, a time of 'inanimate stillness' and 'motionless torpor', when man's
presence 'seems an intrusion on the dreary solitude of this wintry desert, which
even its native animals have for a while forsaken'.

A number of improvements had been made for wintering. These included the
positioning of Mr Sylvester's stove right at the bottom of the hold – 'a con-
trivance of which I scarcely know how to express my admiration in adequate
terms', wrote Parry. For many, this was their third Arctic winter, so that some
novel form of entertainment was required. Captain Hoppner's idea of a mas-
querade, 'in which every man might find a character for himself, and thus
become the hero of his own imagination'[14] proved a great success, officers and
men both joining in.

> Admirably-dressed characters of various descriptions readily took their parts, and
> many of these were supported with a degree of spirit and genuine humour which
> would not have disgraced a more refined assembly . . . Ours were masquerades with-
> out licentiousness – carnivals without excess.

As captain of the *Fury*, this was Hoppner's fourth Arctic voyage and his sketches illustrate Parry's account of this voyage, which was published in 1826. Schools
for the seamen were set up again on a voluntary basis aboard both vessels, while

religious instruction was zealously given by William Hooper (Purser) in the *Hecla*, to which, thought Parry, was owing 'the constant yet sober cheerfulness, the uninterrupted good order, and even, in some measure, the extraordinary state of health which prevailed among us during the winter'. The observatory was set up on the shore and before long seven or eight 'detached houses', whose needles measured magnetic intensity, formed a 'scattered village'.

Twelve polar bears were killed during the winter and fed mainly to the 'Eskimos' dogs', which had been brought out, presumably from England. Six pups were born. One or two foxes were caught – one becoming a pet aboard ship, while three hares, an ermine and a few mice made up the total number of quadrupeds 'at this desolate and unproductive place'. When the weather became warmer, three land journeys were made 'to extend our geographical knowledge', while a small black whale was killed for the sake of its oil. The ships were released from the ice of Port Bowen on 20 July, after much laborious sawing and towing by officers and men.

Parry sailed south along the formidable west coast of Prince Regent Inlet with the intention of looking for inlets perhaps leading to the west. The vessels had to navigate in heavy ice but, nevertheless, Elwin Bay, Batty Bay and Cresswell Bay were discovered, named and charted on the east coast of 'North Somerset', where 'traces of our old friends the Esquimaux' were found on the shore, in the form of old stone circles. The season turned out to be a warmer one, melting the snow and encouraging moss and other plants to grow. Great lumps fell from the tall limestone cliffs revealing fossils of 'countless myriads of shell-fish and marine insects which once must have existed on this shore'.

A fierce northerly gale on 31 July 1825 brought the *Fury* and *Hecla* into dangerous conflict with the ice, the *Fury* almost at once being forced on shore, though she floated off at high tide. The ice closed in again rapidly with a change of wind, and both vessels were beset. The *Hecla* struck the ground several times and then became immovable. Parry described how 'The *Fury* continuing to drive, was now irresistibly carried past us', only narrowly escaping a collision. Shortly afterwards, a large floe forced her against grounded ice on the beach, after which she began to leak a good deal. At high tide, both vessels floated free and the *Hecla* was immediately driven to the south for two or three miles. Parry was informed by Captain Hoppner in the early hours of 2 August by telegraph that the water in the *Fury* was gaining on two pumps. He rowed to the stricken vessel 'and found four pumps constantly going, to keep the ship free, and Captain Hoppner, his officers and men, almost exhausted with the incessant labour of the last eight-and-forty fours'. Parry and Hoppner went by boat along the shore to search for a make-shift harbour, where the *Fury* might be repaired and they discovered a more shelving part of the beach, where three grounded icebergs might provide shelter while the *Fury* was careened so that the carpenter could get at the hull and repair the leaks. 'Wild and insecure as, under other circumstances, such a place would have been thought, for the purpose of heaving a ship down, we had no alternative . . .', wrote Parry. No sooner had the crews begun to set sail, in order to reach this place, than the ice surrounded the ships again and the *Fury* was forced violently on shore during the night of 2 August.

Four pumps had to be kept going while some of the *Fury*'s dry food was transferred by boat to the *Hecla*. Some heavy iron items and other non-perishables were landed in order to lighten her. This work continued on 4 August and that night a heavy cable was taken round one of the grounded icebergs. The two vessels finally arrived at the make-shift harbour next morning, but there was still a great deal of ice there and very shortly after their arrival, the ice closed in again.

Parry explained how a small basin was formed where the ships could be secured. Anchors were 'carried to the beach, having bower-cables attached to them, passing quite round the grounded masses, and thus enclosing a small space of just sufficient size to admit both ships. Empty casks and spars kept the cables afloat, so that they might resist the ice pressure just below the water surface. Tents were erected on the shore to receive stores from the *Fury*, while everything was removed from her upper deck and landed. Captain Hoppner and the officers worked at the ice saw to avoid damage to the rudder. The two carpenters worked on the boats while the armourers forged bolts ashore. 'In short', wrote Parry, 'every living creature among us was somehow or other employed, not even excepting our dogs, which were set to drag up the stores on the beach; so that our little dock-yard soon exhibited the most animated scene imaginable.'

The multitude of necessary tasks continued, until the *Fury*'s crew transferred to the *Hecla* on 16 August, while her officers moved to tents ashore. At high tide on the 18th the labour of heaving down the *Fury* began, but had to be interrupted and the gear adjusted. Just when the work began again a blizzard arose, creating a considerable sea, so that everything came to a halt. Parry found:

> The officers and men were now literally so harassed and fatigued as to be scarcely capable of further exertion without some rest . . . I noticed more than a single instance of stupor amounting to a certain degree of failure in intellect, rendering the individual so affected quite unable at first to comprehend the meaning of an order, though still as willing as ever to obey it.

The gale blew stronger during the day and night of the 18th destroying the grounded bergs on which the make-shift harbour depended, and slackening the cables which could no longer keep out the encroaching ice.

After consulting with Captain Hoppner for much of the night in his cabin, Parry spoke to the ships' companies of his intention to prepare the *Hecla* for sea and to see the topgallant yards crossed before they slept. The *Fury* was to some extent prepared and made stable, with the idea of towing her into the ice for temporary repairs and then to a place of security. The vessel was 'thrummed' (a sail was passed under the keel and made fast around the hull) to try to reduce the leaking. The *Hecla* got under sail on the 21st to avoid more heavy ice, which threatened to drive both ships on shore, but scarcely an hour later, the *Fury* was driven firmly aground, just as the tide was starting to fall. All hands went aboard the *Hecla* and it was not long before five miles of pack ice lay between the two ships. Soon this had increased to twelve miles, although to the south, the sea

HMS *Terror* (Captain George Back) in the ice of Foxe Basin, 1836–37. She emerged 'crazy broken and leaky' from the terrible pressure. (Oil painting by First Lieutenant William Smyth, NMM, BHC 3655)

Phoenix, *Talbot* and *Diligence* passing a 'remarkable iceberg' during their voyage to meet the Franklin search squadron, Commodore Sir Edward Belcher, in 1854. (By Captain E A Inglefield of HMS *Phoenix*, NMM, PT 2735 CT)

Sledge party returning over the sea ice, through summer melt-water, during the Franklin search expedition, 1852-54, commanded by Sir Edward Belcher. (Watercolour by Lieutenant W W May of HMS *Assistance*, NMM, PW 7058 CT)

The *Fox* in Arctic seas. Sledging from winter quarters of 1858–59, Captain McClintock and Lieutenant Hobson discovered
[remainder of caption illegible] ... (Oil on canvas, artist NMM, BHC 2251)

appeared open. Captain Hoppner and Parry visited the *Fury* in two boats but found her forced even further up the beach and after several hours' inspection Parry received the opinions of Captain Hoppner, Lieutenants Austin and Sherer and Mr Pulfer, the carpenter, which confirmed Parry's own belief that they would have to abandon the *Fury*, there being no means of saving her. With 'extreme pain and regret', he made the signal for the *Fury*'s officers and men to retrieve their clothes and belongings from ship and shore. One of the midshipmen, Berkley Westropp, described the 'melancholy disorder' and 'bustle and confusion' which he observed while guarding the spirits on shore. He relates how eventually a last order was given, commanding the boats to leave the ship. From these, the light of early morning showed the distant *Hecla* dancing 'on the glassy surface of the deep, giving to the scene an air of solemnity . . . only interrupted by the noise of the seamen's oars'. He turned to gaze upon the *Fury*, her colours 'waving in melancholy grandeur' and gradually receding from his sight. Soon the *Hecla* was 'pursuing her trackless course for England', taking home 'those who had so often walked the *Fury*'s deck, in proud confidence of future fame', with the news of her misfortune.[15] Parry's third and last attempt to find the North West Passage had come to an end.

Beechey's Voyage to Bering Strait 1825-28

The Admiralty had prudently despatched HMS *Blossom* to the North Pacific, in retrospect rather optimistically to await the emergence of the *Fury* and *Hecla* of Parry's third Arctic expedition and of the boats from Franklin's second overland expedition into the North Pacific. Her Captain was F W Beechey, Franklin's second-in-command in HMS *Trent* in 1818 and Lieutenant in the *Hecla* with Parry in 1819-20, during his first spectacular voyage. A number of the dramatic plates in Parry's first narrative were from sketches by Beechey, as are those in Beechey's own narrative of the Pacific voyage, together with those of William Smyth (Admiralty Mate) and Beechey's younger brother, Richard Brydges Beechey (Midshipman), both of whom the Captain thanked in his introduction 'for the devotion of their leisure time to drawing'.[16] Young Midshipman Beechey later became a successful professional marine painter.[17]

The *Blossom* was in service from 1806 to 1848. She was rated by the Admiralty for the voyage as a Sloop of War, and was strengthened to withstand ice floes, though not as heavily as the *Hecla* and *Fury*, which were intended to winter.[18]

The *Blossom* departed from England in May 1825, rounded Cape Horn, then proceeded to chart various islands in the Pacific, including Pitcairn where they met the surviving mutineer John Adams from the *Bounty* and all sixty-six healthy inhabitants of the island. On arriving at the Russian port of Petropavlovsk in Kamchatka, in late June 1826, where they were hospitably entertained by the Governor, Beechey learnt of Parry's return to England after the wreck of the *Fury*. The *Blossom* passed through Bering Strait and arrived at Chamisso Island in Kotzebue Sound on 25 July 1826, fifteen days later than the date of their agreed

'Tracking the barge round Cape Smyth' (Alaska) during the voyage of the *Blossom* 1825-28. (From F W Beechey's *Voyage to the Pacific and Beering's Strait*)

rendezvous with Franklin. There was, of course, no sign of him. Kotzebue Sound had been explored by Otto von Kotzebue, the Russian navigator, during his voyage in the *Rurik* in 1815-18 and there would have been a copy of his three-volume Narrative aboard the *Blossom*. They reached Captain Cook's Icy Cape (on the coast of what is now Alaska) on 13 August 1826 and as they proceeded along that coast, bottles were deposited for Franklin's overland party containing messages in English and Russian. The usual exchange of goods from their 'baidars', large skin boats, was made with the Eskimos who lived in this part of what was then Russian America. These boats and the people themselves are described by Beechey and a vocabulary of their language was published in Beechey's second volume, mainly of those in Kotzebue Sound. Though Franklin never reached the western end of the North West Passage Beechey's voyage was not all in vain. A further length of northern coast was surveyed by sending off Thomas Elson, Master of the *Blossom*, on 17 August, in the barge, along the coast to the north-east. Although no sign of Franklin's party was seen, that well-known future landmark in western Arctic voyages, Point Barrow, was reached and named after Sir John Barrow of the Admiralty, 'to mark the progress of northern discovery on each side of the American continent which has been so perseveringly advocated by that distinguished member of our naval administration'. Point Barrow is only 146 miles from Franklin's Return Reef, his furthest west from the mouth of the Mackenzie River. Elson Bay, to the east of Point Barrow, was named after the barge's commander.

The 'barge' was, in fact, a decked topsail schooner designed and built at Woolwich Dockyard, which was small enough to sail close to the shore, where the *Blossom* could not go. The Eskimos hereabouts were found to be audacious and prone to close bargaining and thieving and in view of their numbers Elson thought it prudent to leave Point Barrow before any open hostility occurred, so no record for Franklin was left and neither were lengthy observations of the eastward trending coast made. Point Barrow's latitude (71°23′31′′N) was determined and shown to be the most northerly part of the American continent so far surveyed. The coastal voyage south to the *Blossom* was made with great difficulty – a contest of will and wits played against the changes of wind and the encroachments of the ice. The barge had to be 'tracked' from the shore and cliffs, at one stage with the help of more modest and friendly Eskimos.

As a result of the surveys by the *Blossom* and by the barge a further 126 miles had, in Beechey's words, 'been added to the geography of the polar regions', leaving as we have seen only 146 miles between Point Barrow and Return Reef unexplored. After spending the winter carrying out her duties in warmer waters to the south, the *Blossom* called again at Petropavlovsk, where Beechey was pleased to see in the hospitable Russian governor's garden a monument to Captain Charles Clerke, who succeeded Cook after his death during his third voyage, and another to Vitus Bering, the Dane in Russian service, after whom the strait is named. However, he was 'mortified' to find that the 'respectable inhabitants of the place' preferred their own dishes made from seals' flesh to the turtle soup made by the *Blossom*'s cook from a live turtle caught on a tropical island! Lieutenant George Peard, whose journal has been published by the Hakluyt Society, gives an interesting account of the two visits to Petropavlovsk, during the first of which they met Baron Ferdinand von Wrangel, the Arctic traveller, and were reminded of home on hearing the cuckoo. The *Blossom* passed through Bering Strait again in 1827 and proceeded to the north after entering Kotzebue Sound. Fog, ice and gales made navigation difficult and only one bottle was deposited for Captain Franklin. On returning south to Kotzebue Sound, two shipwrecked mariners were seen, waving a white cloth to attract attention. Not knowing whether these men belonged to Franklin's party or were the crew of *Blossom*'s barge, a boat from *Blossom* was sent with blankets and provisions. Beechey was distressed to discover that the barge had been wrecked and three men drowned in the sound, after having navigated only just beyond Icy Cape with Lieutenant Belcher in command. For his 'strenuous exertions to save the crew, and his resolute conduct towards the natives, after he was thrown amongst them', Beechey praised Belcher for his 'humanity and courage'. Later known for his survey work and for his rather disagreeable character, Belcher comes into this story again, as commander of the what he called the 'last of the Arctic voyages'.

The *Blossom* passed through the chain of the Aleutian Islands where thick fog, together with strong and uncertain currents, made navigation tricky. The *Blossom* returned to England on 12 October 1828, after a voyage of three and a half years, during which she sailed 73,000 miles in every climate. Eight members of the ship's company had been lost by illness, four shipwrecked, one went missing, one drowned in a lake and another lost overboard in a gale. 'To individuals', wrote Beechey, 'nothing probably can compensate for these losses; but to the community, considering the uncertainty of life under the most ordinary circumstances, the mortality which has attended the present undertaking will, I hope, be considered compensated by the services which has been performed by the expedition'.

Captain Lyon's Disastrous Voyage 1824

Complementary to Parry's, Franklin's and Beechey's expeditions was that of Captain G F Lyon, who had commanded *Hecla* during Parry's voyage of 1821-23 and who had written such a lively account of it. The Admiralty sent him in 1824 to connect Point Turnagain, Franklin's furthest east on the mainland of North America, with Repulse Bay, to the north west of Hudson Bay, visited by Parry and Lyon in 1821 *en route* to Fury and Hecla Strait. Lyon was instructed to sail to Repulse Bay in the *Griper* (180 tons), then to cross the Melville Peninsula and continue westwards along the coast to Point Turnagain. What Sir John Barrow had called the 'defective geography' of America meant that it was not known at the time that this proposed journey would have involved not only crossing what was later called the Rae Isthmus, between two arms of the sea, but also the base of the Boothia Peninsula, which was explored by John and James Clark Ross in 1829-33.

The *Griper* never even reached Repulse Bay during what proved to be a disastrous voyage. The old gun brig was quite unequal to navigating these stormy seas. Having taken on supplies at Stromness in the Orkney Islands, including two strong Shetland ponies, for the land expedition, the *Griper* was towed across the Atlantic by the *Snap*. In Hudson Strait the officers and men, the ponies and other livestock were given 'a run ashore' on an ice flow. A meeting with the natives of the Savage Islands also took place, Captain Lyon finding these people spoke the same language as those of Igloolik. Four puppies were bought 'as an incipient team for future operations'. The pigs and ponies were exhibited to the natives who, with 'a loud laugh and shout announced their satisfaction at having seen two new species of Tooktoo (reindeer)'.[19]

Lyon found the old charts of Southampton Island (the large island to the north of Hudson Bay) most inaccurate, so that the hand lead had to be kept sounding near the coast. In addition, the compasses became erratic and unreliable, so that they had to depend on celestial bearings, whenever these could be obtained. On 12 September, they were far up Roe's welcome (the sound between Southampton Island and the mainland) and at the entrance to Wager Inlet experienced a perilous storm and a shortage of water, because of which the Shetland ponies, great favourites with all hands, had to be shot.

The *Griper's* dull sailing became a danger because she could not work off a dangerous lee shore. Both bower anchors were therefore let go at the onset of a sudden northeasterly gale, sails furled, and the lower yards and topmasts struck leaving the *Griper* pitching in the heavy seas. E N Kendall, who later accompanied Dr Richardson as surveyor on Franklin's second overland expedition, described the horrors of that night in a letter to his mother:

Never shall I forget the dreariness of this most anxious night. Our ship pitched at such a rate, that it was not possible to stand even below, while on deck we were unable to move without holding by ropes which were stretched from side to side. The drift snow flew in such sharp heavy flakes, that we could not look to windward, and it froze on deck to above a foot in depth. The sea made incessant breaches and the temporary warmth it gave while it washed over us, was most painfully checked by its almost immediately freezing on our clothes. To these discomforts were added the horrible uncertainty as to whether the cables would hold until daylight, and the conviction also that if they failed us, we should instantly be dashed to pieces; the wind blowing directly to the quarter in which we knew the shore must lie. Heavy floes drifting down on the ice-encrusted ship endangered the anchor cables.

Kendall continued:

The hurricane blew with such violence as to be perfectly deafening, and the heavy wash of the sea made it difficult to reach the mainmast where the officer of the watch and his people sat shivering, completely cased in frozen snow, under a small tarpaulin, before which ropes were stretched to preserve them in their places. I never beheld a darker night, and its gloom was increased by the rays of a small horn lantern which was suspended from the mizen stay to show where the people sat.[20]

By the early morning all the anchor cables had parted and the *Griper* lay broadside to the sea. Fortunately, a change of wind at slack water enabled two trysails to be set with great difficulty, the gunwhales being underwater and the steeply sloping decks almost too slippery to stand on. Captain Lyon summoned all hands and told them that he would turn south, out of the Welcome. The men's sufferings were great, exposed for two nights and days to the freezing sea, with neither rest nor hot meals. The officers were asked to give their opinions as to the course to be adopted for the voyage. They all decided for England, at once, because the *Griper* had lost her anchors.

After a slow and stormy crossing of the Atlantic, the battered and leaking old gun brig ran into Portsmouth Harbour on 10 November, five months after leaving Deptford, after a heroic voyage, which sadly had added little to the chart. Lyon found himself blamed by the Admiralty and he was not offered a new appointment. Parry expressed his opinion of the Admiralty's conduct in a letter to his brother:

I cannot express the indignation with which I view this too common attempt on the part of the Admiralty, to let the blame for failure lie on any shoulders but their own. This is certainly the case now, with respect to the Griper, a vessel of such lubberly, shameful construction as to baffle the ingenuity of the most ingenious seaman in England to do anything with her . . . a good vessel would not have incurred the same risk . . ., and *it is the Admiralty* with whom the principal, original and most glaring fault lies.[21]

Off Lyon went to Mexico as a Commissioner of the Real del Monte Mining Company and in 1828 his *Journal of a tour in Mexico . . .* was published. He died four years later. Sadly, his wife died in 1826, a year after their wedding, so he never had children to tell about the Eskimos.[22] One wonders whether it was his wife Lucy, who wrote the well-illustrated little children's book by 'A Lady', entitled *A peep at the Esquimaux . . .*, published in 1825, in which the Eskimo boys and girls provide a lesson for English ones.[23]

CHAPTER 8

John and James Clark Ross: Four Winters in the Arctic 1829-33

We have seen earlier how Captain John Ross suffered the ignominy, on the return of Parry's expedition of 1819-20, of hearing how the *Hecla* and *Griper* had sailed right through his supposed 'Croker Mountains' and into Lancaster Sound. He was never given another appointment by the Admiralty and he joined the ranks of a vast number of unemployed naval officers. He was put on what was called 'half-pay', which was, in fact, better than it sounds. For Ross, who had served in the navy for thirty-three years and was a junior captain, it meant a reduction from 12 shillings a day to 10 shillings and sixpence. He became greatly interested in the development of steam navigation in the years that followed the Arctic expedition of 1818 and in 1828 he published his book, which had the lengthy title, *A treatise on Navigation by Steam; comprising a History of the Steam Engine, and an Essay towards a System of the Naval Tactics Peculiar to Steam Navigation, as Applicable both to Commerce and Maritime Warfare.* In these same years, he also built North West Castle, his house on Loch Ryan at Stranraer, which incorporated many nautical features. It now forms part of a large hotel.

Franklin's future second wife, Jane Griffin, met John Ross the year after his return from the Arctic and described him as 'short, stout, sailor-looking . . . his features are coarse and thick . . . Yet notwithstanding his lack of beauty, he has a great deal of intelligence, benevolence and good humour in his countenance'.[1] In contrast, she is said to have called James Clark Ross 'the handsomest man in the navy', an opinion that is borne out by his splendid portrait of 1833. This same young man sailed with Parry on the three North West Passage expeditions and also on a fourth, of 1827, the aim of which was to travel over the sea ice from Spitsbergen to the North Pole.

John Ross's second Arctic voyage met with no more success as far as discovering and navigating the North West Passage than his first in 1818. However, like them, it added pieces to the geographical jigsaw and was remarkable on two counts: first, no less than four winters were spent in the Arctic and, second, James Clark Ross sledged to the North Magnetic Pole, an attainment of considerable scientific importance. Their descendant and biographer tells how it began.

Early in 1828, John Ross submitted to the Admiralty a plan for an Arctic expedition in a steam vessel. He claimed that a steamship of shallow draft would be superior to a sailing ship in approaching unknown coasts and that a steamship could force her way through relatively thin ice that would stop a sailing ship; moreover, since right ice conditions were usually the result either of no wind or of a northerly (and therefore adverse) wind, a sailing ship was often unable to take advantage of a clear sea or of leads through the ice. Ross was also strongly of the opinion that all the ships used in the expeditions of the past ten years had been too large.[2]

This proposal, and two by Franklin, was turned down by the Admiralty, official interest in the North West Passage, as Franklin suspected, having waned, and as the Board of Longitude was abolished in 1828, rewards for northern discoveries became null and void. After various other approaches, John Ross persuaded his old friend Felix Booth to finance the expedition. Booth was then Sheriff of London, whose fortune came from the manufacture of Booth's gin. His name was later added by Ross to the map of the polar regions in the form of Boothia Felix, the Gulf of Boothia and Felix Harbour. Booth agreed to contribute a large sum anonymously, to which John Ross added £3000 of his own money. It so happened that James Clark Ross had also been on half pay since his return from the attempt on the North Pole and his promotion to Commander in the Royal Navy. By this time, after so many years in the Arctic, he had begun to consider expeditions to be his birthright and was happy to join his uncle in this new venture.

James Clark Ross, the most experienced of all the 'Arctic Officers' of the nineteenth century. The dip circle symbolises his reaching the North Magnetic Pole from the *Victory*. (Oil by John Wildman, NMM, BHC2981)

A paddle steamer, the *Victory*, which had been carrying mail to the Isle of Man, was bought by John Ross. In being fitted for the voyage, a number of new features to the machinery were added and the sides were raised 5½ feet, increasing her tonnage, and consequently her draft, from 85 to 150 tons. Parry spent a day on board and, although confident that Ross would succeed if anyone could, felt that there was 'in the whole thing, rather too much that is new and untried; and this is certainly not the kind of service on which novelties of that sort ought first to be tried'.[3] Many naval officers without employment, including Back and Hoppner, were eager to join, and a whaling vessel, the *John*, was bought to carry the stores; the Admiralty contributed a small decked vessel, named *Krusenstern* by Ross, as well as two of the boats built for Franklin's second overland expedition. And so, on 23 May 1829, after being seen off by Franklin and a number of naval and French dignitaries, the old campaigner set off in his new contraption, down the Thames to the sea.

Parry had been forced to abandon the exploration of Prince Regent Inlet, owing to the wreck of the *Fury*, which incidentally, Ross attributed in the Introduction to his narrative, to her drawing 'eighteen feet instead of eight'.[4] Parry had been preoccupied with his endeavours to save the *Fury*, but had noted indications of ice free waters further south. It was therefore possible that a westward passage might exist there. Ross felt it his duty 'to decide that question in the first place', and then to turn his attention 'to the next opening further north. Since this was a private venture, he had of course no official instructions to follow. As for scientific work, several learned societies replied to his letters 'requesting to know in what manner I could aid them in their several objects of pursuit'. Like Parry's, the expedition was well supplied with instruments and had enough food for three years.

The *Victory* arrived at Gravesend, on the lower River Thames, where she anchored to await the turn of the tide and to take on a new pilot, and it was here 'that the constructors of our execrable machinery, Messrs. Braithwaite & Erickson left us'. With these words, John Ross gave the readers of his *Narrative* an early hint as to the troubles that were to follow. Felix Booth and his nephew hailed a fishing boat next morning 'and took leave of us; little foreseeing at that time the length of our separation, and the doubts hereafter to arise whether we should ever meet again on this side of eternity'. Ross had known that there were defects in the machinery, but, with the voyage well and truly under way, he discovered more. For instance, a pump had to be kept going because the boilers leaked so much, despite dung and potatoes being put in them on the manufacturer's instructions. 'It was moreover impossible', he wrote, 'for the men to remain, for any length of time, at this work, in a place where the temperature was above 95°: while, although they performed it without murmuring, they soon became exhausted, as I was fully convinced by the fainting of one of them, whom it therefore became necessary to bring on deck before he could be recovered'.

Worse was to come for one of the men, however. The *Victory* had proved a good sailer, if the paddles were lifted out of the water, when a breeze sprang up.

She rounded Lands End and put into the Isle of Man, where improvements were made to the machinery. All seemed to be going well on passage to Ross's Loch Ryan, on the coast of Galloway, the Ross family's homeland in western Scotland, when on 9 July,

> at ten in the morning, our principal stoker, William Hardy, came up from the engine room. On the deck, unassisted, and alone, and though without complaint or exclamation, presenting his left arm, shattered, and nearly severed above the elbow.

He had slipped owing to the motion of the vessel and his arm had become entangled 'between the guide wheels and the frame'. Ross lost no time in deciding that an amputation was necessary and though the surgeon had not yet joined the expedition his instruments, bar the saw and medicine chest, were on board. Although he would have been more at ease 'cutting away half a dozen masts in a gale', Ross performed the amputation, using 'such knowledge as the sight of amputations in my naval service', plus any reading he had done. Once ashore, the patient was taken to Ross's house at Stranraer and put under the surgeon's care; he eventually returned to a post with his original firm.

A further examination of the boilers and machinery served to convince them 'still more that we must consider ourselves in future, as dependent on our sails, for such progress as it should be our good fortune to make'. Owing to the mutinous conduct of the crew of the *John*, the *Victory* had to progress on her own, the *John* being left behind in Scotland. Ross was pleased with the conduct of his own people. These consisted of three mates, a carpenter and his mate, two engineers, three stokers, a steward, a cook and nine seamen. Commander James Clark Ross was second in command, while William Thorn, formerly Ross's purser in the *Isabella*, was third. Captain Ross, his nephew and Mr Thorn all served without pay. The surgeon was Mr George Macdiarmid. Thomas Blanky, the First Mate, later sailed as Ice Master of HMS *Terror* (Captain Crozier) on Franklin's last expedition, 1845-48. Thomas Abernethy, the Second Mate had served under Parry in 1827. He later sailed in HMS *Erebus* with Captain James Clark Ross, to the Antarctic 1839-43; with Captain John Ross again in the *Felix*, 1850-51, in search of Franklin and likewise in the *Isabel* (Captain Inglefield) in 1852.

On nearing Cape Farewell (Kap Farvel), the southern tip of Greenland, warm clothes were issued. After divine service on Sunday 5 July, a piece of ship's timber was picked up, full of treenail holes and covered with 'marine animals' of various sorts and therefore given as a prize to Commander Ross, such creatures being his special study. The *Victory*, with the little *Krusenstern* in tow, proceeded northwards along the west Greenland coast, putting into the harbour of Holsteinborg (now Sisimiut) amid a multitude of kayaks and a plague of mosquitoes. They were welcomed by the Danish governor and the Danish pastor, from whom they learnt that the stores, hull and rigging of a wrecked English whaler, the *Rookwood*, had been left in the governor's charge and were for sale. Ross therefore bought some stores and the whaler's mizzen mast, which was to replace the *Victory*'s foremast. At dinner ashore, John Ross was able to converse

The two Eskimos, Ikmalick and Apelaglu, drawing maps aboard the *Victory* during Captain John Ross' voyage of 1829-33. The kindness and gentleness of the Inuit was much appreciated by Ross and company. (From Sir John Ross' *Narrative*)

in Danish with the pastor and his wife, because of his service in the Baltic. In this way, and while dining later with the governor and his family, much was learnt of life in this Danish settlement, where the summer was the mildest ever experienced. Winter was said to be the healthiest season, while chest complaints were prevalent in the summer. Ross dryly remarked that 'the patients cannot at least suffer much from medicine, since the nearest medical person is two hundred miles off, at Baal's river; and even there, his practice is not extensive enough to afford him the means of doing much harm'. The governor presented the expedition with six Eskimo dogs, which proved useful later.

Crossing Baffin's Bay turned out to be not unlike a Mediterranean cruise with blue skies, gentle breezes, and the men scrubbing the decks in bare feet. The occasional iceberg served to remind them that they were in high latitudes, and also provided them with drinking water and fresh water for the boilers. Even the engine worked well enough during calms, driving the vessel at over one knot, and as the *Victory* neared the western land on 6 August, it excelled itself by running continuously for twenty-four hours. The entrance to Lancaster Sound had of course a particular and painful significance for John Ross. In 1818, he had reached the entrance but had gone no further on seeing ice and what he called the 'Croker Mountains' barring his track, but through which Parry sailed the following year.

Little ice was encountered until they entered Prince Regent Inlet and the smaller pieces were easily fended off by *Victory*'s paddles. On 12 August they were near Fury Point, where Parry's ship had been wrecked four years earlier. There was no sign of her. As the *Victory* eventually neared the spot, those not needed to work the ship climbed to the masthead to look for the wreck. Commander Ross, who had been the *Fury*'s lieutenant, went in a boat to find a good harbour (bounded by icebergs) just south of Fury Beach. On landing, after the crew had been ordered a good meal and a rest, Captain Ross, Commander Ross, the Purser and the Surgeon 'found the coast almost lined with coal' from the wreck. There was one tent still whole, though even that had been torn by bears. James Ross could not find his notebook and bird specimens which he had left in a pocket near the door. On the other hand, the canned meat and vegetables, which had been piled in two heaps, were found to be quite untouched by the bears, not at all rusted and still wholesome. 'Had they [the bears] known what was within, not much of this provision would have come to our share, and they would have had more reason than we to be thankful for Mr Donkin's patent', remarked Captain Ross. The wine, spirits, bread, flour, cocoa, lime juice, pickles and even the sails were largely in good condition and from these materials, deposited on that far distant and icy shore, all their wants for over two years were supplied items 'for which we should have searched the warehouses of Wapping or Rotherhithe: all ready to be shipped when we chose, and all free of cost; since it was the certainty of this supply . . . that had formed the foundation of the present expedition'. After embarking a proportion of the gunpowder, the remainder was destroyed, at Parry's request and in accordance with their own sense of what was right, so that no harm could be done to the Eskimos.

They proceeded to the south, beyond Parry's furthest, hoping that their course would lead to the North American mainland. They failed to discern Bellot Strait (the strait between Somerset Island to the north and what Ross named the Boothia Peninsula to the south) but Parry's Cresswell Bay was seen to be a deep inlet. Formal possession was taken of the 'new-discovered land' on 16 August, 'with the usual ceremony', when the colours were displayed, and the King's health and that of Felix Booth were drunk.

Sometimes beset and drifting in the ice, sometimes proceeding by sail or stem, by the end of August the *Victory* had navigated more than 100 miles to the south of Fury Point. A splendid harbour 'not exceeded by any in the world' was charted and named Elizabeth Harbour, after Sheriff Booth's sister. On 12 September, the *Victory* and the *Krusenstern* had a fortunate escape from being driven on the rocks with the rapidly moving ice. No description in words, or depiction with the pencil, observed Ross, could convey the frightful scene to the readers of his book, familiar only with the level ice of lakes and canals at home.

> But let them remember that ice is a stone; a floating rock in the stream, a promontory or an island when aground, not less solid than if it were a land of granite. Then let them imagine, if they can, these mountains of crystal hurled through a narrow strait by a rapid tide; meetings as mountains in motion would meet, with the noise of thun-

der, breaking from each other's precipices huge fragments, or rending each other asunder, till, losing their former equilibrium, they fall over headlong, lifting the sea around in breakers, and whirling it in eddies; while the flatter fields of ice, forced against these masses, or against the rocks, by the wind and the stream, rise out of the sea till they fall back on themselves, adding to the indescribable commotion and noise which attend these occurrences.

Ross paid tribute to the *Victory*, saying that her shallow draft and the way she had been strengthened were tremendous advantages. 'It is plain,' he wrote, 'that either of the ships employed on the former expeditions must have been here lost, from their mere draft of water, since they would have struck on the rocks over which we were hurried by the ice; while, however fortified, they would have been crushed like a nutshell, in consequence of their shape.'

In discussing whether Ross were correct in his judgement, the maritime historian A W H Pearsall has pointed out that, while Ross was undoubtedly far-sighted in pioneering the use of steam in the Arctic, his advocacy of smaller ships (as here) was more questionable. While these would require fewer men (and therefore fewer stores) and were less likely to go aground, as Ross said, this last advantage was not generally required in an area of deep water. 'Moreover, the degree to which ships became frozen in may have overshadowed the purpose of the voyages, which was actually to sail through the North-West Passage, and for sailing a full and active crew was obviously required . . . it was rough justice that although arranging to have the paddle wheels unslippable to avoid damage from ice, he made a bad choice of engines for his *Victory*, as they proved useless, and led to her loss for just the reasons he attempted to avoid, frozen in, in a remote region from which she could not escape under sail'.[5]

At the end of September 1829, Ross summed up their situation with some observations about navigating these icy seas. He maintained that a ship should not hesitate to enter the pack when the ice was moving along the shore and the ship was near to the land, though the watchwords of the Arctic mariner should always be 'caution and patience'. Their position towards the southern end of Prince Regent Inlet was, according to Ross, 'three hundred further miles than any preceding expedition, [and] not more than two hundred and eighty miles from the coast laid down by Captain Franklin'. They were, in fact, roughly south west of *Fury* and *Hecla* Strait in what Ross called the Gulf of Boothia. In proceeding southwards, cairns and posts had been erected in prominent positions. However, the great encumbrance was the ship's engine, since it took up two-thirds of the tonnage and, being a constant trouble, required four men to attend to it. Ross decided that 'in future our ship was to be a sailing ship, and nothing more', and the boilers would be taken to pieces, with a view to landing them, once the *Victory* was frozen in for the winter.

On 2 October, preparations began for wintering, since it was clear that no further progress was possible. In Ross's words, 'the prison door' had shut upon them for the first time and by 7 October the *Victory* had been hauled along a channel sawn in the ice into what appeared to be secure winter quarters. No open water was visible and only snow upon the land. At this point in his narrative, Ross wrote his view of the winter scene.

> Amid all its brilliancy, this land, the land of ice and snow, has even been, and ever will be a dull, dreary heart-sinking, monotonous waste, under the influence of which the very mind is paralyzed, ceasing to care or think . . . for it is but the view of uniformity and silence and death . . . where nothing moves and nothing changes, but all is for ever the same, cheerless, cold and still.

In preparing the *Victory* for wintering the provisions were found to be enough to last for nearly three years. On 20 October, the last of the engine was hoisted out, to everyone's relief, and then the galley was moved to the men's quarters to give them the benefit of the warmth. A novel and useful device was to place iron tanks upside down on the upper deck over the cooking area where the steam was caught and condensed into ice rather than in the ship. The issue of grog was stopped, since there was only one year's supply which might be needed for parties travelling overland, or in case of shipwreck.

In early January 1830, a group of thirty-six Inuit arrived, with whom friendly contact was made, the experience of Commander Ross proving helpful. They were all good-natured, well fed and clothed, and Ross expressed his satisfaction at meeting them and remarked that 'it was to the natives that we must look for such geographical information as would assist us in extricating ourselves from our difficulties and in pursuing our course'. The usual visits to the ship and the exchange of gifts took place, and the individual who had most cause to be thankful for their visit was Tulluahiu, and Estamo who had lost half his leg to a bear. The *Victory*'s carpenter made him a wooden one, bearing the ship's name, to which was later attached a foot. Before the expedition left for England, several spare legs were given to him.

On the important matter of the lie of the land, the Eskimos were found to be familiar with quite distant shores, including Repulse Bay. The best draughtsman proved to be Ikmallik, who earned the name of 'Hydrographer'. Another able draughtsman was Tiriksiu, the wife of the man with the wooden leg. 'I soon found too,' wrote Ross, in his somewhat ponderous style, 'that this personage, woman though she was, did not want a knowledge of geography, and that, also, of a different nature from what she might have acquired in an English boarding school, through the question book and "the use of the globes" '. He went on to say that Tiriksiu 'perfectly comprehended the chart' and, besides drawing one similar to Ikmallik's, added more islands, day's journeys and places where food might be found.

However the chart they drew, on which appear place-names in Inuktitut and in English, shows no sea way at the southern end of Prince Regent Inlet/Gulf of Boothia, the way the *Victory* had been heading in the search for the North West Passage, to link up with Franklin's furthest east, Point Turnagain, on the north coast of America. The *Victory* was unable to navigate any further south than her first winter quarters in Felix Harbour and it fell largely to Dr John Rae to survey the southern coast on foot in later years from Repulse Bay, although James Clark Ross did chart a portion of the coast to the south of the *Victory*.

During their first winter, a good stock of clothes and skins and a number of dogs were acquired by barter from the natives, so that Ross, and more particularly James Clark Ross, possessed a team of ten good dogs and the right clothing for the country. With the realisation that there was no passage to the south came the need to explore westwards and also to look northwards again, making a more precise survey of the coast in order to find the strait, which the Inuit said existed, suitable for the passage of a ship. By this they must have meant Bellot Strait which was not discovered until twenty years later, during the Franklin Search.

*   *   *

In 1830, the Rosses made a number of journeys across the neck of the Boothia Peninsula, a chain of narrow lakes which John Ross later called the Isthmus of Boothia, in company with their Inuit guides and friends. James Clark Ross discovered 'King William's Land', an island of special importance in this story, and during May and June 1830 he sledged across the ice of what is now called James Ross Strait, west of the Boothia Peninsula, skirting Matty Island. He followed the northern coast of 'King William's Land', naming its northern point Cape Felix and reaching Victory Point on its west coast, from which there was a view of what James Ross called Point Franklin. With the irony of fate, it was not far from here that Sir John Franklin was to die aboard HMS *Erebus* in June 1847. As with his other journeys, James Clark Ross's account of this journey was published in his uncle's narrative and its significance makes it worth close scrutiny.

The party which left the *Victory* on 17 May 1830 consisted of four men, including Thomas Abernethy, the Second Mate, one man-hauled sledge and another pulled by eight dogs. They carried three weeks' provisions, instruments, clothes and a skin boat, presumably an umiak, and travelled at night when there was less glare from the sun. When they reached the sea, after crossing the Boothia Peninsula, the sailors gave three cheers, 'for it was the ocean that we had pursued, the object of our hopes and exertions; the free space which . . . was to have carried us round the American continent, which ought to have given us the triumph for which we and all our predecessors had laboured so long and so hard'. Following the west coast of Boothia for two or three nights, the party struck out across the sea ice to the west and after hacking through a 30-foot hummock encamped on Matty Island. From its north shore, they could see 'a great extent of ocean, terminating in heavy packed ice', whose hummocks showed James Ross that they were indeed 'on the boundary of the great northern ocean'. Freezing fog made their clothes so heavy and stiff that they could hardly move and putting these on next morning was 'difficult and painful', but with a little courage and exertion they got going again. They soon discovered 'an excellent harbour, could such a harbour ever be of any use'. At the end of the night's sledging, they would burrow into a snow drift, using the boat for a roof – 'a house, which with a little pardon for the want of precision in the term, might be called subterranean.'

After some ten days' laborious travelling over the rough sea ice, having crossed what was later called James Ross Strait, past Matty and Tennent Islands, James Ross was in doubt as to their actual position.

> The question with me was, whether we were in reality skirting a continent, or whether all this irregular land might not be a chain of islands. Those unacquainted with frozen climates like the present, must recollect that when all is ice, and all one dazzling mass of white, when the surface of the sea itself is tossed up and fixed into rocks, while the land is on the contrary, very often flat, if not level; when, in short, there is neither water nor land to be seen, or when both are equally undiscriminated, as well by shape as by colour, it is not always so easy a problem as it might seem on a superficial view, to determine a fact which appears, in words to be extremely simple.

We know now that these were islands and James Ross was wise to take the safe option and retain all his provisions though their weight was considerable and the dogs consequently exhausted; only one of which could still pull towards the end of May. With the approach of the melt season, when travelling would become impossible, it was essential to explore as much as possible. Proceeding north-westwards along the coast of what we know is King William Island, Ross was eager to ascertain whether it would turn to the southwest, towards Point Turnagain. Yet he was strangely reluctant: 'Will it be believed,' he wrote 'that I was not anxious to complete the survey of the north coast of America, that with so important an object almost within my very reach, I was not desirous to attain this great triumph?' The men were keen to continue and volunteered to go onto half rations, and so extend their journey for two more days. Having established a depot, they pressed forward and at midnight on 29 May, reached Cape Felix, the northern tip of King William Island, named by Ross, of course, after Felix Booth, that 'singularly generous and spirited individual, whose fame and deeds will go down to posterity among the first of those whose characters and conduct have conferred honour on the very name of a British merchant.'

From Cape Felix, the land trended southwest, while to the north 'the vast extent of ocean then before our eyes, assured us that we had at length reached the northern point of that portion of the continent which I had already ascertained with so much satisfaction, to be trending towards Cape Turnagain'.

However, in words that were later to have a particular significance in view of the fate of Sir John Franklin's ships, the *Erebus* and *Terror* in 1847-48, James Ross described the pressure of the sea ice upon the shore.

> The pack of ice which had, in the autumn of the last year, been pressed against that shore, consisted of the heaviest masses that I had ever seen in such a situation. With this, the lighter floes had been thrown up, on some parts of the coast, in a most extra-ordinary and incredible manner; turning up large quantities of the shingle before them, and, in some places, having travelled as much as half a mile beyond the limits of the highest tide-mark.

The party made a laborious journey of 20 miles to the southwest, crossing a great deal of hummocky ice. They were well pleased with having 'rounded the northernmost point of this part of the continent', as Ross believed – wrongly of course – and with finding that the coast trended 'in the desired direction'.

They were now only 222 miles distant from Cape Turnagain, roughly the same distance that the party had come from the *Victory*, 'with the main object of the expedition, almost, it may be said, within our reach'. Yet they were forced to return. The same number of days 'would have enabled us to do all that was remaining, to return triumphant to the *Victory*, and carry to England a truly worthy fruit of our long and hard labours'. Ross felt that only those who had been placed in the same circumstances could 'conceive the intensity of this regret and the severity of this disappointment'.

> But these days were not in our power; for it was not days of time, but of the very means of existence that were wanting to us. We had brought twenty-one days' provisions from the ship and much more than the half was already consumed, notwithstanding the reductions which had been made.

They had reached their present point after thirteen days, on only eleven days' provisions. They were 200 miles from the *Victory*, by the shortest route, and even 'a very scanty allowance' would eke out the provisions for only ten days.

James Ross and Abernethy, after whom Ross named Cape Abernethy, left the remainder of the party to rest for the day and travelled quickly, and lightly laden, southwest along the land. At midnight on 29 May, they climbed 'a stranded mass of ice about forty feet high' from which they could see to the southwest, a point of land some 15 miles away, at the end of a wide bay, where the ice was heavy and closely packed. There was an island about eight miles off, and they wondered whether the point might not in fact be an island too, but there was no time to struggle across the rugged ice and find out.

> We now therefore unfurled our flag for the usual ceremony, and took possession of what we saw as far as the distant point, while that on which we stood was named Victory point; being a 'ne plus ultra' of our labour, as it afterwards proved, while it will remain a standing record of the exertions of that ship's crew. The point to the southwest was also named Cape Franklin . . . on Victory point we erected a cairn of stones six feet high, and we enclosed in it a canister containing a brief account of the proceedings of the expedition since its departure from England.

At 1 am on 30 May, Ross and Abernethy turned their backs on this furthest point of their journey and rejoined the others at 6 am. The first piece of driftwood found since leaving the ship made a fire on which to cook a hare and two grouse. 'Everything thus united,' related Ross, 'to make this a marked day and, such animals are we, in spite of ourselves, that the rare occurrence of a hot supper and a glass of grog made us for a moment forget all our disappointments, and rather caused us to feel pleasure that we were now returning home, than regret that, in so doing, we were renouncing the very object of our long anxiety and hard pursuit'. On the following page of his account of this journey, James Ross gave the latitude and longitude of Victory Point and the estimated position of Cape Franklin; and these two places and the cairn feature poignantly in the later tragedy of Sir John Franklin's last expedition.

An artist's imaginative portrayal of the attainment of the North Magnetic Pole by James Ross on 1 June 1831. (From Robert Huish's account of John Ross' voyage of 1829–33, NMM, C8411)

The party was very tired and the remaining dogs quite exhausted. Wellington Strait, between Matty Island and the east coast of the much larger King William Island (the mainland of North America as Ross thought it) was traced and then they struck out east across what is called on Captain Ross's chart, 'Poctes's Bay' (with a dotted line along its supposed south coast to indicate that it was uncharted.) Seeing Cape Isabella cheered them on and they reached the coast of Boothia Peninsula to find that the supplies left for them by Captain Ross had been largely eaten by the Eskimos. However, they were amply repaid in fresh fish and though the melting snow made travel difficult, the skin boat came in useful to transport the supplies 'on this amphibious portion of our journey'. The party sighted the ship at 7 am on 13 June, when James Ross 'issued the last remaining dram to the party, and, hoisting our flag, we arrived on board at eight, all in good health, though much reduced in appearance'.

*   *   *

Preparations had been made in their absence to repair the *Victory* and the little *Krusenstern* (which had been sunk by the ice) for departure to the north. However, the ice never relented and the winter of 1830–31 was passed near to the previous winter quarters. The most important of the sledge journeys made during the following summer was by James Clark Ross, with Blanky, Abernethy and a small party to the North Magnetic Pole. The earlier observations of Franklin, Parry, Sabine and others had enabled its position to be calculated, although, unlike the north and south geographical poles, it never stays still, but migrates over the years. While this journey has no direct bearing on our story, it was a notable scientific achievement. James Clark Ross had made careful observations in the magnetic observatory to pinpoint the position of the North Magnetic Pole as far as the instruments permitted. After crossing the Boothia Peninsula to the western ocean, the party travelled northwards up the coast and at 8am on 1 June 1831 arrived at the 'calculated place'. This was a goal from which he did not have to turn back. 'I believe I must leave it to others,' he wrote, 'to imagine the elation of mind with which we found ourselves now arrived at this great object of our ambition: it almost seemed as if we had accomplished everything that we had come so far to see and to do; as if our voyage and all its labours were at an end, and that nothing now remained for us but to return home and be happy for the rest of our days'. This was on 1 June 1831, but they faced another dreary winter at Victoria Harbour, only some 15 miles further north than their old winter quarters. 'On the men,' John Ross wrote, 'the effect was tangible . . . When we first moved from our late harbour, every man looked forward to his three years' wages, his return to England, and his meeting with friends and family; the depression of their spirits was now proportionate'. During this winter of 1831-32, the mariners' dread disease of scurvy made its first appearance.

Christmas Day 1831 was celebrated in the cabin of the *Victory* with a round of preserved beef left on Fury Beach eight years before, 'which, with some veal and some vegetables – was as good as the day on which it was cooked'. Ross went on to speculate in his book as to 'whether the preservation of this meat, thus secured, be interminable', since what they brought home was in 1835 as good then as when it had been made in 1823. Since the flavouring of hare soup and puree of carrots, for example, had not lessened during those eight years, might not these foodstuffs last for ever, always supposing that the containers would last too?

During the winter, Ross concluded that the *Victory*, in her over-secure anchorage, should be abandoned and that boats, sledges and provisions be taken forward to the north, before the melt season arrived. The aim was to reach Fury Beach for supplies and for the boats still there. The health of Ross and the ship's company was not what it was; an old wound of his had begun to bleed – a sign of scurvy. By 29 May 1832, everything had been landed from the *Victory* which could be of use either to the expedition if forced to return or to the Eskimos. 'The colours were therefore hoisted and nailed to the mast', wrote Ross, 'we drank a parting glass to our poor ship, and having seen every man out, in the evening, I took my own adieu of the *Victory*, which had deserved a better fate'. She was the first vessel he had ever abandoned during his long sea service of forty-two years. 'It was like the last parting with an old friend' to leave the 'solitary, abandoned, helpless home of our past years, fixed in immovable ice, till time should perform on her his usual work.'

After a laborious journey, with a largely debilitated crew relaying most of the way, the whole party reached Fury Beach on 2 July. The first task was to construct a large house (Somerset House) of wood and canvas. A 'luxurious supper' from the *Fury*'s supplies was greatly relished. The *Fury*'s three boats, one of which had been badly damaged by the ice, were repaired, strengthened and rigged for the voyage to Lancaster Sound. However, heavy ice put an end to their first attempt in August 1832 to sail up Prince Regent Inlet – 'a succession of hopes and disappointments severely tried the patience of all'. On 7 October, they returned to Somerset House 'our labours at an end, and ourselves once more at home', where a fox had until then been resident. Another winter was endured. It saw the lamented death of the carpenter, Chimham Thomas, 'from scurvy, in addition to a worn-out constitution . . . the first of our losses . . . attributed to the climate and our peculiar situation'. In May 1833, work began on transporting provisions northwards, to the place where the three boats had been left the previous year. The party, which set out on 8 July, included three heavy invalids who could not walk and others who could just manage to get along, but not help to pull the three sledges. Having arrived at the boats, Ross found duties for the men to keep up their spirits while waiting for the ice to move. On 15 August the boats were launched, the stores and the sick embarked and they were truly off at last, trending northwards. This was an open ice year so that they were able to enter Lancaster Sound, which was filled (instead of ice) with water, which was 'navigable, and navigable to us, who had almost forgotten what it was to float at freedom on the seas'. On 17 August they made a run of 72 miles, at the end of which they pitched their tents on a beach west of Cape York. By dint of long hours of rowing, the boats passed eastwards across Admiralty Inlet and towards the entrance to Lancaster Sound.

In the early hours of 25 August, when all except the lookout were asleep in the tents, a sail was seen. The boats were launched with little delay and they set off in pursuit of the ship, which a breeze caused to sail away. After some anxious moments it fell calm and the three boats began to gain on another ship, which, after sighting them, hove-to, and lowered a boat. The mate presumed they had lost their ship, which Ross confirmed, before asking the name of his ship and requesting that they might be taken aboard.

> I was answered that it was 'the Isabella of Hull, once commanded by Captain Ross': on which I stated that I was the identical man . . . and my people the crew of the *Victory*. That the mate . . . was as much astonished at this information as he appeared to be, I do not doubt; while with the usual blunderheadedness of men on such occasions, he assured me that I had been dead two years.

The mate left for the ship 'repeating that we had long been given up as lost, not by them alone, but by all England'. Soon the rigging was manned and three cheers given, followed by a 'hearty seaman's welcome from Captain Humphreys'.

> Unshaven since I know not when, dirty, dressed in the rags of wild beasts instead of the tatters of civilization, and starved to the very bones, our gaunt and grim looks, when contrasted with those of the well-dressed and well-fed men around us, made us all feel . . . what we really were, as well as what we seemed to others. . . . Every man was hungry and was to be fed, all were ragged and were to be clothed, there was not

one to whom washing was not indispensable, nor one whom his beard did not deprive of all English semblance. All, everything was to be done at once; it was washing, dressing, shaving, eating, all intermingled . . . while in the midst of it all there were interminable questions to be asked and answered on all sides.

The *Isabella* left Davis Strait on 30 September, landing at Stromness in the Orkney Islands twelve days later. Captain Ross and the officers and men of the *Victory* arrived on 18 October in the whaling port of Hull, from which the *Isabella* had sailed. News of their miraculous survival had preceded them, so that the Mayor and Corporation and other worthies gave them a civic welcome. The freedom of the ancient city of Kingston-upon-Hull was conferred on Captain Ross. Soon afterwards, he was presented to William IV, the Lord High Admiral, at Windsor Castle and there the King gave Ross permission to dedicate to him his *Narrative of a second voyage in search of a North-West Passage and of a residence in the Arctic regions during the years 1829, 1830, 1831, 1832, 1833,* published in London two years later. Ross was knighted, James Clark Ross promoted to Captain, and Felix Booth given a baronetcy. Ross was able to make satisfactory arrangements for the payment of his crew by the Admiralty. Sir John Barrow wrote a caustic but anonymous review of Ross's book in the *Quarterly Review* of 1835 in which he also reviewed a somewhat scurrilous account of the expedition by Robert Huish, supposedly from the 'original documents' of William Light, the steward, which was also published in 1835.

The Appendix to the *Narrative* goes far beyond the usual scientific appendices found in similar volumes. Lively pen portraits and pictures of the 'Eskimos found in the territory of Boothia Felix' bring them to life, and Ross stresses the point that these people, unlike those of Igloolik (as portrayed by Lyon) looked carefully after their elderly folk, perhaps because they lived where food was plentiful. The zoology of the voyage includes notes on the animals such as the Arctic Hare and Arctic Fox, which were tamed and kept as pets; the Surgeon's report contains some interesting remarks about the diet of the native people. Two men died from diseases from which they were suffering at the outset of the voyage. The short biographies of the seamen are interesting too, and, give life to those who are usually anonymous in most other narratives. Finally, Ross evidently could not resist publishing a letter about one of the numerous men who wished to join the expedition. This individual said he could cook, had been on voyages to the East Indies, and could make 'portable soup'. He had been told by a person appearing in a dream, 'go with Captain Ross, he will be crowned with *success*'. However, instead of the man turning up to join the *Victory*, Ross received the following letter from his wife:

April 9, 1829

Sir,

I have just found out that my husband has made an agreement with you to join your expedition, through a dream, *without consulting me*; I must beg to tell you,

'The Victory's crew saved by the Isabella' of Hull (whaler) in August 1833, after four years in the Arctic, having been given up as lost 'by all England'. (From Sir John Ross' *Narrative*)

Sir, that he shall not go – I will not let him have his clothes. He must be mad even to think of leaving a comfortable home, to be frozen in with ice, or torn to pieces with bears; therefore, I am determined he shall not leave Gosport, so I hope you will not expect him.

Yours, Sir, etc., and so forth,
Mary L.

George Back Descends the Great Fish River, 1833–35

With no news of the Rosses after their departure in the *Victory* in 1829, anxiety slowly increased. Eventually, Dr John Richardson, who had taken part in both Franklin's overland expeditions, offered early in 1832 to lead a search party. Likewise, Commander George Back, then in Italy, travelled home to volunteer as well. The Government was willing partly to finance a search expedition, providing considerable private funds were raised too, and a 'Committee for promoting the Arctic Expedition by Land', consisting of a number of prominent persons, first met late in 1832. Under the Colonial Office, the Hudson's

Bay Company became the formal organisers of the proposed expedition, 'issuing Back with a commission under its seal that would enable him to obtain provisions and stores from the company's posts. It also provided two boats, two canoes, and 120 pounds of pemmican'.[6] Back was also given authority by the Admiralty to seek help in Canada, where more men were to be recruited besides the three who left England with him and the young surgeon-naturalist Dr Richard King in February 1833.

Back had reasoned that the Rosses were most likely to make for Fury Beach and subsist on the shores there. His first instructions were therefore to reach it by way of the unexplored 'Thlew-ee-choh-desseth or Great Fish River, which is believed either to issue from Slave Lake, or to rise in its vicinity, and thence to flow with a navigable course to the northward, till it reaches the sea'.[7] M J Ross has aptly summarised the first season of this expedition, as follows:

> Back arrived at Fort Resolution on Great Slave Lake on 8 August [1833] and left four days later with four men, including an Indian guide, to seek the Great Fish River. Weaving his way for hundreds of miles through lakes, forests, and rocky streams in pursuit of the headwaters of a river that might prove unnavigable or flow in the wrong direction [perhaps to Hudson Bay], Back had the satisfaction of discovering the source himself while temporarily separated from his party. He confirmed the size of the river after a few days of survey, but his progress was soon cut short by rapids, which his canoe was too weak to negotiate, and he took his party back to Fort Reliance [at the eastern end of Great Slave Lake], the new base that had been built in his absence. There the party spent a winter more uncomfortable than had been expected, because of the shortage of game.[8]

This shortage naturally affected the Indians as well as the relief expedition and Dr King praised the 'noble conduct' of Akaitcho, 'during this appalling season of calamity'. He 'proved himself well worthy of the rank of chief of the Yellow Knives, and was in every way the firm friend of the expedition'. He endeavoured to mitigate his tribe's distress, by 'hunting early and late every day'. However, Back found that age had lessened the old chief's authority and that he had grown 'peevish and fickle'. It was here that Back received the sad news of the death of Augustus, his friend and former interpreter, who had lost his way and died of cold and hunger in a snow-storm, having set out from Hudson Bay in order to join the expedition. 'Such was the miserable end of poor Augustus!' wrote Back, 'a faithful, disinterested, kind-hearted creature', whose qualities had won Franklin's, Richardson's and Back's own respect and regard during earlier expeditions. Back later met Green Stockings, whom he immediately recognised despite her assertion that she was an old woman now. She was surrounded by her children and was still the beauty of the tribe, being not at all displeased 'like all belles, savage or polite' when Back sketched her portrait.[9] Presumably one of these children was Hood's offspring.[10]

After the safe arrival of the Rosses in England the character of the expedition changed. A letter which reached Back on 30 April 1834 from the chairman of the search committee, Sir Charles Ogle, dated 22 October 1833, told him of the return of the Rosses (which was celebrated in a bowl of punch) and instructed him to turn his whole attention to the second object of his expedition, which was to complete the coastline of the northeastern extremity of America. 'You will observe,' the letter confirmed, 'from the enclosed abstract of Captain Ross's proceedings that this, also, is become an object of comparatively easy acquisition'.

> By proceeding first to Point Turnagain, and thence eastward to an obelisk in about 69 °37′N and 98 °40′W, which marks the termination of Captain Ross's progress – or, *vice versâ*, by proceeding first to this obelisk, and thence westward – it is believed that you may accomplish all that is now wanting in one season . . .

> Your choice of routes will of course depend on the point where the Thlew-ee-choh joins the sea; If, as Governor Simpson imagines, it falls into Bathurst's Inlet, and is identical with Back's River, you will of course proceed thence to the eastward . . .[11]

The news that members of the Ross expedition were safely home enabled Back to reduce the scale of his own expedition, so that only one boat was taken. The party of twelve, besides Back and King, consisted of three artillery men and seven voyageurs plus a small terrier. On 4 July 1834, they embarked on the Thlew-ee-choh (Great Fish, later Back River) and after twenty-five days' travel, they sighted a far distant 'majestic headland . . . to the north' from the wide channel into which the river had broadened. The water in this channel was salty, so that they knew they had reached the sea. George Back described the course of the Great Fish River as follows, on arriving at Victoria Headland and the estuary of the river:

> This then may be considered as the mouth of the Thlew-ee-choh, which, after a violent and tortuous course of two hundred and thirty geographical miles, running through an iron-ribbed country without a single tree on the whole line of its banks, expanding into fine large lakes with clear horizons, most embarrassing to the navigator, and broken into falls, cascades, and rapids to the number of no less that eighty-three in the whole, pours its waters into the Polar Sea in latitude 67 °11′0′N and longitude 94 °30′0′W.[12]

Dr Richard King gave a very similar description of the course of the river, except that he gave its length as 530 geographical miles. King's book, which is somewhat discursive and, by today's standards, opinionated, devotes considerable space to the animals and birds encountered, linked by sections relating to the affairs of the expedition. His last chapter set out proposals for a small expedition down the river to the polar sea, with himself as leader. He also pointed out the accuracy of the Indians' 'testimony . . . that the river, after running east for a long way, would ultimately cut its course through high rocks and flow north to the sea'. Looking at the map, one sees that the river does just that, as Back and King discovered, whereas it might well have continued eastwards and drained into Hudson Bay. The river was in flood on their descent to the sea and much lower on their return. King described one of the numerous difficult channels. This one was met on 22 July 1834.

Victoria Headland at the mouth of Back's Great Fish River, seen by George Back and Richard King after their perilous journey downstream, in 1834. (From George Back's *Narrative of the Arctic Land expedition to the mouth of the Great Fish River*)

Having secured the boat in a small bay, we proceeded to examine what was supposed to be a fall, from its roaring, hollow noise, but which proved to be a succession of cascades and rapids, presenting as terrific a sight as could well be conceived. The water rushed with impetuous and deadly fury between four mountains of reddish granite, extremely barren and naked, and from six to eight hundred feet high. An insulated rock, about three hundred feet high, situated in the very centre of the torrent, expanded the foaming river to a breadth of four hundred yards; where, from the inequalities of the sunken rocks, a surge was raised so overwhelming, that huge masses of ice were swallowed up, and in a moment afterwards tossed high into the air in innumerable splintered fragments.[13]

The difficulties of the river's descent were extremely hard on the boat; sometimes it was 'hurled by the force of the current against the projecting rocks with a force that threatened instant destruction, while at other times it was swept in the very centre of the raging stream'.[14] The river has been descended only a few times since Back's expedition, and his maps 'remained the only ones in use until as late as 1948.'[15]

The Great Fish (Back) River debouched into a long and wide bay – Chantrey Inlet – in which was an island, which Back named after the good people of Montreal. It features later in the Franklin story. To reach Point Turnagain, as instructed, the party would have had to navigate first northwards to the mouth of the inlet and then westward along the coast of the mainland, just where (in both places) the ice blocked their passage. Back did detect, nevertheless, between the mainland and King William Island, a strait, later named Simpson Strait. To north and east, there appeared to be open water. Back surmised that eastwards there could be a strait or 'southern channel' leading to Prince Regent's Inlet and therefore cutting through Ross's Boothia Felix (now Boothia Peninsula). It appeared that 'Poctes's Bay', shown with a dotted line on Ross's chart as a continuation of King William Land as far as the Boothia Peninsula, did not exist.

Sir John Barrow was to write an almost exultant letter to John Murray, the publisher, dated 8 September 1835, in relation to Back's belief that an eastern strait existed, on the publication of Sir John Ross's narrative.

> Somebody tells me that John Ross's second Humbug is out – if so, could you borrow a copy for a few days. I have long letters from Back who has completely demolished his Boothia Peninsula etc. etc. I suppose you [the *Quarterly Review*] are nearly out or I think half a sheet might be advantageously employed in holding up the charlatan a little more than we have done.[16]

On 16 August, the party left the north coast and returned up river to Fort Reliance for the winter. In the spring, Back set out for England via Montreal and New York, leaving Richard King to take charge of the rest of the party and return via the Hudson's Bay Company outposts and York Factory.

Back's *Narrative of the Arctic Land Expedition*, published in 1836, is one of the finest travel books of the nineteenth century. There followed from its publication a renewed interest in Arctic exploration, which led to another naval expedition, similar to that of Lyon in the *Griper* (1825). It was proposed by the Royal Geographical Society to the Colonial Secretary and approved by the Admiralty.

George Back in HMS *Terror* 1836-37

Although Back sailed in a far stronger and more suitable vessel than Lyon's old gun-brig, the *Griper*, his voyage of 1836-37, with a similar aim, was just as disastrous. HMS *Terror* was a bomb vessel of 340 tons, with a crew of sixty. The First Lieutenant was William Smyth, who had been with Beechey in the *Blossom* and who had just returned from crossing the Andes and sailing down the Amazon. The Second Lieutenant was Owen Stanley, subsequently Captain of HMS *Rattlesnake*, which surveyed Torres Strait and Louisiade Archipelago. The Mate was Robert John LeMesurier McClure, later to be hailed as the discoverer of the North West Passage during the voyage of HMS *Investigator* in 1849-54. McClure's inclusion in the party was to lead him on the road from obscurity to dazzling heights. In June 1836, when staying with friends, on his way to visit his recently bereaved mother and sister in Ireland after an absence of nine years, McClure was introduced to a senior naval officer who might help to advance him in the Service. He learnt that nothing could be done for him in his then post as Chief Mate of a revenue cutter, but that his promotion 'might almost be reckoned a certainty' if he joined the *Terror*, then fitting out for her Arctic voyage. He was only allowed four hours to decide, 'so that in the space of a short time the whole career of my life was altered, my promised visit to my mother

'The Crew of His Majesty's ship *Terror* breaking a passage in the Ice', water-colour by William Smyth, First Lieutenant, during the voyage of 1836-37, commanded by George Back. (NMM, PAD 9071)

and dear sister annulled and in three days I was installed in my new office . . .'[17]

She sailed from the Medway in June 1836 for Repulse Bay, north of Southampton Island, to the northwest of Hudson Bay. The aim was to haul boats to the sea across the Melville Peninsula, then to survey its western shores, south of Fury and Hecla Strait, and continue westwards to Point Turnagain along the north coast of America, thus completing, at last, the charting of the whole from east to west. The idea must have been based on Back's opinion that a strait existed through Ross's Boothia Felix to the south of the *Victory*'s winter quarters, thus making the peninsula an island. He never got near enough to see if he were correct in this assertion. The *Terror* was beset in September 1836, near Frozen Strait, after entering Foxe's Channel, and never reached Repulse Bay.

The vessel drifted in the grip of the sea ice for the entire winter, somehow withstanding its terrible pressure. Despite this, plays were performed by both officers and men, and evening schools were held. In fact, of the mixed crew of whalers, colliers and Jack Tars, only three or four could not write. Fortunately, the *Terror* escaped from the pack ice near the western entrance to Hudson Strait in July 1837, still encased in part of a floe, eventually emerging 'crazy, broken and leaky'[18] and in no condition to continue exploring. Some of the crew were suffering from scurvy, so that Back had little choice but to try and reach home. With her hull 'frapped', or bound together with chain cable, she only just survived the passage and was run aground on the sandy shores of Lough Swilly on the Irish coast in early September 1837. This was by no means the end of the

'Sketch of the *Terror* showing the courtyard and snow walls built round the ship'. (From Owen Stanley's sketch book kept during the expedition of 1836-7, commanded by George Back. (NMM, D49980-11)

Terror. She later ventured into the pack ice of the Southern Ocean in company with HMS *Erebus* during James Clark Ross' celebrated Antarctic expedition of 1839-43 and it was in these two stout ships that Sir John Franklin was to seek the last link in the North West Passage in 1845. They were both to leave their timbers amid the ice of the Arctic seas.

These bomb vessels were in many ways ideally suited to polar exploration. Originally built to withstand the recoil of their heavy artillery they were strong and sturdy and were better suited than most vessels to bear the crushing pressure of ice. They were also roomy and buoyant and so ideal for carrying men and stores, while in their new-found roles as survey and exploring vessels, their slow speed was no disadvantage.

Back had written of the *Terror* during her outward voyage in 1836, 'deep lumbered though she was, and though at every plunge the bowsprit dipped into the water, she yet pitched so easily as scarcely to strain a ropeyarn'. When the weather improved, 'the royals and all the studding sails were for the first time set, and the gallant ship in the full pride of her expanded plumage floated majestically through the rippling water.'[19] 'Sturdy and seaworthy, but crowded with men, stores and provisions, these little ships are remembered for their feats of exploration rather than for their prowess in war. How appropriate it is that their names survive on features of the regions they did so much to discover.'[20] The most famous of these features were of course Mount Erebus and Mount Terror the volcanic peaks on Ross Island in the Antarctic named by Captain James Clark Ross.

The damage to the sternpost and after run of *Terror*. This sketch was taken in turn from an outline made by Lieutenant Smyth, using a camera lucida. (From George Back's *Narrative of an Expedition in* HMS *Terror*)

CHAPTER 9

Dease and Simpson along the North Coast of America 1836-39

Through the remarkable travels by boat, on foot and by umiak of Peter Warren Dease and Thomas Simpson, both officers of the Honourable Hudson's Bay Company, under whose auspices their journeys were made, whole new stretches of the coast of North America were charted. It fell to these two men (particularly Simpson) to continue Franklin's westward survey, beyond his Return Reef to Point Barrow and subsequently to travel eastward, well beyond Franklin's Point Turnagain, making some significant discoveries, the most notable being the more easterly coast (beyond Richardson's 'Wollaston Land') of the large island which they called 'Victoria Land', after the young Queen Victoria, who had recently ascended the British throne.

We have noted the coalition of the North West Company and the Hudson's Bay Company which occurred towards the end of Franklin's first tragic overland journey of 1819-21. This union greatly facilitated his second and successful journey of 1825-27. By the time Dease and Simpson set out to finish the task begun by Franklin, fur trading in the Company's territory of Rupert's Land and further west over the Rockies to the Pacific had been vastly reorganised by the short, tough, despotic, illegitimate Scot, Governor George Simpson, who became known as the Little Emperor. As a bachelor, Simpson had travelled widely, getting to know not only the country itself, but the officers and servants of the company, some of whom he pensioned off in the cause of economy and efficiency. For the same reason, the transport system was completely changed. It was dominated to the east of the Rockies by the York boat while the colourful light canoe was retained 'as a special conveyance for the Governor, for senior officers on important missions and for vital packets of letters'.[1] The Governor had his own piper, Colin Fraser, during his long journey of 1828. Fraser would signal Simpson's approach to the trading posts by preceding him in full Highland costume piping 'Highland marches which must have stirred the souls of the Scots at the posts, and must have moved the Indians deeply too!'[2] The songs of the voyageurs or the skirl of the pipes – what music in the wilderness!

The younger cousin of the Governor was Thomas Simpson, who had studied for four years at King's College, Aberdeen, between 1824 and 1829. Governor Simpson had been impressed by him while on a visit to his aunt in Dingwall, and

had encouraged him to travel out to 'the wilds of the New World', in the anticipation of 'rapid promotion and handsome emolument'.[3] In June 1829, he joined
Governor Simpson at Norway House (the Company's post at the north end of
Lake Winnipeg) as his secretary, accompanying him on visits to other posts in
the territories and taking well to these travels, also learning the business of the
fur trade at York Factory on Hudson Bay, its capital for many decades.

In his account of Captain George Back's expedition down the Great Fish
(Back) River (see previous chapter) of 1833-35, Dr Richard King set out his plans
for another descent of the river, and further explorations. Because of his harsh
criticism of the Hudson's Bay Company, he became *persona non grata* in their territories and this was one reason for the Company's decision to organise an
expedition to complete the survey of the north coast of America. A more important reason was the Company's desire to place itself in an advantageous light
during forthcoming negotiations with the British Government, for the renewal
without liability to tax of the grant of the exclusive trade of Rupert's Land and
the North West territories made freely for twenty-one years to the limited companies in 1821.

Governor Simpson was instructed by the London committee in the spring of
1836 to arrange for an expedition to connect the discoveries of Captain John Ross
with those of Captain George Back, this objective being later extended to connect
the discoveries of Sir John Franklin with those of Beechey in the *Blossom* (as far
as Point Barrow.) Thomas Simpson entered upon its planning 'not only with zeal
and alacrity, but with the highest delight'.[4] His plans were substantially repeated
in the official instructions given to the expedition, the leadership of which was
given to Peter Warren Dease, a long-serving but quiet and reserved Chief Factor
of the Company. It was he who had been left in charge of Fort Franklin on Great
Bear Lake in 1825-26, during Franklin's second overland expedition. The historian of the Hudson's Bay Company described Dease 'as the most active and
effective of four brothers [the sons of Dr. John B. Dease] in the Company's service ... He had great knowledge and experience, and notable 'suavity of
manners' (the phrase is George Simpson's) which admirably fitted him for a
land voyage'.[5]

His young co-leader, Thomas Simpson, was described by his brother as having
a cheerful expression, with twinkling eyes, but a stern mouth, denoting
decisiveness. 'He was brave, judicious, enthusiastic and persevering', with a great
love for his family. The same brother also described him as short in stature, with
a round full face, whose expression was 'open and engaging', with brown curls
clustering 'over a brow of massive breadth'- and as 'a man of great ardour,
resolution and perseverance'.[6] Thomas Simpson was glad to escape from desk
work. A good mathematician, he knew how to take observations for position and
to work up his results into surveys for eventual publication as finished maps,
while his Master's degree gave him a good academic background, as regards natural history and physical science.

Although not a highlander by descent, his upbringing among the Scottish hills and his yearly rambles in Aberdeenshire and Banffshire gave him 'a keen feeling for the scenery of his native district' (within sight of Ben Nevis). During his years at the university, he became leader of the highland students (although speaking little Gaelic) and, in debates, 'he frequently made triumphant comparisons between the proud feelings instilled into the mind of a highlander by a constant contemplation of the grand and romantic scenery of the mountains, and the plodding stolidity of the inhabitants of the lowlands'.[7] His brother, Alexander Simpson, who penned these words, was also in the Company's employ and played some part in the negotiations regarding the Sandwich Islands (now Hawaii). After the violent death of his elder brother, 'the Arctic discoverer', in 1840, Alexander Simpson was to write a book entitled *The life and travels of Thomas Simpson* . . . which was published in London, 1845. This contains many personal opinions as to the expedition, its background and its sequel, but also quotes his letters from Thomas Simpson, which supplement the explorer's own *Narrative of the discoveries on the north coast of America, effected by the officers of the Hudson's Bay Company during the years 1836-39*, published in London in 1843.

The instructions to Dease and Simpson, given by George Simpson, overseas governor of the Hudson's Bay Company, from Norway House on 2 July 1836, were based, as we have seen, on Thomas Simpson's plan. This in turn derived from a proposal by Dr Richardson, but set out on a reduced scale. An expedition was to be fitted out 'for the purpose of endeavouring to complete the discovery and survey of the Northern shores of this continent', a matter of great public interest, which had 'baffled the exertions of many enterprising men' . . . 'I trust', wrote the Governor, 'that the honour of its accomplishment is reserved for the Hudson's Bay Company, through your exertions'.[8] During the first season (1837), the westward journey down the Mackenzie River up to and beyond Franklin's Return Reef was to be undertaken with eight men. Meanwhile, four men would travel 'to the north-east end of Great Bear Lake, and there erect buildings, establish fisheries, and collect provisions for the accommodation and maintenance of the party during the winter of 1837-38'. The next stage of the expedition in 1838-39 would be eastwards from Great Bear Lake, down the Coppermine River to the Arctic Ocean and then along the coast to the mouth of Back's Great Fish River. It was hoped to ascertain whether Ross's 'Boothia Felix' were a peninsula or an island. The instructions also contained advice on the survey of the coast, provisions (pemmican and flour), ammunition, fishing tackle, babiche for snow-shoe lacing and material for building small canoes. Astronomical instruments by Jones of Charing Cross were to be provided for observations and surveys. Place-names should be bestowed on headlands, mountains and rivers. Collections of minerals and plants were to be made and formal possession should be taken of the country 'on behalf of Great Britain, in your own names, acting for the Honourable Hudson's Bay Company'.

Peter Dease departed for Fort Chipewyan on Lake Athabasca in July 1836, while Thomas Simpson spent the autumn at the settlement on Red River, improving his knowledge of astronomy. On 1 December, he began a long

Chief Trader Thomas
Simpson of the Hudson's
Bay Company, who with
Peter Warren Dease,
completed much of the
survey of the north coast of
America from Point Barrow
(Alaska) to Castor and
Pollux River (named after
their boats), 1837-39. There
appears to be no portrait of
P W Dease.

winter journey to Lake Athabasca through the soft snow of the valleys, across
frozen lakes and rivers and over 'the celebrated Portage la Loche' (Methye
Portage), from whose north side there was a fine, but wintry view of the
Clear Water River, previously 'drawn with so much truth and beauty by
Sir George Back'.

Simpson used the carriole for the carriage of his books and instruments and
proceeded on foot, usually ahead, closely followed by the leading dog, which
often pushed his black muzzle forward to be caressed. 'This fondness,' wrote
Simpson, 'usually procured me the close society of a whole posse of them during
the night, which, when not extremely cold, was anything but agreeable.' He
remarked that at the end of this journey to Fort Chipewyan of 1,277 miles,
because of the good treatment they received half the dogs had travelled the whole
way from Red River – 'the longest continuous journey ever performed by the
same dogs'. The others he exchanged *en route*. He himself had made this journey
on foot in sixty-two days.

The early part of the year was spent at Fort Chipewyan, where like Franklin,
Simpson noted the improvement in the treatment of the Indian women by their
men and of the relationship between Chipewyans and Eskimos. He was amused
that even the 'old Canadian *voyageurs*', who while lamenting 'the degeneracy of

their successors,' were themselves 'nothing loath' to add the luxury of tea and sugar to their provisions He also stated that 'A large proportion of the Company's servants, and, with very few exceptions, the officers, are united to native women. A kindly feeling of relationship thus exists between them and the Indians, which tends much to the safety of the small and thinly scattered posts'.

With the arrival of swans and other wild fowl from the south toward the end of April, the melting of the snow to disclose the crimson and purple of cranberry and juniper and the swelling of buds on the willow, it was evident that spring was near. The construction of the two sea going boats of the expedition was finished at Fort Chipewyan in May and because they were identical as well as admirable, they were named *Castor* and *Pollux* after the twins of Ancient legend. Simpson described them as follows:

> They were light, clinker-built craft, of twenty-four feet keel and six feet beam, furnished with wash boards and carrying each two lug-sails. They were expressly adapted for a shallow navigation, by their small draught of water; were payed with a mixture of clear pine-resin, which gave them a light and elegant appearance, and with the coloured earths of the country we manufactured paints for their further decoration . . . Each of the sea-boats was provided with a small, oiled, canvass canoe, and portable wooden frame, which proved highly serviceable in the sequel.

On 1 June 1837, the expedition left Fort Chipewyan, making its way northward into Great Slave Lake, and then entering the Mackenzie River at its head and proceeding rapidly downstream to Fort Norman, west of Great Bear Lake. Further downstream, at the junction of the Mackenzie and Bear Lake rivers, John Ritch, the boatbuilder, left with a small party in the luggage boat for the northeastern (Dease) arm of Great Bear Lake. Here he was to construct what was later called Fort Confidence, the expedition's winter quarters, designed on a small scale by Thomas Simpson. He was also to find and establish a fishery 'and to keep our Chipewyan hunters and the native Indians employed in collecting the meat of the reindeer and musk-ox against our return from the coast'.

Besides trading goods to be given to the Eskimos, the *Castor* and *Pollux* carried altogether thirty bags of pemmican of ninety pounds each and ten hundred-weights of Red River flour. Simpson explained in his *Narrative* that by mixing flour with pemmican into a palatable 'bergoo', or thick soup, a saving of one third was made, the daily allowance per man of three pounds of pemmican being reduced to two. The two steersmen, James McKay (Scottish highlander) and George Sinclair (half-breed), as well as one of the middlemen, Peter Taylor, (half-breed) had been with Back down the Great Fish River in 1834, while François Felix had been with Franklin in 1826. As they sped downstream between the Rocky Mountains and the 'Eastern Hills', 'now shadowed by floating clouds, now reflecting from their snowy peaks the dazzling sunshine, Simpson found the whole scene enchanting. At Fort Good Hope, Dease's son-in-law, Mr Bell, welcomed the party and, because of a recent quarrel between the Loucheux Indians and the Eskimos, no Loucheux were taken on as interpreters.

A more westerly and slightly deeper channel was found through the estuary of the Mackenzie River and during the afternoon of 9 July 'the Arctic Ocean burst into view'. Beyond Tent Island, nineteen Eskimo kayaks caught up with the boats. Presents were given to their owners, who had afterwards to be deterred from following by gunshots over their heads. After pulling along the steep mud banks of the coast, on 10 July the tents were erected at Shingle Point during a gale. Here Eskimo graves and winter huts were seen, together with an umiak frame 24 feet long and a 'large sledge with side-rails, well mortised, and strongly knit with whalebone, so that our Canadians pronounced it made 'comme à Montreal' – the very superlative commendation in their opinion', observed Simpson.

Despite the fog, the party 'twisted and poled' its way between transparent icebergs in many 'fantastic shapes'. Fish was bought from groups of poor, but lively and unintrusive Eskimos, who used a seine of whalebone to catch them. The second group had a tame full-grown seal, which came to the water's edge for food. The party met larger groups near Herschel and Barter islands, with whom they traded for waterproof boots of sealskin. As they pressed on, the 'lofty peaks of the Romanzoff Mountains seemed to look scornfully down upon the little party that now sat at their humble evening meal'. A continuation of the coastal mountains was sighted and named the 'Franklin Range in honour of the distinguished officer whose discoveries we were following up'. Fog, gales and ice made navigation difficult, but on 23 July the party reached Franklin's Return Reef. Simpson attributed their early arrival at this point 'under Providence . . . to our inflexible perseverance in *doubling* these great icy packs, any of which might have confined us a fortnight on the beach, had we chosen to wait for its dispersion . . .' Progress through the ice floes was often made at great risk to the boats and with all the crew, apart from the bowman or steersman out on the ice, using poles to push it aside or to fend off smaller lumps. The alternative, where a narrow channel existed wide enough to take the boats, was a perilous passage among 'the innumerable floating rocks'.

By the end of July further progress in the bitter weather and through the everlasting ice appeared hopeless and Simpson volunteered to complete the journey to Point Barrow on foot. Dease agreed to stay with the boats at 'Boat Extreme', and Simpson, with five men set off to continue westwards on 1 August, an extremely dark and dismal day. They carried enough pemmican and flour for twelve days, the canvas canoe, one kettle and two axes, plus a few trinkets for the Eskimos. Simpson carried the navigational instruments. Another group was encountered, this time of women, children and an old man who, 'sitting under a reversed canoe, was tranquilly engaged in weaving a fine whalebone net'. They expressed great surprise on meeting the first white men they had ever seen. Simpson exchanged the tin pan, which made up his 'whole table service, for a platter made out of mammoth tusk!' It was from these people that Simpson obtained an umiak plus four slender oars and two paddles. This large skin-boat would float in six inches of water. The Kabloonans arranged their 'strange vessel so well that the ladies were in raptures, declaring us to be genuine Esquimaux, and not poor white men'.

Yet again, the ability of the people to delineate the topography of the region came in useful and Simpson persuaded the most intelligent of the women to make a sketch of the inlet in front of them and of the coast beyond.

> She represented the inlet as very deep; that they would make many encampments in travelling round it; but that it receives no river. She also drew a bay of some size to the westward; and the old man added a long and very narrow projection, covered with tents which I could not doubt to mean Point Barrow.

Simpson named the inlet after Peter Warren Dease 'as a mark of true esteem for my worthy colleague'. Freezing fog (and a northeasterly wind) caused them to steer the five miles to the opposite shore by compass alone, the new craft surmounting the waves 'with wonderful buoyancy'.

In the very early morning of 4 August, from the bottom of Elson Bay (earlier named by Beechey), Simpson saw 'with indescribable emotions, *Point Barrow*, stretching out to the northward . . .' They reached it by forcing a way through tough young ice and then through half a mile of heavy ice which touched the shore. On arrival at the long narrow spit, 'seeing the ocean spreading far and wide to the southwest, we unfurled our flag, and with three enthusiastic cheers took possession of our discoveries in his Majesty's name.' There was an extensive cemetery close to their landing place, but contact was soon made with the live inhabitants of Point Barrow, care being taken to avoid a surprise attack, since there were about a hundred of them. However, despite the party's vigilance, the oars were stolen and buried in the sea and sand. They departed in the umiak on 5 August with the impression that some of these numerous natives bore an 'evil intent' regarding them. Before doing so Simpson walked across the point to take bearings for position. The day was fine and he could see a broad shore lead stretching away to the southwest. 'So inviting was the prospect in that direction', he wrote, 'that I would not have hesitated a moment to prosecute the voyage to Behring's Strait, and the Russian settlements, in my skin canoe. I could scarcely, in fact, suppress an indefinite feeling of regret that all was already done'.

However, it was time to head back along the dreary shores to Boat Extreme, where Dease had been taking tidal observations, as did Simpson at Point Barrow, showing that the tides came from the Pacific Ocean. A westerly gale sped the boats towards the Mackenzie, 'running all night under close-reefed sails'. They had some difficulty in crossing the powerful stream of the Colvile River, named after Andrew Colvile of the Hudson's Bay Company even four miles out to sea. The mouth of the river appeared to be at least two miles wide. A small island, which they named Esquimaux Island, was discovered twelve miles offshore, where the water proved to be still fresh. Simpson remarked that the Colvile must be 'the opening described to Augustus, Sir John Franklin's interpreter, by his countrymen in 1826 . . . another proof of the accurate information to be obtained from the Esquimaux'. He regretted that the lack of an interpreter meant they were unable to learn whether the great river provided a link between the north coast and Cook Inlet on the south coast of Russian America (Alaska). What now appears to be called the Colville River has its source in the De Long Mountains, the far western section of the Brooks Range. The Fawn River, near Return Reef, was so named on 8 August after a little fawn (one of the many reindeer or caribou, seen along the coast), which 'came to the tents and was suffered to retreat unmolested'. Soon afterwards they met again some Eskimos who 'had concluded their barter with the Western Eskimos and Mountain Indians'. As a result of this they had acquired 'iron kettles, knives, and other things . . . from the distant Kabloonan, or white men'. If some of these utensils had been manufactured in Russia (as opposed to Siberia), the indirect trade must have extended, mainly overland, across half the world. These people 'knew at once that we had been among the far west Esquimaux', wrote Simpson, 'from the boots we wore, which were of a wider and clumsier shape than their own'.

On 12 August, a fine, calm day, Simpson climbed a hill some miles inland, where his eyes delighted in the scene:

> On either hand arose the British and Buckland Mountains, exhibiting an infinite diversity of shape and form; in front lay the blue boundless ocean strongly contrasted with its broad glittering girdle of ice; beneath yawned ravines a thousand feet in depth, through which brawled and sparkled the clear alpine streams; while the sun, still high in the west, shed his softened beams through a rich veil of saffron-coloured clouds that over-canopied the gorgeous scene. Bands of reindeer, browsing on the rich pasture in the valleys and along the brooks, imparted life and animation to the picture. Reluctantly I returned to the camp at sunset.

The natives of Herschel Island welcomed them back from afar, and after asking about their countrymen to the west, were both delighted and amazed to hear some of their names read out from a notebook. Further on, a large party proved troublesome, though bloodshed was avoided. This caused Simpson to remark, 'Notwithstanding the deceitful good-humour of the Esquimaux, I have no hesitation in asserting that, were they in possession of fire-arms, it would require a stronger force than ours to navigate their coasts'. On 17 August the boats entered the western mouth of the Mackenzie River, where camp was made, having returned from Point Barrow in thirteen days.

The boats were towed up the Mackenzie without incident, the men working alternate hours between 4am and 8 or 9pm. Parties of Loucheux Indians were met, 'whose unobtrusive manners were pleasingly contrasted with the importunate and annoying behaviour of the Esquimaux'. The women, children and baggage were returning from Fort Good Hope on rafts in the form of an A, made of two large logs, joined with a cross bar. The men escorted these rafts in their canoes. Here the party was enlarged by Dease's wife, niece and grand-daughter. After some highly dangerous tracking up Bear Lake River and an icy and hazardous traverse of Great Bear Lake, the expedition reached winter quarters near the mouth of the Dease River on 25 September, being welcomed by Ritch, other comrades and the Hare Indians. 'With feelings of sincere gratitude to the Almighty Protector, we bestowed on our infant establishment the name of Fort Confidence'.

In a letter to his brother at Moose Factory, written towards the end of the west-ward journey in September 1837, Thomas Simpson exulted in its successful result:

> Fortune and its great Disposer have this season smiled upon my undertakings, and shed the first bright beams upon the dark prospect of a North American life. Yes, my dearest brother, congratulate me, for I, and I *alone*, have the well-earned honour of uniting the Arctic to the great Western Ocean, and of unfurling the British flag on Point Barrow.[9]

Dease and Simpson's Eastward Journeys 1838 and 1839

Winter still had to be passed in the far north of the American continent, on the edge of the barren lands to the east, where the prevalent easterly winds blew in icy blasts across the treeless hills. In another letter to his brother from Fort Confidence, dated 29 January 1838, Simpson described how both men and dogs would return frost-bitten from hunting excursions, 'while bringing meat across the elevated and stormy region, where there is not a shrub for shelter'. They lived on caribou and musk ox meat and fish. He had, of course, to write up the results of the 1837 journey, but when tired of 'writing, chart-drawing and astron-omy', he took advantage of 'an excellent little library; which, beside scientific books, and a regiment of northern travels, contains Plutarch, Hume, Robertson, Gibbon, Shakspeare [sic], Smollett and dear Sir Walter [Scott]'. The Scottish highlanders and Orkneymen used the library a lot, but not the Canadians, who were 'deplorably ignorant'.

Simpson went on to say that Mr Dease and he lived together 'on the happiest footing; his old wife, a little grandchild, and a strapping wench, a daughter of his brother Charles' joining their mess. 'Dease is a worthy, indolent, illiterate soul, and moves just as I give the impulse', an uncharitable remark, perhaps a sign of his growing egotism. One did not become a Chief Factor by being indolent and illiterate. Dease, in fact, made an essential contribution to the success of their journeys through his logistical abilities, his tight discipline of the men and his skill at driving the party onwards. Thomas Simpson asked his brother not to worry about the dangers of the next stage of the expedition, which were 'nothing appalling to people who have traversed the interior of this wild country'. Their plans, thanks to his foresight, were 'admirably laid' and must ensure success. 'I am no wild theorist like Dr King'; he wrote, 'all my calculations are based on calculation and knowledge. On that foundation, and a humble reliance on a stronger Arm than man's, do I build my hopes'.[10]

At the end of March, during which month a temperature of minus 60 °F was recorded, Simpson and two men reconnoitred a route between Great Bear Lake and the Coppermine River. On return, he led a party of men and dogs, loaded with provisions and baggage for the summer, to make a depot 15 miles from the Coppermine and 95 from Fort Confidence. Two reliable men were left in charge and a third journey was made to bring up the remaining provisions. During the early spring, news came in letters from home of the death of William IV after whom King William's Land (now Island) had been named and of the accession of the young Queen Victoria in the summer of 1837. As well as taking part in hunting excursions during the winter, Simpson surveyed an arm of Great Bear Lake, previously unknown. Although he had travelled for some 2,000 miles in other regions, 'wearing only an ordinary cloth capot' (hooded overcoat), it was not long before he found that

> the wanderer within the unsheltered precincts of the Polar Circle must be far otherwise provided. Accordingly, on our distant excursions, we usually assumed capots of dressed moose-skin, impervious to the wind, or of reindeer hide with the hairy side outwards, and were provided with robes of the latter light and warm material for a covering at night, when, to increase the supply of animal heat, our dogs couched close around us.

Nevertheless, despite this protection,

> in a stormy, barren, mountainous country, where, in many parts, a whole day's journey intervenes between one miserable clump of pines and the next, we were often exposed to suffering, and even danger, from the cold; and several of our dogs were at various times frozen to death.

The expedition left Fort Confidence for the Kendall and Coppermine Rivers and the Arctic Ocean on 6 June 1838. They found the Coppermine still in full flood, but determined to brave the loose ice on 25 June, come what may. From

Fort Confidence, Great Bear Lake. This sketch of the fort rebuilt in 1848 was drawn by Dr John Rae. (Hudson's Bay Company Archives, Provincial Archives of Manitoba)

Franklin's description, they could anticipate some of the hazards of the lower Coppermine, although his descent had been a month later, when the water level had fallen. Nor were they disappointed. Simpson described the thrill and danger of their passage downstream:

> The day was bright and lovely as we shot down rapid after rapid . . . Shortly before noon we came in sight of Escape Rapid of Franklin, and a glance at the over-hanging cliffs told us that there was no alternative but to run down with full cargo. In an instant we were in the vortex; and, before we were aware, my boat was borne towards an isolated rock, which the boiling surge almost concealed. To clear it on the outside was no longer possible; our only chance of safety was to run between it and the lofty eastern cliff. The word was passed, and every breath was hushed.. The pass was about eight feet wide, and the error of a single foot on either side would have been instant destruction. As, guided by Sinclair's consummate skill, the boat shot safely through those jaws of death, an involuntary cheer arose.

They looked back to see how the other boat had fared and saw it had almost disappeared between the waves. Dease related afterwards that the spray enveloping them had 'formed a gorgeous rainbow round the boat'. Near Bloody Fall, ice blocked the way, but from the hills could be seen 'a wide expanse of sea covered with a dazzling sheet of ice, dotted with dark rocky islands; while far north rose the lofty headlands of Cape Kendall and Cape Hearne'. A large river flowing near the Coppermine was called Richardson River 'after that resolute and scientific traveller'. After five days' detention, an arduous portage of the boats brought them near to the sea and, two weeks later, on 17 July, Dease and Simpson began their second voyage on the 'Hyperborean Sea', this being the first time the Indians had ever sailed on the sea. They were intrigued by the young seals, which they called 'sea beavers'.

Progress was made only with great difficulty and perseverance, the ice lying 'fixed and immovable in the almost innumerable little rocky bays, creeks and coves which indent this part of the coast'. The young ice cut the boats even more than the old, and Simpson considered that copper sheathing would have been desirable. Sometimes the floes had to be pushed away from the rocks to make a passage, before closing like a pair of nut-crackers. On 6 August, Simpson climbed to the top of a high cliff, from which he viewed a prospect of Coronation Gulf 'little calculated to cheer our spirits or to buoy up our hopes':

> The ice-covered gulph, with its innumerable dark, rugged islands, the clouds gloomily gathering over the crescent-shaped mainland, and long files of waterfowl passing aloft to the southward . . . while around flew several large hawks at the danger that threatened their young brood from the intrusion of man . . .

He remarked that in 1821, at the same date, Franklin had found open water. Here is an example of one of the hazards of polar exploration: the state of the ice and its influence on a vessel's progress or an explorer's achievement. Parry, for instance, was fortunate in finding Lancaster Sound pretty free of ice, and he was bold enough to press on and take advantage of this. Day after day passed for Simpson and Dease's party 'in a constant and ineffectual struggle with the same cold obdurate foe'. By 20 August, the usual date for the return of earlier expeditions, they had not yet reached Franklin's Point Turnagain. It was decided that Dease and the boats, 'torn and jagged by the ice', should remain in a little cove which they christened Boathaven. Simpson with five of the Company's servants and two Indians set out on foot to achieve 'at least a *portion* of the discoveries which we had fondly hoped to complete'. The whole expedition was to *rendezvous* at Boathaven on 31 August. While each of the men was loaded with about half a hundredweight, Simpson himself, apart from his gun, carried only a telescope, compass and dagger, so that he could easily climb to high ground, take bearings and see the coast.

During the middle of the day (20 August) they passed Franklin's Point Turnagain, camping later at a flat cape which Simpson named Cape Franklin. As they walked on, some of the men's legs became swollen, because of their heavy burdens, the uneven ground and 'the constant immersion in icy-cold water' while fording the streams. The sea ice remained immovable. Across the water, some 20 odd miles opposite the shore along which they were struggling, could be seen a high, snow-covered coast that Simpson called 'the great northern land'. He hoped they were not about to find that it formed a wide bay, into which they were heading. Fearing a bitter disappointment, he climbed a high cape, but instead

> a vast and splendid prospect burst suddenly upon me. The sea, as if transformed by enchantment, rolled its free waves at my feet, and beyond the reach of vision to the eastward, Islands of various shape and size overspread its surface; and the northern land terminated to the eye in a bold and lofty cape, bearing east-northeast, thirty or forty miles distant, while the continental coast trended away south-east.

The cape on which he stood, Simpson called Cape Alexander, after his brother, and the land to the northward Victoria Land; its eastern termination was named Cape Pelly, after the Governor of the Company. At the other end of the world, Captain James Clark Ross was shortly to discover and name 'South Victoria Land', also in honour of the young Queen, part of the Antarctic Continent – 'the whitest if not the brightest jewel in the crown'. Simpson's little party continued further east along the coast of the mainland, until on 25 September, beyond the Beaufort River, named after the Hydrographer of the Navy, they came to a wide bay, full of islands. Here a 'pillar of stones' was built, their union–jack was hoisted and Simpson 'took formal possession of the country in her Majesty's name'. In the cairn he deposited a short account of their proceedings, during which they had surveyed over 100 miles of coast.

Aware of the importance of saving the boats for a second attempt the following summer, Simpson had made careful note of the course of the Coppermine on their descent. Having picked up Dease's party, he found himself at Bloody Fall the only one of the opinion that the boats could be brought up the river against the current. However, Simpson got his way and the difficult operation was achieved, the river being relatively shallow then. 'Nothing but the skill and dexterity of guides long practised, like ours, in all the intricacies of river navigation could have overcome so many obstacles: it is not therefore, surprising that Dr Richardson's less experienced crews should have found it necessary to relinquish the attempt, even with the "walnut shell" '. The boats were deposited under a cache of heavy stones, where they could be repaired in the spring. On 14 October, after feasting on cranberries, they arrived at Fort Confidence to find all well.

*   *   *

During a miserable winter, when food and game was scarce, the lives of a number of starving Indians were saved. 'Far be it from us, however,' remarked Simspon, 'to arrogate any merit for our exertions in preserving the lives of our fellow-creatures. It is a duty conscientiously fulfilled by every officer in the service when the occasion arrives . . .' News was received of the death of Akaitcho, the old chief of the Copper Indians and the saviour of Franklin's party of 1819-21. During the winter, a dipping needle by Jones (an instrument to measure the direction of the earth's magnetism) arrived from London, as well as periodicals, which 'beguiled the almost insupportable tedium of a second polar winter' beside stormy Great Bear Lake. Some diversion was also provided by three young wolf cubs which Simpson had rescued, but they were repulsed by the dogs and attempts to train them to pull a sledge were unsuccessful. They took refuge at night on top of the woodpile, whence 'their long melancholy howl arose . . . above the clamorous serenade with which the canine species delight to entertain the residents at the trading posts'. Ouligbuck, who had been one of Franklin's interpreters, arrived in the spring of 1839. A spell of unusually fine weather in early June made the snow disappear as if by magic. The Indians and the Company men played games out of doors, while Mr Dease's violin was more often heard of an evening than during the long dreary winter.

Simpson appears to have had some difficulty with Dease in keeping the expedition together during the early winter. However, the receipt after Christmas of commendation for his journey to Point Barrow from the Admiralty and the Colonial Secretary, and the news that the newly formed Royal Geographical Society had awarded him its gold medal, did much to further a third exploring venture and in a joint dispatch from Fort Confidence to the Governor, Chief Factors and Chief Traders of the Northern Department of the Hudson's Bay Company, dated 1 May 1839, Dease and Simpson concluded that 'Our boats are repaired; our provisions are on the banks of the Coppermine; and as soon as that impetuous river bursts its icy fetters in June, the rest of the party will be there, with hopes no wise damped by the hardships and languor of a second Polar winter'.[11]

This third journey in 1839 along the north coast of America was entirely successful, owing to a milder winter and warmer summer. McKay and Sinclair were again the steersmen. An early descent of the Coppermine gave the party time to explore the Richardson River near its mouth and to make contact with some

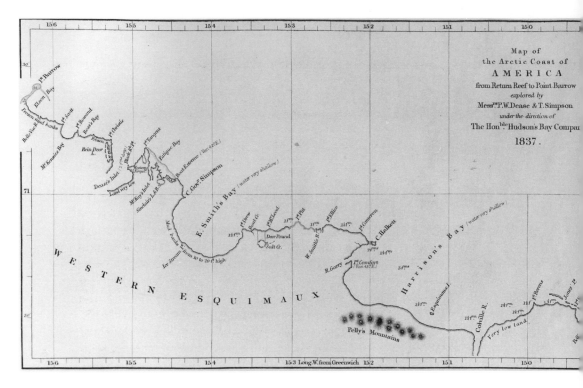

Map showing Dease and Simpson's journey beyond Franklin's furthest west in 1826 (Return Reef) to Point Barrow (Alaska). (Published in the *Journal of the Royal Geographical Society*, 1838. (Hudson's Bay Company Archives, Provincial Archives of Manitoba)

Eskimos there, through Ouligbuck, whose 'sonorous voice' they heard across the water. Of them, Simpson remarked: 'If these poor people were not far more industrious, provident and ingenious than the Indian tribes of the interior, they could not exist in their bleak, barren, country', and he contrasted the 'slender, agile figure' of the Indians with the 'square, rugged forms of these natives of the sea'. Friendship was cultivated between the Indians of the expedition and the young Eskimos while one of the older measured Dease for a pair of boots, which he undertook to have ready on his return. These people hunted seals from the offshore islands in winter and reindeer inland during the summer.

Reaching Cape Barrow on 18 July, it was with 'astonishment and delight' that from its 'rugged heights', they saw that Coronation Gulf was partly free of ice, 'whereas long after this period the year before the whole party might have crossed it on foot'. Proceeding beyond Simpson's furthest point of 1838, in clear weather, the party was able to unravel the intricacies of the coast and numerous islands of the 'stupendous bay' which Simpson had just sighted in 1838. The largest island was named after Lord Melbourne, the British Prime Minister, and one of the bays Labyrinth Bay. As for a North West Passage, Simpson remarked that no ship would steer for shores so full of hidden dangers and that Cape Alexander would be the first approachable point. The whole of the indentation of the coast further east was to be named Queen Maud Gulf sixty years later by

Roald Amundsen. Proceeding along the eastern coast of the gulf, along the west coast of the Adelaide Peninsula, they passed another island, about the size of Melbourne Island, which they named O'Reilly Island. This island was later to feature in the story of Sir John Franklin's last expedition.

They expected to have to round James Ross's Cape Felix, the most northerly point of what Ross called King William Land (now Island), but were surprised and delighted to find a more southerly strait leading to the 'much desired eastern sea' and to the mouth of Back's Great Fish River. On 11 August, they passed through Simpson Strait, as it was afterwards called. The 'glorious sight' of the eastern sea was first viewed by Simpson from the summit of one of the islands, which 'joyful news made even the most desponding of our people' forget for the moment how far away they were from winter quarters. At length, in cold dense fog, they reached Point Ogle, on the northwest corner of the Adelaide Peninsula, which had been named by Back, after descending the Back or Great Fish River in 1834. The steersmen, McKay and Sinclair, had been there at the time, but did not immediately recognise the place, because of the thick fog. However, on 16 August, when, with flags flying, the little boats were beached on Montreal Island in Chantrey Inlet, McKay located a cache left on their earlier visit. Besides gun-powder, fish hooks, chocolate and other items, there were two bags of pemmican. Known by the voyageurs as 'taureau' (ox), the pemmican was 'literally *alive*, and it was wittily remarked, "L'isle de Montreal sera bientôt peuplée de jeunes *taureaux*" '. As he had found on previous occasions, Simpson's observations for position agreed with Franklin's and not with Back's, with which he found a difference of 25 miles.

In reaching the estuary of Back's Great Fish River, the objects of the ex-pedition, sent out in 1836, had been attained. By their exertions, Simpson, Dease, and their comrades had surveyed the north coast of America from its fur-thest west at Point Barrow to link with Back's discoveries of 1834. However, the question still remained as to whether Ross's 'Boothia Felix' were united with or divided from the mainland. This could perhaps be determined by crossing Chantrey Inlet and proceeding further east. When this was put to the men and its importance explained, they all agreed to go on. When the fog cleared, the 'pic-turesque shores of the estuary' were disclosed. To the south, Victoria Headland could be recognised from Back's 'exquisite drawing'. After supper, the little boats bore away for the opposite side of Chantrey Inlet, which was reached on 17 August after six hours' hard rowing. 'It was a lovely night', wrote Simpson, 'The fury of the north lay chained in repose. The Harp, the Eagle, the Charioteer, and many other bright constellations gemmed the sky and sparkled on the waters, while the high Polar star seemed to crown the glorious vault above us'.

Soon after sunrise Simpson climbed some 200 feet to the summit of a remark-able headland, which was named Cape Britannia, and here a great conical cairn was built 14 feet high, fit to withstand the fury of countless storms, unless dis-mantled by the Inuit. An account of the expedition's discoveries, in a sealed bottle, was placed in the cairn, while loud cheers and the firing of guns marked

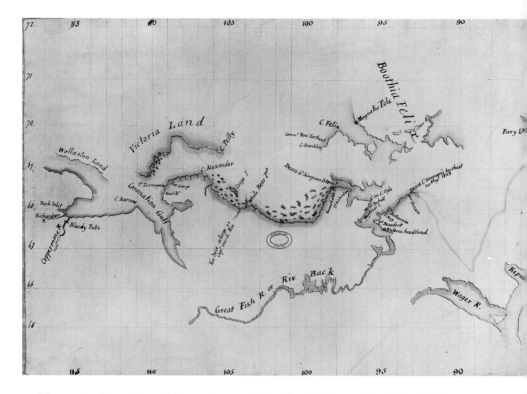

Manuscript chart of part of the north coast of Canada and adjacent islands from Wollaston Peninsula, Victoria Island to Repulse Bay, mainly showing Dease and Simpson's explorations in 1838 and 1839. (Hudson Bay Company Archives, Provincial Archives of Manitoba)

their taking possession of these in the name of Victoria Regina. However, Sinclair's illness, due to the lack of hot food and the warmth of a fire, damped their spirits. There was virtually no driftwood along this coast but with medicine this man 'active, careful and ambitious in the discharge of his duty' was brought round. Finer weather then enabled fires to be lit from moss and dried seaweed, so that food could be cooked and no-one else was laid low.

From Cape Britannia, Simpson had seen the eastward trend of the coast, while to the northwest 'stretched a sea free from ice, and devoid of all land, except what looked like two very distant islands'. Perhaps he was looking up the present James Ross Strait (between King William Island and the Boothia Peninsula) across which on Simpson's map, marked with a dotted line, is shown land to the south of Sir John Ross's supposed 'Poctes Bay'. By 20 August, it was clear that eastward exploration must cease and that the party should begin the long journey to Fort Confidence and Great Bear Lake. The stream which marked the boats' furthest point was named Castor and Pollux River after them, while 'some high blue land' to the northeast was called Cape Sir John Ross. Simpson expressed the opinion that they had almost certainly reached 'that large gulph, uniformly described by the Eskimos as containing many islands, and, with numerous indentations, running down to the southward, till it approaches within forty miles of Repulse and Wager bays'. He was mistaken in this view, since the great bulk of the Boothia Peninsula blocks the bay known to the Eskimos at the southern end of the Gulf of Boothia. He hoped that 'the Honourable Company . . . would not abandon their munificent work till the precise limits of this great continent were fully and finally established'. Simpson's untimely death meant that not he, but another officer of the Company would complete the task.

Before turning for home, the men erected another cairn in commemoration of their visit. Here, as all along this coast were found 'old stone circles, traps and caches', left by the Eskimos, 'but no *recent* traces of inhabitants'. With a following wind filling the sails, the old boats made good progress, though in a heavy sea, Ooligbuck and Hope (an Indian) suffered greatly. Simpson remarked that the crews 'though good men and true in their way' were by no means all good sailors. He observed that besides the steersmen, there were only 'two Europeans in each boat entitled to the name'. The other six – 'a Canadian, an Iroquois, a Cree, two Hare Indians, and an Eskimo, knew about as much of handling a sail, as they did of geography or geology'.

On 24 August, the party crossed what was later called Simpson Strait from which they named the Adelaide Peninsula (after Queen Adelaide, the widow of William IV). They traced for 60 miles what Simpson called 'the southern shore of Boothia' – in fact the southern shore of King William Island and the northern coast of Simpson Strait – until it turned up to the north. James Ross's pillar (cairn) was only 57 miles away and the magnetic pole ninety miles to the north-northeast. The coast was 'low and uninteresting, but abounding in reindeer, musk-cattle and old native encampments'. Out to sea, ice could be seen, while 'vast numbers of snow-geese passed high overhead in long triangular flights, bound for milder skies'. At the southwest corner of what was later called King William Island, the men built another tall cairn while Simpson took observations. The point was named Cape Herschel, after the eminent astronomer. Less than ten years were to elapse before this cape and the coasts of the strait were to be the scene of the last agonies of the men of Sir John Franklin's expedition of 1845-48.

Crossing Simpson Strait again, the party retraced their outward track, but more to seaward. By early September, frozen water and snow falls warned them of winter's approach. Despite this, they crossed over from Melbourne Island to the southern shore of Victoria Land (now Island), 20 miles away. During a cold night, the phosphorescent waves appeared quite brilliant. 'The boats seemed to cleave a flood of molten silver', wrote Simpson, 'and the spray dashed from their bows before the fresh breeze, fell back with glittering showers into the deep'.

Dease and Simpson reached the bold southern coast of Victoria Land, finding deep water offshore. On 7 and 8 September, they crossed 'two magnificent bays', which were named after the Duke of Cambridge and the illustrious Duke of

Wellington. The channel between these two bays and the Kent Peninsula was later named Dease Strait. HMS *Enterprise* (Captain Richard Collinson) was later to winter at Cambridge Bay during the Franklin search. After landing for breakfast at Wellington Bay, Simpson walked along the shore and found there some interesting caches left by the Eskimos, for whom three or four awls and a few iron hoops were left, happily to surprise them on their return. The furthest southeastern cape of this great island was named Point Back and their furthest west Point Parry. Another headland was named Cape Louis-Philippe after the King of France. The boats had coasted Victoria Land (Island) for over 150 miles; 'It probably exceeds Boothia in size', observed Simpson, 'and is separated from it by a wide arm of the sea, down which came the heavy press of ice that detained us in the beginning of August'.

This is Victoria Strait, between Victoria Island and King William Island on the modern chart into which are squeezed ice floes from M'Clintock Channel and Franklin Strait. It was to this heavy ice that the *Erebus* and *Terror* were to be abandoned in 1848. Simpson surmised that a similar strait must divide Victoria Land from 'Wollaston Land' to the west, discovered by Dr John Richardson. This is not so and the Wollaston Peninsula is now shown on the map as part of Victoria Island. Numerous deer, hares, foxes and ducks were seen on Victoria Land, while great white owls 'sat perched on every knoll'. On the morning of 10 September, the expedition left 'this noble coast' for Cape Barrow, on the mainland, 50 miles away to the south-southwest.

The little boats 'old and worn-out as they were crossed this truly magnificent strait' in a great style. On making their landfall at Wentzel River at the end of the day, a great deal of driftwood was found strewn on the beach. 'Our poor fellows absolutely capered and whooped for joy,' wrote Simpson, 'and enjoyed once more the luxury of a rousing fire, to which we had been strangers since crossing Bathurst Inlet in July.' Making their way in wintry weather along Coronation Gulf, 'unremittingly night and day, fair and foul, whenever the winds permitted', the boats entered the mouth of the Coppermine River on 16 September 1839 'after by far the longest voyage ever performed in boats on the Polar Sea', totalling no less than 1,408 geographical, or 1,631 statute miles.

On their way upstream towards Bloody Fall, the first thing that met their eyes was a pair of boots hung on a long pole. These were the boats which had been commissioned by Dease in June from one of the Eskimos and, as Simpson remarked, this showed an 'extraordinary trait of good faith'. One of the boats was left at the Fall for the Eskimos, with all her gear, as well as surplus pemmican. After an icy winter journey up the Coppermine River, when Ouligbuck and the two Hare Indians proved to be poor 'crag climbers', the second boat and everything, except a lump of pemmican per man, books, instruments and necessities, were shared between Larocque and Maccaconce, the two faithful Hare Indians. After floundering across the Barren Grounds and embarking in a boat left by Ritch for them at Dease River, the expedition arrived at Fort Confidence on 24 September, to a welcome from him and the other 'solitary inmates'. Two days

Fort Simpson on the Mackenzie River, 1852, established earlier, but since 1823 known as Fort Simpson, after Governor George Simpson of the Hudson's Bay Company. (Pen and ink drawing by Alexander Hunter Murray, from Hudson's Bay Company Archives, Provincial Archives of Manitoba)

later, Fort Confidence was abandoned to the Indians and the members of the expedition made their various ways home.

*   *   *

His cousin, the Governor, was knighted, but Thomas Simpson had not long to savour the expedition's remarkable success. Writing from Fort Simpson, on the Mackenzie River in October 1839, he had proposed to the Directors of the Hudson's Bay Company in London that he should lead a small expedition to complete the surveys beyond Castor and Pollux River as far as Fury and Hecla Strait. Winter quarters would be at Fort Reliance and the way to the Arctic coast would be down the Great Fish (Back) River. Mackay and Sinclair, 'the only steersmen in the country who are acquainted with the long and dangerous navigation of the Great Fish River' were prepared to go.[12] However, the letter accepting his proposals, written in London on 3 June 1840, never reached Simpson and he set out from Red River for England via the United States at about that date. He died at the age of thirty-two in a brawl on the American prairies, beyond the Company's jurisdiction. The circumstances were unclear and the matter has never been resolved. He was buried in the churchyard of the Red River colony. Largely through his brother Alexander's good offices, Thomas Simpson's *Narrative of the discoveries on the north coast of America* . . . was published in London in 1843, having been revised for the press by Colonel Edward Sabine. Unlike the narratives of Franklin, Parry, Sir John Ross and others, the only illustrations in his book are two maps at the end. Two years later, Alexander Simpson published *The life and travels of Thomas Simpson, the Arctic discoverer* (London, 1845). This gives the Simpsons' family background, publishes personal letters and official dispatches from the expeditions, analyses the evidence about Thomas's death and caustically attacks the injustice of the Hudson's Bay Company in 'withholding from his heirs the rewards which he had won by his past services'.[13]

As this last book was going to press, in March 1845, Alexander Simpson added a thoughtful 'Postscript on Arctic discovery', of several pages. This was occasioned by the news that the British Government was 'to send out another maritime expedition . . . for the discovery of a North Polar passage between the Atlantic and Pacific Oceans'. This, of course, was Sir John Franklin's expedition of 1845-48. Alexander Simpson discusses his late brother's claim already to have discovered such a passage, having connected the surveys of Beechey, Franklin and Back along the 'Arctic American Sea-board' through 'sixty-two degrees of longitude'. However, as he observed, 'The only possible point on which a doubt can be hung . . . is, whether he reached the same sea which Sir John Ross sailed down in the Victory . . . and which Parry saw before him from the western extremity of the Straits of "the Fury and Hecla" '. As we have noted before, it was all a question of whether Ross's 'Boothia Felix' were connected with the mainland by an isthmus, or whether, as the Simpsons thought, there existed the 'Straits of Boothia', connecting Prince Regent Inlet with Thomas Simpson's furthest east, the Castor and Pollux River.

Alexander Simpson also commented on the possible route of another seaborne expedition and on likely winter harbours on the south coast of Victoria Land or on the mainland. He thought that, in the spring and early summer, the officers might make 'pedestrian journeys to the northward' and also examine two known copper deposits. In a footnote, he remarked:

> It would much facilitate and increase the prospect of success of such journeys, if a few men accustomed the travelling with dogs and snow-shoes were shipped, instead of the crews being composed solely of genuine *Jack Tars*, good men and true, in their own element, but, of course, perfect novices in this mode of travelling. In the Orkney Islands there could be found many men who have wintered in the fur countries bordering on 'the barren grounds', hence well qualified to travel the *warmer* bays of the Arctic Ocean.

He concluded by stressing that his brother's success had provided 'convincing evidence' of September's being in fact *'the month most propitious to Arctic navigation'*.

Thomas Simpson died in his youth, at the peak of his passion and abilities for polar exploration and, as L H Neatby, the Arctic historian points out, his death was a double tragedy. Had Simpson's explorations continued in the same area, he might have been able to avert the Franklin tragedy thus saving those who were to perish on King William Island.[14]

CHAPTER 10

Sir John Franklin's Last Expedition 1845-48

On his return from the overland expedition of 1825-27 to trace the north coast of America westwards from the Mackenzie towards Point Barrow and eastwards to the mouth of the Coppermine, Franklin had written a long and elegantly produced narrative, published by John Murray in 1828. Soon after his return from the second overland expedition, he put forward a proposal to the Lord High Admiral to complete the survey of the north coast of America, which was promptly and decisively rejected by the Admiralty. He, equally promptly and decisively, went off on an interesting visit to St Petersburg, where he met the Tsar and Tsarina with whom he conversed about his travels along the north coast of the furthest of their dominions – Russian America. In 1828 he became engaged to Miss Jane Griffin, a London solicitor's daughter and woman of great vivacity, loyalty, intellect, spirit and charm. She loved travel and had a great bump of curiosity about the world, keeping numerous diaries which now line the shelves of the manuscripts' repository at the Scott Polar Research Institute, Cambridge.

Her *joie de vivre* and desire to share the experience of travel with Franklin is shown in a letter written during her own visit to the Baltic and Russia in 1828, before they were married:

> I should rejoice to see with you the same things for the first time, to help or be helped by you in every little difficulty, to become acquainted together with the same people, to be the objects of the same hospitality and kindness, and to witness with pride and sympathy that your claims to interest and esteem are acknowledged in a foreign land as well as your own.[1]

Their wedding took place near London on 5 November 1828, and the honeymoon was spent partly in Paris, where Franklin was invited to dine with the *savants* of France while Jane Franklin attended *soirées* given by the ladies of Paris and they both much enjoyed the theatres and opera. In August 1830, he was appointed by the Admiralty to command HMS *Rainbow* in the Mediterranean, where he spent the years 1830 to 1833 concerned especially with the affairs of Greece. Franklin had been knighted in 1829 and on his return from Greece he was made a Knight Commander of the Guelphic Order of Hanover. The medal which he received then would play its part in the saga of the Franklin Search.

After a number of years on half pay, in March 1836 Franklin accepted the Lieutenant-Governorship of Van Diemen's Land (now Tasmania). Since the sailing of the First Fleet of vessels taking out convicts from England to New South Wales in 1788, other convict settlements had been founded, including that of Van Diemen's Land, named by Tasman, the seventeenth-century Dutch navigator. These colonies were increased, as the years went by, with free settlers and the convicts themselves who often formed the staff of private households, could earn their freedom with good conduct, although some, who had committed heinous crimes, were kept in penal servitude.

Sir John Franklin found these years from 1836 to 1843 very trying ones and he was eventually, although unjustly, recalled by the Colonial Secretary in London. The happiest occasions for him were no doubt the reception of scientific exploring expeditions, such as Dumont d'Urville's in the *Astrolabe* and *La Zélée* and particularly that commanded by his old friend and brother-officer Captain James Clark Ross in *Erebus* with *Terror* (Captain F R M Crozier). Ross hoped to plant the union flag on the South Magnetic Pole in the Antarctic but because a great range of mountains lay between the ships and the magnetic pole, and because he could find no secure winter quarters, Ross was disappointed. However, its approximate location was ascertained from numerous observations made in the southern hemisphere. The geographical results of his circumnavigation of the Antarctic were quite outstanding, and included the discovery, already noted, of South Victoria Land.

This scientific expedition of 1839-43 needed a magnetic headquarters. In January 1840, Lieutenant-Governor Sir John Franklin received official notice from London that this was to be in Hobart and he set about getting the framework of the observatory constructed, ready for Ross's arrival in August 1840. Ross received a warm welcome from the Franklins and after he had chosen the site, two hundred convicts were set to work to construct Rossbank – the observatory named after Sir James Clark Ross, at Lady Franklin's suggestion.[2] A ball was given aboard the *Erebus* and the *Terror*, which lived for a long time in the memories of the belles of Hobart, their escorts and families. The Royal Society of Tasmania, and its journal, owe their foundation to the Franklins, Sir John being a Fellow of the Royal Society of London. Efforts to establish a college of further education in the end fell through, but the Reverend J P Gell, who came out to Van Diemen's Land for this purpose, became Franklin's son-in-law, by marrying his daughter, Eleanor. The faithful seaman, John Hepburn, accompanied the Franklins to Van Diemen's Land and became Superintendent of Point Puer, the convict establishment for boys.

Franklin's departure from Tasmania was witnessed by dense crowds lining the route and cheering him as he walked, in full naval uniform wearing his orders and medals, towards the barge that was to take him aboard a waiting vessel. The people of Tasmania were later to subscribe £1700 to the Franklin Search and the Tasmania Islands in the Arctic were named in their honour. His statue (erected at public expense) stands in Franklin Square, in the centre of Hobart. Sir John Franklin is not forgotten in Hobart even now.[3]

*　　*　　*

Franklin got no satisfaction from Lord Stanley, the Colonial Secretary, on his return to London and when another seaborne expedition to find the North West Passage was proposed, by Sir John Barrow in 1844, Franklin was eager to command it and return to his own profession, far from the ferment of colonial affairs. Sir John Barrow was still the Second or Executive Secretary of the Admiralty and it was he who had been largely responsible, as we have seen, for promoting the series of naval expeditions in search of the North West Passage and of overland ones to define the north coast of America. The books which he wrote on the Arctic voyages, one published in 1818 and the other in 1846 provide seamarks, as it were, of the progress made in delineating the Arctic archipelago, its channels, and the coast of the mainland.[4] The map in the 1818 volume shows only the points reached by Cook, Hearne and Mackenzie, whereas in that of 1846, nearly the whole north coast of America is drawn, as well as the north and south coasts of a number of the large Arctic islands.

It can be seen from the map published in the *Geographical Journal* on the centenary of Franklin's departure in 1845, in the words of Dr R J Cyriax, the historian of Franklin's last expedition, that north of the North American mainland an 'unexplored quadrilateral' existed, 'the northwest corner being formed by Banks Land, the northeast by Cape Walker, the southwest by Wollaston Land, and the southeast by King William Land ... an area of about 70,000 square miles. If ships, sailing southwards and westwards from Barrow Strait or Melville Sound, could pass through this unexplored quadrilateral to the American mainland the problem of the North West Passage would be solved. Since Parry had found that the ice increased both in extent and in closeness from Barrow Strait to Melville Island, an attempt to sail southwards and westwards from near Cape Walker seemed more likely to succeed than one made farther to the west'.[5] Cape Walker is situated on a small island off the north coast of Prince of Wales Island, west of Somerset Island. This approach was suggested by Sir John Barrow in 1836, during his Presidency of the Royal Geographical Society (which he founded) and again in 1844, when it was accepted by Lord Haddington, First Lord of the Admiralty.

On the return of the *Erebus* and *Terror* from the Southern Ocean, Captain F W Beechey (of the *Trent* and the *Blossom*) suggested that a fresh attempt in those ships, to be fitted with engines, should be made to reach the North Pole. Whereas there was agreement among those concerned that Arctic exploration should be resumed, Sir John Barrow, supported by Sir Edward Parry, Captain Francis Beaufort (Hydrographer of the Navy) and Colonel Edward Sabine (the authority on terrestrial magnetism) believed that the North West Passage should be attained first.

Barrow's 'Proposal for an attempt to complete the discovery of a North West Passage' was submitted to Lord Haddington, First Lord of the Admiralty, in December 1844, only a month before Barrow's resignation at the age of eighty. It is a persuasive document and it begins:

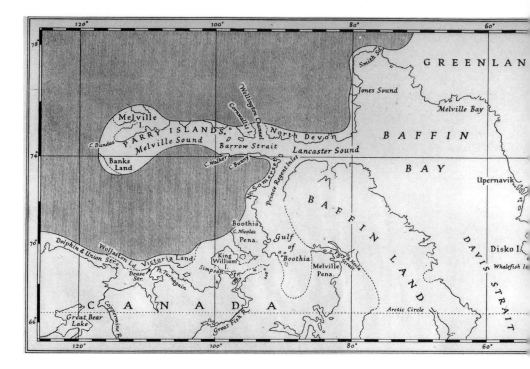

The North West Passage region as known in 1845. (*From Geographical Journal*, article by
R J Cyriax and James Wordie, Vol 106, 1945, p169–97)

There is a feeling generally entertained in the several scientific societies, and individuals attached to scientific pursuits, and also among officers of the Navy, that the
discovery, or rather the completion of the discovery, of a passage from the Atlantic to
the Pacific, round the Northern coast of North America, ought not to be abandoned,
after so much has been done, and so little now remains to be done; and that with our
present knowledge no reasonable doubt can be entertained that the accomplishment of
so desirable an object is practicable.

He continued as follows:

The case stands thus: since Captain (now Sir Edward) Parry on his first voyage passed
Lancaster Sound, and proceeded without interruption to Melville Island, the same
Sound as has been repeatedly passed by himself, by Ross, and several whalers, and may
therefore be considered passable in all years; and this Sound is one of the open gates
of the passage to Behring Straits, which is the other gate, and has also been passed to
a certain extent along the coast of America. There remains therefore to be navigated,
on the Polar Sea, the distance between the meridian of Melville Island and that of
Behring Straits, which is about 300 leagues [900 nautical miles] . . .[6]

He appeared to argue that there was no land lying between Cape Walker in the
north along a diagonal line reaching the mainland of America in about 120 °W,
just beyond Dr Richardson's discovery of 'Wollaston Land' (now the Wollaston
Peninsula of Victoria Land). According to Cyriax, Barrow believed that 'Banks
Land' (seen indistinctly to the south by Parry from Melville Island), 'Wollaston
Land' and 'Victoria Land' were small islands. 'It may be presumed, therefore',
Barrow wrote in the same proposal, 'that a distance of 300 leagues on a clear sea,

keeping midway between the supposed Banks' Land and the coast of America, would accomplish an object which, at intervals during 300 years, has engaged the attention of crowned heads, men of science and mercantile bodies, whose expectations were frequently disappointed, but not discouraged'.

Barrow then briefly reviewed the advantages that had come from the voyages of the Elizabethan seamen and referred to Baffin's discovery of

the great opening of Lancaster Sound . . . [which] has in our own time been found to lead into the Polar Sea, through which the North-West Passage from the Atlantic to the Pacific will one day be accomplished, . . . and which, if left to be performed by some other power, England by her neglect of it, after having opened the East and West doors, would be laughed at by all the world for having hesitated to cross the threshold.

The 'other power' was, of course, Imperial Russia. He had used this argument before, when endeavouring to promote the Arctic voyages of 1818, observing then that it would be 'somewhat mortifying if a naval power of but yesterday should complete a discovery in the nineteenth century, which was happily commenced by Englishmen in the sixteenth'.[7]

Barrow maintained that the matter would be settled during a voyage lasting only one year and costing therefore a third of the recent Antarctic expedition. It would also extend the scientific work of that expedition by helping to complete the magnetic survey of the world, while its ships, the *Erebus* and *Terror*, were already fitted out for use in icy seas. Many officers, experienced in polar navigation, would be 'ready and willing to embark on an expedition for completing the North West Passage'. Sir John Barrow was to die before the Franklin tragedy unfolded and there is, therefore, an ironic ring to his words, in this same proposal, maintaining that there could be 'no objection with regard to any apprehension of the loss of ships or men', and that 'neither sickness nor death [have] occurred in most of the voyages made into the Arctic regions, north or south.'[8]

The Prime Minister, Sir Robert Peel, asked Lord Haddington for certain points to be clarified regarding the scientific aspects of the proposed expedition and the feasibility of Barrow's plan. In a letter to Haddington of 27 December 1844, Sir John Barrow again expressed his optimism as to the short time necessary to navigate those 900 miles. He added that 'a time of profound peace, and the finances of the country in a flourishing state' seemed the right moment to set out his plan. This would be to the benefit of the Navy since it was 'admitted on all hands that the Arctic expeditions have produced a finer set of Officers and Seamen perhaps that in any other branch of the Service; and we have much need of encreasing [sic] such men, now that Steamers are supplanting our best Seamen'. He ended by naming seven of the Arctic officers whose opinions might be sought.[9]

It is worth drawing attention to Barrow's point that the Arctic was a good training ground, something that is often forgotten by writers on polar history. In time of peace, particularly the long decades during Queen Victoria's reign of over sixty years, some of the best officers and men of the Royal Navy pitted them-

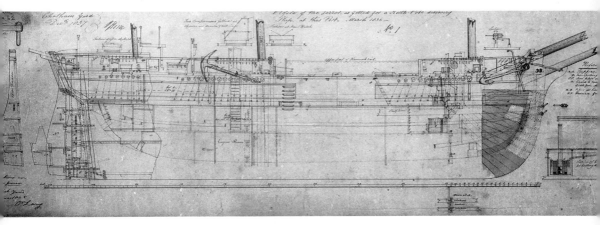

Originally built as a bomb vessel in 1812 at Bideford in Devon, this draught shows the *Terror* strengthened for service in ice. She had not long returned from James Ross' celebrated Antarctic voyage, in company with HMS *Erebus*, when both were recomissioned in 1845. (From the National Maritime Museum draughts collection)

selves against the Arctic and Antarctic, when there were few other enemies to fight. Sir Albert Hastings Markham in later Victorian times considered the creation of another generation of Arctic officers to be one of the most important results of the Nares expedition of 1875-76, and it is true that all the officers of the *Alert* and *Discovery*, bar one who was killed earlier, achieved flag rank (ie became Admirals.) His cousin, Sir Clements Markham, who had taken part as a young man in the Franklin Search, played the principal role in urging the renewal of Antarctic exploration by the Navy in the last decade of the nineteenth century. 'The real objects' of an Antarctic expedition, he maintained, would be 'geographical discovery, and the opportunities for young naval officers to win distinction in time of peace.[10]

It seems that only three of the Arctic officers cited by Barrow were asked to give the Admiralty written reports on his plan and in view of its importance to our story, that of Sir John Franklin is quoted below in full.[11]

21 Bedford Place,
Russell Square.
24th January, 1845

MY LORD,

In obedience to your Lordship's commands I lose not a moment in giving my written opinion on the questions your Lordship did me the honor of putting to me this morning.

1st. As to whether I consider the question of a N.W. Passage as one which ought to be entertained; to which I have no hesitation in answering in the affirmative, for the following reasons.

The discoveries of Parry and Ross have narrowed the parts in which the passage should be sought, to two at farthest, viz. that space between Cape Walker and Banks Land of Parry; where I should recommend the trial first to be made, and in case of the Passage not being found in that direction, then, to the Northward by the Wellington Channel.

The ships commanded by these officers had not the advantage of Steam and I need hardly say that the benefits to be derived from the aid of such a power are incalculable. Having pointed out to your Lordship to-day some of these advantages I will not dwell farther on this matter than to say the addition of steam to the ships is in my opinion indispensable. It is gratifying also, to know that it may be efficiently applied to the ships without destroying their capacity for stowing the requisite stores and provisions.

If the proposed expedition should unfortunately not be entirely successful in effecting a passage, it must contribute to our Geographical knowledge, and it cannot fail to make important additions to the series of Magnetical observations which are now carrying on in every part of the world.

I conceive that the greatest impediments from Ice will probably be met between the 95th and 125th degrees of Longitude, the latter meridian being passed, I should expect to find the ice less heavy and such as may be penetrated with comparative facility. We know of no Islands to the North-Westward of 120°.

Should there be any who say of these Arctic Expeditions to what purpose have they been? I should desire them to compare our present map of that region and of the northern coast of America, with that of 1818 when these expeditions commenced. They will find in the latter only three points marked on the coast of America, and nothing to the Northward of it. Surely it cannot be denied that so large an addition to the Geography of the Northern parts of America and of the Arctic Regions is in itself an object worthy of all the efforts that have been made in the course of former expeditions.

> I have the Honor to be
> My Lord, Your Lordship's
> most obedient Servant
> JOHN FRANKLIN
> Captain, RN

However, it is worth remembering that Franklin had earlier argued, as a result of discoveries made while tracing the north coast of America in 1825-27 that 'the best means of effecting the North-West Passage in a ship' would be from the Pacific, via Bering Strait, contrary to Parry's considered opinion that the attempt should be made from the Atlantic. He set out his argument in the last pages of his weighty narrative of the second overland expedition as follows:[12]

The prevalence of northwest winds during the season that the ice is in the most favourable state for navigation, would greatly facilitate the voyage of a ship to the eastward ... It is also well known, that the coast westward of the Mackenzie is almost unapproachable by ships, and it would therefore, be very desirable to get over that part of the voyage in the first season.

Captain Sir John Franklin,
Commander of the expedition of
1845-48, the last sent by the
Admiralty to find the North West
Passage. He was then nearly sixty
years old. Photograph taken before
the expedition sailed by William
Beard. (NMM 9191)

Probably, he thought, because the boats had kept to the shallow coastal flats, he
had not noticed the easterly current observed by Parry flowing through Fury and
Hecla Strait and by Kotzebue through Bering Strait. If such a current were
prevalent 'throughout the Polar Sea', he continued, 'it is evident that it would
materially assist a ship commencing the undertaking from the Pacific, and keeping in the deep water, which would, no doubt, be found at a moderate distance
from the shore'. Franklin made a particularly interesting remark when he wrote:

> The closeness and quantity of the ice in the Polar Seas vary much in different years;
> but, should it be in the same state that we found it, I would not recommend a ship's
> leaving Icy Cape earlier than the middle of August, for after that period, the ice was
> not only broken up within the sphere of our vision, but a heavy swell rolling from
> the northward, indicated a sea unsheltered by islands, and not much encumbered
> by ice.

If following this route via Bering Strait, he would find 'a wintering place' east of
Cape Bathurst en route for Dolphin and Union Strait, through which he would
pass. The 'confidence and safety' of the men engaged on the voyage would be
increased 'if one or two depots of provisions were established in places of ready
access, through the medium of the Hudson's Bay Company'. He ended his narrative of 1828 with these words:

Captain F.R.M Crozier, second-in-command of the expedition of 1845-48 and Captain of HMS *Erebus*. He had considerable previous experience in the Arctic and had just returned from the Antarctic expedition of 1839-43. Photograph by Beard, May 1845. (NMM 9191)

Arctic discovery has been fostered principally by Great Britain; and it is a subject of just pride that it has been prosecuted by her from motives as disinterested as they are enlightened; not from any prospect of immediate benefit to herself, but from a steady view to the acquirement of useful knowledge, and the extension of the bounds of science. Each succeeding attempt has added a step towards the completion of northern geography; and the contributions to natural history and science have excited a general interest throughout the civilised world. It is, moreover, pleasing to reflect that the loss of life which has occurred in the prosecution of these discoveries does not exceed the average number of deaths in the same population at home under circumstances the most favourable. And it is sincerely to be hoped that Great Britain will not relax her efforts until the question of a north-west passage has been satisfactorily set at rest, or at least until those portions of the northern shores of America, which are yet unknown, be laid down in our maps; and which, with the exception of a small space on the Asiatic continent eastward of Shelatskoi Noss, are the only intervals wanting to complete the outline of Europe, Asia, and America.

Both Parry and Sir James Clark Ross endorsed Barrow's view as to the route to be followed, while Ross also supported Franklin in suggesting that Wellington Channel (on the north side of Barrow Strait) might be tried, if the more southerly one proved impossible. As Comptroller of Steam Machinery for the Navy, Parry

Captain James Fitzjames, second-in-command of HMS *Erebus* and third-in-command of the expedition of 1845-48. Although he had no Arctic experience, Sir John Barrow thought Fitzjames should have commanded it. Photograph by Beard, May 1845. (NMM 9191)

strongly emphasised the value of installing steam engines with movable propellers.

These reports and that of Colonel Sabine on the gains to be made in the science of terrestrial magnetism, together with a favourable resolution passed by the Royal Society, must have helped to persuade Sir Robert Peel to give his consent. The decision came just before Sir John Barrow retired. The *Erebus* and the *Terror* would be re-equipped, but who would be chosen to lead the expedition? Sir James Clark Ross was undoubtedly the most suitable, being relatively young (in his mid-forties) and vastly experienced in polar exploration. However, on hearing confidentially that another Arctic expedition was in prospect, he wrote to Sir Francis Beaufort, Hydrographer of the Navy, saying that he had 'great and well-founded objections' to returning 'so soon to the severe and arduous service' to which he had already devoted twenty-four years of his life, especially as Sir John Franklin was eager and 'pre-eminently qualified' to command it. In addition, the fitting of the ships as steamers would be a measure to which he could not consent and which would alone lead him to decline 'an honor which a few years ago was the highest object' of his ambition.[13] Another reason was probably his recent marriage. Jane Franklin wrote to Ross hoping if he himself did not wish to take the command, her husband would 'not be put aside for *his age and inexperience*'. She thought Franklin would only go if he felt equal to the task, and continued:

'Captain Sir John Franklin's Cabin, in the *Erebus*', shown in the *Illustrated London News*, 1845. In the expectation that the expedition of 1845-48 would sail through the North West Passage into the Pacific, the Admiralty supplied charts of both Atlantic and Pacific oceans. (NMM neg 57/227)

what weighs most upon my mind is that at the present crisis of our affairs and after being treated so unworthily by the Col. Office, I think he will be deeply sensitive if his own department should neglect him and that such an appointment would do more perhaps than anything else to counteract the effect which Lord S's injustice and oppression have produced. I dread exceedingly the effect on his mind of being without honourable and immediate employment and it is this which enables me to support the idea of parting with him on a service of difficulty and danger better than I otherwise should – and yet not well.[14]

After some discussion, it was decided by the Admiralty that Franklin, who was fifty-eight, should have the command in *Erebus*, and that Captain Francis Rawdon Moira Crozier, ten years younger, should sail in *Terror*, as second-in-command, as he had with Ross in the Antarctic. Crozier had served in three of Parry's four Arctic expeditions, and had also sailed with Ross in the *Cove* to rescue a number of whaling vessels beset in the ice in Davis Strait, a taxing voyage lasting from January to August 1836, and for which Crozier was promoted. His particular expertise was in terrestrial magnetism. During the visits of the *Erebus* and *Terror* to Van Diemen's Land (Tasmania), Crozier fell in love with Franklin's niece, Sophia Cracroft, who rejected him.

Sir John Barrow had wanted Commander James Fitzjames to lead the expedition. He had been a junior officer in the Euphrates Expedition of 1835-37, an extraordinary episode in the Great Game between Great Britain and Imperial Russia, and he had also served in China. He was considered too young for the command, but he sailed in the *Erebus* with Franklin. In the preface to his *Voyages of discovery and research within the Arctic regions, 1818-45*, Barrow praised Fitzjames' zeal and alacrity, his good humour and ever cheerful disposition which had made him 'an universal favourite in the navy'. He had earlier rescued a man from drowning, at great danger to himself, for which he was awarded the medal of the Royal Humane Society. His letters, full of fun and high spirits, were sent home from Greenland, and, together with a faded rosebud in a tiny envelope, they still survive.[15]

The twenty-one junior officers were largely recommended to the Admiralty by James Fitzjames, presumably because Franklin must have been out of touch with the younger generation and Crozier too perhaps. Seven of the officers as a whole had already been in the Arctic. Besides Franklin and Crozier, these were Lieutenant Gore, who had been Mate in *Terror* 1836-37; Mr Osmer, Paymaster and Purser, who had been a clerk in the *Blossom* under Beechey, during the voyage to Bering Strait; Dr Alexander Macdonald, Assistant Surgeon, who had sailed on a whaling voyage in 1840; James Reid, Ice-Master and experienced whaling captain; and Thomas Blanky, Ice-Master, who had served as an Able Seaman in the *Griper* (Captain Lyon), 1824, and on Parry's fourth Arctic expedition, 1827, and also as Mate in the *Victory*, under Sir John Ross, 1829-33, during which expedition he did some sledge travelling.

Captain Crozier's experience of navigating in ice was the longest and the most recent. Sir John Franklin's had been twenty-seven years earlier, in the *Trent*, which had only ventured a short distance into the multi-year ice of the central polar basin, although of course he had great experience of overland travel and had journeyed by boat among the offshore ice of the north coast of America in the 1820s. He no doubt owed his appointment partly (this being a seaborne expedition) to his ability to look after his men and inspire their affection and respect, and to his knowledge of the difficulties and dangers of the Arctic and how to withstand them. Crozier was in Italy when the expedition was first under consideration and had written in December 1844 to Sir James Clark Ross:

> I hesitate not a moment to go second to Sir John Franklin, pray tell him so; if too late I cannot help it. Of course I am too late to volunteer to command but, in truth, I sincerely feel I am not equal to the leadership. I would *not* on any terms go second to any other, Captain Parry or yourself excepted.[16]

In his masterly account of Franklin's last expedition, R J Cyriax provides short biographies of all the junior officers, in addition to longer summaries of the careers of Franklin, Crozier and Fitzjames. He also lists the one hundred and twenty-nine officers and men who sailed in the *Erebus* and *Terror* from Greenland (five men returned to England before then.) There was a Surgeon and an Assistant Surgeon for each ship, one of whom, Dr Harry Goodsir, of Edinburgh, had published a number of original papers on zoology and pathology. He succeeded his elder brother, Professor John Goodsir, as Conservator of the Museum of the Royal College of Surgeons of Edinburgh. He was the *de facto* naturalist of the expedition, described by Fitzjames as 'perfectly good-humoured', 'very well-informed', a 'pleasant companion' and an 'acquisition to the mess'. Dr Alexander Macdonald, Assistant Surgeon of the *Terror*, was probably a fellow-student of Goodsir and in 1838, he had been awarded a silver prize-medal. Lieutenant John Irving of the *Terror* was another Scot, who had emigrated to New South Wales for six years, but returned to the Navy in 1843. The Surgeon of the *Erebus*, Dr Stephen Stanley, probably a Londoner, had published an article on a rare surgical condition. Fitzjames described him as thoroughly good-natured and obliging.

Lieutenant Graham Gore of the *Erebus* had taken part in the Battle of Navarino in 1827 and fought later in China. Fitzjames described him as a 'man of great stability of character, a very good officer', with the 'sweetest of tempers', saying too that he played the flute extremely well and could draw sometimes 'very well' and at other times 'very badly', but that he was 'altogether a capital fellow'. Lieutenant H T D Le Vesconte, a Jersey man, had fought too in China. Lieutenant J W Fairholme, also of the *Erebus*, had had an adventurous career. One of the missions of the Victorian navy was to stamp out the slave trade, and when second-in-command of a captured slave-ship in 1838, Fairholme was himself captured by Moors after the vessel was wrecked on the African coast, but was rescued by some French negroes. In 1841, he accompanied an expedition up the Niger River in three small steamers, with the aim of exploring this great river and making treaties with the African kings, but so many succumbed to fever, including Fairholme, that the mission was abandoned.[17]

It is through Cyriax's brief biographies, which include Fitzjames' comments on his shipmates, that the officers of *Erebus* come to life. It is fortunate too, in this regard, that daguerreotypes taken by William Beard, an early photographer, still exist and were later engraved for the *Illustrated London News*, 13 September 1851. Sir John Franklin is there in cocked hat, as is the gallant Fitzjames. Of the *Terror's* officers, only Crozier was portrayed. His honest, somewhat anxious face, looks out from under a large peaked cap. Among the others who were photographed, one of the Mates of the *Erebus*, Edward Couch, was described by Fitzjames as a 'little, black-haired, smooth-faced fellow – good-humoured in his own way; writes, reads, works, draws, all quietly. Is never in the way of anybody, and always ready when wanted . . ' The Paymaster and Purser, Charles Osmer, 'was full of quaint, dry sayings', according to Fitzjames, and was 'always good-humoured' and 'laughing'. Last, Fitzjames considered the Ice-Master (or Greenland Pilot) James Reid, the most original character in the officers' mess, 'rough, intelligent, unpolished, with a broad North-Country accent, but not vulgar, good humoured and honest-hearted.'[18]

In the fitting out of the *Erebus* and *Terror* for the Arctic expedition, the greatest innovation was the introduction of auxiliary steam power, in the form of two railway engines, with screw propellers that could be lifted out of the water when the vessels were under sail. As we have seen, Parry was at the time Comptroller of Steam Machinery for the Navy, and he saw the advantages of steam in polar navigation, as had Sir John Ross. The Admiralty's Instructions to Franklin of 5 May 1845 included a paragraph about this:

> As however, we have thought fit to cause each ship to be fitted with a small steam engine and propeller, to be used only in pushing the ships through channels between masses of ice, when the wind is adverse, or in a calm, we trust the difficulty usually found in such cases will be much obviated, but as the supply of fuel to be taken in the ships is necessarily small, you will use it only in cases of difficulty.[19]

The engine of the *Erebus* came from the London and Greenwich Railway, while that of the *Terror* was probably from the London and Birmingham Railway. Both were 20hp. The trials on the River Thames were satisfactory. Lieutenant Irving of the *Terror* wrote home on 16 May, the day after the *Terror*'s trials:

> We tried our screws and went four miles an hour. Our engine once ran somewhat faster on the Birmingham line. It is placed athwart ships in our afterhold, and merely has its axle extended aft, so as to became the shaft of the screw. It has a funnel the same size and height as it had on the railway, and makes the same dreadful puffings and screamings, and will astonish the Esquimaux not a little. We can carry twelve days' coal for it, but it will never be used when we can make any progress at all by other means.[20]

It seems that Irving's sketch shows a funnel 'far too tall for any railway'.[21] The engine-room in each ship was placed abaft (behind) the mainmast and took up the whole width of each vessel, being 13ft high and 8ft long. A shaft tunnel 31½ ft long ran between the engine and the 7ft diameter screw. Coal bunkers holding 25 tons of coal were installed nearby. An engineer and two stokers were appointed to each ship, at the usual rate of double pay for the ships' companies of the Arctic expeditions. The installation of the engines must have made the living quarters very cramped indeed. The cabins were to be warmed by an apparatus circulating hot water, presumably in pipes. So that the *Erebus* and *Terror* should not be either dangerously overloaded or under-supplied, a transport, the *Barretto Junior* (Captain Edward Griffiths) was to accompany them as far north as was prudent.

The vessels were amply provisioned for three years as follows:

> Biscuit (36487lbs) Flour (136656lbs) Pemmican 1203lbs. Beef in 8lb pieces 32224lbs. Pork in 4lb pieces 32000lbs. Preserved meat 33289lbs. Sugar 23576lbs. Preserved vegetables 8900lbs. Concentrated spirits 3684 gallons. Wine for the sick 200 gallons. Suet 3052lbs. Raisins 1008lbs. Peas 147 bushels. Chocolate 9450lbs. Tea 2357lbs. Lemon juice 9300lbs. Concentrated soup equivalent to 20463 pints. Vinegar 1326 gallons. Scotch Barley 2496lbs. Oatmeal 1350 gallons. Pickles 580 gallons. Cranberries 170 gallons. Mustard 1000lbs. Pepper 200lbs.[22]

This list is abridged from a slightly more detailed one compiled by Dr R J Cyriax. He tells us that 'the soups were either vegetable or gravy, chiefly the former; the preserved vegetables were potatoes, carrots, parsnips, and 'mixed'; the preserved meats were boiled and roast beef, boiled and roast mutton, seasoned beef, beef and vegetables, soup and bouilli (soup containing stewed meat), veal and ox-cheek, all supplied by a contractor. The pickles were 'mixed' cabbage, onions and walnuts.

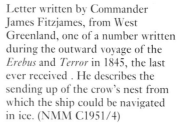

Letter written by Commander James Fitzjames, from West Greenland, one of a number written during the outward voyage of the *Erebus* and *Terror* in 1845, the last ever received . He describes the sending up of the crow's nest from which the ship could be navigated in ice. (NMM C1951/4)

The pemmican was prepared apparently under the personal supervision of Sir John Richardson at the Royal Clarence Yard, Gosport.

Amongst other articles supplied were 7088lbs of tobacco, 3600lbs of soap and 2700lbs of candles. Cyriax also reconstructed a typical week's victualling. Each man would receive a daily allowance of 1lb of biscuit or flour, 2½ ounces of sugar, ¼ ounce of tea, 1 ounce of chocolate and 1 ounce of lemon juice. On Mondays and Fridays, ¾ lb of salt beef would be served; on Wednesdays and Sundays, ¾ lb of salt pork; and ½lb of preserved (tinned) meat on Tuesdays, Thursdays and Saturdays.[23]

Besides food for the body, there was food for the mind in the form of libraries on board each ship of some 1200 books. These included the usual narratives of previous polar expeditions, geographical and nautical journals, technical works on steam engines, as well as *Pickwick Papers* and *Nicholas Nickleby*, the *Ingoldsby Legends*, and volumes of *Punch* (the humorous and satirical magazine.) For the evening schools to be held during the winter for the seamen, the Admiralty supplied seventy slates, slate pencils, and two hundred pens, besides ink, paper and arithmetic books. Religious works were supplied by friends and societies. Each ship was presented with a hand-organ by subscribers, while Mr Beard, who had photographed Franklin, Crozier and the officers of *Erebus*, supplied a daguerreotype apparatus.[24]

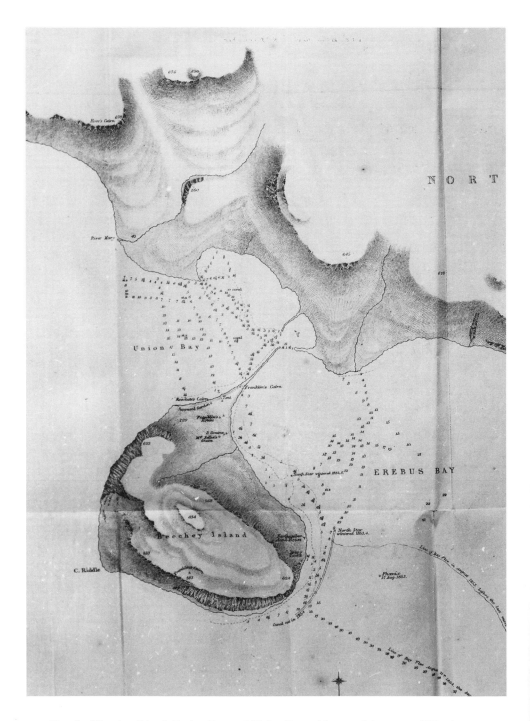

Detail of Beechey Island, Erebus Bay and Union Bay, with part of the coast of 'North Devon' Island from the chart of Erebus Bay, surveyed by Commander W J S Pullen of the *North Star*, 1854. (Parliamentary Papers, Arctic Blue Books)

Thus lavishly provisioned and provided, the last of the British Admiralty expeditions to seek the North West Passage proceeded down the Thames to the sea. The date was 19 May 1845. The First Sea Lord, a member of the Board of Admiralty, a Lieutenant-General and the aged Sir John Barrow had inspected the *Erebus* and *Terror* on 24 April. Another inspection followed an official entertainment in honour of Sir John Franklin, attended by most of the senior Arctic officers. On Sunday 18 May, the day before the expedition's final departure, Sir John Franklin read Divine Service aboard *Erebus*, a moving experience not only for the ships' companies, but for his wife and Sophia Cracroft, the niece beloved by Captain Crozier. The *Erebus* and *Terror* departed with the good wishes and good will of the nation. Visitors to the ships praised the arrangements and the alacrity, keenness and efficiency of the officers and men, especially Sir John Franklin.

Sir John Franklin was a Vice-President of the Royal Geographical Society and some days after his departure, Sir Roderick Impey Murchison, its President, in Cyriax's words, 'voiced the opinion of the entire nation when he said':

> As far as depends on my judicious and enterprising friend Sir John Franklin, and his energetic officers and seamen, I have the fullest confidence that everything will be done for the promotion of science, and for the honour of the British name and Navy, that human efforts can accomplish. The name of Franklin alone is, indeed, a national guarantee; and proud shall we geographers be if our gallant Vice-President shall return after achieving such an exploit, and gladly I am sure would we then offer to him our Presidential chair as some recompense for his arduous labours.[25]

Calling at the Orkney Islands, where the two tugs were sent home, the *Erebus* and *Terror* proceeded northwards, accompanied by the transport *Barretto Junior*, from time to time throwing overboard a number of printed forms in six languages enclosed in copper cylinders, which recorded their progress. Only one of these was ever recovered from the sea.

At the Whalefish Islands in Disco Bay on the west coast of Greenland, the stores from the transport were transferred to the exploring ships in early July, so that they had a full three years' supplies. Franklin's last despatch to the Admiralty and personal letters from him and the ships' companies were taken home by Lieutenant Griffiths. Their friends and families expected next to hear from them via Petropavlovsk on the Pacific coast of Siberia. Among the mail must have been Dr Goodsir's report of dredging live creatures from the sea bottom at the depth of 300 fathoms, soon after rounding Cape Farewell, published in *Annals of Natural History* for 1845. The ships were sighted by two whaling vessels at the end of July: the *Enterprise* of Peterhead (Captain Martin) and the *Prince of Wales* (Captain Dannett) of Hull. Both found that all was well. This was the last occasion on which the officers and men of the *Erebus* and *Terror* were seen by their fellow-countrymen. They disappeared completely.

*   *   *

In view of the weary years that it took to solve the mystery of their disappearance, it is as well to see what was in Franklin's mind when he was about to depart from

Greenland. His letter to his old friend and companion of his Arctic journeys, Dr John Richardson, throws much light on this. It was dated 7 July 1845 from the Whale Fish Islands, Disco Bay. After mentioning Goodsir's work in the field of Natural History and other matters, Franklin wrote:

> I have been thinking much of the probability of there being a chain of islands, if not a continued shore, which connects Wollaston Land with that of Banks as I remember you always imagined would prove the case. I cannot else see how the musk oxen got to Melville Island, which cannot swim far, I suppose. These would hardly cross over the ice, though the Reindeer would; besides, the latter animals can swim, and would perhaps cross over wide channels.
>
> Should there exist a chain of islands in the direction we are speaking of I shall consider the circumstance as favourable and that we shall have the best prospect of getting to the westward through the channels between them. I cannot agree with Sir John Barrow in supposing that the open water is to be found apart from land. I shall, of course, despatch parties in boats and by land to examine into and find out passages in places where it may be difficult and only productive of delay in taking the ships . . .
>
> I admit with you that Regent's Inlet seems to be the most certain way of attaining [the coast of America] . . . , but the more I reflect upon the voyages hitherto made into that inlet the more convinced I am that James Ross and Parry are right in supposing that ships of our size if they even once got down among the islets and strong tides at the bottom of that Inlet, they would never be got out again. The coast in that part must be surveyed in boats. But once to the west of Point Turnagain our ships might with safety go. Should we be entirely obstructed in forcing our passage between the parallels of Banks and Wollaston Lands, we must try the Wellington channels or some other of the channels to the North, but I cannot find any good reason for [supposing that] we are to find open water th[ough Barrow *w]ill* have it . . .
>
> I have an excellent set of officers and men who have embarked with the best spirit in the cause. It will be my study to keep them united and happy, and to encourage them while they put forth their own strenuous endeavours – to commit the issue of their safety to God.[26]

With the help of a letter to another old friend dated 10 July 1845, we can picture Franklin in his cabin aboard *Erebus*. At one table, he told Parry, a lieutenant was busy making a draft chart from his survey of the Whalefish Islands. At the same table sat Mr Goodsir examining under the microscope the rare and unknown creatures dredged from the bottom of the sea, some of which had 'too long names' for Franklin to write. Goodsir was sketching and describing them straight away, while the colour was still fresh. On another table lay 'lots of skinned birds, the handiwork of the surgeon, who is skilled in such subjects'. Franklin said he was encouraging the officers to specialise in one branch or another of the work, from which they should 'ultimately reap real substantial benefit'. His own concern was to train and oversee these gentlemen, rather than do the work itself. Packed in neat tin cases around the deck of his cabin, were the ships stores of preserved potatoes. From this description, wrote Franklin, Parry should 'be able to bring me before your mind at this moment, and, in turning my head, I recognise *you*, like as life in your picture'. As with Richardson, he commended his 'dearest wife and daughter' to Parry's kind regards', and the expedition to the care of the Almighty. The letter

An artist's impression of Sir John Franklin's funeral. From Sherard Osborn. 'The last voyage of Sir John Franklin', Part 2. *Once a Week*, 29 October 1859)

was published over ten years later in Edward Parry's memoirs of his father.

Wishing that the engine were back on the railway in England, sad at being spurned by Sophy Cracroft and missing his old friend and commander immensely, Captain Crozier wrote from the Whalefish Islands to James Clark Ross saying 'What I fear is that from our being so late, we shall have no time to look round and judge for ourselves, but blunder into the ice and make a second 1824 of it. James, I wish you were here, I would then have no doubt as to our pursuing the proper course'.[27] As his biographer remarks, James Ross must have had mixed feelings, as his two great friends sailed into the unknown. His baby son was then nearly a year old.

The extent and complexity of that maze of islands – the Canadian Arctic archipelago – was only to be fully revealed in the early twentieth century. The map on page 170 shows its geography as perceived in 1845. Franklin's ships were indeed still venturing into the unknown, despite the relatively short distance of some 600 miles to be navigated between the northern and southern charted coasts. Least known of all were the ice conditions, changing with each year. Some channels and straits nearly always lose their ice in the late spring. Others are churned and choked by heavy floes even in the height of summer. Franklin had no helicopters to act as scouts and no images from satellites to help him choose the way.

CHAPTER 11

The Franklin Search Begins

After the excitement of departure, Jane Franklin took her step-daughter, Eleanor, aged 21, to visit France for the first time; and then to Madeira and the United States. In August 1846, they headed homewards, hoping for news; in December, Lady Franklin expressed her fears to Sir James Clark Ross, and the hope that he would be the man to search for the expedition, if need be.[1]

For Jane, and for all the friends and relatives of the ships' companies, the following year, 1847, was one of dashed hopes and terrible anxiety. Sir John Ross wrote to the Admiralty in January and February urgently suggesting a relief expedition, but their lordships resolved to await the results of an appeal to the Arctic whalers. However, Sir John Richardson met Sir George Simpson, the Governor-in-Chief of Rupert's Land (the territories of the Hudson's Bay Company) in April 1847, during the Governor's visit to England, from whom Richardson received a warm reception and expert advice. Because provisions at the company posts were unusually low, owing to the failure of the bison hunt on the Saskatchewan, Sir George recommended that a large supply of pemmican should be manufactured in England to support an overland relief party in 1847 and 1848 and to leave caches for Franklin.

The Admiralty gave permission for this to be done at the Royal Clarence Yard in Gosport (across the harbour from Portsmouth). A total of 17,424lbs were made from the best kiln-dried beef and suet and transferred to canisters weighing 85lbs each, some being sweetened with sugar and others having currants added. 1847 was the year the Irish potato crop failed and Sir John Richardson wrote, 'various temporary expedients' had to be used in drying the meat, since the 'whole Clarence Yard establishment' was at that time 'fully occupied night and day in preparing flour and biscuit for the relief of the famishing population of Ireland'.[2] The Admiralty also ordered four boats to be built, suitable for both river and sea navigation, able to carry cargo and as light as possible in view of the portages. Five seamen and fifteen sappers and miners were chosen by Richardson because he had found that seamen marched badly, especially when carrying a load and because the 'intelligent artisans' could be used 'for repairing the boats, working up iron, constructing the buildings of our winter residence; or making the furniture'. Together with the boats, pemmican and other supplies, the men sailed in the Hudson's Bay Company's ships from the Thames on 15 June 1847, but did not arrive until September at York Factory,

Jane Griffin (later Lady
Franklin) as a young woman. She
inspired search expeditions for
more than ten years after the
disappearance of her husband.
(Author's collection)

the Company's main port of entry on Hudson Bay, because of bad ice conditions.
They were consequently delayed in making their way inland, and passed the winter of 1847-48 in the Company's post, Cumberland House.

Meanwhile in England, Sir John Richardson received letters from army and
naval officers and from civilians, who wished to join him. Amongst these were
'two clergymen, one justice of peace for a Welsh county, several country gentlemen, and some scientific foreigners, all evidently imbued with a generous love of
enterprise, and a humane desire to be the means of carrying relief to a large body
of their fellow creatures'. However, it was only on the return of the last whalers
from Davis Strait, bringing no news of Franklin, that a second officer was
appointed by the Admiralty, with the consent of the Hudson's Bay Company. He
was Dr John Rae, a Chief Trader, whom Richardson had recommended.
Accomplished and resolute, Rae had spent fifteen years in Rupert's Land and
had just completed a successful expedition, under the auspices of the Hudson's
Bay Company, exploring the limits of Prince Regent's Inlet.

One's heart warms to Sir John Richardson, who, at the age of sixty was prepared to set out across North America on an arduous and trying journey to find
his old friend and chief, Sir John Franklin. He was able to do so, secure in the
knowledge that his new wife would look after his young family kindly and well.
Her mother was staying at the time with them at Haslar, where Richardson held

the post of physician from 1838-55 at the Royal Naval Hospital. She wrote in her diary 'It is only necessary to see the invariable cheerfulness and goodness of Sir John Richardson in his own house, and his attention to those most dependent on his kindness, to form a true value of his admirable character. I saw him at a time of great excitement, just about to leave his happy home and part with all he loved most on earth, to fulfil what he considered a sacred duty'.[3]

He and Dr Rae travelled by steam packet from Liverpool to New York, arriving in early April 1848. Besides their personal baggage, they took with them a few astronomical instruments, needed to determine their positions, and four pocket chronometers, one of which was lent free of charge by Mr Frodsham, the maker. It had already been used on Parry's and Ross' voyages. A number of meteorological and magnetic instruments, besides 'an ample supply of paper for botanical purposes, a quantity of stationery, a small selection of books, a medicine chest, a canteen, a compendious cooking apparatus, and a few tins of pemmican' made up the rest of their baggage, which altogether weighed more than 4000lbs.

The geographical and scientific appendix to Richardson's narrative takes up about a third of the book and ranges far more widely than the results of observations with the instruments and materials he specifies above, and the expedition contributed greatly to the sum of knowledge of the North American Arctic, despite its lack of success in finding the *Erebus* and *Terror*. Richardson's keen interest and sharp eyes with regard to Natural History is evident in the narrative, and there are chapters on the 'four Aboriginal Nations' met by the expedition, including the Inuit.

This overland expedition of Richardson and Rae was part of a three-pronged plan by the Admiralty to relieve Franklin, detained somewhere in the Arctic between the Atlantic and Pacific Oceans. HMS *Plover* (Commander T E L Moore) sailed first, on New Year's Day 1848, needing to reach Bering Strait that summer, to be joined later by HMS *Herald*, which was already in the Pacific. She carried orders to search the coast of Russian America (Alaska) by boat as far as the Mackenzie River. Second, Richardson and Rae, were to travel overland, then down the Mackenzie to the Arctic Ocean and eastward along the coast to the Coppermine River, a journey which Richardson had made in 1826. They were to cross over to 'Wollaston Land' and search its shores. Last, Sir James Clark Ross also volunteered to search, and lay depots, from the Atlantic end. He was given command of HMS *Enterprise* and HMS *Investigator*, of 450 tons and 400 tons respectively, newly constructed for the Admiralty at Blackwall and Greenock. They carried six months' provision for Franklin as well as their own stores for three years. Both were well strengthened for use in ice. Two steam pinnaces were also provided. Ross evidently believed, as Dr. Cyriax pointed out, that the *Erebus* and *Terror* were beset in the extremely heavy 'polar' ice, which he alone of all the Arctic officers had seen both at Cape Dundas, Melville Island with Parry in 1819-20 and from the west coast of King William Island, during his sledge journey from the *Victory* in May 1830.[4]

Ross' ships were ordered to examine Lancaster Sound, Barrow Strait and Wellington Channel, should they arrive early enough, as well as the gaps between Cape Clarence and Cape Walker. The *Investigator* was to winter near Cape Rennell (North Somerset). A sledge party in the spring would explore the adjacent coast and the west coast of 'Boothia Felix', while another should search to the south of Prince Regent Inlet. The *Enterprise* was to winter much further west – at Parry's old winter quarters on Melville Island or on Banks Land, which he had seen to the south, across what was later to be called M'Clure Strait. Parties from the ship were to travel south across the blank space on the chart to Cape Bathurst or Cape Parry on the American mainland, and southeast towards Victoria Land and Wollaston Land to help Sir John Richardson in searching the latter. Depots were to be laid to help and direct the lost expedition.

Such was the three-pronged search for the missing ships and men, plans which would have effectively operated to cover Franklin's route in a good ice year, when there is plenty of open water. However, Captain F W Beechey, who had earlier commanded the *Blossom*, suggested in April 1847 that a boat should be sent down the Great Fish (Back) River, as part of a more extensive search. A descent of that long, tortuous and difficult river was also vehemently advocated by Dr Richard King, who had accompanied Back in 1833-35. King had a very high opinion of his own capabilities and unfortunately 'by the tactless and egotistical phrasing of his letters' to the authorities, he 'virtually ensured that no-one would listen to him'.[5] Both Parry and Sir James Clark Ross, the Admiralty's main advisers, were of the opinion that Franklin would never attempt the ascent of that river because of the difficulty of navigation, the lack of food *en route*, and because no post of the Hudson's Bay Company stood nearby.

However, Lady Franklin expressed her doubts as to the completeness of the Admiralty's plans in a letter to James Clark Ross of 18 December 1847. Her words were to be shown as strangely and sadly prophetic by the time the fruitless search for her husband was virtually complete in 1859.

> You will hardly forgive me if I tell you that I feel something is still wanting to the completeness of the expeditions and you will be thinking that Dr King has been exciting a most mischievous & unjustifiable influence on my mind. Of Dr King himself I wish to say nothing. I do not desire that he should be the person employed, but I cannot but wish that the Hudson's Bay Company might receive instructions or a request from Govt. to explore those parts which you and Sir J Richardson cannot immediately do & which if done by you at all can only be when other explorations have been made in vain. And then does he *not* say truly, it will be *too late*? I will agree with you on the great improbability of their being in such & such positions, but who can say they may not be found (if found at all) in the most unlikely place?[6]

And so began the search for the lost ships and their companies, which was to last for more than a decade.

*   *   *

Some forty expeditions, both official and private, joined the search, mainly British, but including at least two from the United States and the participation of two young naval officers from France during the years 1848 to 1859. It marks the end of the centuries-old English, and subsequently British, endeavour to find the North West Passage and it also marked a change in method. No longer were ships to force their way through the ice seeking a sea route linking the two great oceans. They still had to battle with the ice and find safe winter harbours, but they then acted as headquarters from which boats and travelling parties could search the adjoining coasts as minutely as weather, ice, muscle-power and provisions allowed. Nor were observations of meteorology and magnetism and other sciences forgotten.[7] To the long spring and summer sledge journeys (some over 1000 miles), we owe the mapping of the vastly complicated Canadian Arctic archipelago. Throughout the years of the Franklin Search, one can picture Jane Franklin cajoling or pleading with the Admiralty and even with the Prime Minister and the President of the United States of America, writing numerous letters to the 'Arctic Officers' of the Navy, corresponding with the Masters of her own search expeditions and keeping numerous diaries and letter-books.

During the first attempt to succour Franklin in 1848-49, Sir James Clark Ross experienced a frustrating and difficult voyage in the *Enterprise* and *Investigator*, owing to ice blocking the way westward and their being forced to winter in Port Leopold, at the northeast tip of North Somerset. Sledge parties travelled with difficulty south to Fury Beach, where Parry's stores were found to be in order, and down Peel Sound to what Ross named Cape Coulman, along the unexplored west coast of North Somerset. Of this new strait (Peel Sound), Lieutenant Francis Leopold McClintock, who was experiencing his first Arctic expedition, wrote, 'Our opinion . . . was that any attempt to force a ship down it would not only fail, but lead to almost inevitable risk of destruction, in consequence of its being choked up with heavy ice'.[8] Little did he or Ross realise that it was down this very strait that the *Erebus* and *Terror* had sailed to their doom in 1846, no doubt in open water that year.

Though Ross had bought no dogs, he did introduce a type of sledge which was based on those of the Inuit and which he had made on board ship. The sledging routine was to travel at night, when the sun was less powerful and the snow harder. Ross went ahead to reconnoitre, while McClintock followed with the sledges, each drawn by six men. Ross would walk round any large bays, surveying them as he went, while the others took the more direct route. Some 150 miles were added to the chart by this expedition, but no trace of Franklin was found. Nevertheless, before departing from Port Leopold, a large depot was left in a house built there by the expedition and one of the steam launches was also left, having been lengthened sufficiently to transport the crews of the *Erebus* and *Terror* as far as the entrance to Lancaster Sound to meet the whalers.

It proved impossible to spend a second season in the Arctic, since the ships (the *Enterprise* and *Investigator*) were beset in the ice and drifted eastwards for 250 miles, and were only released in September 1848 near Baffin Bay. They

Dr (later Sir) John Richardson, surgeon and naturalist, who at the age of sixty, left his family to search overland, with Dr John Rae, for Sir John Franklin, in 1848. He had earlier taken part in both Franklin's overland expeditions. (Author's collection)

reached England in November, both officers and men having suffered badly from scurvy. This was due mainly to the poor quality and inadequacy of the provisions, including the lemon juice from Sicily, which had lost most of its anti-scorbutic qualities in preparation. As a result, the provisioning of subsequent naval search expeditions was greatly improved. The experience of sledging gained with Ross, who had spent so many years of his life in the polar regions, was to prove invaluable to a new generation of 'Arctic Officers' of the Royal Navy, among them McClintock and McClure. However, he did not teach them to drive dogs, having bought none in Greenland, perhaps because only he and Abernethy had learnt the art. A further and more direct consequence of the voyage was the despatch of the supply ship *North Star*, by the Admiralty, in May 1849 to meet HMS *Investigator*. Her captain was James Saunders, a Master in the Royal Navy. The *North Star* was forced to winter in northwest Greenland, but then drifted westwards and eventually left a depot of provisions in Navy Board Inlet, off Lancaster Sound, arriving in England in September 1850.

Lady Franklin sent a letter to James Clark Ross by the *North Star* in which she told him that she had visited Lady Ross, who was 'kind and generous enough to say she was glad you were going to stop out a 2d. Winter'. Jane Franklin had been very taken with his two 'sweet children', James and Anne, one being 'an interesting and most promising boy', while his little sister was 'so very pretty' and very like her father. She wrote also of the Admiralty and of Sir John Ross's interviews with the First Lord regarding where the lost ships might be. She said that she often thought of 'poor Captain Crozier', who had 'seemed so ill and dispirited when he left'.[9]

This letter stayed with the *North Star* during the Arctic winter and only reached Ross on that vessel's return in 1850. Far more poignant are those written by Jane to her husband, which were brought back to her unopened, time after time. She was to demonstrate her abiding love for Franklin in almost ceaseless activity during the decade after his disappearance by organising her own expeditions and in urging the Governments of both Great Britain and the United States to do likewise. Her biographer quotes a few lines from one of these letters, which put her love and her faith into words.

> I desire nothing but to cherish you the remainder of your days, however injured and broken your health may be – but in every case I will strive to bow to the Almighty Will, and trust thro' His mercy for a blessed reunion in a better world! . . . I live in you my own dearest – I pray for you at all hours.[10]

Throughout these years, and later in life, Jane Franklin found a faithful friend, travelling companion and amanuensis in her niece Sophia Cracroft, who seems to have accompanied her everywhere. Of her aunt, Sophy wrote to the absent Franklin early in 1850:

> You may wonder at my saying that even you do not know your own wife, but in as much as her devotedness, courage and fortitude, and extraordinary mental endowments have never been tested as of late, so you have never known the full extent of her

'The *Enterprise* and the *Investigator* in the Valley of the Glaciers, Greenland, 1848' Watercolour by W H Browne, Lieutenant in the *Enterprise*, during the Franklin Search Expedition, commanded by Captain Sir James Clark Ross. (NMM, PY 0066)

rare qualities. I cannot express to you how entirely I honour as well as love her..
Throughout the length and breadth of the land is she honored and respected . . . and
this, notwithstanding the most shrinking anxiety to avoid notice . . .'[11]

A great lover of travel throughout her life (despite rats in her cabin on the Nile),
Jane Franklin was quite prepared to set off with Sir John Richardson to search
for her husband. She had instead to wait while others searched: sometimes her
own captains, sometimes naval officers sent by the Admiralty and sometimes the
officers of American vessels, whose owner Henry Grinnell answered her appeal
with action. In all there were some forty expeditions, during the years 1848 to
1859, whose journeys and fortunes have been told in many a book from the 1850s
to the present day. It is almost as difficult for the writer to plot a course through
this literature as it was for sailors to navigate and chart the icy seas and lands of
what was eventually revealed as the Canadian Arctic archipelago.

However, all this activity, positive as it was in the way of geographical
discovery contributed largely to prove a negative, ie where Franklin had *not* been.
The winter quarters of the *Erebus* and *Terror* in 1845-46 were found quite early
on in 1850, but no record was retrieved disclosing where the ships were heading.
The next important step was the purchase by Dr John Rae in 1854, from a band
of Eskimos, of a cap band, a medal, and other small items, which had clearly
belonged to Franklin or his men. By then it was unlikely that any of the lost
expedition had survived and it fell to Sir Leopold McClintock after the Crimean
War of 1854-56 to gather up numerous other relics and the vital last record,
which showed that King William Island was the scene of the tragedy and that
some of Franklin's men had completed a North West Passage, thus 'forging a last
link with their lives'. During these years, two more North West Passages were
discovered by McClure in HMS *Investigator*, linking the western search from the
Pacific with that from the Atlantic. The Franklin Search seems to have been
bedevilled to some extent by the theory of the 'open polar sea', some searchers
believing that the missing expedition had gone north up the Wellington Channel
(mentioned in Franklin's orders) to proceed westwards through a polar basin
clear of ice.

The first news of Franklin's winter quarters of 1845-46 was brought to
England by the *Prince Albert*, a schooner of 80 tons, in the autumn of 1850.
Sponsored by Lady Franklin and by public subscription, the expedition spent
only one summer season in the Arctic. Her captain was Charles Forsyth. At Cape
Riley, on Beechey Island, an appendage of the much much larger Devon Island
along the north shore of Barrow Strait, a message left by Captain Erasmus
Ommanney in HMS *Assistance* earlier in the summer was found. This reported the
discovery of signs of the expedition on Beechey Island. The *Prince Albert* brought
back pieces of rope and canvas and some meat bones from Cape Riley. Alone
among the fifteen vessels in the Arctic during the summer of 1850, the little
Prince Albert had been sent in the right direction. Drafted by Jane Franklin,
Forsyth's orders were to sail down Prince Regent Inlet, to cross North Somerset
and then to proceed down Peel Sound and what was later called Franklin Strait,

beyond the point reached the previous year by James Clark Ross, less than 200 miles from King William Island, off which the *Erebus* and *Terror* had been abandoned in 1848. It was a disappointment to Jane Franklin that the *Prince Albert* had navigated only some 70 miles down the inlet when stopped by ice.

The *Prince Albert* had left from Aberdeen in June 1850, when two other small vessels, the schooner *Felix* and her tender the yacht *Mary* (12 tons), had already departed from Loch Ryan on the west coast of Scotland. The schooner *Felix* was commanded by another veteran, even older than Richardson, Sir John Ross, aged 72. His patron, Sir Felix Booth, had been willing to support the expedition, but died suddenly and then, understandably, the Admiralty turned Ross's offer down, though it was willing to approve his plans. Eventually, the Hudson's Bay Company launched an appeal to which it subscribed generously and Ross himself succeeded in raising funds by writing to various prominent persons, including the Duke of Wellington and Lord Palmerston. From one of these, Lord Hardwicke, he received the following reply.

> A man at your time of life undertaking on his own means so severe and arduous a service, is a rare and splendid example of devotion to friendship and science. If my refusal to subscribe toward it would *stop you*, I would act on this selfish and stingy suggestion; but as I see by the subscription list you are likely to gain the required sum, I shall give my mite to so good a cause. You will therefore find £50 at your disposal at Messrs. Cocks & Co. 43 Charing Cross . . .[12]

The *Felix* was newly built and strengthened at Ayr and was, of course, named after Sir Felix Booth. Her crew of twelve whalers from Peterhead and particularly another polar veteran, Thomas Abernethy, were all drunk on departure, but, despite this rather inauspicious beginning, the *Felix* and the *Mary* caught up first with the *Prince Albert* and then with the other vessels engaged in the search, off Greenland, in early August. A Danish-speaking Eskimo interpreter named Adam Beck had been appointed by Ross (who was fluent in the Scandinavian languages) earlier in the voyage.

The ships ahead consisted of a naval squadron commanded by Captain Horatio Austin in HMS *Resolute*, accompanied by HMS *Assistance* (Captain Erasmus Ommanney) both sailing ships of over 400 tons. They were escorted by two screw steamers, the *Pioneer* (Lieutenant Sherard Osborn) and the *Intrepid* (Lieutenant Bertie Cator) both of 400 tons, 60hp and 150ft long. The *Resolute* and *Assistance* were manned by sixty officers and men, while the steamers carried thirty. Two other vessels were sent by the Admiralty. These were the brigs HMS *Lady Franklin* and HMS *Sophia*, both with appropriate figureheads, that of the *Lady Franklin* being Hope leaning upon an anchor. They were under the command of Captain William Penny, the Aberdeen whaling master, a rough diamond who had gone to sea at the age of twelve. Unlike the younger Scoresby, and perhaps through the help and encouragement of the two ladies, who took a great liking to him, Penny was given a naval commission. He could claim to have made the first effort to contact the *Erebus* and the *Terror*, during the summer of 1847 by sailing into Lancaster Sound.[13]

The remaining 'discovery ships' sailing, or more often towing and tracking, towards the North Water – the usually ice-free sea at the head of Baffin Bay – were the *Advance* and *Rescue*, which formed the first Grinnell expedition, commanded by Lieutenant E J De Haven, USN, who had taken part in the United States Exploring Expedition of 1838–42 and therefore had experience of navigation in ice. The *Advance* and *Rescue* were hermaphrodite brigs, the first of 140 tons, the other of 87 tons, both well strengthened for use in ice. The *Advance* was manned by four officers and thirteen men, while the *Rescue* carried four officers and twelve men. The surgeon of the *Advance* was Dr Elisha Kent Kane, who wrote a beautifully illustrated account of the expedition and who was to lead the second Grinnell expedition in search of Franklin in 1853–55. The diary by the first officer of the *Rescue*, Robert Randolph Carter, has been published recently.[14]

This American expedition was equipped and sent in response to Jane Franklin's plea. It was unofficially aided by Congress, manned by naval personnel and financed largely by Mr Henry Grinnell of New York. Her biographer tells us that in March 1850, Jane Franklin began a correspondence with Henry Grinnell which was to last for more than twenty years. The American vessels had left New York on 22 May 1850, only to encounter a heavy squall, which sent all their well-wishers home, apart from Mr Grinnell and his sons in a 'beautiful pilot boat', which continued in company for three more days.[15]

In Baffin Bay, the steamers of Captain Austin's squadron proved their worth in towing not only their consorts, the *Resolute* and *Assistance*, 'our bluff bowed worse halfs' as the *Pioneer*'s captain described them, but the smaller British vessels towards Lancaster Sound. They also succeeded in making progress through the pack by charging and re-charging the floes, in the manner of modern icebreakers. One of the midshipmen in the *Assistance*, Clements Markham, described in his diary how they worked through the ice for thirty-two days in July and August 1850.

> From this time [10 July], till we got into the North water (which generally makes from Cape York to Ponds Bay) it was incessant but very agreeable work. Cutting docks, tracking along the edge of the floes, pressing into narrow lanes of water, blasting the ice with powder, sometimes stopped altogether and nipped by two floes; sometimes sending the steamers to charge the ice at full power, playing rounders, chasing bears, shooting little auks: with lovely weather, incessant daylight and strange fairy like scenery.[16]

A combination of great experience in ice navigation, an iron will, and enthusiasm for the course, as the search for Franklin came to be known, kept Captain Penny well to the fore, despite being dependent on sail alone.

The gallant little American brigs, without the benefit of steam and not much larger, as Dr Kane pointed out, than those of Frobisher and Baffin so long ago, suffered a delay of five weeks on the northward track. The doctor was busy not only sketching with his pencil, but writing his journal, which became the basis for his best-selling book during the voyage. Sitting, during a calm, on a rock in 'Bessie Cove' to the far north of Baffin Bay, he was struck with the Arctic originality of every thing around. It was midnight, and the sun, now to the north, was hidden by the rocks; but the whole atmosphere was pink with light. Over head and around me whirled innumerable crowds of Auks and Ivory gulls, screeching with execrable clamor, almost in contact with my person. On the frozen lake below, contrasting with its snowy covering, were a couple of ravens, fighting zealously for a morsel of garbage; and high up, on the crags above me, sat some unmoved phlegmatic burgomasters [Glaucus gulls].[17]

Smith Sound, at the head of Baffin Bay, was later to be the route to both triumph and tragedy for Dr Kane and for subsequent American expeditions.

From Lieutenant Sherard Osborn, Captain of the screw steamer *Pioneer*, we have an observant, lively and perceptive account of the Franklin Search in the years 1850-51. In his book, *Stray leaves from an Arctic journal*, first published in 1852, his comments are at times as sharp as the bow of his ship, but always good humoured. Of the *Resolute* and *Assistance*, both barque-rigged, with 'their hulls strengthened according to the most orthodox arctic rules', to such an extent, he remarked that

instead of presenting the appearance of a body intended for progress through the water, they resembled nothing so much as very ungainly knife-trays, and their bows formed a buttress which rather pushed the water than passed through it.[18]

In a personal letter Osborn likened the towing of the *Resolute* and *Assistance* by the *Pioneer* and *Intrepid* to 'leashing two Hippopotami to a couple of Greyhounds'.[19] However, he praised the internal fittings of the vessels as 'most perfect', and the 'most comfortable' ever to winter in the ice.

Hot air was distributed by means of an ingenious apparatus throughout the lower deck and cabins. Double bulkheads prevented the ingress of unneccessary cold air. A cooking battery, as the French say, promised abundance of room for roasting, boiling, baking, and an arrangement for thawing snow to make water for our daily consumption. The mess places of the crew were neatly fitted in man-of-war style . . . A long tier of cabins on either side showed how large a proportion of officers these vessels carried; but it was so far satisfactory, that it assured us of a division of labour, which would make arctic labours comparatively light.

Osborn refers presumably in the last sentence to the need for the officers to lead the numerous 'travelling parties' to be despatched from the ships. There were spacious captains' cabins and gun-rooms large enough to seat all the officers for meals.[20]

The *Pioneer* and *Intrepid* were sister vessels, used previously to transport cattle and rigged as three-masted schooners. Their decks and frames were doubled with tough planking. They were strengthened internally at the bow, and because a few 'catastrophe-lovers' in England had 'consigned Franklin to death because he had steam-engines and screws', special precautions were taken to ensure that the vessels would 'still be left fit to swim' in the event of the ice's tearing off the screw, rudder and sternpost. Other wiseacres had curled their lips 'in derision and pity', when Osborn spoke of 'cutting and breaking ice with an iron stem'. Internally, the arrangements were much as those, in the ships, although there

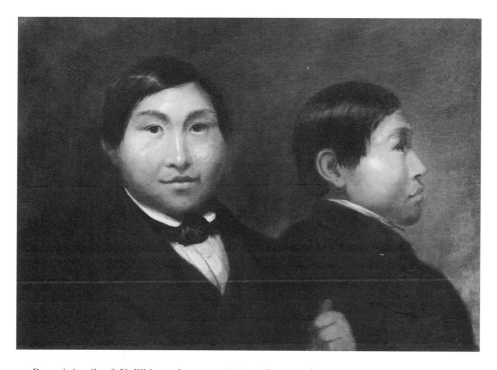

Portrait in oils of Kallihirua, the young Eskimo from northwest Greenland, who was befriended by Captain Ommanney of HMS *Assistance*, during the Franklin Search expedition of 1850-51 and afterwards in Canterbury, England. (NMM, BHC2813)

were difficulties because the 'large mass of cold iron machinery acted as a rapid refrigerator'. In addition, from the small place in the bows occupied by the men to the officers' cabins aft, there was a deadweight of up to 300 tons of coal.

Captain Ommanney landed from the *Assistance* at Cape York, where a young man named Qalasersuaq, anglicised as Kallihirua, joined the ship as interpreter. He became a great favourite with his shipmates and eventually trained in Canterbury at St. Augustine's Missionary College, as Captain Ommanney's protégé. His death in Newfoundland, still as a very young man, greatly saddenned his friends there and in England. Further north, in Wolstenholme Sound or Fjord, the recently vacated wintering place of HMS *North Star* (Captain Saunders) in 1849-50 was discovered in what is called North Star Bay. On its stony shore, there is a gravestone 'set in the top of a massive heap of boulders . . . with the beautifully carved inscription, 'SACRED to the MEMORY of Wm. Sharp of HMS North Star: who departed this life Nov, 1849 aged, 26 years.'[21]

This discovery did much to convince Ommanney and the other captains (apart from Sir John Ross) of the untruth of the assertion made by Adam Beck, a Greenland Eskimo and Ross's interpreter, that in 1846 two ships had been wrecked on the north west coast of Greenland, and that some of the men had been murdered by the natives, while others had drowned.[22] There were three

other tombstones of seamen from the *North Star*, but more tragic remains were
found in a hut where, in the words of one of the search squadron:

> Huddled together in numbers lay a heap of human beings, neglected and abandoned,
> as if the angel of death had taken possession of the land . . . It was a sight that struck a
> chill through the heart, and one that cannot easily be effaced from the memory. Age
> and youth; the manly father by his stalwart son; the tender mother by her cherished
> babe, lay here without distinction of years, of sex, of relationship.[23]

These were Greenlanders (Inughuit), struck down by famine or an epidemic,
perhaps contracted from the *North Star*. After this distressing visit Austin's
squadron and their fellow searchers were able to enter Lancaster Sound, and proceed westwards. As the American brig, *Advance*, was driven ahead in a gale on 21
August, she came up to a topsail schooner which was 'fluttering over the waves
like a crippled bird'. It turned out to be the *Felix* and her tender, commanded by
Sir John Ross, whom Dr Kane described as follows:

> He was a square-built man, apparently very little stricken in years, and well able to
> bear his part in the toils and hazards of life. He has been wounded in four separate
> engagements – twice desperately – and is scarred from head to foot. He has conduct-
> ed two Polar expeditions already, and performed in one of them the unparalleled feat
> of wintering four years in Arctic snows. And here he is again, in a flimsy cockle-shell,
> after contributing his purse and his influence, embarked himself in the crusade of
> search for a lost comrade. We met him off Admiralty Inlet, just about the spot at which
> he was picked up seventeen years before.[24]

All the vessels engaged in the search sooner or later penetrated Barrow Strait as
far as Beechey Island, which is what the French call a *presque-île*. Less than two
miles wide, with steep cliffs or terraces culminating in a plateau about 800 feet
high, it is joined by a low gravel isthmus to its large neighbour, Devon Island.
Union Bay was given its name in 1850, because so many of the search vessels met
there. Nearby is Cape Riley, a bluff headland rising to some 700 feet and it was
here that the first signs of the missing expedition were found on 23 August 1850
by Captain Ommanney. He had landed with a party of officers a mile from Cape
Riley and was walking on the beach under the Cape, when they came across 'fragments of Naval Stores, portions of ragged clothing, preserved meat tins etc.',
which must have been there for three years at least. The articles were collected
and a search was made for a record, but none was found. The party's own record
was left in a beacon on the cape, as Ommanney reported:

> A Cairn being seen on the summit of Beechey Island, the Steam Tender [*Intrepid*] was
> pressed through the packed ice to examine it in the full confidence that some docu-
> ment would be found, containing information of the missing Expedition . . . but on
> pulling down the Cairn to my great disappointment no record could be found, altho'
> it was carefully examined and the site dug out with a spade. A few small shot were
> found lying on a stone which formed the top of the Cairn, it was rebuilt and a docu-
> ment deposited in it.[25]

During the morning of 27 August Captain Penny, Sir John Ross, and
Commander Phillips (Ross's second-in-command) were conferring with Captain

De Haven and Dr Kane, the Americans, as to the best way to search further when a messenger was seen, making all haste over the ice. 'Graves, Captain Penny! Graves! Franklin's winter quarters!' he shouted. Between Cape Riley and Beechey Island lies Erebus Bay, named after Franklin's ship. It was on the low terraced land on the northern part of Beechey Island that the expedition's winter quarters were discovered. The inscriptions, cut by a chisel on the wooden head-boards, commemorated John Hartnell, died 4 January 1846; W Braine RM, died 3 April 1846, both from the *Erebus*; and John Torrington, died 1 January 1846 on board *Terror*. The burial mounds were arranged in a row, facing Cape Riley. The first two were protected with limestone slabs. According to Dr Kane, the third was not so well finished as the others, 'but its general appearance was more grave-like, more like the sleeping place of Christians in happier lands'. The engraving in Dr Kane's narrative, entitled 'Beechy [sic] Island – Franklin's first winter quarters', done from a sketch by the American surgeon, shows one of the most romantic and evocative of polar landscapes. Here are the three graves of Franklin's men, set on an icy shore, backed by beetling cliffs and lit by a full moon, half obscured by the clouds. This was drawn by the artist, James Hamilton, from Dr Kane's sketch.[26]

Unfortunately, these sad mortal remains have not been allowed to rest in peace on the desolate and lonely shores of Beechey Island. The exhumations by Dr Owen Beattie in 1984 and 1986 were done to test his theory that high levels of lead in the bodies contributed to the disaster of the lost Franklin expedition of 1845-48 and this appears to have been confirmed by work on the samples removed during the autopsies of the three bodies buried on Beechey Island.[27] The disinterments demonstrated the careful way that the burials had been per-formed, with copper plaques on the coffins of Torrington and Braine. That of John Hartnell bore no plaque and the grave had already been disturbed. A letter of 1852 in the archives of the Hydrographic Office, Taunton, cited by Beattie and Geiger, revealed that this had been done by Captain E A Inglefield, one of the naval officers.

Another letter from Inglefield to John Barrow of the Admiralty, dated 14 September 1852, described how on arriving at a snow-covered Beechey Island on 7 September he found that Captain Belcher had not examined the graves, which Inglefield resolved to do on his own responsibility. He landed with a party of his officers only, as he did not want 'to engage the superstitions feelings of the sailors by allowing the crews of either ship to know what we did'.

We started with Pick axe and shovel, the ground like flint striking fire with each blow from the Pick, six of us worked unremittingly till the perspiration at last bathed the lid of the coffin of poor Hartnell – Poor fellow. I was most anxious to have examined the body that the cause of death might be ascertained, but our utmost efforts had been exhausted and to lay bare the middle of it to take off the copper plate that was nailed on the lid and to discover that no relic had been laid with him that could give a clue to the fate of his fellows was all our strength and the intense cold that had set in with mid-night permitted our doing. The coffin was decently covered with blue cloth and white

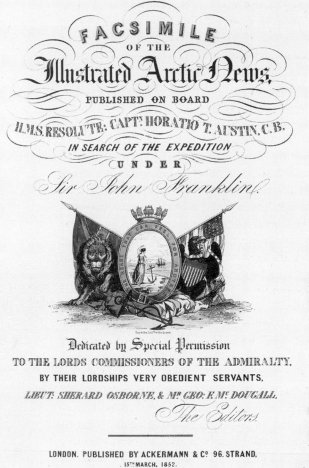

FACSIMILE OF THE *Illustrated Arctic News*, PUBLISHED ON BOARD H.M.S. RESOLUTE: CAPT: HORATIO T. AUSTIN, C.B. IN SEARCH OF THE EXPEDITION UNDER *Sir John Franklin*.

Dedicated by Special Permission TO THE LORDS COMMISSIONERS OF THE ADMIRALTY, BY THEIR LORDSHIPS VERY OBEDIENT SERVANTS. *LIEUT: SHERARD OSBORNE, & M.R GEO: F. M.c DOUGALL, The Editors.*

LONDON. PUBLISHED BY ACKERMANN & C.º 96. STRAND. 15.TH MARCH, 1852.
By Appointment
TO HER MAJESTY THE QUEEN, H.R.H. PRINCE ALBERT, H.R.H. THE DUCHESS OF KENT & THE ROYAL FAMILY.

Title page to the published version of the *Illustrated Arctic News,* the magazine first produced aboard *Resolute* (Captain Austin) searching for Franklin, 1850-51. With both officers and men contributing, such papers were a feature of British polar expeditions. (NMM, PX8005)

tape was nailed round the edges. The copper plate and the cloth or rather some small portions I have preserved. A piece of the cloth I enclose you.

Inglefield finished his account of this midnight excursion with a plea to Barrow.

All this I am telling *you* only, and I beg you will use your own discretion in keeping it to yourself or communicating it, as the prejudices of some people would deem this intended work of charity sacrilege: It was one o'clock ere we got on board.[28]

The letter from Captain Inglefield to the Hydrographer of the Navy, Rear Admiral Sir Francis Beaufort, also dated 14 September 1852, as quoted by Beattie and Geiger, provides a different version. It relates that only Inglefield and Dr Sutherland, the surgeon of his ship, the *Isobel*, were there. 'My doctor assisted me, and I have had my hand on the arm and the face of poor Hartnell. He was decently clad in a cotton shirt, and though the dark night precluded our seeing, still our touch detected that a wasting illness was the cause of dissolution.' Inglefield described the 'curious and solemn scene on the silent snow-covered sides of the famed Beechey Island, where the two of us stood at midnight. The pale moon looking down upon us as we silently worked with pickaxe and shovel at the hard frozen tomb . . .'[29]

This attempt to exhume one of the bodies took place two years after the graves had been found. The reason for it, as Inglefield implies, was that despite a profusion of evidence in the way of scraps of blue cloth, canvas, cordage and paper, preserved meat cans, sledge tracks, coals, wood shavings and the graves themselves, no record could be found indicating the intended direction of the *Erebus* and *Terror*, and indeed whether they had departed and not sunk at their anchorage, as some came to suspect. One of the more curious finds was a pile of some six hundred preserved meat tins 'arranged in regular order', which had been emptied and were 'now filled with limestone pebbles, perhaps to serve as convenient ballast on boating expeditions'.[30] Even more puzzling, indeed tantalising, was the cairn 'mounted on a high and conspicuous portion of the shore, and evidently intended to attract observation; but, though several parties examined it, digging round it in every direction, not a single particle of information could be gleaned'. To the writer of these words, Dr Kane, and to other searchers, including, as we have seen, Captain Ommanney, its discoverer this appeared extraordinary; and 'for so able and practiced an Arctic commander as Sir John Franklin, an incomprehensible omission'.[31]

However incomprehensible this may appear to us too, a detailed study by Dr R J Cyriax, the historian of the expedition of 1845-48 and of the Franklin Search, led him to the opposite conclusion that:

> . . . Franklin cannot justifiably be blamed for having omitted to leave records on the shores past which he sailed, for this omission was neither exceptional nor contrary to his orders . . . Sir John Richardson stated that 'it was understood' that Franklin would 'cause piles of stones or signal posts to be erected on conspicuous headlands at convenient times'. If no 'convenient times' arose, no records would have been left.[32]

An interesting point was made by one of the Arctic officers, Sherard Osborn, who wrote to John Barrow, junior, on 15 August 1852: 'We have turned every stone . . . without finding any record, which is incomprehensible to me. Unless indeed they had built the Cairn, with an intention of leaving a record before starting – the ice opened since they bolted without leaving time, for it would take at least 1½ hours to reach the summit of Beechey Island, where they have built their cairn.'[33]

All sorts of things were found on Beechey Island, including a pair of cashmere gloves, on which were stones to stop them blowing away and, which had been lying there since 1846, when their wearer put them out to dry. They were taken up carefully by Sherard Osborn, whose subsequent experience led him to conclude that there was always a hasty departure in the anxiety to leave the prison of winter quarters and that people left 'too well pleased to escape to care much for a handful of shavings, an old coal-bag, or a washing tub'.[34]

The dates on the three graves showed of course that the *Erebus* and *Terror* had wintered at Beechey Island, having presumably found no open water in 1845 to the south and west of Cape Walker, which lies north of Prince of Wales Island on the southern shores of Barrow Strait. Franklin's orders directed him in this eventuality, to try for a passage up Wellington Channel, on the north shore, between Devon and Cornwallis islands, discovered but not entered by Parry in 1819 and 1820. We know from the two Franklin records deposited on King William Island that this was done and that the ships turned south after reaching latitude 77 °N thus circumnavigating Cornwallis Island (between Devon and Bathurst islands). This was not repeated for another century.[35] As Cyriax points out, the ships were by then in Barrow Strait about 100 miles to the west of Beechey Island, but quite rightly during the outward voyage Franklin must have decided that secure winter quarters would be found on that island.

Not knowing, of course, that Franklin's ships had gone south after leaving winter quarters, a considerable effort was put into a search to the north.

The *Felix* (Captain John Ross) and the *Lady Franklin* and *Sophia* (Captain Penny) had found good winter quarters in Assistance Bay, Cornwallis Island, whereas the naval squadron, commanded by Captain Austin, in navigating further to the west, was beset off Griffith Island (a small island south of Cornwallis Island in Barrow Strait) and had to winter there.

The American vessels were not intended to winter, but they were caught in the ice of Wellington Channel and drifted as far north as latitude 75° 24´, where new land was sighted (the northwest corner of Devon Island) and named after Henry Grinnell 'in honor of the head and heart of the man in whose philanthropic mind originated the idea of this expedition, and to whose munificence it owes its existence'.[36] The Americans were destined to be carried by the ice for a thousand miles along Parry Channel, far from their 'English friends' in a way which reminded Dr Kane of the situation of Back's *Terror* in 1836. On 23 September he wrote in his diary:

> How shall I describe to you this pressure, its fearfulness and sublimity? . . . The voices of the ice and the heavy swash of the overturned hummock-tables are at this moment dinning in my ears. 'All hands' are on deck fighting our grim enemy . . . No vessel has ever been caught by winter in these waters. We are lifted bodily eighteen inches out of the water. The hummocks are reared up around the ship, so as to rise in some cases a couple of feet above our bulwarks – five feet above our deck . . . often ten and twelve feet high . . . Add to this darkness, snow, cold, and the absolute destitution of surrounding shores.[37]

The recently published diary of Robert Randolph Carter is a contrast to Kane's polished and evocative prose. It is colloquial and candid in its comments, quite often amusing too. For example, he describes Captain Austin as 'the jolliest old Englishman ever seen' and is unashamably envious of the roomy, clean, well-heated 'splendid craft' of the naval squadron, in contrast to 'Poor Rescue, the smallest, dirtiest unhappiest little boat.'[38] Amid more terrifying scenes, still prisoners of the ice, the two brigs eventually passed eastwards into Davis Strait. The *Advance* reached New York on 30 September 1851 and the *Rescue* on 7 October, to be welcomed home from the pier-head by Henry Grinnell. They had survived a perilous voyage, but they had not found Franklin.

*   *   *

Nor, of course, had the other wintering expeditions, although they made strenuous efforts to do so by sending out what were called 'travelling parties' from the ships in the spring of 1851. But first of all Beechey Island was combed and combed again for a record which might indicate where these travelling parties should go. As Sherard Osborn put it:

> Everyone felt that there was something so inexplicable in the non-discovery of any record, some written evidence of the intentions of Franklin and Crozier on leaving this spot, that each of us kept on returning to again search over the ground, in the hope that it had been merely overlooked in the feverish haste of the first discovery of the cairns . . .[39]

In September, winter came upon the naval squadron. Early in the following month, Lieutenant McClintock of HMS *Assistance* urged the need to send depot-laying parties on the intended search routes of spring 1851. McClintock and Dr Bradford set out towards Melville Island (far to the west, where Parry had wintered in 1819-20) and Lieutenant Aldrich set out towards Lowther Island, while Lieutenant Mecham was to search for traces of Franklin between Assistance Harbour and Cape Martyr. Sherard Osborn described his own short autumn journey with Mr May of HMS *Resolute* along the shores of Cornwallis Island.[40] On one of the terraces they came across a conical stone building of twenty feet in circumference, whose builders, he remarked, must have known the strength of an arched roof to withstand heavy snowfalls. They had used 'much skill and nicety' in placing the limestone slabs to preserve its conical form. The growth of moss indicated that the ruin had been built long ago. Many such deserted dwellings and caches were seen by the searching parties, and there is a record of those 'Esquimaux remains discovered by our travelling parties' in *Arctic miscellanies*, the newspaper produced by the officers and seamen of the search expedition.[41]

Not long after leaving the ruin, Sherard Osborn's party stopped for the night. 'Four of us (for, in arctic travelling, officer and man are united by the common bond of labour) erected the tent over a space which we had cleaned of the larger and rougher pieces of limestone . . .' Cooking was done on a boat's stove, which measured eighteen by nine inches burning *lignum vitae*. Meanwhile, Osborn took his gun and struck inland across a landscape of the dead:

> No pen can tell of the unredeemed loneliness of an October evening in this part of the polar world; the monotonous, rounded outline of the adjacent hills, as well as the flat, unmeaning valleys, were of one uniform colour, either deadly white with snow, or striped with brown where too steep for the winter mantle as yet to find a holding ground . . . The very wind scorned courtesy to such a repulsive landscape, and as the stones, before the blast, rattled down the slope of a ravine, it only recalled dead men's bones and motion in a catacomb.

Gloomy thoughts were banished near the tent – 'the pemmican is all ready, sir'. However, the 'greasy compound', instead of being made supposedly of the best rumpsteaks and suet, to the party's 'then untutored tastes' it appeared to consist of 'broken down horse and Russian tallow'. After six tablespoonfuls they had eaten enough. Osborn commented that the day would come when, 'hungry and lean', they would devour a pound of it and find it delicious!

After the meal, a waterproof sheet was spread over the pebbles and each man got into his sleeping bag, 'in order that the operation of undressing might be decently performed'. Jackets and wet boots were their pillows, and strong smelling wolfskin robes were laid over and under the sleeping bags. Pipes were then lit and the grog ration served out and, while the cook was clearing up and making ready for the morning, as well as securing the food on the sledges from bears or foxes,

> many a tough yarn is told or joke made. . . . The cook reports all right, comes in, hooks up the door, tucks in the end of the fur robe, and seven jolly mortals, with a brown-holland tent over their heads and a winter's gale without, try to nestle their sides amongst the softest stones, and soon drop into such a sleep as those only enjoy who drag a sledge all day, with the temperature 30° below freezing point.

Breakfast in the morning consisted of boiling hot chocolate, served with frozen pork and biscuit, and during a day of calm, then a gale, they completed the circuit of the bay without finding any trace of Franklin and arrived at the ships on 12 October 1850, the last of the autumn sledge journeys. From these small beginnings, we shall see that many notable journeys were subsequently made.

Meanwhile, with the onset of winter, the vessels were housed–in and the upper decks cleared of lumber, so as to make space for exercise in bad weather under the awning. The stoves and warming apparatus were set to work and the boats were secured on the ice and 'masts and yards made as snug as possible'. In addition, 'rows of posts [were] placed to show the road in the darkness and snowstorms from ship to ship; holes cut through the ice into the sea, to secure a ready supply of water in the event of fire; arrangements made to insure cleanliness of ships and crews, and a winter routine entered upon'. The seamen exercised their ingenuity in the building of snow walls, posts and houses, as well as 'obelisks, sphinxes, vases, cannon, and, lastly, a stately Britannia, looking to the westward'.

As the long Arctic night began in early November, with the last sight of the sun, in 74½° North latitude, Sherard Osborn observed that

> light-hearted and confident as we felt in our resources, one could not but feel, looking upon the dreary scene which spread around us on every side, how much our lives were in His hands who tempers the wind to the shorn lamb; and wanting must he have been in feeling who did not offer up a heartfelt prayer that returning day and returning summer might find him able and fit to undergo the hardship and fatigue of journeys on foot, to seek for his long-lost fellow seamen.[42]

The winter gave full scope to the talents of officers and men of the naval squadron in the performance of theatricals (with the making of scenery and costumes), the production of two newspapers (one illustrated), a voluntary evening school, lectures by the officers, a musical society consisting of officers and men

'HMS *Assistance* and *Pioneer* breaking out of winter quarters,' by W W May. Despite breaking out of the ice on this occasion, the vessels were eventually abandoned. (NMM, PT2914 CT)

'who never sang before, and maybe . . . will never sing again', a glee club, an instrumental band and a wonderful fancy dress ball in which Captain Austin retained his incognito as an 'odd figure uttering the cry of "old chairs to mend!" until his 'well known laugh' revealed 'our ever-cheerful Commodore'.[43] Captain Austin's dinner parties were a great aid to morale and there appears to have been a degree of socialising between the naval vessels and even with those of Captain Penny and Sir John Ross, 20 miles away.

We are told by Clements Markham that Captain Horatio Thomas Austin was a 'stout little man, with florid complexion, bright eyes and curling iron-grey hair . . . A great talker, energetic and of undoubted ability', he was 'fond of detail, and carefully considered every point himself'. He was the son of Nelson's coxswain and had served in the *Chanticleer* (Captain Henry Foster) during her scientific voyage to the South Atlantic and Southern Ocean, and under Hoppner in the *Fury*, 1824-25. He was an enthusiast for the use of steam and had commanded the navy's first steam vessel *Salamander*.

> A very experienced officer, he based his decisions on wide knowledge, though he was a little narrow in his views. But for managing the internal economy of a ship, and organising the details of an expedition, he was admirable. Captain Austin was genial and warm-hearted.[44]

The Captain of *Assistance*, Erasmus Ommanney, had taken part in the Battle of Navarino and had served under James Clark Ross in HMS *Cove*, 1836, during a winter voyage to rescue the whalers in the Arctic. He had played an active part in the relief of famine in Ireland by the Navy in 1847. 'He was a little man, with rather a black face and fishy eyes . . . Very ambitious, but without capacity to match, he was at the same time kind-hearted and good-natured . . .'[45]

The same writer (Clements Markham), who was a midshipman during this naval expedition of 1850–51, thought that Sherard Osborn, Captain of *Pioneer*, should have commanded it. 'He was its greatest ornament and its historian, full of enthusiasm and knowledge.' However, he may not have made 'sufficient allowance for a man so differently constituted as old Austin. They did not hit it off. But their collisions struck off sparks which threw light around'.[46] We shall hear more of Francis Leopold McClintock, Captain of the *Intrepid*.

Sherard Osborn wrote a lively book, full of good humour, called *Stray leaves from an Arctic journal*, about the expedition, some of which is quoted here. Another lively publication was *Arctic miscellanies*, the newspaper produced during the expedition and published later in London. In it are contributions from the officers and seamen, as well as Sir John Ross and others. Osborn observed the editors of the newspapers floundering to write a leader, and their 'sailor contributors, whose hands were more accustomed to the tar-brush than the pen' turning out 'flowing sentences by the aid of well-thumbed dictionaries'. Perhaps his best sketch is of the sailors:

> On wooden stools, leaning over long tables might be seen a row of serious and anxious faces, which put one in mind of the days of cane and birch – an arctic school. Tough old marines curving 'pothooks and hangers' as if their very lives depended on their performances, with an occasional burst of petulance, such as, 'D—— the pen, it won't write! I beg pardon, sir; this 'ere pen will splutter! Or some big-whiskered top-man, with slate in hand, reciting his multiplication table, and grinning at approval; whilst a 'scholar', as the cleverest were termed, gave the instructor occasionally a hard task to preserve his learned superiority.

We see another side to the British sailor in the appearance of the three graves of Franklin's men on Beechey Island. Writing when the Royal Navy kept the peace of the world, Sherard Osborn described them as 'scrupulously neat', like 'all that English seamen construct'.

> Go where you will over the globe's surface – afar in the East, or afar in the West, down among the coral-girded isles of the South Sea or here where the grim North frowns upon the sailor's grave – you will always find it alike; it is the monument raised by rough hands, but affectionate hearts over the last home of their messmate; it breathes of the quiet churchyard in some of England's many nooks . . . and the ornaments that nature decks herself with, even in the desolation of the frozen zone, were carefully culled to mark the seamen's last home.

These same seamen formed the backbone to the travelling parties which sledged north, south, and west of the winter quarters in search of Franklin, of whom, alas, they found no further trace. From the cairn erected by the men of the *Erebus* and *Terror* on the southern edge of the plateau at the height of Beechey Island, there was a view up and down Barrow Strait. One wonders how often Sir John Franklin and Captain Crozier climbed up to prospect the ice, when awaiting the release of the ships in the early summer of 1846. This would have been their view:

To the west, the land of Cornwallis Island stretched up Wellington Channel for many miles, and Cape Hotham locked with Griffith Island. In the southwest a dark mass of land showed, Cape Walker, and from Cape Bunny the southern shore of Barrow Strait spread itself until terminated in the steep wall-like cliffs of Cape Clarence and Leopold Island.[47]

Leopold Island was barely 40 miles away, looking ridiculously close on a fine day. It was there that Sir James Clark Ross wintered in 1848-49, little knowing that Franklin's own winter quarters of three years earlier had been so near. To the searchers of 1850-51, Cape Walker was an obvious goal, across Barrow Strait to the south because Franklin's orders were to proceed southwest from that point towards the mainland of North America, which he knew so well. Cape Walker is situated on Russell Island, a small island lying off the north coast of Prince of Wales Island. Surely he must have built a cairn and deposited a record there.

It has been pointed out by Clive Holland, the author of the massive chronology of Arctic exploration, that the methods of travel of the 1850-51 expedition, 'though extremely laborious, became the pattern for the Navy's famous sledge hauling tradition. These methods, introduced largely by Lieutenant (later Admiral Sir) Francis Leopold McClintock were such an improvement on earlier efforts as almost to eclipse these.[48] Holland summarises the methods devised largely by McClintock, as follows. They

> involved using a team of six or seven men led by one officer to haul each sledge. For each major journey one 'extended' travelling party was accompanied along part of the route by one 'limited' party carrying additional provisions and often laying depots in preparation for the main party's return. Each sledge was given its own name, flag and motto to aid morale.[49]

The sledges and equipment for Austin's squadron had been brought from London (unlike those of Captain Penny, made during the winter on board the *Lady Franklin* and *Sophia*). These naval sledges were ingeniously made in Woolwich dockyard of tough and well-seasoned wood. In Sherard Osborn's words:

> They were shod with iron, and the cross-bars or battens which connected the two runners, and formed the floor upon which the load was placed, were lashed in their places by us when required for use. At the four corners of the sledges light iron stanchions dropped into sockets, and formed the support for the sides of a species of tray or boat, capable of serving to ferry the sledge crew across water in an emergency, as well as to keep the provisions and clothing in it dry.

The 'boats' made of oiled canvas were preferred to those of gutta percha. The sledges weighed 120lbs and each one carried equipment amounting to another 320lbs consisting of blankets, sleeping bags, a tent, floor cloth, shovel, cooking apparatus, clothes and other personal effects such as soap and a comb, spare boots, bandages and other first-aid equipment, including opium, spare amunition and, last but not least, kites and string. In addition to this there were the provisions. The daily scale of provisions was: 1lb of pemmican, 6 ounces of boiled pork, 12 ounces of biscuit, ¾ gill of concentrated rum, ½ ounce of

'Beechey Island: Franklin's first winter quarters', 1845-46, discovered by the
search expeditions of 1850-51. Drawn by James Hamilton from the sketch by
Dr Kane, surgeon of the first US Grinnell Expedition. (Plate from E K
Kane's *Personal Narrative*, NMM, D928)

tobacco, 1 ounce of biscuit dust, ¾ ounces tea and sugar, ¾ ounces of chocolate
and sugar on alternate days, ½ ounce of lime-juice. The complete load of a long-
party (long distance) sledge, dragged by seven men, is given as 1408lbs which
works out at 201lbs per man. The officer carried a gun, powder and ball, telescope, compass and notebook. All were heavily clad against the cold.

Sherard Osborn provides much more interesting detail of the sledges and
sledging, including the names of the fifteen sledges and their mottoes. Captain
Ommanney's long-party sledge, *Reliance*, had the Latin motto, *Domine dirige nos*
(Direct us O Lord), while Lieutenant W H Browne's supporting sledge
Enterprise had the longer motto:

Gaze where some distant speck a sail implies,
With all the thirsting gaze of enterprise.

These formed part of the southern division of seven sledges, making for Cape
Walker and beyond, led by Captain Ommanney, with Lieutenant Osborn as
second-in-command. Osborn's long-party sledge was the *True Blue*, and its
motto *Nil desperandum*.

A northern division of two sledges under Lieutenant R D Aldrich (sledge *Lady
Franklin*, with supporting sledge *Hotspur*), was to travel past Byam Martin Island
up the unexplored channel between Bathurst and Melville islands in order to
intercept the *Erebus* and *Terror* had they sailed north up Wellington Channel for

Bering Strait. A western division, under Lieutenant F L McClintock (sledge *Perseverance*), and consisting of five sledges, was to make for Parry's furthest, Melville Island. A depot 40 miles in advance laid in the autumn for this party, had been replenished by G F McDougal, after depredations by Polar Bears. Osborn goes into some detail to explain how the use of supporting parties and depots enabled long distances to be travelled.

The sledges were mustered on 12 April 1851, at –50 °F, before marching 'with due military pomp' to the starting point off Griffith Island, in two columns under the senior officers. However, records Osborn,

> Our sense of decorum was constantly overthrown by the gambols of diverse puppies given to us by Captain Penny, with small sledges attached to them, their food duly marked and weighed, with flags and mottoes, perfect facsimiles of our own, which were racing about, entangling themselves, howling for assistance, or else running between the men's legs and capsizing them on the snow, amidst shouts of laughter, and sly witticisms at the *tenders*, as they were termed.

After lunch and an inspection, Captain Austin made a speech which, according to Osborn, 'buttered us all up admirably'. He thanked McClintock, 'to whose foresight, whilst in England, and to whose valuable information collated during his sledging experience under Sir James Ross in 1849, we were now indebted for the perfect equipment we now had with us'.

In the evening of 15 April, all hands were present to hear 'our warm-hearted leader' read a short prayer, then off went the sledges charging the huge hummocks in their paths, 'officers encouraging and showing the way; the men labouring and laughing' wrote Osborn – 'seven red-faced mortals, grinning and up to their waists in snow'. The southern division made an icy passage across Barrow Strait, many suffering from frozen feet, as white and cold as blocks of ice so that some invalids had to be sent back, reluctantly, to the ships. Cape Walker was reached at last through 50-foot ridges of ice. Made of red sandstone, the cape was found to be about 1,000 feet high. No cairn had been erected there by Franklin, but Lieutenant Browne was sent to examine the channel to the south (Peel Sound), whose eastern shore had already been searched for a certain distance by Sir James Clark Ross. As Sherard Osborn wrote, 'Franklin's remains were found in after years just 200 miles down this very channel'. The search party built a cairn to record their visit and left a depot of Halkett's india–rubber inflatable boats.

These were, of course, early days in the Franklin Search, or relatively so, when there was still hope of finding the crews of the *Erebus* and *Terror* alive. In praising the 'indomitable spirit of our seaman and marines,' Sherard Osborn had this to say:

> On them fell the hard labour, to us fell the honours of the enterprise . . . yet none excelled the men in cheerfulness and sanguine hopefulness of a successful issue to our enterprise, without which, of course, energy would soon have flagged. Gallant fellows! They met our commiseration with a smile, and a vow that they could do far more. They spoke of cold as 'Jack Frost', a real tangible foe, with whom they could combat

and whom they would master. Hunger was met with a laugh and a chuckle at some future feast, or jolly recollections, told in rough terms, of bygone good cheer; and often, standing on some neighbouring pile of ice, and scanning the horizon for those we sought, have I heard a rough voice encouraging the sledge-crew by saying 'Keep step, boys! Keep step! She (the sledge) is coming along almost by herself: there's the Erebus's masts showing over the point ahead! Keep step, boys! Keep step!

On the north west coast of Prince of Wales Island the *True Blue* pulled by Osborn's sledge crew parted company with Captain Ommanney's *Reliance* on 17 May. While the latter explored the channel to the southward, which proved to be a wide bay, later named Ommanney Bay, Osborn and crew attempted to penetrate further to the west, across the northern reach of what is now M'Clintock Channel, whose huge and tortured masses of ice were first seen by James Clark Ross off King William Island and in whose unrelenting grip the *Erebus* and *Terror* were perhaps still held in 1851, to the south of where Osborn tried to cross. He gave up the attempt when progress became more and more laborious and it was evident that the sledge would not stand the strain for long. Being 300 miles from the ships, the risk was too great to continue.

The party led by Lieutenant McClintock made a fine journey to Melville Island, Parry's furthest west. It was thought that if Franklin had sailed north up Wellington Channel and had been beset further west, he and the crews of the *Erebus* and *Terror* might have retreated south towards the American continent across Melville Island. Game in the form of polar bears and musk oxen were shot by McClintock's party for fresh food and fuel, whereas on Ommanney's and Osborn's journey there had been little sign of wildlife.

McClintock's biographer and messmate, Sir Clements Markham, who was a midshipman in HMS *Assistance*, makes a point of saying that the officer leading each sledge party would haul on the drag ropes with the men, unless he were needed to find the route. At the end of the day, in the tent, the officer would write up his journal and would wind the chronometer. His rest would be broken to take astronomical observations, presumably at noon, as it was usual to travel by night and sleep in the day. Markham also provides short pen portraits of James Wilkie, the captain of the *Perseverance* sledge and of the three other seamen and two marines, who took part in McClintock's memorable sledge journey of 770 miles in 80 days, the longest so far. He tells us that two out of the six later gave their lives in the search for Franklin.[50] The party rounded Cape Dundas, Parry's furthest west, sledged up Liddon's Gulf to Bushnan Cove and crossed overland to Winter Harbour. There, the huge sandstone block known as Parry's Rock, 10 feet high and 22ft long, still bore Fisher's inscription, on which no lichen had grown in the thirty years since it was done. A tame white hare lived beside the rock, which McClintock persuaded the men to leave rather than take home as a pet. Disappointed at finding no traces of the lost expedition, although surprised to find the tracks of Parry's cart appearing freshly made, McClintock's party left Melville Island on 6 June and after wading and struggling through bitterly cold melt-water pools on the ice floes, they arrived alongside HMS *Assistance* to an enthusiastic welcome.

The remaining parties examined lengthy stretches of coastline, but were equally unsuccessful in finding traces of Franklin. 'In all', writes Clive Holland, 'the season's activities added to the map the northern half of Prince of Wales Island, most of Cornwallis Island, the southern half of Bathurst and Melville Islands, most of Byam Martin Island, and in Barrow Strait, the coasts of Griffith, Lowther, Garrett and Russell islands'.[51] Sir Clements Markham praised the 1850-51 naval squadron as follows:

> Of all the Arctic expeditions, Captain Austin's expedition was the happiest, the healthiest, the best administered, and the most successful. It performed all, and more than all, that had been planned by its chief, being the utmost that could be done from its base with the means at its disposal. Its sledge travellers, in their searches had covered 7,025 statute miles on foot, and discovered 1,225 miles of new land.[52]

Markham wrote these words near the end of a long life, but the little book, *Franklin's footsteps*, which he published on his return from the expedition, as a midshipman, bears this out.[53]

Captain Austin concluded that Franklin could not be west of Lancaster Sound, because his retreat would have been to Barrow Strait. He therefore resolved to search Jones Sound (north of Lancaster Sound), before returning home. He ignored the channel leading southwards from Barrow Strait, which was named after the Prime Minister, Sir Robert Peel, because, wrote Sir Clements Markham years later, with some sarcasm, 'such great authorities as Sir James Ross, Sir John Richardson and Sir George Back declared that it was quite out of the question that Franklin should have taken that route. So it remained out of the question'.[54]

Captain Austin searched Jones Sound with the two steamers, *Pioneer* and *Intrepid*. The sound had in fact been penetrated some 150 miles by the whaler *Prince of Wales* (Captain Lee) in 1848, one of whose seamen was aboard HMS *Pioneer* in 1850-51, as ice quartermaster. The two steamers of Austin's squadron were prevented by ice from running that far up Jones Sound, but enough was seen of the bold landscape, in conjunction with the travelling reports from Captain Penny's expedition, to convince Sherard Osborn that only a narrow stretch of low land divided Jones Sound from Wellington Channel.

The homeward voyage of the *Resolute*, *Assistance*, *Pioneer* and *Intrepid* took a month from northern Baffin Bay. In Woolwich, all but one member of Captain Horatio Austin's Arctic happy family were paid off and dispersed.

Captain William Penny 1850-51

Let us turn back now to Captain William Penny and Captain Alexander Stewart commanding HMS *Lady Franklin* and HMS *Sophia*. Sledging equipment had not been provided for them, although they had been otherwise well fitted out with clothing and preserved food. The tinned carrots and the 'Hotch Potch', provided by Mr Hogarth of Aberdeen, seem to have been especially good. Harry

Goodsir, the brother of Dr R A Goodsir, surgeon of the *Lady Franklin*, sailed with Franklin, as we have seen. Hoping to find some traces of the missing expedition, Goodsir accompanied Captain Penny in 1849 to Lancaster Sound, on a whaling voyage. His book, published in 1850, gives an account of this.[55] The surgeon of the *Sophia*, Dr Peter Sutherland, who had sailed in 1845 to the Davis Straits whale fishery, as it was called, published an obervant narrative of Penny's search voyage, in 1852.[56]

With this narrative we can follow Captain Penny's little ships into their winter quarters, working westwards from Beechey Island. On 8 September 1850 the *Sophia*'s bows 'were encrusted with ice, and the rigging of the bowsprit was fantastically fringed with pendant icicles, which appeared like so many rows of frightful teeth moving furiously over the surface of the water and ready to seize any unfortunate thing that might come within reach of their horrid grasp'. On 12 September, anchors were dropped in Assistance Bay, for the first time since leaving Aberdeen. The surgeon showed his enthusiasm for dredging soon afterwards, working with bare hands among the mud and slime, and remarking that a 'whole volume might be written on a single haul of the dredge'. He later made a collection of Arctic plants and much admired the transient beauty of their flowers. The Eskimos, and the ancient ruins on Cornwallis Island, also fascinated him.[57] In early October, Dr Sutherland witnessed the release of two carrier pigeons by Sir John Ross. They had been placed in cages attached to balloons, to be liberated by the burning of a slow five-foot long match twenty-four hours later, when Sir John estimated they would be able to alight on a whaling vessel for a passage to England. One of them is said to have arrived home, without its message. Some days later, an Arctic fox, wearing a collar and disc, which had been attached to it by HMS *Assistance* was caught. It was hoped that members of the lost expedition might capture these foxes – further afield of course – and learn from the disk the whereabouts of the squadron. Sutherland wrote at length about the schooling which was organised for the men. All the surgeon's pupils were interested in geography, from voyaging in many parts of the world. By the end of the winter, about a dozen would be able to navigate a ship across the seven seas. The regular theatrical productions helped to alleviate the boredom of wintering in the Arctic. Sir John Ross particularly enjoyed these, tapping his foot to the music.

Early in 1851, Captain Penny began preparations for travelling on the sledges which had been made by his blacksmiths, sailmakers and carpenters, while Johan Carl Petersen, the Danish interpreter, trained the dogs and advised on the sledging equipment. An official with the Greenland administration, his expertise proved to be of great value during the Franklin Search. It was agreed between Captain Austin and Captain Penny that the latter should search Wellington Channel, while the naval squadron would do the rest. The *Felix* stayed in the background, with one really severe case of scurvy and others recovering after an outbreak during the winter. However, Commander Phillips did make what Captain Penny dismissed as a pointless attempt to cross 'the trackless and barren' top of Cornwallis Island, a mission said to be unworthy of his zeal and talents.[58]

The handwritten drawing includes:

— Winter Quarters —

— Despatches leaving H. M. S. Assistance, by balloon & fox — 13

— Reference —

...aptain Ommanney —	6 - 1st Lieut —	12 — H. M. St Pioneer —	16. H. M. S. Assistance
Balloon filling —	7.7.7.7. Men erecting fox —	13 — Pilot balloon —	17. Snow statue of Britannia
Medical department —	8 — Fox —	14. Cape Martyr —	18. Unfinished north of art.
Observatory —	9 — Cylindrical tin case —	15 — Thermometers on a	19. Cape Hotham much
...ar whose turn it was,	10 — Captain Austin. C.B —	black surface —	refracted
...have a ship —	11 — H. M. S. Mosquito —		

give the view taken

'Despatches leaving HMS *Assistance* by balloon and fox'. Original drawing by Clements Markham in his *Arctic Journal*, 1850-51. (Royal Geographical Society)

Six of Penny's sledges set out from Assistance Bay on 17 April, every face beaming with delight, both officers and men doing the hauling. To negotiate the rough and uneven ice, up to twenty men were required for each sledge. Sir John Ross, aged 74, did not accompany them out of the bay, but Sutherland would 'never forget the venerable appearance of his grey locks, as he waved his hat, or fur cap, with its light blue veil, and joined heartily in the cheers of those we left on board'.

This was on 20 April, Easter Sunday, when prayers were said and thoughts were given to the cathedrals and country churches at home on that special day. As the sweat trickled down their cheeks in the effort of hauling the sledges, they hoped to be forgiven (being Scots) for travelling on Sunday. They suffered tremendous thirst, as the improvised 'conjurors', or stoves, were unable to melt snow quickly enough. It was so bitterly cold that a flask of frozen water, placed under the surgeon's armpit took two or three hours to melt. Terrible cold was experienced during the following three days. The men of the naval squadron suffered badly from frostbite, and one died. But Dr Sutherland watched over his men so carefully that not even a finger nail was lost, despite the temperature being 60 °F below the freezing point of water for three days. In his book, he recorded his recipe for success on sledge journeys – mainly the preparations beforehand but 'above all, the constant and watchful eye, which the officer keeps over his men, guarding them, and caring for them, as if they were parts of himself, yet without being too familiar with them'.[59] On 13 June 1851, after travelling 450 miles in forty days, Dr Sutherland arrived back at the ships in Assistance Bay.

The sledge parties of Captain Stewart and Dr Goodsir, having departed in early May, also returned to the ships in the second half of June. They had searched much of the eastern shore of Wellington Channel as far as Cape Becher (along the west coast of North Devon Island) and the eastern and northern shores of Cornwallis Island, on the western side of the channel.

Captain Penny himself, with Petersen, departed on 9 May, with two dog sledges along the east coast of Cornwallis Island. They discovered and reached Baillie Hamilton Island across the ice to the north of the channel, naming some conspicuous snow-clad mountains 'Sir John Barrow's Monument' on 'Prince Albert Land' (now Grinnell Peninsula) and naming a small island after Barrow's son and namesake. Penny was astonished to find open water at what he called Point Surprise in the high latitude of 76 °N, where there were walruses, eider ducks and gulls. Here, he would have given five thousand pounds, he said, for a boat in which to continue the search for Franklin, but he was forced to turn back, dividing Petersen's sealskin robe *en route* among the ravenous dogs, and reaching the ships on 20 May.

Determined not to give up, Captain Penny had a sledge made big enough to carry the largest six-oared whaleboat, enabling him to start again for the northern reaches of Wellington Channel on 11 June. Eight men, including Penny, dragged the boat sledge, accompanied by a 'fatigue party' with dogs. Despite wet sleeping bags and wet ground sheets in the tents, causing night cramps, and the heavy labour, the men never complained. Each one, remarked Penny, 'seemed to think it rested with himself to solve the fate of our missing countrymen'. Nearly a week later, the first man out of the tent called out, 'The water! The water!' The support party was then sent back, the boat loaded with forty days' provisions, the sail hoisted and Penny and seven sailors were launched into their true element again. Despite snow, rapid tides, gales, ever-moving ice floes and what Penny called a 'left-handed sort of wind', a good deal of searching and exploration was done. The newly discovered channel to the northwest of Baillie Hamilton Island was named 'after our illustrious and much beloved sovereign', Queen Victoria; the strait south of the island was later named after Maury, the well known oceanographer, by the Americans. The wide stretch of water between northeast Bathurst Island and another *presqu'île* (a very large one), now the Grinnell Peninsula of Devon Island, was later named Penny Strait. Capes on the opposite and most distant coasts of the Queen's Channel were called after Sir John and Lady Franklin. As a whaling captain, Penny was used to sea ice and its perils but even he described the situation in mid-channel off Hamilton Island as 'truly fearful', likening the break-up of the sea ice to an earthquake, some floes rising to 20 feet and then 'tumbling down with tremendous crashing and rending'. On the same occasion, they got into an 'unpleasant situation', between a perpendicular snowy cliff and the sea ice, which was pressing up 'with a loud grinding noise, and tumbling over in huge blocks upon the terrace on which we had taken shelter'. No-one slept that night 'owing to the terrifying and groaning noise', of the churning floes.

Despite contrary winds, fierce squalls and torrents of rain, the search continued over rough shingle in patched and mended boots along these unknown shores. On 5 July, a piece of English elm, 'quite fresh' was picked up. Penny described it as 'much reduced in weight and weatherworn by exposure to the atmosphere'. He was convinced that it indicated the passage of Franklin's ships in the neighbourhood of Baillie Hamilton Island, where it was found. However, Sir John Richardson's examination of the wood in England, concluded that although it was indeed English elm, it had no connection with the missing expedition.[60]

Cairns were built along the party's route until it reached Cape Becher, Captain Stewart's furthest point, where the men were disappointed to find Stewart's cairn, not one built by Franklin. Viewing the great expanse of open water to the northwest, Penny concluded that the missing ships must thereby have sailed beyond his reach, although he also pointed out that had Sir John Franklin left documents, they would surely have been deposited upon Cape Becher or Dundas Island.

Another of his conclusions was an interesting geographical one.

That there is a large Arctic Sea beyond this channel, in which the ice is constantly in motion, there can be no doubt: for where could all the ice have gone to? Where does the comparatively fresh driftwood come from? It must be America or Siberia, and that through a body of drifting ice.

It was a struggle for Captain Penny to relinquish further search, but with only one week's provisions left, he had to turn back on 20 July. The party travelled south by boat as far as Abandon Bay. (The boat they left was found a century later by a party from the Geological Survey of Canada. From the various articles strewn about the wreck, they removed a serviceable boat-hook to carry their radio aerial.)[61] Penny's party then made a watery journey to the ships, helped with supplies from a depot laid by Captain Stewart at Cape De Haven and later a boat also left for their use. Soaked to the skin and almost bare foot, they reached the ships on 25 July, thankful to the Almighty for their preservation.

Meanwhile, Captain Austin had been growing increasingly anxious for Captain Penny's return. As party after party had come back to his ships, with no news of Franklin, the search up Wellington Channel was the last hope. Dr Sutherland visited the naval squadron on 14 July at the invitation of the officers of the *Pioneer*. Its commanders, Captain Austin and Captain Ommanney met him, asking straight away, 'What of Penny?' However, observed Sutherland their anxiety stemmed not from a concern for Captain Penny, but for themselves. Should Mr Penny not return, it might be necessary to make a protracted search for his party, involving, maybe, a second winter in the Arctic.

Despite the efforts of the naval surgeons, there were several invalids in the squadron, whose ulcers (following frostbite) refused to heal, while one, George

The ice saw in use. The 34-foot long saw was mounted on a tripod to cut a passage for the ship through the sea ice. (Owen Stanley's sketch book kept during the voyage of the *Terror*, 1836-37, NMM, D4980-20)

Malcolm, Captain of the hold of *Resolute* had died. Captain Austin, who, according to Sutherland, 'looked upon those under his command, one hundred and seventy-nine men, like a fond parent', could not be blamed for his fears for them, should another winter be required. Dr Sutherland encountered a great depression of health and spirits among the squadron and instead of glowing faces, full of hope on setting out on the sledge journeys in the early summer, he found 'a powerful reaction' (since their labours had proved fruitless) in both officers and men. All longed for home.

Dr Sutherland saw some of the recently returned officers busy on their travelling reports and charts and he makes some pertinent remarks as to how mistakes can inadvertently creep into the charts, often through too much reliance on the chronometer – sometimes a 'treacherous friend' – and he had his own recommendations for accuracy, not least by using the sun. He also witnessed the inspection of the *Pioneer* by Captain Austin, who praised Osborn for the good order in every department. 'Each man, as his name was called, doffed his cap to his commander, and walked across the deck from port to starboard', presumably to show his fitness, only one being off-duty with frost-bitten toes However, Sutherland was critical of the fact that while six medical officers accompanied the naval squadron, there was not one chaplain for the 180 men.

Captain Austin and Captain Ommanney were far from keen to spend a second winter in the Arctic while, in contrast, Captain Penny believed there was still much to be done in the direction of Wellington Channel, ideally with a steamer and the little *Sophia*. However, he was conscious of the responsibility that a decision to remain for a second winter would place on his and Captain Austin's shoulders, but also aware of their duty to the members of the missing expedition. When the two leaders actually met to discuss these weighty matters, Captain Penny failed to convince Captain Austin, in the absence of the discovery of any records deposited by Franklin, of the need for further search up Wellington Channel, while Penny's small squadron had not the resources to remain on its own. Profiting from Petersen's good advice and help, says Dr Sutherland, they had already travelled on foot or by boat, some 2,000 miles, following the coasts of every island, bay and channel, of which over 700 were of newly discovered land. And so Captain Penny, with a sad heart gave the order to weigh anchor and set sail for England.

During the homeward voyage, the dogs on board the *Sophia*, becoming oppressed by the heat, lay panting on the deck by day and then spent the night fighting, so much so that Captain Stewart decided to destroy some of them. Dr Sutherland remarked that 'to the man who had charge of them, and who had watched over them during the long winter, it was a source of great grief and not a few tears'. Only four were kept alive, to fight and to roam the decks. The surgeon went on to say that everyone felt a sense of shame at this 'deed of extermination', which took the lives of 'the poor brutes that had served us so faithfully, and had been our companions for such a length of time . . .'. On the expedition's return, Captain Penny presented a very special dog, Sultan, to John Barrow, who described him as a 'splendid Eskimo Dog, King of the Pack. He saved the life of one of Ross' seamen by his sagacity'. However, 'He was not suitable for London!! and got me into trouble – and I sent him back'.[62] Curiously enough, Tommy, another of Penny's dogs, was stuffed on his death and is now in New Zealand.[63]

Captain Penny was both upset and indignant that his efforts were not altogether appreciated by the Admiralty, and he failed to obtain command of another search expedition. Penny – that 'generous-hearted seaman' returned to his whaling and to other causes. However, it is worth noting that when he sent John Barrow a painting of the *Lady Franklin* and the *Sophia* some years later, his accompanying letter asserted that these 'two little vessels' (and Barrow's advice) enabled 'a N.W. passage and an arctic ocean . . . to be found' by way of Wellington Channel. The vessels were also, Penny maintained, 'the first to bring home the intelligence that the scientifick [sic] theory of Sir John Barrow was no longer so . . .'.[64]

We shall see that Captain Penny's conviction that Franklin's ships had sailed up Wellington Channel was subsequently found to be correct.

CHAPTER 12

The Search for Franklin from the Pacific

When Captain Henry Kellett, in command of HMS *Herald*, surveying in the Pacific Ocean, reached Petropavlovsk, eastern Siberia, on 23 June 1849, seeking news of the depot ship HMS *Plover*, stationed to the north, he was amazed to find an English yacht, the *Nancy Dawson*, at anchor alongside several American whalers. A newly-built schooner of 163 tons, flying the burgee of the Royal Thames Yacht Club, she had left England some time late in 1848. Her owner was Robert Shedden, who had served as a midshipman in the Royal Navy during the Napolenic Wars, and he offered to place his yacht under Kellett's command to assist in the search for Sir John Franklin.[1]

The *Plover* had not touched at Petropavlovsk, but had wintered on the coast of the Chukchi Peninsula, to the north where she found and named Providence Bay (now Bukhta Provideniya) and where friendly relations were established with the Chukchi villagers and from which bay travelling parties searched for Franklin. *Plover* eventually arrived at the rendezvous of Chamisso Island, Kotzebue Sound (Alaska) in mid July 1849 and was joined by the *Herald* next day. *Nancy Dawson* came up soon afterwards and the three sailed in company as far as Wainwright Inlet to the north, working their way past great herds of walrus, numerous seals and whales and sighting the occasional American whaler. The Eskimos on the coast proved anxious to trade, particularly for tobacco and beads. Knowing that the waters beyond Point Barrow were shallow and shoaling, Kellett ordered Lieutenant W J S Pullen to begin his boat expedition, in search of Sir John Franklin, from there.

The *Nancy Dawson* accompanied the boats beyond Cape Barrow for some 50 miles, keeping an eye on them in case of Eskimo hostility and helping in other ways. In rounding Cape Barrow she became the first ship to enter the Beaufort Sea, and here Shedden's crew began to mutiny. Being ill with tuberculosis and seeing he could do little more, he deposited a cache of provisions and began the return voyage. When HMS *Herald* and the *Nancy Dawson* met on their way south, Captain Kellett took off three mutineers and put his Second Master in charge of the yacht, with orders to rendezvous at Mazatlan in Mexico. Here Shedden died soon after arrival on 13 November 1849. Captain Moore of the *Plover* and Lieutenant Pullen both greatly appreciated Shedden's kindness and help. He was buried in Mexico, but a tablet in his memory, commemorating his valiant efforts in search of Franklin was erected in 1851 in the church of

Weston Underwood, Buckinghamshire. The tablet was no longer to be seen a century later states A G E Jones.

*   *   *

Two naval vessels, the *Enterprise*, Captain Richard Collinson, and the *Investigator*, Commander Robert McClure, departed from England in January 1850. These had only recently returned with Sir James Clark Ross from his fruitless search expedition of 1848-49. They had been re-equipped in some haste between November 1849, when Ross returned, and January 1850, when they set sail from England on a voyage of many thousands of miles to reach Bering Strait, via the Straits of Magellan, and the whole length of both the Atlantic and the Pacific Oceans. A steamer, the *Gorgon*, was to tow them through the southern straits and as far north as Valparaiso on the coast of Chile. However, such were the difficulties of towing in the long swell of the Pacific that the *Enterprise* and the *Investigator* parted company and were never to meet again.

They missed their *rendezvous* in the Sandwich (now Hawaiian) Islands and sailed northwards independently, towards Bering Strait and Point Barrow, the 'ice gate' into the Beaufort Sea, towards the western end of the North West Passage. The Admiralty's orders had urged Captain Collinson to 'bear in mind that the object of the Expedition is to obtain intelligence, and to render assistance to Sir John Franklin and his companions, and not for the purpose of geographical or scientific research'.[2] It was for this reason that, after waiting for five days at Oahu for Commander McClure in the *Investigator*, he left the islands, with the intention, authorised by the Admiralty of taking the depot ship, HMS *Plover* (Commander T E L Moore) into the ice, failing the arrival of the *Investigator*. The latter would then act as a reserve, further south, off the coast of Russian America (now Alaska.) Collinson's orders also warned him against allowing the *Enterprise* and the *Investigator* to separate.

Commander McClure arrived at Oahu the day after the *Enterprise* departed, and he left with little delay for Bering Strait, arriving at Cape Lisburne (the next *rendezvous*) a week before the *Enterprise*. Blessed with a fair wind, he had taken the bold course of passing through the chain of the Aleutian Islands, rather than round them, as Collinson and most previous navigators had done. The Admiralty had stationed two vessels in the North Pacific. One was HMS *Herald* (500 tons), commanded by Captain Henry Kellett, which was detached from her surveying duties further south during the years 1848, 1849 and 1850 to assist the *Plover*, a storeship (213 tons) which had left England in January 1848 on the long voyage to the North Pacific, at first to await the *Erebus*' and *Terror*'s exit from the North West Passage and subsequently to keep a lonely vigil during the winter and to send out parties by boat and on foot in the spring and summer, searching for traces of the missing expedition. On the departure of the *Herald* for England, vessels from the Pacific squadron went north each year to contact the *Plover* until 1854, when she was condemned and sold in San Francisco. Captain Rochfort Maguire had replaced Commander Moore in 1852.[3]

Commander McClure in *Investigator* met the *Herald* at Cape Lisburne on 31 July 1850. He endeavoured to persuade Captain Kellett (who had done survey work in China with Captain Collinson and thus knew him well) that the *Enterprise* must have preceded the *Investigator* into the ice. Kellett thought this most unlikely, in view of McClure's swift passage. In addition, he did not believe that Collinson would depart without leaving instructions for his junior officer. Unfortunately, and presumably because the *Investigator* had proved to be much the poorer sailer during the voyage, Collinson had made no provision in his instructions to McClure for such an event. McClure declined to wait even for the 48 hours that Kellett wished and sailed away. McClure's journal[4] for 31 July concerning the encounter records that at 8am, near Cape Lisburne, a strange sail was sighted, which proved to be *Herald*. At 9.30, 'Hove to and went on board, and most kindly received by Capt. Kellett, who congratulated me on the shortness of our trip from Wahoa'. He had not seen the *Enterprise*, a fact which McClure attributed to the foggy weather of the previous fortnight, 'allowing her to pass unnoticed'. The *Herald*'s crew manned the rigging 'and gave us three hearty cheers, which was responded to by our little band with heartfelt emotions'. Three members of Kellett's crew were allowed to volunteer to complete the complement of the *Investigator*, making her 'truly efficient for any service'. The gift of a sheep was 'of inestimable value' as McClure had 'foolishly come from Wahoa, without any'. Kellett accompanied McClure back to the *Investigator*, wishing 'to see the arrangements of a vessel destined to withstand not only a polar winter, but the still more dangerous antagonist, the polar ice'. The *Investigator* made sail at 2pm with the *Herald* in company. McClure's journal continued:

> In the afternoon the Herald signalized me to remain forty eight hours in case Enterprize had not passed, a delay I was not at all inclined to submit tacitly to, as I am well aware the value of time in a navigation amongst Ice is indispensable, a day lost might be that of a whole season, in consequence of my remonstrance I was permitted to proceed and at 11.30p.m. parted company with the Herald, and now make the best of my way to the N.E. where I expect to meet Enterprize, in the neighbourhood of Point Barrow, stopped by the Ice.

McClure interpreted his instructions as indicating that the *Investigator* would probably form a 'detached part of the expedition', since he thought the two vessels were unlikely to meet at Cape Lisburne.[5] As the editor of Collinson's journal concluded, 'This was certainly a very strong step for the junior vessel of an expedition to take', as well as 'a great stretch of the power he [McClure] accidentally possessed at the moment'. He quotes the remarks of Dr Armstrong, the surgeon of the *Investigator*, that, 'Two ships are always sent on Arctic expeditions for mutual succour and support, and for salutary controlling influences, no less than for the social effect'.

By sailing away, Commander McClure condemned both ships to winter alone.

He was able to pass through the ice gate at Point Barrow and enter the Beaufort Sea a whole year earlier than Collinson, thus becoming the first (apart from Franklin) to connect the eastern and western ends of the North West Passage. Lacking a second commander in the *Enterprise* and following the death in Russian America of one of his best lieutenants, Collinson must have suffered a particularly lonely and responsible command. One wonders whether McClure ever regretted his action during the dark days of the third winter, when it seemed certain that his crew would meet a fate similar to that of Franklin's men. It is worth noting that twenty years after these search expeditions, when the Admiralty despatched what really was the last of the Arctic voyages, in *Alert* and *Discovery*, under Captain G S Nares' command in 1875-76, the *Alert* proceeded through what is now Nares Channel (between northwest Greenland and Ellesmere Island) to reach a very high northern latitude, while her consort wintered further south, within striking distance, but ready to carry both crews home, should the need arise.

It is remarkable how much good fortune attended McClure (at least at first) and how much bad luck affected Collinson. Had, for instance, Collinson spoken with Kellett in the *Herald* as he made his first passage up Bering Strait in August 1850, he would have heard that the *Investigator* was ahead of him and might have persisted longer in endeavouring to round Point Barrow. When he did hear (at Port Clarence), he sailed north again, but then returned to the coast of Russian America, where in October he put a party ashore (Lieutenant Barnard, Adams the assistant surgeon and one of the seamen) at Mikhailovskiy Redoubt (now St Michael on Norton Sound), one of the Russian trading posts. The little party were to investigate native reports of white men being seen in the interior. When the *Enterprise* returned after wintering in Hong Kong, Collinson found that Barnard had been killed in a massacre of one Indian tribe by another. His loss was much felt by his captain and shipmates in the *Enterprise*. The mysterious strangers were almost certainly traders from the Hudson's Bay Company.

*   *   *

After rounding Point Barrow, *Investigator* sailed east following the flat and featureless coast of what was then Russian America, along which had travelled Sir John Franklin and Messrs Dease and Simpson. The vessel was navigated between the shallows near the shore and the grounded or floating ice to the north. In crossing an open sea opposite Cape Parry, new land was discovered, which McClure called 'Baring Land', but which was really the southern end of Banks Land, seen thirty years before by Parry from Melville Island. McClure discovered Prince of Wales Strait, between Banks Island and Victoria Island, which they penetrated to a point only some 30 miles from its junction with Viscount Melville Sound, being stopped by heavy flocs at 73 °10′N. The *Investigator* wintered in the strait near Princess Royal Islands and was not released from the ice until mid-August 1851. However, during the previous

October, McClure and the second Master, Stephen Court, reached the north-western point of Prince of Wales Strait and looked across the ice-choked sound to Melville Island, some 60 miles away. It was a proud moment for McClure, for with his own eyes he could see the last link in the fabled North West Passage, sought by British seamen for nearly three hundred years, but the elusive Passage was to prove as difficult for him to navigate as it had always been.

In the spring, sledging journeys were made up and down the Prince of Wales Strait and along the coasts of Victoria Island and Banks Island, but no trace of Franklin was found. One party narrowly missed meeting Dr John Rae, who visited the southern shore of Prince Albert Sound only ten days after the party had reached their furthest point along the northern shore. During the summer of 1851, McClure made a second effort to pass north into Melville Sound, but the *Investigator* again met the heavy floes of multi-year ice and could go no further. Her Captain therefore turned her about, and sailed west round Nelson Head and Cape Kellett on the southwest coast of Banks Island, then northwards along the narrow lane of water off the west coast between the shore and the massive floes of oceanic ice. The *Investigator* eventually rounded the northwest cape of Banks Island, despite heavy ice, to enter what was later called M'Clure Strait. The diary of the Assistant Surgeon, Henry Piers, gives an idea of the strain suffered by both the *Investigator* and her crew. On 19 August 1851:

> At about 9.30 or 9.45 our stern-post took it with a slow, steady and powerful pressure, the whole ship trembled under the struggle for mastery and never with us before has her strength been so thoroughly tested: the mizzen mast was seen to shake; the bells rung or chattered; the Boatswain, who was confined to his bed, dressed himself and came on deck, for he told me afterwards he could not remain below, as he expected every minute a *visitor* in his cabin ... Biggs too, a Marine and Captain's steward, thinking the cabin was coming in, seized the captain's packed carpet bag and ran to the ladder with it.[6]

A month later, the *Investigator* found a haven on the north coast of Banks Island, which McClure named Bay of Mercy, where they wintered securely in 1851–52. Although their food allowance was reduced, musk oxen, caribou (reindeer) and hares partly made up for the deficiency. The following spring, McClure sledged across the strait to Winter Harbour, on Melville Island, where he deposited a record giving the position of the *Investigator* in Mercy Bay.

The Assistant Surgeon of HMS *Investigator*, Henry Piers, as we have seen, kept a journal of the voyage which has survived (despite McClure's orders that all records should be abandoned with the ship). On 16 February 1852, towards the end of the second Arctic winter, Piers described the routine of a winter's day and compared the dull lethargy of the men (which he attributed to monotony and a reduced food allowance) to their cheerful and lively disposition of the year before, when dance, song and comic scenes enlivened the whole lower deck:

> ... but let anyone imagine a ship frozen up, with the deck covered with snow a foot or 18ins deep, and covered over exactly like a booth, a temperature of –30 or –40 with strong wind, and notwithstanding every part being closely stopped to keep out the

'The perilous position of HMS *Investigator*' (Captain McClure) nipped by two large floes off Banks Island, drawn by Lieutenant S Gurney Cresswell, during the Franklin Search expedition 1850-54. (NMM, PX7015)

wind & snow, the fine snow drift still finding its way through & covering everything, the wind howling through the rigging at the same time: let him picture to himself then this covered deck lit by a single candle in a [storm] lantern; five or six officers walking the starbourd side & maintaining some conversation and twenty or thirty men, perfectly mute, slowly pacing the port side – all muffled up to the eyes and covered with snow drift or frozen vapour visible about the dark parts of their dress – he will then have some idea of many of this winter's day's exercise, and I think he will consider it cheerless & dismal enough.[7]

On 10 March 1852, Piers reflected on the stealing of a loaf of bread:

This is the third or fourth case of theft of provisions since we have been on reduced allowance; but if the crime can admit of any extenuation I think it should in the case of this ship, for although to be on two-thirds for a week or fortnight in a temperate or tropical climate may not be so bad, to be so not only week after week but month after month in a climate like this, where there is such a great and constant expenditure of animal heat; to be frequently very hungry and always ready to eat, so that a meal is no sooner finished than a person feels that he should like to repeat the pleasure, though his only prospect is the next limited fare; to be slowly, yet perceptibly, losing flesh, strength and spirits, must, when added to the other circumstances attending such a long, dreary & monotonous voyage be very trying to many fore-mast men.[8]

The Assistant Surgeon's diary demonstrates the level to which the 'Investigators' had been reduced during the winter of 1851-52. Things could only get worse from hunger, scurvy and depression during the winter of 1852–53, when the Mate and one of the seamen became insane, the Mate aggressively so. In March of 1853, McClure made preparations for part of the crew to leave the ship. A letter was written in April 1853 by Captain McClure to his old commander, Sir George Back, with whom he had sailed in HMS *Terror*, more than ten years before. It provides a short 'on the spot' account of the *Investigator*'s proceedings. Presumably McClure prepared it for one of the parties to take with them on their retreat to England, before the *Investigator* was relieved. In it he explained how they had accidentally 'tumbled through this long sought for North West Passage, indeed two of them. Their groundings and the problems of navigation as he 'groped and grappled' his way long the shallow shore were outlined, plus the horror of upsetting one of the ship's boats which contained 12 months' provisions – when lightening the ship – which was the prelude to the terrible shortages of food they later experienced. Encounters with the Eskimos, not altogether happy ones, were also described. Of the passage northwards up the west coast of 'Baring' (ie Banks) Island, he wrote, 'No idea can be formed unless witnessed of the stupendous masses of ice with which this terrible polar sea is entirely filled. We were actually squeezed through it and frequently so close to the cliffs that the vessel had to be listed over to prevent the boats being carried away at the davits by projecting rocks'. He asserted in his letter that shortages were compelling him to send half his crew home, some via the Mackenzie River and the rest by Baffin Bay.[9]

*   *   *

Unknown to Captain McClure and the 'Investigators', in the spring of 1852, the Admiralty had sent out a third naval search squadron under the command of Captain Sir Edward Belcher. Their orders virtually divided the four vessels into an eastern and a western division: the *Assistance* and *Pioneer* were to search Wellington Channel, for traces of Franklin, while the *Resolute* and *Intrepid* were to deposit supplies of provisions, fuel and clothing on Melville Island, for Collinson and McClure. The store ship *North Star* was to remain at Beechey Island. The *Resolute* (Captain Kellett) and the *Intrepid* (Commander McClintock) reached Parry's old winter quarters at Winter Harbour, Melville Island, in early September 1852, where they left a depot. Unable to find cairns erected by parties from either the *Enterprise* or the *Investigator*, Captain Kellett secured the *Resolute* and *Intrepid* in winter quarters at nearby Dealy Island, an islet off the southeast coast of Melville Island.

Once frozen in, he sent travelling parties to lay depots for the spring journeys. One of these was led by Lieutenant Frederick Mecham, who was later to make two remarkably long sledge journeys in 1853 and 1854. During his return from laying a depot at Liddon Gulf, he made a close inspection of Parry's famous rock at Winter Harbour. He was amazed to find on its summit McClure's record recounting the discovery of the North West Passage and giving the *Investigator*'s position in the Bay of Mercy. This news was greeted with great joy in Captain

Kellett's squadron, followed by anxious debate as to how to reach the *Investigator* in the spring before she was abandoned, or, on the other hand how to intercept her, supposing she had broken free from her captivity and had proceeded elsewhere.[10]

The senior officers, Commander McClintock and Lieutenant Mecham, therefore chose routes that would cut across the *Investigator*'s track should she sail northwest of Melville Island and it fell to the second lieutenant of the *Resolute*, Bedford Pim, and Dr Domville to travel south with nine men, a man-hauled sledge and a dog sledge across the strait towards Banks Island. They left on 10 March 1853 (very early in the season) to the cheers and prayers of their shipmates. The journey was a difficult one, across high irregular hummocks under overcast skies, in low temperatures and occasional thick snow. Pim's sledge lost its lee runner in 'gliding off a glassy hummock', so that he took over Domville's dog sledge, with two men to make his way to the Bay of Mercy, leaving the surgeon to return to Melville Island with a heavy load of provisions (1,700lbs) and a broken sledge. The carpenter's mate repaired the sledge, so that it could bear one half of the load, and they proceeded by relays back to Cape Dundas. Domville concluded at the end of this journey, undertaken so early in the year, that travelling could be done at any season, provided there was enough daylight and the party was in good health. Men's constitutions could adapt, provided the clothing were suitable and the food plentiful. In reporting to Captain Kellett, the surgeon continued: 'By your directions our resources in these respects were ample: the *clothing* being light and warm, not impeding the motion of the limbs during exercise by day: the double tent and buffalo skins forming an adequate covering by night; and the diet of good quality, the supply being equal to the demand, and consisting of a large proportion of animal food . . . namely pemmican, the best adapted for the process of assimilation . . .'.[11]

Meanwhile, on the opposite side of the strait on 6 April 1853, Pim was approaching the Bay of Mercy and seeing no cairns, assumed that *Investigator* had made the NorthWest Passage. Here in his own words is what happened next:

> Having seen nothing to indicate the vicinity of the 'Investigator' I now made up my mind that she had left the Bay, and accordingly steered right across it with the intention of tracing the whole coast line in search of her cairns. At 2PM when already half way over Rt. Hoile reported that he saw something black up the Bay. Upon looking through the glass I made out the object to be a ship, and immediately altered course for her, weather gradually clearing. 3.0 PM, left the sledge and went on in advance. 4.0 PM, observed people walking about and made out a cairn and staff on the beach. The old floe still continues, it is therefore not difficult to understand the reason of the ship being still here. 5.0 PM, arrived within 100 yds. without being observed, then however two persons taking exercise on the ice discovered that I did not belong to their ship, upon beckoning they quickly approached and proved to be Capt. McClure and Lt. Haswell, their surprise and I may add delight at the unexpected appearance of a stranger (who seemed as it were to drop from the clouds) it is needless attempting to describe. One of the men at work near them conveyed the

Captain Sir Robert McClure of
HMS *Investigator*, which
discovered two North West
Passages during the Franklin
Search expedition of 1850-54,
painted by Stephen Pearce.
(NMM, C819)

news on board and in an incredible short time the deck was crowded, every one that
could crawl making his appearance, to see the stranger and hear the news. The scene
which then presented itself can never be effaced from my memory nor can I express
any idea of the joy and gladness with which my arrival was hailed.[12]

McClure and the first lieutenant had been walking on the floe discussing how
best a grave could be dug in the hard frozen ground for one of the seamen who
had died (the first to do so) the previous day. In Captain Kellett's words:

Seeing a person coming very fast towards them, they supposed he was chased by a Bear
or had seen a Bear. Walked towards him – on getting within a hundred yards they
could see from his proportions he was not one of them. Pim began to screech and
throw up his hands (his face as black as your hat.) This brought the Captain and Lt.
to a stance as they could not hear sufficiently to make out his language. He was a
considerable way ahead of his sledges – a solitary man – and that man as black as old
Nick [the Devil]. McClure says he would have turned and run if he saw a tail or a
cloven hoof. At length Pim reached the Party – quite beside himself, also stammered
out on McClure's asking him, who are you and where you from? Lt. Pim answered,
Captain Kellett. This was more inexplicable to McClure, as I was the last person he
shook hands with in Behring Strait; he at last found that this solitary stranger was a
true Englishman – An Angel of Light, he says.[13]

Dr Alexander Armstrong, the senior surgeon of *Investigator*, must have been
below deck when Lieutenant Pim arrived at 4pm, on 6 April. The news 'flew
with the rapidity of lightning from stem to stern', wrote the doctor, after its at

first being thought 'either a mistake or a joke'. But the joyful shout from the handful of men on deck confirmed the news. There followed a rush of men from down below to the hatchways and the deck.

For 'three long and dreary years', the 'Investigators' had been alone in the icy seas and Lieutenant Pim (in the doctor's words) was 'the first of our countrymen we had seen, or whose voice we had heard' for all that time. Soon the sledge 'drawn by five Esquimaux dogs and two men' (Thomas Bidgood and Robert Hoyle) arrived as well, to be greeted 'by three as hearty cheers as ever came from the lungs of British sailors'. Dr Armstrong recorded in his personal narrative of the voyage the debt of gratitude owed by all the 'Investigators' to Lieutenant Pim, who had volunteered for the duty and who had undertaken the journey so early in the year, when the temperature measured 50 °F below zero. In addition, wrote the surgeon, 'nothing could exceed the kindness and warmth of feeling he showed', particularly when distributing small gifts, of which they stood in need:

> But when he saw us sitting down with starved aspect on the morning after his arrival, to what was denominated breakfast (a cup of weak cocoa without sugar, and a moiety of bread) his feelings overcame him; he rushed to his sledge, then out on the ice, brought a large piece of bacon, placed it before us, and gave us the only breakfast we had known for many a long day.[14]

Dr Armstrong recorded that Bidgood and Hoyle were moved to tears.

On 7 April, Captain McClure, another officer and six men set off with Lieutenant Pim, Bidgood and Hoyle to cross the strait, in order to communicate with Captain Kellett, the senior officer, at Melville Island. They arrived on 19 April. Continuing his letter to Barrow, Kellett declared: 'This is really a red letter day in my voyages and shall be kept as a Holy day by my Heirs and successors for ever.' On 2 May, a second party arrived led by Lieutenant Gurney Cresswell (whose sketches were engraved after his eventual return to England in 1853, having made the first traverse of the North West Passage). He was accompanied by Piers, the Assistant Surgeon, Johann Miertsching, the Moravian Interpreter, who was very upset at having to leave his precious journals and collections behind in the Investigator; and lastly, the Mate, Mr Wynniatt, whose mind was deranged and who had been troublesome during the journey, as well as the vacant but inoffensive Bradbury. Four or five men of the twenty-four sailors were carried on sledges and all were afflicted with scurvy to a greater or lesser extent. Miertsching recorded that the few healthy men often had to drag the sledges over the hummocks crawling on hands and knees, while crossing the 80 miles to the ships at Dealy Island.

No doubt hopeful of completing the Passage, McClure did not want to desert his ship. After much discussion, however, Kellett gave orders to do so, if the medical officers considered that the 'Investigators' were not fit enough to stand another winter or if less than twenty officers and men volunteered to remain. Dr W T Domville of the *Resolute* and Dr Armstrong of the *Investigator* duly examined the brave but enfeebled crew. Only four of them offered to remain for another winter and so the gallant *Investigator* was abandoned in the Bay of Mercy and was left cleaned and, with hatches and gangways secured, ready for any ship-wrecked mariners to occupy. On 19 May, McClure had travelled back across the ice to his ship, after six weeks' absence and it was only then that the men were placed again on full rations. Three graves on the beach, a depot, a cairn on the hill and a tablet to their shipmates' memory remained in Mercy Bay beside the *Investigator*.

On 3 June 1853, after a last inspection of the ship, Captain McClure addressed a few words – 'not complimentary', said Dr Armstrong – to the men and all were piped to join their sledges on the ice.

> The white ensign of St George was hoisted at the peak, and the pendant at the main, which flaunted gaily in the breeze as we stepped over the side of the ship that had so long been our home, never to visit her again . . . As we stood on the ice, and took a last view of our fine old ship, we could not but do so with a grateful recollection, considering how far she had borne us, through what dangers she had carried us, and the safe asylum she had so long afforded us. But while we entertained those feelings . . . we felt that the time had come . . . to abandon her, and consequently we could feel no regret at leaving a ship where every form of privation had been so long endured.[15]

The extent of that privation is vividly described by Miertsching, who from the other side of the ice-bound strait on the deck of the *Resolute* watched his shipmates from the abandoned ship coming very slowly over the ice. He went out with Captain Kellett to greet them. They provided 'a melancholy spectacle' he would never in his life forget.

> Two sick men were lashed onto each of the four sledges; others, utterly without strength, were supported by comrades who still preserved a little vigour; others again held onto and leaned on the sledges, and these were drawn by men so unsteady on their feet that every five minutes they would fall and be unable to rise without the help of their comrades, the captain, or one of the officers.[16]

Their desperate condition reminded Miertsching of the lost Franklin expedition also and led him to think that 'had not our gracious and merciful Lord and Saviour intervened, and, by bringing these ships at the right time, cancelled our intended long journey at the last moment, we must all have perished miserably on the frozen sea'. He found that Captain McClure had not retrieved his journal, but was resigned to its loss in view of the plight of the men. McClure offered to lend him the ship's journal, so that he could reconstitute his diary, which he did. L H Neatby, his translator and editor, has pointed out that Miertsching, a pious German evangelist from the Moravian brotherhood in Labrador, was in a different category from the naval officers, who had also been ordered to leave their journals behind, and might have been afforded the privilege of keeping his for this reason. Neatby also observes that the 'suspicion that the captain was doing his utmost to conceal the cost of his daring voyage in human suffering is strengthened by the circumstance that, when the abandoned ship was visited in the following spring, the officers' journals could nowhere be found'. Dr Armstrong, continues Neatby, probably owed the retrieval of his journal to Dr Domville, who was under Kellett's orders.[17]

From the time of their arrival at Dealy Island, the 'Investigators' were cared for by the warm-hearted Captain Kellett, the *Intrepid* being turned into a hospital ship. Their trials were not over, however, and it was only Lieutenant S Gurney Cresswell, with Wynniatt and Bradbury, who arrived home in England in the autumn of 1853.[18] After many vicissitudes, the surviving officers and men followed them a year later. Miertsching saw the little crowd of wives and children, who had assembled at Sheerness in Kent to welcome home their husbands and fathers. 'Unhappily more than one mother with children . . . received from the captain the heart-breaking intelligence that the father had *not* come back, but had found rest in an icy tomb! . . . With the deepest sympathy men saw the heart-broken and sorrowing widows and orphans leaving the ship'.

At the end of October 1854, when a court martial had honourably acquitted McClure for the loss of the ship, the crew were paid off, after nearly five years of Arctic service. A short note in the *Illustrated London News* reported the presentation by the crew to Dr Alexander Armstrong, senior surgeon of the *Investigator*, of 'a gold chronometer and gold chain, valued at seventy guineas, as a testimony of their sincere respect and affection . . .' A testimonial signed by each of the men accompanied the gift which was presented by a deputation of ten at the Ship Inn, presumably in Sheerness, in the presence of a number of Dr Armstrong's brother officers. He replied with a short speech of thanks.

> The men then turned round to Lieutenant Bedford Pim and said, 'If it had not been for you, Sir, many of us now present would never have seen Old England again. All of us look upon you as a deliverer, and we shall never forget the joy we felt when you reached us.' Lieutenant Pim answered:- 'Thank you my lads. I shall never forget our meeting. I congratulate you on your having escaped a similar fate to that of Sir John Franklin; I hope you will now enjoy yourselves to your hearts content . . . and next spring I dare say we shall meet again under the walls of Cronstadt, perhaps in St Petersburg itself.[19]

Pim referred of course to the outbreak of the Crimean War in March 1854. A parliamentary committee later awarded £10,000 to the officers and men of the *Investigator* for the discovery of the North West Passage, but nothing to the men of the *Resolute,* a decision which upset Captain Kellett. Captain McClure was knighted on his return and his journals, edited by Sherard Osborn, went into four editions. The only other published account was by Dr Armstrong, until Professor Neatby translated and edited Miertsching's diary. The following paragraph from Neatby's epilogue to Miertsching is worth quoting in connection with McClure.

> Miertsching's portrayal of this celebrated seaman clarifies the impression that the careful reader gets from Osborn's glowing but somewhat evasive panegyric and from the guarded hostility of Armstrong. He was aloof, unstable at times, with a driving ambition, coupled with more selfishness and less scruple than quite befitted his rank and profession. Yet he was not a wholly unpleasing character, not unworthy of the honours he obtained. His remoteness was due more to insecurity than to lack of feeling . . . In an emergency he could overcome his diffidence and appeal to the men with force and emotion. If the lack of confidence between himself and his officers was

a fault, it serves to emphasise the resolution with which he maintained discipline for a long period of hardship and privation . . . He had much luck in his historic voyage, but the use he made of it marks him as a brave and skilful navigator.

Captain Collinson's Voyage 1850-55

Captain Collinson, McClure's senior officer, had arrived after him at Point Barrow as we have seen and only learnt later that the *Investigator* had preceded the *Enterprise* into the Beaufort Sea. In a private letter to John Barrow from Port Clarence at the end of the ice navigation season, September 1850, Captain Collinson expressed his satisfaction 'that one vessel most likely has accomplished a main object of the voyage and that a wintering place has been obtained to the eastward of Point Barrow' . . . The *Enterprise* had also in 1850 penetrated 70 miles to the east of the point, but was 'headed back by a barrier resting so close to the shore as to demand my serious thoughts whether we had season enough left to push for Cape Bathurst.'

This was not thought practicable in the written opinions of the officers, including the two ice-mates, so Collinson tried for open water further north, 'although I am not of the [open] Polar basin theory'. Lack of success in this direction simply convinced him 'that if we want to get to the east^d we must go inshore and there I hope McClure is at present'. He was pleased that they had not been 'completely frustrated'. This letter to the younger Barrow was signed 'Your disappointed friend, R Collinson'.[20]

Collinson wintered in Hong Kong and returned to the North Pacific in the early summer of 1851, rounding Point Barrow at the end of July. The *Enterprise* followed in the wake of the *Investigator* up Prince of Wales Strait, but like her, failed to penetrate the oceanic ice blocking its northern exit. Collinson found evidence of the *Investigator*'s wintering in Prince of Wales Strait and also endeavoured to pass up the west coast of Banks Island, but was stopped by heavy ice. The *Enterprise* therefore turned south and found safe winter quarters in Walker Bay, Victoria Land, not far from the southern entrance to Prince of Wales Strait. In the spring of 1852, sledging parties searched in various directions for Franklin, partly duplicating the earlier journeys from the *Investigator*.

Here again, Collinson was plagued with bad luck. A party led by the mate, M T Parkes, crossed Melville Sound in May 1852 to leave a record at Parry's Winter Harbour on Melville Island. The ice was so tumultuous and uneven that they deposited their sledge and set out carrying racoon skins, sleeping bags and provisions on their backs, but the men became so tired, snow blind and lame that Parkes went on towards Winter Harbour alone. Hearing the howling of Eskimo dogs and seeing sledge tracks, he felt obliged to turn back, being in no state to meet the natives, on his own and having left the only gun with the men. These, however, were no Eskimos, but Captain McClure's party from the *Investigator*, then in the Bay of Mercy. Parkes deposited a record near Point Hearne, short of Winter Harbour, which was unfortunately never found by any of the sledging parties from the eastern Arctic. The *Enterprise* therefore wintered near the southern coast of Banks Island, quite unknown to the 'Investigators' to the North.[21]

Captain Collinson had been so worried about the sledging party, that for some days after their return, on waking in the morning, he had to convince himself that it was not a dream. The *Enterprise* was released from the ice in early August 1852. She searched Prince Albert Sound on the west coast of Victoria Land, proving that Wollaston, Prince Albert and Victoria lands were all one. The ship then passed south and east round the Wollaston Peninsula, through Dolphin and Union Strait, Coronation Gulf and Dease Strait to find winter quarters for 1852-53 in Cambridge Bay. This was a very considerable feat of navigation to take a vessel of over 400 tons, propelled only by wind or pulled by boats, through these uncharted and hazardous waters, where the compass is unreliable, and there are frequent fogs and storms during the navigable season. Only boats and canoes had earlier explored the narrow channel along the north coast of America, which Sir John Barrow described in 1846 as 'one continued series of rocky islets, with channels between them mostly choked with ice, the sea beyond them also covered with ice, in the shape of floes and hummocks; reefs of rocks parallel with the beach, their intermediate channels shallow, and in many places not navigable even by boats; the weather foggy and stormy with violent gales of wind.'[22]

Captain Collinson's brother and the editor of his Arctic journal, Major General T B Collinson, Royal Engineers, writing in 1889, just over a decade before Roald Amundsen's successful navigation through these waters of the North West Passage in the *Gjøa* had this to say:

> The bold adventure of the *Enterprise* in entering this discredited pass in the Arctic Sea fully confirmed all the former records as to its troubles and dangers, and yet demonstrated practically that it is navigable for ships; and it even gave the captain the conviction that it was the one most favourable line in which to look for a useful north-west passage.[23]

There were hazards enough, continued General Collinson, but there was one great advantage – a reasonably open sea.

> So great is the gift of a clear water channel in Arctic voyaging, that Captain Collinson did not hesitate to propose, after he had gone to Behring Straits again, to take his ship back through the same channel; and afterwards in England, he undertook to carry a steamer through it and come out in Baffin Bay in one season.

The *Enterprise* wintered in Cambridge Bay, whose neighbourhood as we have seen, had been surveyed by Messrs Dease and Simpson by boat in 1836-37. In his journal, Collinson paid tribute to the value of Simpson's chart, 'being only surprised that with the means at his command, he could have accomplished so much'. Before winter set in, Collinson and a sledge party of seven men set out on 1 November 1852 to visit the mainland, looking for cairns and depositing information. One of the men, Able Seaman William French, had visited Melville Island with Lieutenant Parkes, so that, as his captain remarked, he linked in person the discoveries of Parry and the American continent. During the winter, as in the previous one, parties of Eskimos visited them. Two dogs were bought from

'HMS *Enterprise* entering Dolphin and Union Strait, September 1852', during the Franklin Search expedition of 1850-54, Captain Richard Collinson. Though explored earlier by boat, the *Enterprise* was the first ship to pass through the hazardous channels off the mainland of North America. (Frontispiece to Collinson's *Narrative*, published 1889

them, as well as venison, meat for the dogs and a salmon of 39lbs, which was at first taken for a large log of wood being carried on the steward's shoulder! Collinson described the visit in January 1853 of some children:

> On the 27th we had a little girl who . . . could not have been above eight years old, who being taken much notice of, the next morning we had children of all ages from infancy to manhood. One little boy of four years old was attired in a bear skin suit of one piece, which served for hat, stockings and everything else; how he got into it was a mystery at first, until his mother showed the invention. One small thing, not yet capable of walking, poked out its naked hand every now and then from its mother's hood, where it was carried at the back of the head, the temperature being at the freezing point of mercury, that is to say, 71 ° below the freezing point of water.

Collinson remarked on the good clothing and 'fine, healthy, ruddy appearance' of these kind-hearted and inoffensive people, whose complexions contrasted strongly with the sallow ones of his crew, after a winter spent by candlelight. Unfortunately, since Miertsching, the interpreter, was in the *Investigator*, little could be learnt from them, despite the use of Captain Washington's *Esquimaux and English vocabulary for the use of the Arctic expeditions*. (Published for the Admiralty in 1850, this pocket book had been compiled from various authorities by John Washington, later Hydrographer of the Navy.) One of the ice mates, G Arbuthnot, got a number to draw the coastline. The results agreed with each other, but did not correspond with its trend, as later traced by Collinson.

Arbuthnot thought that they indicated the whereabouts of a ship, but Captain Collinson was sceptical of this. What appeared to be relics of Franklin's ships – two painted pieces of door frame, bearing the broad arrow (the Queen's mark) – were found in July 1853, on the nearby Finlayson Islands, in Dease Strait.

*   *   *

Little did Collinson know, as he sledged that summer, first east and then north along the west coast of Victoria Channel, that another searcher after Franklin had preceded him. This was Dr John Rae, the great Arctic traveller and a Chief Factor of the Hudson's Bay Company. We have seen that he and Dr (later Sir) John Richardson failed to discover any traces of the *Erebus* and *Terror* during their joint expedition along the north coast of America from the Mackenzie to the Coppermine river in 1848. Richardson (then 61) returned to England the following year, leaving Rae to continue the search. Because only one boat remained, only one officer was required in 1849 and Richardson decided that Rae (aged 35) should be that officer. His 'ability and zeal were unquestionable' and he was 'in the prime of life and his skill as a hunter fitted him peculiarly for such an enterprise.'[24] Rae therefore again descended the Coppermine to the sea, but was prevented that year, by the ice in Dolphin and Union Strait, from crossing over as instructed to Wollaston Land (now the Wollaston Peninsula of Victoria Island). His spring and summer journeys of 1851 were remarkable ones. The boats for this Franklin search expedition down the Coppermine and across to the southern shore of Victoria and Wollaston lands were built by the carpenter and fitted out at Fort Confidence on Great Bear Lake to designs drawn by Rae, no doubt from his Orkney childhood. In a private letter to Sir George Simpson, Governor of the Hudson Bay Company's territories, written on 23 April 1851 at Fort Confidence, before setting out, Rae wrote:

> Had any uninterested person been witness of my numerous avocations for the past 3 or 4 months, it is very certain he would have enjoyed many a hearty laugh at my expense. Nothing from the securing of the buttons and seams of my travelling *breeks* to the splicing, fitting and serving of our boats' rigging but I had my hands at. Such duties and occupations for a C.F. [Chief Factor] may be thought infra dig. by my brother-*officers*, but I care little about that as long as the work is done to my mind. I cannot avoid saying a word in praise of our boats which please even me who am somewhat particular in such matters. They are really pretty looking craft, and what is better they seem well suited for their purpose.[25]

The boats were not to be employed until the summer when the ice would have largely broken up and in the spring of 1851, Dr Rae crossed over the ice-bound strait to Wollaston Land, whose south and west coast he searched as far as Prince Albert Sound, an area reached from *Investigator* by Lieutenant William Haswell only ten days before. Then, picking up the boats near the mouth of the Coppermine towards the middle of June, Rae took them along the south side of Coronation Gulf and Dease Strait as far as Cape Alexander, at the northern tip of the Kent Peninsula on the mainland. It was here that he made a crucial decision: to cross the strait to Victoria Land at its narrowest point, although tempted to continue eastward by an 'open passage of a mile or more in width'. His official report to the Hudson's Bay Company continued:

> Had Geographical discovery been the object of the expedition, I would have followed the coast eastward to Simpson Strait, and then crossed over towards Cape Franklin [on King William Land.] This course however, would have been a deviation from the route I had marked out for myself, and would have exposed me to the charge of having lost sight of the duty committed to me.[26]

Had Dr Rae in fact deviated from his chosen route, he would have solved the mystery of Franklin's disappearance.

In the two boats, Rae and his men crossed Dease Strait to Victoria Land and began the examination of its southeast coast, beyond the stretch explored earlier by Dease and Simpson. They continued northwards, first by boat and then on foot; Point Pelly was their last sighting to the north along the dreary, flat, stony and uninteresting shore. In attempting to avoid this by cutting inland, Rae wore out in two hours 'a pair of new moccasins with thick undressed Buffalo skin soles, and stout duffel socks . . . and before the day's journey was half done, every step I took was marked in blood'. Rae noted the presence of beautiful snowy owls along the shores of Victoria Land, while stranded along the coast were 'large pieces of very heavy ice thrown up in great confusion'. This must have been the same type encountered earlier by James Clark Ross and the *Erebus* and *Terror* off the west coast of King William Land. Again on 15 August, Rae had thoughts of crossing Victoria Strait by boat in the lea of Admiralty Island to Point Franklin 'only forty miles distant', but the quantity of ice foiled three attempts to penetrate to the eastward.

New ice and old ice hampered their return journey, but two apparent signs of the *Erebus* and *Terror* were discovered, as the boats crept southwards along the shore, in the form of a piece of pine nearly six feet long and a piece of oak nearly four feet long. The first was stamped with the broad arrow and appeared to be part of a small flagstaff, while the other was evidently a stanchion. Rae concluded that these pieces of wood, found in the latitude of 68 °52′N, longitude 103 °20′W, must have been carried with the heavy ice along a channel which he supposed (correctly) to exist between Victoria Land and North Somerset. Dr Rae summarised the results of the spring and summer operations in 1851 as follows:

> . . . a journey on snow and ice of 1080 statute miles, and a boat voyage along the Arctic Coast, going and returning of 1390 statute miles; the tracing and laying down correctly . . . six hundred and thirty miles of previously unexplored coast, along the Southern shores of Victoria and Wollaston lands . . . This I believe the most quickly performed Arctic journey on record.[27]

*   *   *

Two years later, along these shores, in the spring of 1853, came three sledges from *Enterprise*, named *Enterprise*, *Victoria* and *Royal Albert*. Led by Captain Collinson, each was manned by a team of eight, accompanied by nine dogs altogether, whose names were Sandy, Daddy, Bevis, Fagan, Bill, Jacka, Cribbage, Hook and Hatchett, which were generally loosed when a bear was seen. The sledge *Royal Albert* had been made on board, the others at Woolwich Dockyard. Since driftwood was likely to be scarce, a novel method of cooking food – with 'fire balls' – had been improvised. Made of a mixture of old rope, oil, saltpetre and resin, it was found that ¾lb of this composition thawed the snow or ice and boiled eight pints of water in half an hour, when the temperature was – 30 °F. Three pounds weight, plus one barrel stave, would cook two meals daily for each sledge party.

Captain Collinson and his men left the *Enterprise* on 12 April and were tracing the shores along which Rae's party had sailed or rowed when, on 6 May, three cairns were found, with no indication of their builders. Two days later, they 'came in sight of a beacon and found a notice' deposited by Dr Rae, which outlined his 1851 journey. In his journal, Collinson's reaction, finding once again that he had been forestalled, reads merely, 'Thus we became acquainted that our field of research had been examined; but having eight days' provisions left we set off with the hope of extending the exploration seventy miles further and camped at 5.15'. Their furthest north was reached on 10 May, when they found they were on an island, 'with no land in sight, except in the direction we had come from'. This island, to the northeast of Rae's Point Pelly, Collinson named after his native Gateshead, on Tyneside. Here, he remarked, 'the appearance of the pack to the N.E., N. and N.W. forbid all hope of penetrating even with our light load through it.' In the cairn, built in latitude 70 °26′N, longitude 100 °47′W, a record was placed and they began their return journey.

As Captain Collinson's brother T B Collinson remarked in one of a number of perceptive notes: 'Thus these two explorers [Rae and Collinson] were unconsciously close on the track of the object of search, and both had the ill-luck to go along the west side of Victoria Strait, passing only 30 miles from the spot on the opposite side where there was lying all the time the boat containing the last remaining corpses of the Franklin expedition'. He credited Dr Rae with very nearly completing a North West Passage by boat and blamed Captain McClure for the unfortunate separation of the *Investigator* from the *Enterprise*:

> For, if he had waited, it is reasonable to suppose that the two vessels would have proceeded together up the Prince of Wales Strait (as they did separately), and that in 1852 they would have gone together along the coast of America to the eastward (as the *Enterprise* did) and in the spring of 1853, having double the number of sledges, the E. side of Victoria Strait would have been examined as well as the W. side (which was all the *Enterprise* could do) and therefore the remains of the Franklin Expedition . . . on the coast of King William's Land would have been discovered in 1853.

During the summer at Cambridge Bay, more than 1,500 salmon were caught, of which 1,200 were salted and dried for the homeward voyage. *Enterprise* got under way in early August 1853, and encountered considerable difficulties in making for the west; on 24 August, when attempting to navigate among heavy floes, she lost two bower anchors in the space of two hours. Sometimes both blasting with

'Sledging over hummucky ice' (during the Franklin Search expedition of 1850-54 in *Investigator* (Captain McClure). The ice pressure forms great ridges, making sledge travel laborious. (NMM, D897)

gunpowder and sawing with the giant ice saws were tried in vain. The *Enterprise*, barred from further progress, spent her third Arctic winter, 1853-54, in Camden Bay, not far from the Romanzoff Range and west of Herschel Island, off the north coast of what is now Alaska. In October and November, seventy-six sledge loads of wood were collected from the shore for the winter. The hind leg of a bear had been saved for Christmas Day 1853, but 'was pronounced not to equal either Sir J Richardson's admirable pemmican or Mr Gamble's excellent preserved meat', so that the dogs came in for most of it. With a pint of wine apiece, the seamen fared almost as well as the officers, since the latter's private stocks were by then nearly exhausted. A skittle alley, a billiard room and an observatory were built, as in previous winters, of snow and ice on the floe, while the plays performed on board provided the usual welcome diversion for performers and spectators alike.

Apart from a death from dropsy and scurvy and a serious case of tuberculosis, the winter health record and that of the voyage in general were good. Collinson suffered from scurvy during the first winter of 1851-52 and during the sledge journey of spring 1853, and even thirty years after his return his teeth and gums were still affected.[28] The Sylvester's stove underwent repairs in January 1854 and once installed again, the heat it diffused throughout the ship dried the moist atmosphere in the dripping wet cabins and lower deck. Another useful piece of equipment, one of Halkett's india-rubber boats, which had been invaluable during the preceding years, also showed its age by bursting one of its patches when among the ice, though a nearby floe provided a refuge.[29]

As the weather warmed and flowers carpeted the land in July, a large party of forty-one natives in two umiaks arrived. They quickly made themselves at home, but were not so well behaved, in Collinson's words, 'as our acquaintances of Victoria Land showing a strong disposition to appropriate every article'. One of the boys wore several buttons inscribed with messages regarding *Investigator*, *Enterprise*, *Plover*, the Eastern Search and depots of provisions in 1850, 1851 and 1852. The visitors produced a printed paper a year old, dated HMS *Plover*, 4 July 1853, saying that the *Investigator* had not been heard of. A much more recent message, dated 'Fort Youcon', 27 July 1854, less than a month earlier, was handed to Collinson by the chief of a party of Rat Indians, who were trading with the Eskimos of Barter Island and who had come from the Hudson's Bay Company's post inland. It said that a message from *Plover* of April 1854 had been delivered there by the Rat Indians on 27 June 1854. Meanwhile, Captain Collinson had sent Lieutenant C T Jago with a whaleboat and six men to communicate with the *Plover* at Point Barrow, but Jago found that *Plover* had recently departed for Port Clarence, leaving a house and a depot.

The *Enterprise* rounded Point Barrow and escaped through what Collinson's brother called the 'ice gate' in early August, and at last lost sight of the pack, 1,164 days since rounding Point Barrow in 1851, out of which period, Collinson remarked, only for 38 days was it absent. 'With deep gratitude to Almighty God for having preserved us,' he wrote, 'we experienced with unfeigned pleasure the rolling swell of the open ocean, and bade adieu without regret to the cares of ice navigation.' On their way south, they sighted the first sail seen for three years and received news of the *Investigator*, along with newspapers, pumpkins and potatoes from the American whaling vessel *James Andrews*, whose captain Collinson strongly recommended to round Point Barrow for whales. Unfortunately, it was just Captain Collinson's bad luck to miss the *Plover* again at Port Clarence, so that the *Enterprise* had again to run up to Point Barrow, meeting the pack once more, in order to find her, Captain Maguire having on board all their letters and dispatches. He went on board off Point Barrow and found Captain Collinson and his officers and crew all in good health. Maguire and his crew had been stationed at Point Barrow since 1852 and now that the *Enterprise* was known to be safe, the *Plover* could leave too. Some time was therefore spent landing the vessel's housing rafters and other lumber, no longer of use to them, but greatly prized by the natives of Point Barrow and there was much bustle and bargaining and generous heaping of presents upon their Eskimo friends by the seamen.[30] At Port Clarence, the two ships spent some days in company, transferring provisions, making arrangements for their homeward voyages, and carrying out magnetic observa-

Lieutenant Cresswell's party leaving Mercy Bay to cross M'Clure Strait and reach the *Resolute* (Captain Kellett) before the *Investigator* was finally abandoned on 3 June 1853. Drawn by Lieutenant S Gurney Cresswell (Scott Polar Research Institute)

tions with the instruments from the *Enterprise*. The *Plover*'s last action before her departure for Valparaiso was on 16 September when 'a Native O-mi-ak' was obtained 'for Captain Collinson to take home as a specimen of Esquimaux Naval Architecture'. He had already collected two skin boats from Cambridge Bay, and from Barter Island for the British Museum. Captain Maguire dined aboard the *Enterprise* at Captain Collinson's invitation, after which he took his leave.

Enterprise called at Hong Kong on her homeward voyage, and, while rounding the Cape of Good Hope, learnt in early February 1855 from a steamer that Dr Rae had discovered relics from the missing ships. With this information, Captain Collinson regretted that he had not been able to understand the natives of Cambridge Bay and had also been unable to detach a sledge party to examine the east coast of Victoria Strait (the west coast of King William Land, off which the *Erebus* and *Terror* had been beset).

The *Enterprise* met with no fanfares on her arrival in England in May 1855. Apart from having so nearly missed ascertaining Franklin's fate, there had been trouble between the Captain and some of the officers, a number of whom he suspended in the spring of 1853. Collinson wanted these dealt with by court martial but the Admiralty, tired of the expense and anxiety of the Franklin Search and with the Crimean War to fight, did not wish to pursue the matter. Collinson's brother and editor makes some interesting remarks about the additional labour and responsibility, which accrued to Captain Collinson because of the death of one officer and the suspension of others. He also wrote:

> The captain of the *Enterprise* was a man of most tender heart and generous disposition, but his strong sense of duty to the service gave him a decided and somewhat severe manner; and the reserve that always envelopes the commander of a warship is necessarily increased under such circumstances.

On the posthumous publication of Captain Collinson's journal in 1889, Admiral Sir G H Richards, a greatly respected Arctic officer, described it as 'a record of patient endurance and unflagging perseverance, under difficulties and trials which have perhaps never been surpassed . . .' He went on to say that of the various Arctic voyages of modern times, in his view that of the *Enterprise* was the 'most remarkable of them all'.

> There was no turning back, nor, in the mind of the leader any thought of turning back, until all resources had been exhausted. In its relation, no exaggerated or sensational pictures are drawn: a plain unvarnished tale, almost too plain. Of how many others can this be said?

After noting the unique nature of the *Investigator*'s voyage, Admiral Richards continued:

> Honours were conferred, and deservedly so, on McClure . . . but why the leader [Collinson] was thrown into the cold shade of neglect, almost contumely, when two years later he returned, having accomplished far more, and was only unfortunate in not finding Franklin's parties . . . when he reached almost in sight of their lost ships is only to be accounted for by one of those gusts of popular impulse, which at times blind men's understandings, and obliterate their better judgement, until in the end injustice becomes more expedient than honourable recantation.[31]

The cloud of despondency and anxiety following Collinson's return from the Arctic eventually lifted, and he was knighted in 1875 on the recommendation of the Admiralty for his Arctic service. He was Deputy Master of Trinity House for a number of years. For the infant Hakluyt Society, he edited the Arctic journals of Sir Martin Frobisher 1576-78. It was also he who organised the presentation to John Barrow, junior, on 28 June 1856, of a testimonial to which nearly all the officers employed in the polar sea subscribed, as an appreciation of Barrow's assistance and kindness. The list of thirty-seven names included Dr John Rae.[32]

CHAPTER 13

The Expeditions of Kennedy, Belcher, Inglefield and Kane 1851-1854

Beside the River Thames at Greenwich, in front of the former Royal Naval College, there is a large obelisk erected in 1853 by his English friends to the memory of another martyr to the Franklin Search – a young French naval officer, Joseph René Bellot. After the return in October 1850 of the first search expedition in the little *Prince Albert* sent by Lady Franklin (unfortunately not having carried out her instructions, but bringing some actual relics of the missing ships from Cape Riley), Lady Franklin resolved that the little vessel of 90 tons should be sent off again in the spring of the following year. Her choice of commander was an unusual one. William Kennedy had been an officer of the Hudson's Bay Company, in one of whose posts, Cumberland House, Rupert's Land (now Saskatchewan), he was born in 1814. The son of Chief Factor Alexander Kennedy and a Swampy Cree woman named Aggathas, he was educated in Orkney and joined the company's service at the age of 18. However, disliking the use of alcohol in the fur trade, he resigned in 1846 and for two years, 1848-50, he was captain of a boat on Lake Huron.[1] He thus had little, if any, sea-going experience, nor was he, according to Jane Franklin's biographer, 'of the stuff of which leaders are made', but so impressed were Lady Franklin and her advisers by Kennedy's 'integrity and earnestness' that they were 'blind to his defects'.[2] Frances Woodward, author of *Portrait of Jane*, remarks that Kennedy's expedition was 'perhaps a more striking instance even than McClintock's of that impulse of chivalry which animated the Franklin Search'. In the preface to his book when referring to Lady Franklin, Kennedy expressed his 'admiration of that universal and unexampled devotion with which she has sacrificed her health, her strength and all her worldly means to the search for her distinguished husband and her gallant friends and countrymen.'[3]

Equally unusual was Lady Franklin's choice as second-in-command of the *Prince Albert*. He was *Enseigne de Vaisseau* Joseph René Bellot. In his mid-twenties, Bellot's character was said to be 'sad and thoughtful', but 'his spirit gay'. To Jane, says her biographer, this was 'an irresistible combination' and she 'delighted to call him her "French son" '. Bellot refused to accept any payment for his services, and he later told her that, after their meeting, he joined the search 'with all my feelings, with all the dutiful warmth of a son'. Another

Monument erected by his 'English friends' to Enseigne de Vaisseau J R Bellot of the Imperial Navy of France, who was drowned during the Franklin Search. It stands on the waterfront at Greenwich. (NMM, B9910/5)

example of devotion, this time to his old chief, was to be seen in the supercargo, 'dear old John Hepburn', as Lady Franklin called him, 'who would not be left behind'. By then in his early sixties, he had served in HMS *Trent* and on the overland expedition of 1819-22, and had accompanied the Franklins to Tasmania. Kennedy writes of him as the 'faithful attendant and sharer in the perils and privations' of Sir John Franklin's first tragic journey, going out 'in his old age as the best tribute he can render of his affection for his ancient commander'.

Lady Franklin and Sophia carried out much of the business side of the expedition at Aberdeen and in Stromness (Orkney), as they did later in 1853 for the abortive search expedition, under Kennedy, via the Pacific, in the *Isabel*.[4] The *Prince Albert* made her final departure from Stromness on 3 June, watched by Lady Franklin and her niece. The French flag was flown, as well as the British and 'Our parting with our dear little French friend was really painful – he sobbed like a child as he took leave of my Aunt', wrote Sophy Cracroft. 'It was some time before he got courage to say the word. We are really *very* fond of him – his sweetness and simplicity and earnestness are most endearing.'[5] Kennedy considered Bellot 'the noblest, the greatest and best of our little band'.[6]

Sad to say the expedition accomplished little beyond the discovery of a narrow passage, Bellot Strait between North Somerset and the Boothia Peninsula, which became an important link in the North West Passage. The *Prince Albert* wintered in Batty Bay, south of Port Leopold, North Somerset. A sledge party visited Fury Beach where they found Parry's stores, left 30 years ago, quite wholesome, but no traces of Franklin. A second very early start, using snow houses not tents, on 28 February 1852, took them with dogs, which later existed on 'old leather shoes and fag-ends of buffalo robes', across Peel Sound and Prince of Wales Island, as far as Ommanney Bay. Returning via Cape Walker, they travelled some 1,100 miles, but did not fulfil Lady Franklin's hopes and examine the coast of Peel Sound further south than Ross had done, in which direction, as we have seen, she believed Franklin could have gone. On the return of the *Prince Albert* to Britain, Bellot tried unsuccessfully to persuade the French Government, under the Emperor Napoleon III, to join in the Franklin Search. Sad to say, Bellot was drowned in the Arctic while carrying despatches for Sir Edward Belcher during the Franklin Search expedition of 1852-54. Jane Franklin was, of course, extremely upset about this, at a time when her own cup of sorrows was brimming over, and it emerged that the young man, who was only 27 when he died, was almost the sole support of his mother and five sisters. After the monument had been built at Greenwich, the remaining one thousand pounds subscribed by the public was divided between them. Bellot's journal of the 1851-52 expedition, prefaced by an essay on his life and work, was published in Paris in 1854. An English edition followed the next year. William Kennedy's 'short narrative' of the *Prince Albert*'s second voyage appeared in 1853.

Belcher's Squadron 1852-1853

The commander of the third naval squadron to search for the missing ships was Sir Edward Belcher, who was well known for his survey work in various quarters of the globe, and for his irascible temperament. He was instructed by the Admiralty to search for Franklin up Wellington Channel, as Captain Penny had advocated, and to establish depots on or near Melville Island for the benefit of the *Enterprise* and *Investigator*, which had not been heard of since 1851 and 1850 respectively. The squadron consisted of five ships: the *Resolute* (Captain Henry Kellett) and the steamer *Intrepid* (Commander Leopold McClintock), which formed the western division; the *Assistance* (Belcher) and the steamer *Pioneer* (Lieutenant Sherard Osborn) forming the eastern division, together with the *North Star* (Captain W J S Pullen). The *North Star* was to remain at Beechey Island, as a sort of communications headquarters and depot ship. Commenting on his orders regarding Collinson in a letter from Melville Bay, Belcher asked the former Secretary to the Admiralty, J W Croker, 'Will any one come for me?'[7]

Sir Edward Belcher's reputation as a fine surveyor with a tyrannical disposition is well known. The historian of the Admiralty Hydrographic Service observed that Belcher 'was evidently a hard task-master, as shown by the comment of a brother officer', made in 1845. 'How unfortunate it is that such a capital fellow for work should be such a devil incarnate with his officers'.[8]

Another former Hydrographer of the Navy, G S Ritchie, also commented on Belcher's appointment by the then ageing Hydrographer, Sir Francis Beaufort:

> This time Beaufort's choice of a leader seems almost unbelievable; every ship Belcher had commanded he had made a hell afloat. The humanity, the tact and the leadership which men like Parry, James Ross and Austin had shown to be vital in the Arctic were beyond the reach of Belcher, no matter how he tries to explain away his failures in his account of the expedition which he titled *The Last of the Arctic Voyages*.[9]

Belcher's instructions, dated 16 April 1852, were from five Lords Commissioners of the Admiralty (Northumberland, Hyde Parker, Phipps Hornby, Thomas Herbert and Alexander Milne), not from Beaufort and they are printed in his book, *The Last of the Arctic Voyages* which is dedicated 'by permission' to Beaufort, 'under whose generous sympathy and unfluctuating patriotism the various expeditions engaged in search of Sir John Franklin and his gallant associates have been chiefly planned and executed'.[10] There is no doubt that the book, published in two volumes, is a fine one, amply illustrated with colour plates, charts and wood engravings. It is in distinct contrast to Collinson's plain tale. It contains a useful glossary of Arctic terms and notes on Natural History by Sir John Richardson and others.

The frontispiece to Belcher's narrative shows the squadron leaving the Nore in April 1852. The vessels were well provided with good food, libraries, printing presses and apparatus for preserving specimens of natural history. As in the previous naval expedition, Woolwich Dockyard furnished the 'tents, sledges and general equipment', while magnetic instruments and special thermometers were also embarked. Twenty-five 'silken wrought banners for the sledges, by ladies deeply interested in our success' were presented shortly before departure. Gunpowder for blasting the ice was later taken aboard. The crew, of whom Belcher wrote, 'A finer body of men never trod the decks of any of Her Majesty's ships of war', were paid on departure, six months of this being in advance, with double pay during the expedition. Despite temptation none deserted.

The squadron followed the usual route across the North Atlantic and up the west coast of Greenland and on 4 July 1852, Belcher wrote to J W Croker from *Assistance* in Melville Bay on the northwest coast of Greenland at latitude 76 °N: fourteen whalers were docked nearby, while earlier they had passed the wreck of the *Regalia*, a whaler from Kirkaldy, which had been 'nipped', the ice having gone through both her sides. Belcher described how 'Kellett has been very ill, *all but gone*, but is now himself again and the life of the party. His ship got a severe nip (*all but* also) last week and lost her rudder. So you perceive that we have dangers on this side of the Sound'.[11]

In a postscript to this letter Belcher explained how he hoped to discover documents near Beechey Island, since he had been told by members of the previous expedition that a proper search had not been made because they had had no tools to break up the frozen ground.

Another letter from the same locality, written by Commander G H (later Sir George) Richards to John Barrow paints a graphic picture of their situation. In it

The Arctic Council, 1851, painted by Stephen Pearce. The Hydrographer of the Navy, Sir Francis Beaufort, who planned much of the search for Franklin, is seated centrally, surrounded by some of the most prominent 'Arctic Officers' of the Royal Navy. Portraits of Sir John Franklin, Captain Fitzjames and Sir John Barrow hang on the wall. (National Portrait Gallery, London)

he refers to the destruction of the American whaling barque *M'Lellan* in a heavy nip on the previous day. '*We* are *all right*', he wrote, 'North Star has lost a Cathead by the wreck of the Yankee being jammed down, on top of him, but that is a trifle and can easily be replaced'. He went on to write that 'the *Element* we are in is of so uncertain a character and the changes in it so frequent and so varied that it is impossible to say what may happen the next hour'. The letter continued on 9 July: to describe how everything of any use had been got out of the hold of the wreck, mainly bread, coal, oil, molasses and some ice gear.

> It is a novel scene this – more than 90 Boats on the floe, with their sails rigged for Tents and the Crews all in them, their chests and bags strewn on the Ice round them and evincing a degree of indifference and recklessness I should say only to be attained by long practice. The Masters only seem to take any interest in the affair and they may be seen roaming round their vessels casting anxious glances at them as any motion is observed in the floe.

The *Resolute* and *Assistance* he said, were in the same predicament as the whalers, but were better able to stand very heavy pressure; 'but in case of necessity we are quite prepared and could be on the Ice with all our boats, six weeks provisions or more, and a limited supply of clothing in less than ten minutes'. Otherwise, every spare moment was being devoted to the equipment of the travelling parties,

A group of officers of the Franklin Search expeditions, from the *Illustrated London News*, left to right: Lieutenant Osborn, Mr Allard, Commander McClintock, Mr Pullen, Commander Richards. (Author's collection)

although not enough buffalo robes for use as tent bottoms had been supplied.

He continued the letter on 17 July, after eight more tedious days passed near Cape Walker (on the northwest coast of Greenland). The ice by then had loosened and he was greatly relieved that the whalers were safe. 'Our American friend has disappeared beneath the Ice after having afforded us a good deal of fire wood and a little provision'.[12]

Richards was not only good at describing the voyage: he was also extremely perceptive of the shortcomings of Belcher. As Admiral Ritchie writes:

> Commander George Richards . . . really knew his Belcher. He had served with him in *Sulphur*'s commission and it is not surprising that he decided to keep a diary of every happening on board. Richards was determined that if, on return to England, Belcher court-martialled his officers, as was his habit, the facts of every situation should have been recorded on the spot . . . It does not need an exhaustive study of this diary, or more than a casual perusal of Belcher's book, to make one realise that Richards acted as the buffer, and by his tact and his knowledge of Belcher, maintained the peace.[13]

Richards' letter is headed 'HMS Assistance, In the Pack. Lat. 75 °15′N'. It must have been written in early July 1852. While making very slow progress in *Assistance*, since the *Pioneer* (Lieutenant Sherard Osborn) was elsewhere, Belcher observed in his book that vessels for this service should be independent screw steamers, accompanied by the [sailing] ships as transports or depot vessels. The officer commanding should be in the steamer. Hailing and straining the lungs to people always half deaf, is not pleasant to either party, and is productive, by repetition of orders, when not heard or not obeyed, of very unpleasant feelings.

The squadron was reunited at Beechey Island on 11 August and though a thorough search was made of various localities, still no records of the missing expedition were found. An attempt was made to dig up the graves, but these were found so firmly frozen that the effort was discontinued. Belcher's conclusion was that some disaster had taken place there.

On 14 August 1852, the senior officers dined with Belcher and the various instructions were gone over before the squadron separated into its two divisions – eastern and western. The crews were then assembled on the floe under the union flag to be addressed by Belcher and given a printed copy each of the 'beautiful prayer composed by the Rev. H Lindsay for the commencement of travelling'[14]. This then was the parting of the ways. The *Assistance* (Captain Sir Edward Belcher) and *Pioneer* (Lieutenant Sherard Osborn) turned northwards into Wellington Channel, while *Resolute* (Captain Henry Kellett) and *Intrepid* (Commander McClintock) endeavoured to pass westwards to Melville Island.

Assistance and *Pioneer* were fortunate in finding open water in Wellington Channel. They passed into the Queen's Channel, then further north to discover Northumberland Sound (named by Belcher after the Duke of Northumberland, who presided over the Board of Admiralty). This extensive sound is situated on the northwestern coast of the Grinnell Peninsula, Devon Island. Winter quarters were established in the north of the Sound and the elegant little folding chart in Belcher's narrative, entitled 'Plan of Northumberland Sound, Prince Albert Island', gives the position as 77 °52′N, 97 °W. Belcher moved Captain Penny's place-names for Sir John and Lady Franklin 'to the limiting points of the Queen's Channel', but retained almost all those further south. By 20 August they were frozen in.

On 23 August, before winter truly set in, a party of twenty-seven men with three sledges and a boat explored to the northeast. The so-called sledge-boat *Hamilton* was one of four, built of canvas and laminated board, from the modified design of a Norway boat, for use in light ice-travelling – a 'brown paper boat', as Belcher called her. He maintained that 'she did her duty well with those who knew how to manage her'. To the north of winter quarters, at 'Village Point', a large cairn was built, mainly from the remains of an 'Esquimaux encampment'. In Belcher's description of this deserted site, so far to the North, he explained how 'Great ingenuity and labour had been exerted' in the construction of the houses . . . their foundations were laid at least three feet below the ground . . . These foundations were of stone, in double walls, with the interval filled in with fine clay and gravel. The doors faced to the east, and evidently had the long passages usually appertaining to those of settled habitations in Greenland'. He noted that the building stones were larger, and different from any others found on the Point. One doorway still had a lintel over it. Most of the houses (one of which is sketched in his book) were oval in form, with doorways about three feet wide by two and a half high.

Belcher described in some detail the practicalities of camping during the sledge journeys. The men would wriggle into their 'chrysalis' bags under which was an oilskin canvas, spread over the snow, and a buffalo-robe acting as a carpet. The officer slept on the windward side and the cook beside the tent door, being the first to wake to the 'ominous snuffling' of a polar bear, of which two were shot on this reconnaissance.

During the boat journeys of late August and early September 1852, parties under Belcher and Richards reached and took formal possession of Exmouth and Table Islands, to the north of the Grinnell Peninsula of North Devon, and of the larger and more distant North Cornwall Island, to which Belcher gave its own Land's End. The channel between these was later named after Belcher. The islands even further north (the Ellef Ringnes group) were only to be explored by Otto Sverdrup in the *Fram* nearly half a century later. Belcher came to believe that this 'great eastern space' of sea connected with Jones and Smith Sounds or even the polar ocean. It hardly needs remarking that no traces of Franklin were found, but according to Belcher the duty of searching was never forgotten.

Inglefield's Voyage in the Isabel 1852

On his return from the *Plover* in the North Pacific in 1851 and before his memorable crossing of M'Clure Strait from HMS *Resolute* to the Bay of Mercy, Lieutenant Bedford Pim visited St Petersburg to see whether a Franklin Search expedition might be organised along the coast of Siberia. The idea was not pursued, nor was another plan put forward by a Mr Donald Beatson, with the result that the screw schooner, *Isabel* (149 tons, with a small high pressure engine), fitted out for Beatson's project, was left on Jane Franklin's hands. An arrangement between Jane Franklin, the Admiralty and Commander Edward Augustus Inglefield was then made. Inglefield is described by Jane's biographer as 'an elegant young man with a considerable talent in art as in seamanship'.[15] He took over the *Isabel*, provided the crew and paid for further fitments at Woolwich Dockyard, courtesy the Admiralty. Sir Roderick Murchison, President of the Royal Geographical Society, Dr and Mrs William Scoresby, and of course Lady Franklin, came to see the *Isabel*'s departure from the Thames, from where she was towed by the *Lightning*, again courtesy of the Admiralty, as far as Peterhead, the Scottish whaling port. Here additional crew, a crow's nest, ice saws and fresh beef were embarked. There were seventeen officers and crew altogether. Dr Sutherland, who had already sailed on two whaling voyages and with Captain Penny, was the medical officer. Thomas Abernethy, another Arctic veteran, was one of the two ice-masters while the engineer, Mr Bardin, had superintended the building of the engines. All the officers agreed to a lower rate of pay for this search expedition.

The *Isabel,* yacht, making the first entry into Smith Sound at the head of Baffin Bay in 1852, during a Franklin Search voyage, commanded by Commander E A Inglefield. (Watercolour by Inglefield, NMM, C613)

The *Isabel* departed from Peterhead on 10 July 1852. Since the Arctic squadron under Belcher would be fully occupied in and beyond Lancaster Sound, Inglefield's plan was to search Whale Sound, Smith Sound and Jones Sound at the head of Baffin Bay. Although he found no traces of Franklin, as a voyage of exploration it was a great success. Inglefield called his narrative *A summer search for Sir John Franklin, with a peep into the Polar Basin* and it was published in 1853. In one season only it achieved a great deal. Having crossed the Atlantic the *Isabel* sailed up the west coast of Greenland and took on dogs at Upernavik. Whale Sound (Hvalsund) was entered and two nearby islands were named, but the great novelty and excitement was to enter Smith Sound, which according to Inglefield had never been approached within 70 miles since Baffin's voyage of 1616.

On 26 August, near Cape Alexander, at the eastern entrance to Smith Sound, Inglefield wrote, 'We were entering the Polar Sea, and wild thoughts of getting to the Pole – of finding our way to Behring Strait – and most of all of reaching Franklin and giving him help rushed rapidly through my brain.' Again, 'On rounding Cape Alexander, the full glory of being actually in the Polar Sea burst upon my thoughts, for then I beheld the open sea stretching through seven points of the compass and apparently unencumbered with ice, though bounded on east and west by two distant headlands, the one on the western shore was named after His Royal Highness Prince Albert'. In a letter to John Barrow, Inglefield said that he had reached Smith Sound without difficulty (1852 must have been an open ice year) and had found the entrance to be 36 miles wide and not the 'punny ten marked on the charts'.[16]

A fine folding panorama of the east coast in his book, entitled 'Midnight August 26th. 1852', illustrates Inglefield's discoveries and identifies such place-names as the Prince of Wales Mountains, Cape Albert, Cape Frederick VII (of Denmark), Crystal Palace Cliffs and Cape Alexander. He also named Ellesmere Island, which forms the west coast of what is now known as Nares Strait, which extends from Baffin Bay to the Arctic Ocean. Inglefield was of course wrong in believing the *Isabel* had entered the Polar Sea. Later voyages in the nineteenth century showed that in this area its coast was in roughly 80 °N. According to Inglefield, the Hydrographer, Sir Francis Beaufort, called the voyage of the *Isabel* one of the most remarkable on record.

On his way south, Inglefield searched Jones Sound, reaching further to the west (84 °10′W) than Austin had done, but again finding no trace of the *Erebus* and *Terror*. Determined to give Belcher an account of his voyage, Inglefield entered Lancaster Sound and reached snow-covered Beechey Island on 7 September. He found the *North Star* (Captain Pullen) safely secured and waiting for ice to seal them in for the winter. He handed over their letters and despatches and gave them twelve hours to reply. It was in this interval that he excavated Hartnell's grave.

The Second Grinnell Expedition 1853-55

Inglefield in the *Isabel* was followed into Smith Sound a year later by Dr Elisha Kent Kane in the *Advance*, which had searched for Franklin with the *Rescue* in the expedition of 1850-51 commanded by Lieutenant E J De Haven. The generous Mr Henry Grinnell placed the *Advance* at Dr Kane's disposal and she was repaired and refitted at the expense of Mr Peabody of London. The Geographical Society of New York, the Smithsonian Institution, the American Philosophical Society and other learned bodies contributed towards the scientific instruments.

Ten of the party of eighteen belonged to the United States Navy. The others (all volunteers) were chosen by Dr Kane. They joined at salaries much below the usual. Three main rules were enforced, says Dr Kane. These were 'absolute sub-ordination to the officer in command, or his delegate; second, abstinence from all intoxicating liquors, except when dispensed by special order; third, the habitual disuse of profane language'. Kane based his plan on the probability that Greenland stretched further towards the North Pole than any other land, lead-ing directly to the open sea, whose existence he had inferred. The party would navigate as far as possible up Baffin Bay and from there would press on towards the Pole, with boats and sledges, examining the coast for signs of the lost ex-pedition as they proceeded.

The *Advance* departed from New York on 30 May 1853. Kane was given nine Newfoundland dogs by the Governor of Newfoundland and twenty sledge dogs were bought in Greenland. At Fiskernaes on the Greenland coast a young Eskimo hunter, Hans Christian, was taken on and at Upernavik, Carl Petersen, who had been Captain Penny's interpreter and adviser. The *Advance* succeeded in entering Smith Sound, Kane finding some discrepancies between their own and Inglefield's positions. Smith Sound widened into a basin, subsequently named after him. Here the *Advance* found winter quarters, named Rensselaer Harbour where the little brig was laid up and 'which we were fated', wrote Kane in his book, 'never to leave together – a long resting place to her indeed, for the same ice is round her still'. Kane's officers had advocated seeking winter quarters further to the south, but Kane had another object in view, beside the search for Franklin. This concerned the existence of an open polar sea, round about the North Pole, beyond a supposed circumpolar barrier of sea ice lying between latitudes 75 ° and 80 °N. The instructions to Dr Kane from the United States Navy Department dated 9 February 1853 drew his attention to the 'objects of scientific enquiry', which he was to pursue 'particularly to such as relate to the existence of an open Polar sea, terrestrial magnetism, general meteorology, and subjects of importance in connection with natural history'.[17] Inglefield's account of the *Isabel's* penetration into the 'polar sea' doubtless encouraged Dr Kane.

The story of the second Grinnell Expedition made compulsive reading for the American public when told in its leader's *Arctic Explorations* (1856), whose two volumes are supposed to have lain 'for a decade, with the Bible, on almost every parlor table in America'.[18] Apart from the beauty of Dr Kane's romantic landscapes, the narrative tells a harrowing tale of near starvation (including the cooking of rats which plagued the ship), of a near-fatal attempt by half the expedition to reach the Danish settlements in Greenland by boat, of meetings with the Eskimos, of attempts to explore northwards towards the polar sea, and finally of the successful retreat led by the frail but heroic leader towards Upernavik, well over a thousand miles to the south, by sledge and boat in the summer of 1855. A relief expedition, commanded by Lieutenant H J Hartstein, took the survivors aboard at Disko, apart of course from Carl Petersen. They arrived in New York in early October 1855, when their story covered much of the front page of the *New York Times* and other American newspapers, making Dr Kane the hero of the hour.

On his return journey to the United States, Dr Kane learnt of the find by Dr Rae of relics from the Franklin expedition, so far away from where he himself had searched. Because of its mixed objectives and because of the direction in which it travelled, the second Grinnell Expedition may be said more properly to belong to the history of the attainment of the North Pole, rather than that of the North West Passage. In failing health and not long before his death, Dr Kane nevertheless visited a fog-bound London in November 1856, where he met the Lords of the Admiralty and Beaufort's successor as Hydrographer, Captain Washington. He also called on Lady Franklin and met Sir Roderick Murchison, President of the Royal Geographical Society, whose gold medal he received. Together with other members of the Grinnell expeditions and of the relief expedition under Lieutenant Hartstein, Dr Kane was awarded the British Arctic medal of 1818-55 for his efforts in the search for Franklin.

Lady Franklin had offered the command of the *Isabel*, in a last effort to find the records and relics of her husband's expedition, to Dr Kane in June 1856. In her biographer's words:

> He arrived in October, while the book of his voyage was arousing horror at the unparalleled hardships it revealed; obviously he had not recovered from them, but Jane was at first hopeful that 'the air of the old country' would restore him; then she was plying him with cod-liver oil and 'routing out' soothing books for him (including Roget's Thesaurus); then he was ordered to the West Indies [by his doctor] and she could barely be restrained from accompanying him, Sophy said . . . Early next year this very gallant gentleman died – another martyr to the Franklin Search. His book and his death did much to sway public opinion against resuming it.[19]

In 1965, a century later, an important record of the Second Grinnell Expedition was published. It is a translation from the Danish of Carl Petersen's account of the expedition (1856), with additional documentation, admirably edited by Oscar M Villarejo. This 'reveals . . . the high drama of the clash of the two strongest and most commanding personalities among those who sailed in the *Advance*' – Dr Kane and Johan Carl Christian Petersen.[20] On the walls of her house, Upper Gore Lodge, Kensington Gore, now demolished, Jane hung 'all the Arctic portraits'. Dr Kane's was 'framed in gold and crimson velvet to do more honour to him'.[21]

Belcher's Squadron 1852-1853

Meanwhile in Northumberland Sound, on board *Assistance*, Sir Edward Belcher brooded on his equipment. He complained that the delay in his being appointed to command meant that there was little time for thought being given in England to proper equipment. He considered that this was more the province of a 'ship-broker and the higher classes of tradesmen'. With experience, he and his officers now knew what was really required:

> If time had permitted, I could have had the opinions of the best practical men: lighter, better and cheaper clothing would have been prepared for every individual . . . the tents would have been adequate to preserve life, if wrecked, and yet lighter for travelling; the stoves would have been serviceable now and hereafter; the sledges would not have been constructed of soft Canadian elm in the dockyards, but of lance-wood, by some intelligent carriage-builder, and shod with steel instead of soft iron.

Belcher's further complaint was that the squadron was 'totally unprovided' with travelling boots and no advantage had been taken of the experience of the previous expedition. Meanwhile, one shoemaker and a number of sailmakers were 'closely engaged making canvas boots with leather soles'. Some had been made with the seal skins bought in Greenland, which later proved totally useless. None of the clothing actually fitted, and Belcher himself had obtained a suit for travelling from the Governor of one of the Danish settlements. Extra boots and thick gloves should have been provided for the building of cairns like the one on Mount Beaufort. In the next century the Scott Polar Research Institute was founded in Cambridge in 1920 partly to form a repository for information and results from expeditions, so that each could build on the experience of others.

The winter of 1852-53 was taken up with the usual theatricals, a newspaper, evening school and scientific observations, of which last Sir Edward makes some play in his book, though he says nothing of the newspaper (perhaps because it is written largely in the hand of Sherard Osborn). It was called, *The Queen's Illuminated Magazine and North Cornwall Gazette, 1852, 1853.* It was lively and well illustrated and there are playbills between its leaves.[22] He also features the Society of Royal Arctic Engineers, called by Sherard Osborn, the Imaginary Society of Engineers, which met on Monday nights, with the object of enabling the 'Diffident seamen to stir themselves by a course of study which would enable them to enter the "Excellent" (gunnery school) with certain acquirements'. Belcher thought these meetings 'might induce those to think who had never thought before'. Another aim was to provide a forum for discussion. The crew were invited to produce papers on a subject of their choice. Sir Edward Belcher was the President and Commander Richards the Secretary of the Society. At a meeting on 29 November 1852, in 'Main Hatchway Square', Mr Harwood of the *Pioneer* read a paper entitled, 'on the Construction of a Lamp for the Cooking Apparatus of the Travelling Parties, to burn the fat of Animals slain in the chase'.

A party of younger men climbed Mount Beaufort on 18 February and from its summit (1500 feet) were able to see and cheer the sun's reappearance at the end of the winter darkness, during which a temperature of minus 62.5 °F was registered. The spring depot-laying journeys revealed the inadequacies of the cooking lamps issued by the Government, for which ship-made ones were substituted. Belcher, with the sledges *Londesborough, Dauntless* and *Enterprise*, as well as the sledge-boat *Hamilton*, left on 2 May 1853 for the northeast, travelling along the north coast of North Devon, off which they discovered Princess Royal Islands, as far as Cardigan Strait (looking eastward to North Kent Island and northward to the Victoria Islands). Then the party circumnavigated the Grinnell Peninsula by way of Arthur Strait (now Fiord). They discovered graves, and a number of curious, apparently man-made structures – a pile of half a dozen stones, 'constructed with such mathematical ability by the hand of man, that it was at present firm and complete, but tottering if any one stone was abstracted'. They also found a double cone-shaped cairn, as well as a group of Eskimo stone circles. Sketches of the three curiosities appear in Belcher's narrative. Two whale skeletons were found at 80 and at 500 feet above sea level, as well as musk oxen and a number of polar bears and cubs on which the dogs were set. One of these dogs – Punch from Cape York – 'the bravest of his species' among a breed 'as proud as Lucifer' was later taken to England and placed in the London Zoo.

In June, Sir Edward Belcher, Dr Lyall, men and dogs sledged across Belcher Strait to reach the northern islands of Buckingham and Graham, the whole group being named after Queen Victoria. Here, as usual, Sir Edward Belcher, surveyor, ascended a high point to obtain angles with his theodolite. He blamed their 'bad fowling-pieces' for the escape of game to eat and of specimens for the

'National Museums'. On nearing winter quarters in Northumberland Sound, Belcher sent one of the dogs, called Lady Fanny Disco by the men, to the ships bearing a message to warn his steward of the party's approach. They arrived on 23 June 1853, to find that because of the melt season, the *Assistance* 'had exchanged her snow-white bath for the semblance of a filthy farm-yard', and, more important, a despatch from Commander Richards, with news of the *Investigator*, the *Resolute* and the *Intrepid* in the west.

*   *   *

The old 'wooden wall,' HMS *Resolute* (Captain Kellett) and the steam vessel, *Intrepid* (Commander McClintock) formed part of the naval squadron under Belcher's overall command. Their task was two-fold: to search for Franklin after finding winter quarters at, or near, Melville Island and to watch out too for the *Enterprise* and *Investigator*, last heard of in 1851 and 1850 respectively. The squadron was split at Beechey Island in the summer of 1852 with the *North Star* to remain as depot-ship, the *Assistance* and *Pioneer* to form the Northern division, and the *Resolute* and *Intrepid* to form the Western. The dramatic discovery and rescue of the 'Investigators' has already been told, but the fine sledge journeys made by Commander F L McClintock and the less well known G F Mecham were also important aspects of this particular expedition. Among the officers of *Resolute* was Enseigne de Vaisseau Emile de Bray of the Imperial Navy of France, after whom Cape de Bray on Melville Island is named and whose journal was translated into English and published only in 1992 – in contrast to that of Bellot, which appeared in French and English soon after his death.[23] His sledge was named *Hero*, with the motto 'By faith and courage'. His sledge journey got off to a bad start with the sudden death of one of his party, Thomas Coombes, who suffered a heart attack after they parted from McClintock on the west coast of Melville Island. Coombes' grave was later dug with great difficulty in the frozen ground on Dealy Island beside two others there, and De Bray headed the funeral procession, flying his flag at half mast.

Melville Island had been as far west as William Edward Parry had reached in 1819-20. The Franklin Search organised under Captain Kellett's command from

The sledges of the Franklin Search expeditions flew sledge flags, of which this is a surviving example in the National Maritime Museum. It belonged to Lieutenant R V Hamilton's sledge *Hope*. (NMM, A7465)

the winter quarters of the western division in 1852-53 at Dealy Island (an islet in Bridport Inlet on the southeastern shores of Melville Island) was to show that there were other large islands even further west. The largest was Prince Patrick Island, whose barren west coast, fringed with the stupendous hummocks of the polar pack, was searched, for all but 20 miles, by Commander F L McClintock from the north and Lieutenant G F Mecham from the south. One could describe Prince Patrick Island as an island at the edge of the world, like Banks Island, on the rim of the central polar basin. The two large islands to the northeast of Prince Patrick Island, Borden and Brock, were not discovered until the summers of 1915 and 1916, during the Canadian Arctic Expedition led by Vilhjalmur Stefansson. Although the public of Victorian England was not uncritical, particularly when comparing the efforts of the Hudson's Bay Company travellers with those of the Navy, it was Stefansson who began the fashion for decrying the British naval polar expeditions, forgetting that his own explorations were an extension beyond the lands and seas charted by the Royal Navy in the nineteenth century. The west coast of Melville Island itself had not been explored by Parry, neither had its southwestern coast. Between Prince Patrick and Melville Islands lies Eglinton Island, on which Mecham landed a depot and from where G S Nares, Mate, was sent back. Some twenty years later, Nares commanded HMS *Challenger*, during her great oceanographic voyage, from which he was appointed to lead the North Polar expedition of 1875-76.

Musk oxen, caribou, hares and other game provided a good deal of fresh meat for the sledge parties. McClintock had worked hard on improving the sledging methods and instituted the use of light 'satellite' sledges, under six feet long and weighing 14lbs, which could be detached and pulled by two or three men for a week or more, carrying only blanket bags and provisions, to explore bays and inlets, or to hunt. He also extended the length of the autumn depot-laying. According to Clements Markham, his two larger sledges, when loaded, weighed 2,000lbs or 228lbs per man on starting. He later made efficient use of dogs, and published on the subject of arctic sledge travelling on his return.[24]

In his life of McClintock, Markham writes with feeling of the men who dragged the sledges and who often returned to England broken in health. The weeks when they had to walk through the icy melt water, often up to their waists did the most damage. Some of these men he would have known himself, so that they were not just names as they are to us today. For instance, he wrote 'The captain of Hamilton's sledge was that grand old sailor George Murray, who had served in both the expeditions of Ross and Austin, and was the most brilliant contributor to the *Aurora Borealis*'.[25]

On the return journey from Prince Patrick Island, in June 1853, McClintock and his sledge party struggled northwards across deep melting snow to a pleasant-looking island, covered in moss and flowers, which (being born in Ireland like a number of the other Arctic officers) he named Emerald Isle. Markham tells us that McClintock was away from the ships for 105 days, discovering 768 miles of new country and covering altogether 1,210 geographical (1,408 statute) miles.

He described McClintock (his old messmate during the search expedition of 1850-51) as follows:

> He was a wiry little man, with rather bandy legs, and a habit of sniffing, very consci-
> entious and hard working, enthusiastically devoted to the Arctic cause in his quiet way,
> while he secured the attachment and admiration of those under him by his example
> rather than by anything he said. For he was very quiet and a man of few words. His
> talent for organizing work amounted to genius. He was an excellent messmate and a
> thoroughly good fellow.[26]

The officer who led the long complementary sledge journey to McClintock's, whose exploration of the west coast of Prince Patrick Island was completed by Vilhjalmur Stefansson during the First World War, was Lieutenant G F Mecham. Clements Markham described him as

> tall and good looking with a charming smile, clever, humorous and genial. Equal to
> McClintock as an organizer, he had the gift of winning the hearts of men by his sym-
> pathy and bonhomie. He was the *beau ideal* of an Arctic officer, and never had an
> equal. He was a good messmate and one of the best fellows I ever met.[27]

The captain of his sledge was James Tullett, after whom Tullett Point on its west coast was named. As we have seen, Mecham searched the southwest coast of Melville Island and crossed Kellett Strait to Eglinton Island, then across Crozier Channel to the southeast point of Prince Patrick Island (Cape Mecham) and on round Cape Manning and Land's End, along the desolate west coast to Cape Tullett and beyond. At Cape Manning, 90 feet above the sea, and also further inland, Mecham found tree trunks, some with their bark in place. One tree stuck out eight feet from the bank of a ravine, while others were found later measuring four feet in circumference. One was 30 feet long. The second group were about 400 feet above sea level, near the head of Walker Inlet. Similar finds had been made by the 'Investigators' on Melville Island, quite startling ones in a region where the biggest trees (dwarf willow) only grow to some six inches high. Specimens were sawn off and some used for firewood, though they only smoul-dered with little or no flame. Mr Dean, the carpenter, thought the wood was like larch, but it bore a greater resemblance, because of its weight, to lignum vitae or iron wood. Mecham was away from the ship for 91 days (4 April to 6 July 1853) and his party covered 1,006 geographical (1,173 statute) miles discovering much new land. In his 'compendium of travelling operations' (the appendix at the end of his narrative of the voyage of the *Resolute*), G F M'Dougall, Master of the *Resolute*, provides a useful summary of the discoveries, plus tables and diagrams of tents and other equipment.[28]

Describing the extremely heavy ice off Prince Patrick Island, Mecham con-cluded that 'the character and appearance of the pack driven against the land, and in every direction to seaward, thoroughly convinces me of the impossibility of penetrating with ships to the southward and westward, against such tremendous impediments.'[29] Only the advent of really powerful icebreakers in the twentieth century enabled this polar multi-year ice to be navigated.

'HMS *Assistance* and *Pioneer* fast to the floe off Cape Majendie, Wellington Channel 1853'
by Lieutenant W W May. Part of the naval Franklin search squadron under Belcher,
these vessels wintered to the north of Wellington Channels, 1852-54. (Author's collection)

Writing half a century later in 1909, Sir Clements Markham remarked, 'Like
all great discoveries, Prince Patrick Island points to the importance of further
research', in the vast area of the Beaufort Sea, which was to be explored by
Stefansson, during the Canadian Arctic Expedition of 1913-18. Markham
described how the island

> forms the boundary between the Arctic paradise of Melville Island and the polar ocean
> without life. On its east side there are musk oxen, reindeer, and all the Arctic fauna and
> flora, but more scanty. On the west side there is the mighty polar pack with its line of
> ice hummocks grinding up on the shallow beach, with no vegetation and no life . . .[30]

No one, wrote Sir Clements, had been near either island since 1854 and Mecham
had made it clear that no North West Passage would be found that way. These
journeys of Mecham and McClintock were among the longest undertaken
during the years of the Franklin Search and though their discoveries had been
significant no signs of the missing expedition were found.

Lieutenant Richard Vesey Hamilton (sledge *Hope*) led a third search party to
northeast Melville Island, leaving in late April 1853, which explored the Sabine
Peninsula. Hamilton had a sledge and seven men, as well as a satellite sledge; the
captain of his sledge, as we have seen being 'that grand old sailor', George
Murray. He happened to meet Commander Richards of HMS *Assistance*, *en route*
and was able to catch up with Lieutenant Sherard Osborn, who had just parted

from Richards. This was an unexpected reunion of two old friends. Hamilton returned to the ship on 21 June, after 54 days absence and having travelled 568 geographical (663 statute) miles. Two weeks earlier Commander Richards, Belcher's second-in-command aboard *Assistance*, had reached *Resolute* by following the directions placed earlier by De Bray, the French officer, in a cairn. Richards was disappointed to find that his party had been forestalled by the *Resolute* in the search and exploration of Melville Island, but he was able on his return to relate in person to Sir Edward Belcher and his shipmates the good news of the 'Investigators' and of Kellett's ships.

*   *   *

In the spring of 1853, when the search parties were soon to depart from *Assistance* and *Pioneer*, Lieutenant Sherard Osborn, captain of the *Pioneer*, had written to John Barrow putting him in the picture as to the northern division's proceedings till then.

> On the 23rd of August 1852 we reached the head of The Queen's Channel, and on the same night winter came in upon us and we had reached our winter quarters. That season closed with our Autumn parties assuring themselves of our having reached the *Sea*, the Polar Sea I trust, but no Polynia my dear Barrow, no Polynia! I am disappointed in that respect ... As yet no fresh clue has been found, but ahead of us I believe the Erebus and Terror to be and tell Lady Franklin and others that I am hopeful for the issue ... The Future is too big with Hope for me to say more than that I long to see the result of our coming Search.[31]

By 'Polynia', he must have meant a large area of open water. Sadly, his hopes regarding Franklin were not to be realised. However, towards the end of the sledging season, Sherard Osborn began an excited letter from the *Pioneer* to John Barrow, dated 20 July 1853, in which he explained how McClure had discovered a North West Passage

> My dear Mr Barrow,
>
> You will be inundated with news good and bad and I only wish I could see your face when you hear the N.W. Passage has been discovered, and accomplished in a way by that marvellous man McClure. That the Polar Sea has been reached along the North shore of the Parry group. That Jones's Sound has been opened and that our Search has now been connected along a new extent of coastline fringing the Polar Sea from Jones's Sound to a new group of Islands, West of Melville Island. The alloy to all these triumphs is still to be found in the sad fact of no traces of Franklin's squadron. That there are none is a source of sad regret with me, but not of astonishment. The Polar Sea such as we have seen it is studded with islands small and large between which a strong tide exists and an almost perpetual Easterly set, and caught in it, Franklin's ships may have been swept during the winter of 1846, '47 anywhere that one pleases. That he came up here I have no doubt, that he took the Pack I conceive to be equally probable and then the rest may be left to one's imagination. Holding as I do the [sailing] ships in utter contempt as unwieldy masses of wood, especially when leased in couples, I fear the worst, but have kept the latter part of my opinion locked up in my Heart.[32]

He concluded his letter by writing that 'as yet neither self or any officer of *Pioneer* has been in a scrape with the Leader of the Squadron'. Little did he know that he would finish the voyage as Belcher's prisoner!

Earlier in the year, Commander Richards (sledge *Sir Edward*) and Osborn (sledge *John Barrow*) had travelled west from Northumberland Sound along the unexplored north coast of Bathurst Island to reach the northeast tip of Melville Island, where they went their separate ways. Richards visited the *Resolute* and *Intrepid* at Dealy Island, as we have seen, while Osborn retraced their tracks to the north coast of Bathurst Island. He then searched southwards along the east coast of that island (the west coast of the Queen's Channel) to about 75 °50′N. Both he and Richards returned to winter quarters in Northumberland Sound by mid-July 1853. Osborn made a boat journey across the strait and came back to find that the *Assistance* and *Pioneer* were already southward bound, under Belcher's orders, 'as if all was over for poor Franklin's expedition'.

On his return to *Assistance* Richards found the ship 'in anything but a desirable state – discontent and disorganization seemed to prevail, Capt. complaining of officers and officers, of Tyranny and oppression on his part'. Mr Cheyne was under arrest and Richards found it 'very painful to contemplate' another winter with Belcher, who seemed 'much broken down in health' and his temper was 'more than proportionately affected by it'. Osborn and other good men were 'disgusted and almost repenting that they ever joined the enterprise'. His own position was most painful and difficult, since he had to support Belcher *'under any circumstances'*.[33]

They had great difficulty in navigating southwards towards Barrow Strait, and when Richards continued his letter on 31 July, he explained that although the ice was rotten, the *Pioneer* was unable to tow the *Assistance* through it. They were constantly blasting and warping to gain perhaps two ships' lengths in a day, but would be driven back, 'floe and all' for several miles during the night. The rotten state of the ice meant that they could not get a holding for their lines to haul ahead with. By August, beset near Baillie Hamilton Island, Richards wrote, 'we are lying in as helpless a condition as may be, top gall[an]t masts and yards down and Rudder triced up astern'. The next Spring tides would given them a last chance. If that should fail, they would either remain where they were, or be carried down like the *Advance* and *Rescue* of the First Grinnell Expedition. They were 'in the hands of Providence' and when he wrote again a week later, there was still little change. The young ice was making fast, but they were rather better placed, out of the heavy pack. Greater progress was made later in August, but the *Assistance* and *Pioneer* were forced to winter north of Cape Osborn, Devon Island, still in Wellington Channel.

With the return of the sun in February 1854 Richards made a very severe sledge journey to the *North Star* at Beechey Island, 52 miles away 'as the Crow, or rather the Raven flies'. Sir Edward Belcher had been ill, perhaps with scurvy, but was improving. Richards feared that 'with returning strength the demon seems to be getting stronger within him'. The strongest man in the ship had died

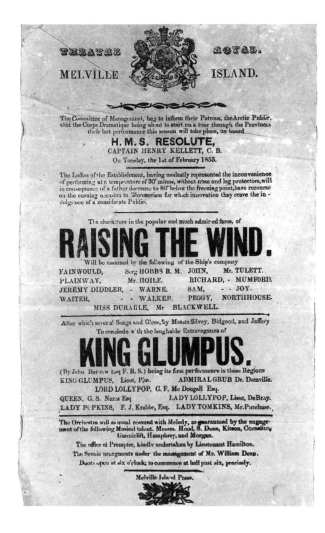

Playbill printed on board the *Resolute* during the winter of 1852-53. Printing presses were provided by the Admiralty on board the Franklin Search vessels for distributing messages to the lost expedition. (NMM, D0943)

earlier in fact from scurvy. In the letter to Barrow, telling him this news, Richards wrote that he would never regret the voyage, which he hoped had made him wiser, if not better. He looked forward to seeing the sun next year from 'the middle of some clover field in Devon'.[34]

The Resolute and Intrepid 1853-54

There were other sledge parties in 1853, one of which was led by Richard Roche one of the two Mates of the *Resolute* to communicate with the *North Star* at Beechey Island. Lieutenant Cresswell accompanied him, bearing Captain McClure's despatches. Cresswell also escorted the other party consisting of Wynniatt and a handful of other invalids, late of *Investigator*. Together they reached England that year, thus becoming the first to travel through the North West Passage. Another small party, with dogs, sledged from Dealy Island to Winter Harbour to move a depot there and to carve the names of the ships on Parry's great sandstone rock. Once all the sledge parties had returned, a reunion celebrated in champagne, Captain Kellett set about preparing the *Resolute* and *Intrepid* for sea.

Before leaving, a well-built stone store house was completed on Dealy Island, on which was still standing in 1978 when it underwent conservation. De Bray recorded on 1 August 1853:

> The store house on Dealy Island is completely finished; it is as comfortable as possible and will certainly be found to be so by those for whom it has been built, if they ever have the luck to reach it. It contains all the provisions, clothing and equipment for sixty men for a winter. A cairn 30 feet high, surmounted by a mast, has been erected on the summit of Dealy Island to serve as a landmark for ships that might pass within sight of the island, and a plaque fixed to one of the sides of the cairn provides directions necessary to locate the house in case it is buried under snow.[35]

The stores were intended for Collinson in the *Enterprise* but the next vessel to pass that way was the *Arctic* (formerly Drygalski's *Gauss*) commanded by Captain J E Bernier on 31 August 1908. Two muskets and two of McClintock's sledges were removed, as were various documents, reproduced in Bernier's report.[36]

The *Resolute* and *Intrepid* made a hurried departure from Dealy Island, being driven out of winter quarters by a strong gale, still encased in the ice floe, which made McDougall think that the same might have happened to Franklin's ships at Beechey Island in 1846. Soon though they were caught again in the pack, and McDougall vividly described the effects of pressure on the *Resolute*, which continued throughout the night of 17 September 1853. There were

> loud rumbling noises, with a succession of sharp reports, not unlike the explosion of artillery; then would follow doleful singing sounds, occasioned by the sudden escape of the pent air . . . breaking suddenly on the stillness of the night, accompanied as they always were by the creaking of beams and bulk-heads, as the vessel laboured beneath the pressure of the moving pack.[37]

Eventually preparations had to be made for a second winter, this time in the pack. On 20 September the topgallant masts and yards were sent down and on 26 September the boats were slung bottom up to their davits, to prevent snow accumulating in them. The housing was then spread over the main and quarter-decks.

Because the *Resolute* had a list to port, snow was spread across the upper deck to make a level surface. On this was laid 'a layer of Arctic cement, composed of water, snow, cinders and gravel, well mixed together, until the ingredients attained the consistency of thick sludgy ice'.[38] On 10 October, banking up around the ship was begun.

> The snow wall was five feet thick; outer side, four feet in height, and sloping from thence to the ice chock. The outer parts were neatly built of blocks of young ice, placed with line and plummet; the space then filled in with loose snow, which by actual experiment, has been found to increase the temperature of the ship's side by nearly 30 °. This increase of heat is not the only advantage, for an additional degree of dryness necessarily follows; so that one comfort, dependent in a measure on those two essential points, is ensured.[39]

A great and useful novelty was the installation of an electric telegraph between the *Resolute* and *Intrepid*.

The Mate of the *Investigator*, H H Sainsbury, who had been in poor health throughout the voyage, died in mid-November 1853. Two days later:

> the funeral service was read on board in a most impressive manner by Captain Kellett and the mournful procession then wended its way to the grave, a hole in the ice, about 250 yards from the ship. The day was cold (–20 °), and misty, and never shall I forget the scene on the ice, as the body, sewn in canvas, with weights attached, was launched through the narrow opening, and disappeared to our view. Within an hour, Nature had placed an icy slab over the grave of our departed messmate.[40]

Captain Kellett had presumed that the ships would reach England in the autumn of 1853. Now that a second winter had to be endured, it was evident that some of the clothing and provisions left for Franklin or Collinson on Dealy Island might have been retained for the 'Investigators', who had left their ship with little beyond what they stood up in. Aboard *Intrepid* also the 'Investigators' had neither warm cabins nor adequate bedding and no more remained to be issued. Because there were more mouths to feed, the daily allowance had been reduced to two thirds. There was plenty of lighting and the crews of the *Resolute* and *Intrepid* had many comforts from England of which the 'Investigators', having departed so much earlier, had no idea. Contact between the two vessels helped to relieve the monotony of the unwelcome extra wintering.

With the return of the sun and the end to the winter darkness, Captain Kellett informed the 'Investigators' that they should prepare for the journey to Beechey Island, so as to sail to England in the coming summer of 1854. Lieutenant Hamilton, who had become a good dog-driver, was to communicate with Beechey Island to inform Belcher of the proceedings of the western division and fate of the *Investigator* and to receive despatches for Captain Kellett in exchange. The dogs were given some good feeds before their departure on 4 March from a stock-pot filled with bread-dust, sealskins, whale-oil, pea-soup and anything else that was edible. A new harness, designed by one of the men, helped them to pull more easily.

By the end of March, Hamilton had not returned so that Captain Kellett kept back the two long-distance sledge parties until early April when Lieutenant Mecham and Krabbé, Master of *Intrepid*, set out with two sledges and fourteen men on 3 April 1854 for Dealy Island, where they were to replenish their provisions from the depot. They were to travel in company along the south coast of Melville Island, then Krabbé would lay a depot for Mecham at Cape Russell, before crossing M'Clure Strait to visit *Investigator*. Mecham would also cross the strait and proceed southwest down Prince of Wales Strait to Princess Royal Islands and as far beyond as was prudent. A search down Peel Inlet (Sound) had also been considered during the winter, to connect Rae and Browne's furthest, but was unfortunately rejected in view of Dr Rae's own forthcoming journey.

Frederick J Krabbé was the grandson of a Danish naval officer who had been taken prisoner during the Napoleonic wars and who had settled in Falmouth. His

'Critical position of HMS *Phoenix* off Cape Riley, on 18 August 1853'. The vessel astern must be the supply ship *Breadalbane*, sunk three days later off Beechey Islands by the ice. A team of divers, led by Dr Joe MacInnis, investigated the wreck in 1980-83. Watercolour by Captain E A Inglefield of the *Phoenix*. (NMM, 416)

father was an Assistant Surgeon in the Falmouth Packet Service. Mecham and Krabbé reached the 'Sailors' Home', as the depot was called on Dealy Island, on 12 April 1854. It was found to be in perfect condition.

On reaching the Bay of Mercy, Krabbé found the tattered ensign and pendant of *Investigator* still flying. He was able to walk up a snow drift to climb on deck. She was slightly heeled over, but there was no sign of ice pressure. The oakum hung very loosely out of most of the seams and the vessel had leaked considerably; water was up to the orlop beams forward, and nearly so abaft. The crew landed all the useful stores they could, though all the spirits, wine and coal and a large quantity of preserved meat were left firmly frozen in the holds. As ordered, Krabbé collected all the medicines on his list, as well as some botanical and zoological specimens.[41] What he did not collect were the journals left behind when the *Investigator* had been abandoned in April 1853 in Miertsching's words, *'because he could not find any!?'* [42]

*   *   *

The object of the other journey, led by G F Mecham, was 'to gain intelligence of *Enterprise*, failing that to leave information for her'. He was to return without fail on or before 10 June.[43] The crew of the sledge *Discovery* were James Tullett,

Thomas Joy, Charles Nisbett, Thomas Manson, Henry Richards, David Ross and Samuel Rogers. Unlike his previous long journey, which covered a great deal of new ground, the present one was along a route traversed already by the 'Investigators'. The victualling for this journey (per man, per day) consisted of

Preserved meat	¾ lbs
Biscuit	1lb
Boiled bacon	½ lb
Concentrated rum	½ gill
Potatoes	2 ounces
Chocolate	1 ounce
Sugar for ditto	1 ounce
Tea	¼ ounce – every other day
Sugar for ditto	½ ounce – every other day

Though not very generous for the extremely arduous sledge-hauling involved, there was usually a chance of shooting bears, seals, caribou, ptarmigan and other game. On the fourth day out, Mecham had to stop the issue of the warmed bacon as it made him and some of the crew bilious. As it was, when 150 miles from the Princess Royal Islands Mecham informed his crew that it was necessary to go on to half allowance in case no food were found at the islands.

Drifting snow and heavy hummocks made travelling across M'Clure Strait difficult, particularly 'old pieces of floe known as polar ice, mingled with pack two or three years' old' forming 'as bad a road as possibly can be imagined'.[44] They had some difficulty in finding the entrance to Prince of Wales Strait. The land was deep with snow. On the thirtieth day out Mecham reached the cairn on Princess Royal Islands and there found the records deposited from *Enterprise* in 1851 and 1852, the boat in good condition and the provisions in a reasonable state. 'A fox visited us', wrote Mecham, 'and committed great havoc among our necessaries; he also in a most daring manner, came up to where the cook was attending to his fires, and ran away with a lump of preserved meat'.[45] Fortunately driftwood was found along the coast, as they had run out of other fuel.

Making a dump of spare clothing and other items, they set off for the island named in Collinson's records where further information could be found. On camping on the thirty-second day (7 May 1854), it was found that the pickaxe had been lost and Mecham got the crew to draw lots for its retrieval. Tullett and Manson drew the unlucky numbers and they had to retrace their steps some 13 miles, making their total distance walked that day to 34 miles. On 9 May the party reached the island and its ruined cairn where they dug for the cylinder containing records of the *Enterprise*; 'the men evinced the greatest excitement and curiosity as I read over the documents, and immediate calculations were made as to the day of our return and the surprise the news would cause'.[46]

Their return to their shipmates was to take longer than any calculation they made. After the men had rebuilt the cairn and buried the records 10 feet away magnetic north on 10 May, the homeward journey began. Mecham placed a bundle of knives and other implements for the Eskimos on whose handles and blades he had cut the position of the *Resolute* and *Investigator*. On their arrival at the Sailors Home, Dealy Island, on 27 May, Mecham found startling orders for them to proceed to distant Beechey Island, on half rations leaving the rum in the depot untouched, and without losing time 'by attempting to reach the ships; they will be by that time abandoned, and their hatchways securely sealed'. Mecham should 'use every exertion to reach Beechey Island with all dispatch' so that his men 'may be exposed as little as possible to the ill effects of travelling after the thaw has commenced'.[47]

In his official Letter of Proceedings Mecham gives no reaction to the sudden and alarming news of the abandonment of the *Resolute* and *Intrepid*. He only remarked, after reading letters not from home but from messmates aboard the ships that 'The accounts of the luxurious feeding up at the ship upon mess stock, Allsopp's ale, and various niceties, produced very watery lips among us, and did not increase our relish for short allowances.[48] He added, ruefully, that they had already been without spirits for three weeks. The daily rum ration, very much a part of naval life at that date, would have been particularly welcome during these dreary and taxing sledge journeys.

Mecham left at Dealy Island an account of his proceedings and a list of the provisions taken from the Sailors Home for the onward journey. He also took away the 'upper part of one pair of sea boots for repairing mocassins'. He left inside 'one sledge bottom, two four-gallon cans and one small sledge', and then blocked up the door and packed up for the journey to Beechey Island of some seventeen daily marches. Wet snow, falling snow, intricate hummocks, thick fog, sore eyes, sore ankles, tattered boots, strong winds and drifting snow did not hinder Mecham's party as much as a shortage of edible provisions and little game. With the help of a sail, they passed both Krabbé and Hamilton's dog team. For the last march, having taken over the dog sledge to hasten their arrival, they were accompanied by a wolf running beside them, 'which kept the dogs in a perfect frenzy of excitement, and one of us at a rapid run'. Arriving at the *North Star*, Beechey Island, at 4.30am they were welcomed by Captain Kellett and all hands. No sooner had Mecham finished telling his tale, than the dogs were on their way to Belcher with the news. Of this journey, Clive Holland remarks: 'By the time he reached *North Star* on June 12, Mecham had completed the longest sledge journey of the Franklin Search, and possibly the longest man-hauling journey on record, a distance of 2,470 km.'[49] In a letter to John Barrow during the homeward voyage Captain Kellett said he believed Mecham's journey to be 'unequalled in Arctic travelling – in 69 days he travelled 1,200 miles averaging per day 18 miles'.[50]

Captain Kellett had planned to remain in the Arctic for a third winter, after sending home the 'Investigators' via Beechey Island in 1854, but Belcher's orders to abandon the two ships were definite. On 30 April, Kellett announced the abandonment. The officers might depart with 45lbs of clothes and necessaries and the men with 30lbs. Most of the invalids were convalescing, but the one still

Sledge parties leaving the *Resolute* and *Intrepid* during the Franklin Search expedition 1852–54, western division, commanded by Captain Kellett. (Plate from G F McDougall's *Narrative*)

seriously ill (Morgan) would have to be carried in a sort of palanquin or cot. A week later, Dr Domville and M de Bray with nine dogs and two sledges accompanied Morgan and most of the other invalids towards Beechey Island, while Lieutenant Hamilton, who had become a fast and skilled dog-driver, left for Dealy Island to deposit a record and to leave orders for Lieutenants Mecham and Krabbé to proceed direct to the island.

Before abandoning the ships in Melville Sound the carpenters caulked the hatchways and skylights and the top hamper was made doubly secure. Souvenirs of loved ones had to be left behind in favour of more practical items. After dining with the officers at 6.15pm on 15 May 1854, Captain Kellett inspected the lower decks, after which the main hatch was secured and the four sledges moved off in funeral order, led by Roche, the junior officer, with the captain in the rear, towards Cape Cockburn. A short distance away the sledge crews halted, unharnessed and gave three hearty cheers for the two ships, 'but though the ice is a good conductor of sound', wrote the Master of the *Resolute*, 'we heard no response'. He expressed the regret they all felt at abandoning 'the staunch old craft to her fate and almost certain destruction'. 'The pilot jack was hoisted at the foretopmast head', he wrote 'and the red ensign and pendant displayed', so that if she had to yield to her 'icy antagonist, she might sink beneath the wave . . . with colours flying'.[51]

Assistance and *Pioneer* (right) at their winter quarters 1853-54, drawn by G F M'Dougall. The 80ft-long Crystal Palace on the right was built out of blocks of ice and intended as a refuge, but it was used principally as a skittle alley, and in temperatures that never exceeded –30 °F. (From Sir Edward Belcher's *The Last of the Arctic Voyages*)

McClintock must have looked back sadly at his 'dear little Intrepid', which he thought of as 'one of those wounded and forsaken dovekies!'[52] Captain Kellett was distressed not only at having to abandon his ships, but because he appeared to be deserting Captain Collinson, whose good friend he was.

Captain Sir Edward Belcher, commodore of the Arctic squadron, believed that by 1854[53] Collinson's *Enterprise* would either have returned to Bering Strait or would have been abandoned, in which case her crew would make their way to England, either overland via the posts of the Hudson's Bay Company, or via the depots left on Melville and Beechey islands and elsewhere among the Arctic archipelago to Lancaster Sound, which was frequented by the whalers. He concluded that he would best meet the wishes of the Admiralty, in view of the fact that four of his squadron of five ships were still beset in the spring of 1854, by withdrawing all their crews and sailing for home, especially since there was still no sign of Franklin. However, despite the Admiralty's wish to end the long and expensive search for the missing ships, Belcher had been given authority to leave one or more vessels and crews, if the safety of others demanded this. In fact, he did apparently consider designating McClintock to remain, but then changed his mind. Belcher gave the order to abandon the *Assistance* and *Pioneer* on 25 August 1854.[53] Hardly had the crowded *North Star* weighed anchor than *Phoenix* (Captain Inglefield) and *Talbot* (Commander Jenkins) were sighted, bringing startling news of the war with Russia and letters from home. Lieutenant Bedford Pim, who had wanted to see the *Investigator* manned with a volunteer crew in the hope of navigating the North West Passage, thought the war might provide 'a chance of wiping off the stigma which will attach to the present Expedition'.[54]

So it was that five of Her Majesty's ships were left imprisoned in the ice, as silent witnesses to what had been. But the *Resolute* was not content to sink into an Arctic grave.

> For the *Resolute* herself, penetrated, no doubt, with the lively feelings of her Commander [Captain Kellett], was not to be left a deserted widow in the frozen ocean. Whether from some magnetic sympathy with him, or from some more natural force, we say not, but apparently about the same time as the crews left Beechey Island, the *Resolute* in her icy bed began to move also, and slowly but securely followed in their track; all through Barrow Strait, through Lancaster Sound, down the west side of Baffin Bay, into Davis Strait, a voyage of 16 months and 12,000 miles; and was then found by an American whaler, complete in all respects, though without a living soul aboard. And finally, having been purchased by the Government of the United States, was restored to Her Royal Mistress as perfect in every respect as on the day she left England, where she should have been honourably preserved, a living evidence of the possible safety of the pack.[55]

Resolute was found by Captain James Buddington of the American whaling barque *George Henry* during a voyage from New London to Davis Straits. On 10 September 1855 at the end of a season of heavy ice and poor catches, Buddington discovered a strange and apparently abandoned ship in the same ice field as he. For six days the vessels drifted towards each other and on the seventh, he sent two mates and two seamen across the ice, who reported on their return that the abandoned vessel was Her Britannic Majesty's Ship *Resolute*. Captain Buddington decided to take his prize to New London, with eleven men from the *George Henry*, though a great deal of work had to be done before the *Resolute* could again sail the high seas. On first going aboard and descending below, he had found the vessel in a lamentable state. In M'Dougall's words:

> The water-tanks had burst, and the hold was full of water, whilst all perishable articles were almost entirely destroyed by cold and damp. Scarcely anything on board, save the salt provisions in casks, and preserved meats in hermetically sealed tins, that had not suffered from the intense hyperborean frost. The cordage, canvas, sails, etc. were all more or less injured, and the gallant Americans had no little difficulty in making the gear they found on board answer the desired purpose of taking the ship into an American port.

The hull itself was in surprisingly good condition despite her journey

> along a track abounding in perils, not only from rocks, shoals, and other dangers which a *ship is heir to*, but those ever moving icy plains and mighty crystal mountains, that sail in undisputed sway, and form the terror of the Arctic Ocean.[56]

THE RETURN OF THE "RESOLUTE."—A GRACEFUL GIFT FROM BROTHER JONATHAN.

After she was abandoned in the Arctic in 1854, HMS *Resolute* drifted with the ice for over 1,000 miles, until found by an American whaler. She was refitted in the United States and sailed back to England, as a gift to Queen Victoria. (Cartoon in *Punch*, 13 December 1856)

After being found by the Americans, *Resolute* drifted southwest in the pack until mid-October, when Captain Buddington began the perilous voyage to New London in a very light and rolling vessel, through a succession of gales. On Christmas Eve 1855, he brought her safely into his home port. Having decided that Captain Buddington should keep his prize, the British Government waived all claim to the *Resolute*, whereupon the Congress of the United States, prompted by Mr Grinnell, purchased her for $40,000. She was then repaired and refitted in one of the navy yards, as a goodwill offering to Queen Victoria and the British people and even books, pictures and musical instruments were carefully restored.

Nearly a year after being discovered among the ice floes, *Resolute* was sailed to England under the command of Captain Hartstein, USN who had earlier gone to the rescue of Dr E K Kane in Greenland. She reached Spithead on 12 December 1856, when the Queen went on board, with other members of the Royal family. Queen Victoria invited Captain Hartstein to dine and spend the night at Osborne, the royal retreat on the Isle of Wight, and also ordered £100 to be shared by the crew.

The Prime Minister, Lord Palmerston, entertained Captain Hartstein at Broadlands, while Lady Franklin gave a *Resolute* Christmas party at Brighton, as well as sending the American crew a well decorated plum cake on Christmas Day. When she visited the ship at Captain Hartstein's urgent invitation, she later received a round robin of thanks for the cake from the crew. Hartstein offered to command any private expedition she should send, or to aid McClintock supposing the latter were sent by the Admiralty.[57]

The restored vessel was formally handed over to Great Britain on 30 December 1856 at Portsmouth. In a closing speech, Captain Hartstein addressed Captain George Seymour of HMS *Victory*, expressing the hope that 'long after every timber in her sturdy frame shall have perished the remembrance of the old Resolute will be cherished by the people of the respective nations'.[58]

Today perhaps, the *Resolute*'s dramatic story might have ensured her preservation but in the nineteenth century that was not to be. However, after long years laid up on the Medway, she was broken up at Chatham in 1880. From her timbers, a 'writing table' was constructed and shipped to the United States, at Queen Victoria's 'gracious pleasure', to be presented to President Hayes.[59] This handsomely carved desk is said to have been discovered in the cellars of the White House by the late President J F Kennedy and brought into use. Still later, the British Prime Minister, Harold Wilson, presented the *Resolute*'s bell to President Lyndon Johnson.

CHAPTER 14

The Discovery of the First Relics
1853-1855

When John Hepburn heard of the return of Sir Edward Belcher 'with all his party safe to their Native Land' he wrote to Sir John Richardson saying he was 'truly glad', but adding 'I had always hoped that some traces at least of our long lost Chief would be found'.[1] News of the lost expedition came unexpectedly soon afterwards, from Dr John Rae, who arrived in London from York Factory in late October 1854, not long after the return of the remnants of Belcher's Arctic squadron.

Dr John Rae's Discovery of the First Franklin Relics 1853-54

Rae had *not* been looking for Franklin during his fourth Arctic expedition of 1853-54. He had obtained approval from the Hudson's Bay Company to sail in boats from York Factory to Chesterfield Inlet (further to the north on the west coast of Hudson Bay), then to travel overland to Back's Great Fish River, descend the river and proceed northwards again, to complete 'the survey of the northern shores of America, a small portion of which, along the west coast of Boothia', being 'all that remains unexamined'.[2] It was thought at the time that 'King William's Land' might be joined eastwards by an isthmus to Boothia, thus making it part of the mainland of North America. Indignant too that the Admiralty had not entirely recognised his discoveries of 1847, Rae wished to settle, finally, the geography of Boothia. In a letter to *The Times* setting out his plans published on 27 November 1852, he stated, 'I do not mention the lost navigators, as there is not the slightest hope of finding any traces of them in the quarter to which I am going'.

Before leaving England, Rae dined with Sir George Back in London and visited Sir John Richardson at Gosport. He met Henry Grinnell in New York soon after his arrival there on 9 April and stayed with Sir George Simpson, Overseas Governor of the Hudson's Bay Company, at Lachine, near Montreal, for several days. While at Sault Ste Marie, McGill College, Montreal, conferred the Honorary degree of Doctor of Medicine upon him. This was, in Rae's words, 'without any examination, which was very fortunate, for a few questions on medical subjects would have floored me'. He added that he would 'now have a title to the name of Doctor, which has so long been given without my having any right to it'.[3] Earlier in the same letter to the younger Barrow, Rae expressed his regret that the 'beautiful Halkett boat' given to him by Barrow had to be left behind in a Liverpool warehouse, because of a strike by railway porters, before the *Europa* departed for America. Regarding his forthcoming survey, Dr Rae observed:

> I often think that your excellent Hydrographer, Sir Francis Beaufort would have pre-ferred that anyone but me should visit that part of the Arctic coast for which I am bound, but neither he nor anyone must fear that I will deviate in the slightest degree from the truth in my report, even should my survey *prove me* to have been in error. My object is to discover facts and to explain them simply and without exaggeration, not to support any theory however probable it may seem.

Arriving at York Factory on 18 June 1853, Rae set off from there with twelve men, three of whom had been with him before, and two boats. North of Churchill they met a party of Eskimos, among whom was William Ouligbuck's son, William Ouligbuck, junior, who had been with Rae in 1846-47 and who joined their expedition as a second interpreter. Beyond Churchill lies Chesterfield Inlet. It was westwards up this stretch of water that Rae had planned to sail, then across unexplored country west again to the Back (Great Fish) River. However, he deviated from this route to ascend a river running first northwest and then northeast from the north bank of the inlet. After 210 miles, the river, which he called the Quoich, became unnavigable and he decided that it was too late in the season to reach the sea. As his biographer points out, had Rae kept to his original plan, he might well have found a route (first traversed in 1902) via Baker Lake to the river and then the coast. He would then have reached 'the place were the answer to the Franklin mystery lay'.[4]

Six men and the first-appointed young and inexpert interpreter were sent back to York Factory, leaving Rae and his party to proceed still further north via Roe's Welcome Sound to Repulse Bay, where they landed on 15 August, finding it a wet and dreary spot. Rae had wintered there in 1846-47 during his first Arctic expedition and his stone house was still standing. After collecting enough fish, game and fuel to supplement the supplies bought with them, Rae decided to remain for the winter. The party lived first in tents and then in snow houses. A carpenter's workshop was constructed of snow, in which the sledges were taken to pieces, reduced in weight and put together again.

On 31 March 1854, having laid a depot earlier along the route, Dr Rae set out for Castor and Pollux River (Thomas Simpson's furthest east, of August 1838) with four men and Ouligbuck, all hauling sledges, since no Eskimos had been found from whom to buy dogs. Soft deep snow made the going tiring and progress was slow until a large lake was discovered, which Rae (remembering his gift of the Halkett boat) named after 'John Barrow Esquire, of the Admiralty', as a mark of respect. Tracks of foxes and the footprints of a solitary partridge were 'the only signs of living thing . . . observed since commencing the traverse of this dreary waste of snow clad country'. On 20 April, seventeen natives were encoun-

tered, some of whom Rae had met in 1847 at Repulse Bay, but no reliable information as to the lie of the land could be obtained, while Ouligbuck had to be
restrained from going off with them.

However, on resuming the journey, a 'very intelligent Eskimo' was met.
He was driving a dog sledge loaded with musk oxen flesh, which he deposited
and joined Rae at his request in order to point out the best route to the west.
Another man then caught them up and in answer to the 'usual questions as to his
having seen "white men" before, or any ships or boats', answered in the negative, 'but said that a party of 'Kabloonans' had died of starvation a long distance
to the west of where we were then, and beyond a large river'. The man did not
know the exact place, had never been there, and was unable to accompany Rae
that far.[5]

Despite the news of Franklin, which he thought too vague to follow up, Dr
Rae's intention was still to reach Castor and Pollux River, which he did after tracing the course of a larger river. This he called the Murchison, after the late
President of the Royal Geographical Society, which had awarded him its gold
medal. At the mouth of the smaller river, there was a pillar of small stones, different from the heaps denoting former Eskimo caches. No document could be
found when the cairn was dismantled, but its latitude agreed with that of
Simpson, although the longitude differed considerably. The cairn must have
been erected by Thomas Simpson to denote his furthest east. The coast was
traced as far northwards as it was prudent to go in view of the heavy travelling
and two disabled men, so that Rae did not reach Bellot Strait, which separates the
Boothia Peninsula from North Somerset Island. The coastline continued northwards, leaving a clear channel, later named Rae Strait, with a loom of land, no
doubt Matty Island and the coast of King William Land, thus known to be an
island, a fact of great importance in the discovery of the North West Passage.
They crossed a large bay, which Rae named Shepherd Bay after the Company's
Deputy Governor, and, interestingly from the point of view of Arctic travel, a
small island at its head, after Bence Jones, 'the distinguished medical man and
analytical chemist', who had prepared an extract of tea for the expedition, which
produced a 'refreshing beverage' even with cold water. Rae found his survey
agreed with that of Sir James Clark Ross, as on previous occasions. Held up again
by bad weather at Point de la Guiche, after sending Thomas Mistegan, 'an Indian
of great intelligence and activity' to inspect and view the trend of the coast for a
further 12 miles, Rae built a cairn and took possession of his discoveries. They
then marched back to the two waiting invalids, whose lives he did not wish to
hazard by completing the survey as far as the Magnetic Pole, Bellot Strait or
Brentford Bay, which he thought might easily have been done.

The party made a much quicker return journey (which included an examination of Pelly Bay, where no westward outlet to the sea was found) to Repulse Bay,
where they arrived on 26 May. The London map publisher and cartographer,
John Arrowsmith of Soho Square, whose 'Map of the countries round the North
Pole' went into numerous editions between 1818 and 1860,[6] produced a large

folding map in December 1854, which was placed with Rae's reports and related correspondence among the Parliamentary Papers. It is entitled, 'Map of the Route of Dr John Rae from his winter hut of 1853-4 at the head of Repulse Bay, to Castor and Pollux River: During this journey he obtained conclusive information of the fate of a portion of Sir John Franklin's expedition'. The map was said to be an 'exact tracing' of Rae's drawing and a fine one it is, showing the course of the Quoich River to the south and the land further north from King William Land in the west to Repulse Bay at the head of Frozen Strait. Dr Rae's journey showed that no isthmus connected King William Land with Boothia, thus placing on the chart an open seaway between the two, which Roald Amundsen passed through during the first navigation of the North West Passage, early in the twentieth century.

However, important as were Rae's geographical survey and explorations, the news he brought back of the Franklin Expedition created a great sensation, even a furore. This was the substance of it, as reported to the Admiralty in a letter headed 'Repulse Bay, July 29, 1854'. The information had been obtained not only from the Eskimo named In-nook-poo-zhee-jook on the outward journey, from whom he bought a gold cap band, but from others who visited him later at Repulse Bay.[6]

> In the spring, four winters past (spring 1850) a party of 'white men', amounting to about forty, were seen travelling southward over the ice, and dragging a boat with them, by some Esquimaux who were killing seals near the north shore of King William's Land (which is a large island.) None of the party could speak the Esquimaux language intelligibly, but by signs the natives were made to understand that their ship, or ships, had been crushed by ice, and that they were now going to where they expected to find deer to shoot. From the appearance of the men, all of whom, except one officer, looked thin, they were then supposed to be getting short of provisions, and purchased a small seal from the natives. At a later date the same season, but previous to the breaking up of the ice, the bodies of some thirty persons were discovered on the continent, and five on an island near it, about a long day's journey to the N.W. of a large stream, which can be no other than Back's Great Fish River (named by the Esquimaux Oot-koo-hi-ca-lik), as its description, and that of the low shore in the neighbourhood of Point Ogle and Montreal Island, agrees exactly with that of Sir George Back. Some of the bodies had been buried (probably those of the first victims of famine), some were in a tent, or tents, others under the boat, which had been turned over to form a shelter, and several lay scattered about in different directions. Of those found on the island one was supposed to have been an officer, as he had a telescope strapped over his shoulders, and his double barrelled gun lay underneath him. From the mutilated state of many of the corpses, and the contents of the kettles, it is evident that our wretched countrymen had been driven to the last resource – cannibalism – as a means of prolonging existence.

Rae went on to report that there appeared to have been no shortage of ammunition and that the Eskimos must have broken up watches, compasses, telescopes and guns, of which Rae saw some and which, together with silver spoons and forks, he purchased. The cutlery bore crests or initials, which he had sketched.

Dr John Rae, a Chief Factor of the Hudson's Bay Company, the resolute and skilled overland traveller, who brought home the first relics indicating the fate of Franklin's expedition, in 1854. (*Illustrated London News,* 28 October 1854. NMM, D899)

> None of the Esquimaux with whom I conversed had seen the 'whites', nor had they ever been at the place where the bodies were found, but had their information from those who had been there, and who had seen the party travelling.[8]

In his letter to the Secretary of the Hudson's Bay Company on the day of his arrival in London, 22 October 1854 (32 days from York Factory in the Company's ship *Prince of Wales*), Dr Rae pointed out that silver spoons and forks bore the initials of several officers of both *Erebus* and *Terror*. He expressed his regret that his expedition had 'been unsuccessful in its object as regards the completion of the survey of the West Coast of Boothia'.[9] The editors of his *Arctic correspondence 1844-55*, Wordie and Cyriax, comment in their introduction regarding Rae's decision to bring to London such news and relics of the lost expedition as he had, rather than proceed in search of more, so that no more search ships should be sent in the wrong direction:

> Rae's return . . . has always been a matter of regret, for a great chance had been lost. No less than five years were to elapse before M'Clintock reached King William Island, and had Rae gone at once to the places indicated by the Eskimos he would almost certainly have obtained more information than M'Clintock and possibly even have found written records.[10]

Rae's report to the Admiralty was published by that body in *The Times* next day. As Wordie and Cyriax have pointed out, its brevity led him to be criticised, because it did not give the full background to the Eskimos' revelations. The sentences regarding cannibalism caused great pain and offence. No less a person than Charles Dickens, in his weekly journal *Household Words*, questioned the report, particularly as regards cannibalism, with great eloquence, citing numerous examples, including Franklin's first overland expedition, where the 'last resource' was not resorted to. He also questioned the reliability of the Eskimos as witnesses and ended by answering the question, 'why care about this?', in these words:

> Because they ARE dead, therefore we care about this. Because they served their country well, and deserved well of her and can ask, no more on this earth, for her justice or her loving-kindness; give them both, full measure, pressed down, running over. Because no Franklin can come back, write the honest story of their woes and resignation, read it tenderly and truly in the book he has left us. Because they lie scattered on those wastes of snow, and are as defenceless against the remembrance of coming generations, as against the elements into which they are resolving, and the winter winds that alone can waft them home, now impalpable air; therefore cherish them gently, even in the breasts of children. Therefore, teach no one to shudder without reason, at the history of their end. Therefore confide with their own firmness in their fortitude, their lofty sense of duty, their courage, and their religion.[11]

In his reply, published in a subsequent issue of *Household Words*, Rae defended his opinions with some skill. He set out the reasons for believing the Eskimos' story (including Ouligbuck's ability as an interpreter) and for not believing that the 'white men' were murdered by them, but died in fact of starvation.[12] This was not Charles Dickens' only involvement with the Arctic. In January 1857, he drew tears from his select, invited audience for his performance as the principal character in his adaptation of Wilkie Collins' *The frozen deep*. Rae did not know until his arrival in England that the British Government's reward of £10,000 for ascertaining the fate of the missing officers and men was still on offer. The company had allowed him time during the weeks after his return, he told John Barrow, to 'satisfy friends and relations of the long-missing party instead of completing his chart and writing up his report for their information'.[13] He was not at all hopeful of receiving the reward. However, after some delay, Rae's claim was accepted, despite Lady Franklin's protests, her main one being that the fate of the expedition had not been fully ascertained. The £10,000 was distributed by the Hudson's Bay Company to Rae (£8,000) and among his men, including those who had returned from Chesterfield Inlet to York Factory in 1853. The relics were considered by the Admiralty 'worthy of a place among the Naval relics already deposited in Greenwich Hospital', and they were placed in the Painted Hall for public inspection.[14]

The Search for Survivors 1855

With its resources stretched by the war against Russia, largely in the Crimea, the Admiralty requested the Hudson's Bay Company as early as 27 October 1854 to follow up the lead given by Rae's discovery and to send an expedition down the Back or Great Fish River. The expedition was to search for any possible survivors from *Erebus* and *Terror*, to ascertain the truth or otherwise of Dr Rae's report and to discover any remains 'which may further explain the proceedings and events which terminated so fatally'. Efforts should be made to find the Eskimos, who had seen and spoken to the Englishmen, to search for records, and to bring home any relics which might shed light on Franklin's fate and that of the two ships. Leaving the detailed arrangements to Sir George Simpson and the Company's servants, the Secretary to the Admiralty expressed their Lordships' view that a wise choice of commander would be made of someone inured to hardships and perils, and used to communicating with the natives. 'It will be an honour to be selected, for it is one in which the feelings of the British nation are deeply interested, and the fate of Sir John Franklin and his men has been regarded for years with intense anxiety both in Europe and America.' The expedition would be paid for cheerfully by the British public, and its members would be well remunerated, with rewards for 'any acts of signal daring and distinguished merit'.[15] Dr Rae did not wish to lead the expedition, but he drew up a list of necessary instruments and other items to be lent by the Admiralty. The list included a copy of Sir George Back's narrative of his descent of the Great Fish River, an Eskimo vocabulary and a Nautical Almanac for 1855, stripped down to essentials, and Admiralty charts. Rae also drew up a 'Memorandum regarding the Efficient Equipment of the Expeditions' in which he recommended Thomas Mistegan and other men, and noted that Chief Trader Anderson of the Mackenzie District knew how to use a sextant. Preparations also included plans to send a second expedition to the Mackenzie River to search for Captain Collinson in the *Enterprise*, but news of his safe arrival in Clarence Harbour pre-empted them.

   With his customary energy and attention to detail, Sir George Simpson wrote from Lachine, on 18 November 1854, to James Anderson and James Green Stewart, appointing them to first and second command of the expedition, which would consist of two officers, twelve canoe men, and two Eskimo interpreters and hunters. He instructed them to depart from Fort Resolution immediately after the opening of navigation on Great Slave Lake in 1855. Three canoes should be taken, with the idea of carrying a large quantity of provisions and of depositing the third, once arrived at the coast, for use in case of accident. Sir George Simpson emphasised the importance of contact with the Eskimos and of treating them liberally. The Company's interests should be subordinated to those of the expedition. William Ouligbuck and another Eskimo would be instructed to leave Churchill during the winter for Athabasca in order to act as interpreters. With them from York Factory would come a Halkett boat left by Dr Rae and gifts for the Eskimos. Any portable relics, especially manuscripts, should be 'purchased at any cost' from the natives, while the mortal remains of those reported to have perished on the Arctic coast in 1850, should be 'decently interred', and covered with a cairn of stones, in which a memorial should be deposited, outlining 'their career and melancholy fate'. The Governor advised Anderson and Stewart to copy Dr Rae's 'admirable tact in command of his people'. Their proceedings would be watched by the whole civilised world.

   The Hudson's Bay Company might be said to have attained its apogee at this period, under the shrewd, able and energetic administration of Sir George Simpson, the overseas Governor. After the union with the North West Company in 1821, its charter was again renewed and greatly extended, giving it a licence

Page from the *Illustrated London News*, 4 November 1854, showing the Franklin relics
bought from the Eskimos by Dr Rae. (NMM, D900)

'for the sole and exclusive privilege of trading with the Indians' over the whole
of British North America, except for Upper and Lower Canada. Its domain eventually stretched from the Atlantic to the Pacific oceans, until in 1870 Prince
Rupert's Land and the North-Western Territories were surrendered to the
British Crown and then transferred to Canada.[16] Simpson's letters to the officers
and others connected with the organisation of the expedition illustrate this mas-
tery – taking Anderson away from the Mackenzie district, transporting Rae's
Halkett boat and other items from Hudson Bay and getting canoes built on lakes
Athabasca and Great Slave. Unfortunately, Ouligbuck was away sealing, while
the attempts by the Admiralty and Lady Franklin to persuade McClure's interpreter, Johann Miertsching, to accompany Anderson and Stewart proved
unavailing. He was still in London on 30 October 1854 when he received a
second letter from the Admiralty. 'Though these offers were most advantageous
to me', he wrote that day in his diary, 'I have answered them with an emphatic
"no" . . . my resolution is fixed: I make no more such polar journeys'. The lack
of an interpreter was to prove a considerable handicap to the expedition as
regards obtaining information about the fate of Franklin.

Chief Factor James Anderson arrived at Fort Resolution on Great Slave Lake

James Anderson, with the Arctic medal which he received after his expedition. (C S Mackinnon collection)

on 20 June 1855, where he found the three canoes ready for use. Although they were of an 'excellent model', with strong frames, the bark was of poor quality, having been procured at short notice. Canoes were employed, rather than boats, because of the amount of portaging involved. Nevertheless, wrote Anderson, they still became very heavy:

> their ladings amounted to 24 pieces of 90 pounds each, and consisted chiefly of provisions, with a good supply of ironworks etc. for the Esquimaux, ammunition, nets, Halkett boat, and the luggage of the party. Double sets of poles, paddles, and lines, were also provided.[17]

Making numerous portages (including the crossing of 3½ miles of mountains) and cutting and pushing the canoes through lake ice, the party pioneered a new route to Back's Great Fish River reaching it on 11 July. Back's narrative proved of great use in making the descent of this dangerous river, but 'notwithstanding the exquisite skill of our Iroquois Boutes [bowsmen], the canoes were repeatedly broken and much strained in the whirlpools and eddies'. One was abandoned. At length, on 31 July, an elderly Inuk and three women appeared who were possessed of various articles 'belonging to a boat or vessel', including a letter-clip dated 1843, but none could be identified as having belonged to a particular individual. The women appeared perfectly to understand Anderson's request for

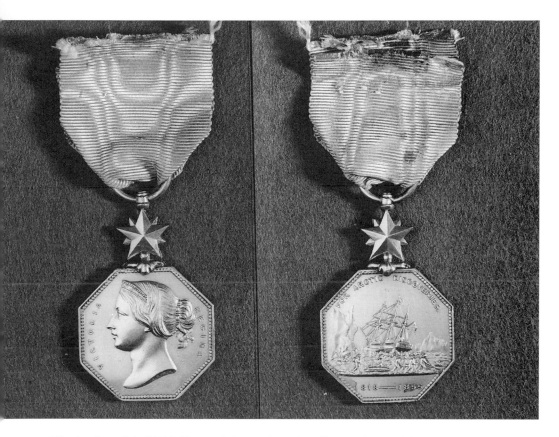

The Arctic medal of 1818-55, awarded not only to the officers and men of the naval expeditions, but to the Americans, the French lieutenants, the Hudson's Bay Company men and the Eskimos, Indians and voyageurs. (NMM, B8032)

letters, notebooks and other printed books and manuscripts 'but they said they had none. They made us understand by pressing the abdomen inwards, pointing to the mouth, and shaking their heads piteously, that these things came from a kayak, the people belonging to which had died of starvation'.

Bitterly regretting the lack of an interpreter, the party could do no more and had to press on. Another small group was met and appeared to relate a similar story. The next day, the party reached Victoria Headland at the river's mouth. A minute search of Montreal Island revealed no bones nor graves, but the planks from a boat, one chip having 'Erebus' carved on it, were found. Part of a snowshoe bore Surgeon Stanley's name. Anderson's journal describes the party's search in torrential rain on the mainland (Adelaide Peninsula) and Maconochie Island despite the danger from closely packed sea ice and the formation of young ice. Because of the ice and the frailty of the canoes, they could do no more. On the homeward journey, further contact with the Eskimos revealed little and the whole party returned to Fort Reliance on Great Slave Lake on 12 September.

Their efforts had, alas, but few results and the mystery still remained to be resolved. However, the expedition did confirm Dr Rae's report, and established that any further search must be in this region.

An intriguing postscript to this expedition relates a possible sighting of one of Franklin's ships. Thirty-eight years later, in 1893, the Canadian geologist and explorer, J B Tyrrell, obtained statements from Thomas Mistegan and two other men who, 'sent northward beyond Montreal Island (or Maconochie Island) . . . saw one of the ships far out in the ice, but returned and reported that they had seen nothing, fearing that if they reported a ship in sight, their masters would take them to it, and they would not be able to get back to Fort Resolution that fall, and would all perish of starvation and exposure'. Tyrrell concluded that it was not impossible that from a high point, they may have seen the boat taken to Starvation Cove or indeed one of Franklin's ships.[18]

We have seen that the departure of Sir John Franklin, commanding HM Ships *Erebus* and *Terror* in 1845, marked the last of the voyages sent by the Admiralty in search of the North West Passage. The expedition of 1855 of Anderson and Stewart marked the end of official involvement in the Franklin Search, for although it was organised by the Hudson's Bay Company, it was financed by the British Government. The year 1855 also marked the official end to both North West Passage and Franklin Search expeditions, through the citation of the medal awarded 'for Arctic discoveries' of 1818-1855, first authorised in the *London Gazette* of 5 May 1857 for British seaborne expeditions, but extended within two years to include the Grinnell expeditions, Franklin's two overland expeditions, a number of private seaborne expeditions, the two French lieutenants, the officers and men of the *Fox* (1857-59) and certain officers and men of the Hudson's Bay Company. Leafing through the list of recipients, one sees many familiar names, including those of the voyageurs Beauparlant and Pierre St Germain, as well as the Eskimo interpreters Augustus, Albert, Junius and William Ouligbuck, senior.[19]

The Arctic medal was a fitting award for the hardships which so many experienced. A letter from Captain Kellett to John Barrow from *Resolute*, 12 April to 2 May 1853,[20] described the arduous work by the men, when hauling the sledges, and raised the matter of a medal.

> I have been a long time at sea, and seen various trying services but never have I seen (for men) such labour and such misery after. No amount of money is an equivalent. The travelling parties ought to have some honorary and distinctive mark; the captain of the sledge something better than the others. Men require much more heart and stamina to undertake an extended travelling party than to go into action. The travellers have their enemy chilling them to the very heart, and paralyzing their limbs; the others the very contrary. I should like to see the travelling men get an Arctic medal. I would gladly give £50 towards it, and I am sure every Arctic officer would be anxious to subscribe, but to be of value it ought to be presented by the authority of Her Majesty.[21]

One Richard Sainthill of Cork finally put forward a proposal in February 1855. His pamphlet shows that the committee which awarded the £10,000 to the

'Investigators' in July 1855 also recommended the award of a medal to 'all those of every rank and class engaged in the several Arctic expeditions'. His postscript of 1 October 1856 confirms the medal to be engraved.[22]

CHAPTER 15

McClintock's Successful Search 1857-59

The naval aspect of the Crimean War required many of the officers who had previously been employed upon Arctic explorations. Captain Ommanney, for instance, was in the White Sea (north Russia) during the war, and one of his cannon balls was said to have been stopped by the Blessed Virgin of the monastery on the island of Solovets. Captain Sherard Osborn served in the Sea of Azov. McClintock, who had been promoted to Post Captain at the age of thirty-five, a very young age, over the heads of 424 seniors, on his return from the Belcher expedition, did not receive a command. He thought that his experience of ice would have been useful in the White Sea or Baltic, but he lacked a patron to advance his career.[1] The end of the Crimean War (during which there had been an action at Petropavlovsk, where the Governor had earlier welcomed the British 'discovery ships' in the North Pacific), encouraged Jane Franklin to renewed efforts. She wrote to the Prime Minister, Lord Palmerston, and had a motion presented in the House of Commons. She asked for the loan of a ship (the *Resolute* being the obvious choice), naval stores and permission for a naval officer to command the expedition. Charles Dickens and many others supported her campaign. Lieutenant Bedford Pim's 'An earnest appeal to the British public on behalf of the missing Arctic expedition', a pamphlet priced at one shilling had gone into at least four editions by 1857. In a well reasoned letter to one of the supporters of the motion (on which the decision was adverse), Lady Franklin pointed out that the Government had decided the matter without the advice of the 'committee of experienced Arctic officers best fitted to advise on the subject', which council had 'hitherto preceded every decision that has been made'. She emphasised that *pecuniary* assistance was not what she required

> since if I can get the loan of one of the Arctic ships now lying in ordinary and fit for no other purpose, her fittings completed in the dockyard, and some of the stores put on board which are now lying waste, my resources will be relieved as much as by money.

Mention had been made, during the debate, of HMS *Resolute*, continued Lady Franklin, but the proposer of the motion had not made use of a document which she had sent him and which had never received the attention it deserved.

> I mean the Resolution of Congress when it voted the money for the purchase and equipment of that ship. The 'Resolution' expressly stated that the object of this noble gift was, not the exhibition of national good will, but simply of sympathy with the cause to which the ship had been devoted.

Sir Francis Leopold McClintock, who travelled great distances in search of Franklin during the naval expeditions and who was successful from the *Fox*, 1857-59, in discovering the expedition's fate. (NMM, BHC 2858)

She concluded by saying that in the event of being driven to the 'painful alternative' of a private expedition, she might well accept Captain Hartstein's 'generous offer' to command it, unless an English officer were allowed by the Admiralty to serve, without jeopardising his naval career.[2]

A final refusal from the Government did not come until April 1857. Almost immediately, Lady Franklin asked Captain McClintock to inspect the steam yacht *Fox*, then for sale and soon afterwards he agreed to command her. His diary of this last British Franklin search expeditions begins:

Dublin, Saturday 18th April 57. Accepted command of Lady Franklin's expedition, applied for 18 months leave of absence for that purpose.

Thursday Evening 23rd recd. a telegraphic message from Lady Franklin stating: 'your leave is granted, the Fox is mine, the refit will commence immediately'

Friday Evening a family gathering at Alfred's

Saturday Morning 25th. started from Dublin to London.[3]

There was little time left to complete all the preparations for an Arctic voyage. Nearly £3,000 was raised by subscription and the Admiralty proved generous with regard to naval stores, clothing, pemmican, instruments and books, while

Captain Collinson took charge of the financial arrangements. A strong and cheer-ful young naval lieutenant, William Robertson Hobson, was appointed McClintock's second-in-command.

One of the most generous subscribers to the expedition was the sailing-master of the *Fox*, a wealthy young man from the merchant navy, Allen Young. He had seen service with the East India Company, had commanded a troopship during the Crimean War, and was considered a very fine seaman. Like the other officers, he renounced his pay during this last Franklin Search voyage. Dr David Walker joined as surgeon, naturalist and photographer, George Brand as engineer; while Captain Penny's and Dr Kane's interpreter, Carl Petersen sailed in his usual role. Of the crew of twenty-five men, seventeen had already taken part in the Franklin Search.

The *Fox*'s velvet furnishings and other fittings as a pleasure yacht had to be removed and she was fitted out for Arctic service by Alexander Hall & Co of Aberdeen where she had been built in 1855. She was a three-masted, topsail schooner of 177 tons, with auxiliary steam power, and she continued to sail main-ly in Greenland waters for a further fifty-five years after the Franklin search voyage.[4]

What were the aims of the voyage of the *Fox* of 1857 to 1859? In the archives of the Royal Geographical Society there is a tiny black-edged envelope inscribed, 'Lady Franklin's letter of Instructions (June 29th. 1857.)' to McClintock. At the top of the list was still the recovery of any survivors, and after that the retrieval of relics. Last, she asked McClintock to try to confirm Dr Rae's report that the Franklin Expedition had, indeed, discovered the North West Passage.

Captain Francis Leopold McClintock was no stranger to Arctic exploration and Jane Franklin had every confidence in him. His sledging journeys, beginning with Sir James Clark Ross in 1848-49 and then during the rest of the Franklin Search, had proved his undoubted qualities, though A G E Jones' biographical article is critical not only of his life, but of the defects of the so-called McClintock system of sledging.[5] In May 1859, when the *Fox* had been nearly two years absent, Captain McClure wrote of him:

> I hope little MacClintock will turn up this year. I have every confidence in his pru-dence and judgment. He will not risk anything without mature consideration. I know him well, if he loses his vessel, depend upon it, his legs will bring him home. He has plenty of physique and lots of endurance and pluck.[6]

At 177 tons *Fox* was within the tonnage advocated by that experienced navi-gator in ice, Dr William Scoresby, who considered a ship between 100 and 200 tons as 'best adapted for discovery in the Polar Seas', considerably less than that of the majority of the naval vessels previously employed. Smaller ships, wrote Scoresby, 'are stronger, more easily managed, in less danger of being stove, or crushed by the ice, and are less expensive, and from their smaller size, they require, of course fewer hands'. Scoresby regarded the rig of a topsail schooner to be suitable for ice navigation 'because of the means of arresting the head-way by backing the top-sails, and for being well-adapted for working to windward in intricate passages'. He also considered fast sailing a great advantage.[7] The *Fox* appears to have met these criteria, although, of course, Scoresby had no part in her refit from luxury yacht to ice-strengthened ship. She had the benefit of a steam engine of 30hp. The refit involved providing the officers with very small cabins like pigeon holes and a tiny mess-room, so that there was more room for stores. Externally the *Fox* was sheathed with stout planking and strengthened internally with 'strong cross beams, longitudinal beams, iron stanchions, and diagonal fastenings'. A massive iron propeller replaced the slender brass one, the false keel was removed, the boiler was enlarged and 'the sharp stem . . . cased in iron until it resembled a ponderous chisel set up edgeways'.[8]

The *Fox* was to need all her strengthening, since she was forced to spend the winter of 1857-58 in the pack. The usual route to Lancaster Sound taken by the whalers and the discovery ships was up the west coast of Greenland and into the North Water or North Main, the ice-free water at the head of Baffin Bay. The *Fox* made satisfactory progress until 17 August, when she was beset until 25 April 1858. In a letter to an old shipmate, Hobson wrote:

> The winter, as you may suppose, was a most dreary one. The ship's position being one of considerable peril and we having the gratifying reflection that we were drifting away from our north . . . Our accumulated drifts came to upward of 1300 miles. I never believed until the day of our release from the pack, that wood and iron could have stood such a pounding as we got when the ice broke up.

Having got up steam, the *Fox* forced her way through the broken pack, as it was borne on the ocean swell.

> Had anything gone wrong with the screw or if for any other cause we had once turned broadside to the sea, goodbye to the Fox and her crew; no earthly power could have saved either.[9]

On 2 October 1857, the barrel organ was erected on the lower deck, to the men's great enjoyment and to the delight of Christian, one of the two Greenland Eskimos, who turned the handle. Out of doors, they played hockey on most evenings. One of the dogs, Harness Jack, so named because he would not allow his harness to be taken off, 'won the esteem of his masters when one of the ladies littered, by constituting himself head of the establishment and preventing all the other dogs from approaching the family cask in which mother and puppies lodged, old Jack took up an uncomfortable position on the outside'. McClintock thought that the pups would have been devoured but for Jack's protection. On 2 December 1857 leading stoker Robert Scott fell down a hatchway. He died, and after the funeral service was buried through a hole in the ice, . His mess mates drew his body on a sledge, to be committed to the deep. McClintock described the burial:

> I know of nothing better calculated to awake serious emotion than such a scene. The lonely 'Fox', with colours half mast high, bell tolling, isolated from the habitable world amid the dark and dreary depth of Arctic winter, the intense chilling cold and death-like stillness of the icy sea over which our little procession marched by the light of the

lanthorns, guided by the direction posts, creates a feeling of awe, which even the most frivolous mind can fail to be impressed by.[10]

During the winter a reading, writing and navigation school had been run for those seamen who wished to attend. Besides keeping the ship clean, the men practised building snow houses and preparing travelling equipment. The officers, after an hour or two's tramping beside the ship or under the housing on deck in the dark mid-winter, would try to while away the hours by reading and talking. However, wrote Allen Young at the time:

> our conversations are miserably worn out; our stories are old and oft-repeated; we start impossible theories, and we bet upon the results of our new observations as to our progress, as we unconsciously drift and drift before the gale. At night we retire to our beds, thankful that another day has passed; a deathlike stillness reigns around, broken only by the ravings of some sleep-talker; the tramp of the watch upon deck, a passing bear causing a general rousing of our dogs, or a simultaneous rush of these poor ravenous creatures at our cherished stores of seal-beef in the shrouds; and, as we listen to the distant groaning and sighing of the ice, we thank God that we have still a home in these terrible wastes.[11]

The shooting by Petersen of the fiftieth seal on 16 November 1857 was celebrated by drinking the bottle of champagne which had been reserved for entering the North Water. McClintock drank the crew's health on Christmas Day and wished them many happy returns, 'but not stuck in the Floe, tho' '. After he had told them that Lady Franklin – the Sailor's friend – would be glad to hear that they enjoyed themselves 'so much and so rationally', they at once proposed that her health should be drunk, coupling with it that of her 'adorable niece', Sophia Cracroft. One of the 'little incidents' that attracted McClintock's attention that day was the men's display of daguerrotypes of their wives, children, sisters and sweethearts, almost all of them being married. His diary also reveals the almost inevitable disciplinary problems during the winter, one of the crew being what he called a 'sea lawyer'.[12]

Freed at last from the menacing grip of the ice, they arrived on 28 April at the west Greenland settlement of Holsteinborg (now Sisimiut), where all nature seemed alive, feeling as if they had risen from the dead. 'We arrived hungry and unshaven, our faces begrimed with oil-smoke, our clothes in tatters', wrote Allen Young, 'the good women of Holsteinborg worked and washed for us, repaired our sadly disreputable wardrobes, danced for us, sang to us, and parted from us with tears and a few little presents by way of *souvenirs*, as if we could ever forget them'.

After a few days in Holsteinborg, where the famished dogs were allowed to gorge themselves on four whale carcases, the *Fox* departed northwards on 8 May, having lost nearly a year by her detention in the pack. Letters sent home must have disappointed Lady Franklin and others anxious for news. McClintock applied for an extension to his leave. The masters of the whaling fleet kindly gave them newspapers and supplied stores, among them a sail and yards given by Captain J Simpson, out of which a main topsail was added to the *Fox*'s canvas.

Often in company with the hospitable whalers, McClintock listened to their experiences in rounding the 'middle ice' between Baffin Island and west Greenland, either via Melville Bay, or later in the season via the southern route.[13]

After long and tedious efforts which included being beset again for a week, McClintock wishing that his vessel were a well-powered steamer, the *Fox* entered Lancaster Sound. Because the easterly winds were filling the entrance to the sound with pack ice, the *Fox* met with unexpected delays, which preyed on her captain's mind. 'These vexatious delays', he wrote in his diary on 16 July, 'are not conducive to sleep; one lies down, but the past, the present and the future occupy the mind; to borrow a phrase, it is a sort of "magic lanthorn represen- tation" carried on mentally, too absorbing to admit of repose until hours have past over'.[14] On Beechey Island, the memorial sent by Lady Franklin inscribed 'To the memory of Franklin, Crozier and Fitzjames and all their gallant brother officers and faithful companions . . .' was placed next to the Bellot memorial. The *Fox* entered Peel Sound, but found fast ice blocking the passage south. McClintock then turned about and tried Prince Regent Inlet, from which they entered Bellot Strait, the passage of 20 miles long, dividing North Somerset from the Boothia Peninsula. 'We feel the crisis of our voyage is near at hand', wrote McClintock on 20 August. 'Does Bellot *Strait* really exist? Poor Bellot himself doubted it, and Kennedy, his commander, could not positively assert that it did. And if there be a strait, is it free from ice?' With much relief, the strait was found to exist – a passage to the western sea. However it had a strong current – 'more like a bore on the Hooghly than any ordinary tide', wrote Allen Young. It carried great masses of ice to and fro along the channel, between bold granite cliffs, making the waterway dangerous to the little *Fox*. After several attempts, the western end was almost reached, but it was quite blocked by heavy ice, with no hope of an exit. McClintock named the wider strait beyond (a continuation of Peel Sound), after Sir John Franklin. Winter quarters were found in a small har- bour at the eastern end of Bellot Strait, which McClintock called Port Kennedy, after the strait's discoverer.

Autumn and winter depot-laying journeys with dogs were made in preparation for the spring of 1859. Hobson led one of these small parties down the west coast of Boothia. The shore ice on which they were camping broke away and was blown out to sea for 15 miles. He had camped, he told a friend, 'with no more idea of danger than I have at this moment, but before I had been 5 minutes in the tent, the cook called out that the ice was breaking up. By the time I got out', Hobson continued, 'we were on a perfect island with a broad lane of dark water between us and the land. The wind which blew nearly a gale was off the shore and away we sailed before it.' His great fear, as the gap widened, was that the rising sea might break up the ice on which they were camped. After an 'anxious and bitterly cold night, a regular crushing match' took place between the floes, which surrounded them. They got back to the land after two days, over some elastic, dangerously thin newly-formed ice.[15] Two magnetic observatories – one of ice for hourly observations and the other of snow – were built at winter

Facsimile of the last record of the Franklin expedition of 1845-48, deposited in a cairn at Crozier's landing place on the west coast of King William Island, after the ships were abandoned in April 1848. The original is in the National Maritime Museum, Greenwich. (NMM, C5561) quarters. The monotony of winter was enlivened by the discovery of a live mouse, which had been encased in a biscuit cask, unopened since leaving Aberdeen. Ravens, their throats ringed by ice from their breath, were the only birds remaining through the winter, but migrating reindeer, as well as hares, foxes and ermines were seen and occasionally shot or trapped.

McClintock summarised the preparations for the long journeys to come from February to July, over the ice in temperatures ranging from 50° below zero to 50° above.

> First our personal apparel, making face-covers, light overall dresses or *snow-repellers* to keep out the penetrating drift-snow; altering and fitting mocassins [sic] and canvas boots, re-sewing everything, and testing the warmth and comfort of the suit by preparatory walks. Secondly, preparing the sledges, re-lashing them, and burnishing the steel shoeing of the runners; adapting and strengthening our small calico tents (mine, which serves for six persons, weighs only 18½ lbs, the poles included); making blanket sleeping bags, and tent robes. And lastly, making bags of the lightest material to hold the provisions, cans for spirit-fuel and for rum, and packages of all sorts; also altering and testing our cooking utensils.

A suit of McClintock's 'snow-repellers' is in the National Maritime Museum, Greenwich.

McClintock and Young were ready to leave the *Fox* on the first sledge jour neys of the year on 10 February 1859, but were detained by bad weather until the 17th. Young crossed over to Prince of Wales Land, where he laid a depot in preparation for his subsequent search and survey of the island. McClintock was accompanied by Alexander Thompson as dog driver, who had accompanied him in 1854, and Petersen of course as interpreter and driver. Petersen was to publish a narrative of the voyage of the *Fox* on his return to Denmark.[16] Petersen had already served under Captain Penny, 1850-51 and Dr Kane, 1852-54. In the portrait which forms the frontispiece to his book he is shown wearing the Arctic medal and a Danish cross. He was rewarded in Denmark with the charge of a lighthouse.

The party travelled for eight or ten hours till dusk each day. The dogs' feet suffered in the low temperatures, so that they could accomplish only fifteen to eighteen miles a day, despite the sledge load of clothing and provisions having been lightened. At the end of a march, a cold two hours was spent building a snow hut, Petersen being the master-mason, while Thompson and McClintock sawed out the blocks of snow, until the walls were nearly six feet high, leaning inwards as much as possible. The small brown tent was laid over the hole to form the roof, since they had not time to spare to complete the dome. Once the snow hut had been built, the dogs were fed, making sure that the weaker ones got their fair share. Then the provisions, sleeping gear, boots, fur mittens and dog-harness were unpacked from the sledges and carried in, after which the door was blocked with snow,

> the cooking-lamp lighted, foot-gear changed, diary written up, watches wound, sleep-ing bags wriggled into, pipes lighted, and the merits of the various dogs discussed,

until supper was ready; the supper swallowed, the upper robe or coverlet was pulled over, and then to sleep.

However, once the cooking was over, or the doorway partly opened, the temperatures fell so low that it became impossible to sleep and mitts had to be put on even when drinking tea. Apart from extra blanket-wrappers and mocassins, they carried no spare clothes.

A bear was shot on the southward journey, giving the dogs, who were suffering still, a chance to eat unfrozen flesh. On 1 March, the little party camped at the supposed position of the Magnetic Pole, where four Eskimos appeared, much to McClintock's surprise and joy. They had been sealing and were returning home, but their village of eight igloos proved too distant to reach that evening, so that for a needle each, they built a hut, large enough to hold both parties, in one hour. The Eskimos would not eat the salt pork, but took a small portion of bear's blubber and water. It may have been on this occasion that McClintock acquired what he called 'the arctic accomplishment' of eating delicate little slices of frozen bear's blubber on biscuit which he greatly preferred to pork.

This encounter turned out to be most rewarding, as far as the objects of the expedition were concerned – a promise of things to come. One of the men was wearing a naval button, which they said came from 'some white people who were starved upon a island where there are salmon (that is, in a river); and that the iron of which their knives were made came from the same place. One of these men said he had been to the island to obtain wood and iron. Some ten miles further south, near Cape Victoria on the south west coast of Boothia, James Ross Strait, McClintock called a halt. Their companions constructed a spacious snow hut for them in half an hour, whereupon he revealed the knives, files, needles, scissors, and beads which they could have in exchange, next morning, for articles belonging to the starving white men.

About forty-five individuals ranging from elderly folk to babies in hoods turned up, and trading began briskly. McClintock bought a number of relics of Franklin's expedition: six silver spoons and forks, a silver medal belonging to the assistant surgeon Alexander M'Donald, part of a gold chain and a few buttons, besides various knives, bows and arrows, made from iron and wood. Two stout pieces of timber, possibly from a boat's keel, formed one of their sledges. McClintock found that all the old people remembered the visit of Sir John Ross's *Victory* some thirty years earlier. One elderly man was called Oblooria and he turned out to have been James Ross's guide, and asked after Ross by his Inuktitut name, Agglugga. The man for whom the carpenter had made a wooden leg appeared to have died.

Next morning, 4 March 1859, McClintock bought a spear from a man 'who told Petersen distinctly that a ship having three masts had been crushed by the ice out in the sea to the west of King William's Island, but that all the people landed safely'. He had not been an eye-witness and because the ship had sunk, they had acquired nothing from her. What they had obtained came from an island in the river, which McClintock appears to have assumed was Montreal

Island. None of the Eskimos saw the Kabloonans, but one man said that some had been buried, while others left their bones on the island where they died. An old man called Oo-na-lee sketched the coastline with his spear in the snow, saying it would take eight journeys to where the ship sank and pointing towards Cape Felix, the most northerly headland of King William Island. McClintock could make little sense of the impromptu chart.

His party returned to the *Fox* as quickly as possible, in good health and with tremendous appetites. Apart from meeting the Eskimos and through them confirming Dr Rae's report, the journey of 360 geographical miles (420 statute miles) had 'completed the discovery of the coast-line of continental America, thereby adding about 120 miles to our charts'. The mean temperature during the journey had been 30° below zero Fahrenheit, or 62° below the freezing point of water. When their faces were cleaned of the soot from the blubber lamp, various scars from frost-bites appeared and the tips of their fingers were calloused from the same cause. Young had been successful in laying his depot on Prince of Wales Island and subsequently sledged the 75 miles to Fury Beach to bring back 1,200lbs of sugar. He had found there still a vast amount of preserved vegetables and soups, which they tried and found good. McClintock spoke to his small crew about his journey and pointed out that one of Franklin's ships still remained to be accounted for.

Hobson, McClintock and Petersen left again on 2 April in a procession of five sledges (one drawn by five puppies that McClintock intended selling to the Eskimos), twelve men and seventeen dogs, of all shapes and sizes. Silk banners flew from the sledges, while the flag of the Royal Harwich Yacht Club was hoisted aboard the *Fox*. On 20 April, at the Magnetic Pole, they met again a dozen of the people encountered earlier at Cape Victoria, from whom some articles were purchased. McClintock discovered that in fact two ships had been seen by the natives of King William Island, and that while one had sunk, the other (which these people had not mentioned in February) was forced on shore by the ice at a place called Oot-loo-lik. Their wood came from this vessel, aboard which the body of a large man with long teeth had been found, according to the childhood memory of a young Eskimo. When a later searcher, Captain C F Hall, interviewed a number of Eskimos in the 1860s, this was repeated. A recent enquirer, David Woodman, has concluded that the ship, in which the decomposing body was found, had been navigated as far as O'Reilly, or more likely, Kirkwall Island, both west of the Adelaide Peninsula; that a few men may have lived on board, leaving one of their party (presumably dead) when they left by boat for the mainland.

At Cape Victoria, McClintock and Petersen's party separated from Hobson, who was to take the northern route and then search the west coast of King William Island for the grounded ship and for records. McClintock followed the more southerly course. Hobson's letter to his old shipmate continues the story:

> On Cape Felix, its northern point, I found the first Franklin traces. There was a large cairn standing and a variety of articles were strewn about it. Three tents had fallen

down over the bedding of the people who had last used them, the poles having been withdrawn, probably for firewood. Three fireplaces were found with fragments of burnt wood, brimstone matches, salt meat bones, feathers etc. in or near them. Judge my disgust when very much against my will I had convinced myself that no paper was deposited there. I think it must have been a shooting station or observatory tracing the coast to the south.

Hobson found two more cairns. In the first nothing was deposited and in the second only a broken pick-axe and an empty canister of coffee.

> The fourth cairn found was at Point Victory where the crews had landed when they left their ship. At this place they seemed to have had a regular overhaul and got rid of all that was deemed superfluous. A vast number of things lay strewn about this cairn and here I found the anxiously sought paper which told us of Franklin's fate and the abandonment of the ships by the survivors of the crews.[17]

The 'anxiously sought paper' was one of two records that Hobson found on King William Island. The second (which he did not mention in his letter), like the first, had originally been deposited in a cairn some miles away by Lieutenant Graham Gore and Charles Frederick Des Voeux, Mate, in May 1847. They had landed with six men by crossing the heavy ice of Victoria Strait, from HMS *Erebus*, which was then beset with *Terror* off the northwest coast of the island. Both records were written on the official forms which were meant to be placed in bottles or cylinders and thrown overboard, for the study of ocean currents. The finder was requested in six European languages to return the form to the Admiralty or to the British Consul at the nearest port, with a note of the time and place at which it was found. At the top of the form were printed headings and lines, to be filled in by the originator with the name of the ship, its position and the date. Both the records found by Hobson were corroded with rust from the tin cylinders in which they were rolled. The entries made in 1847 on both forms are very nearly identical. They read:

> H.M. Ships Erebus and Terror . . . Wintered in the Ice in Lat. 70 °5′N Long. 98° 23′W.

> Having wintered in 1846-7 at Beechey Island in Lat. 74°43′28″ N Long. 91° 39′15″W after having ascended Wellington Channel to Lat. 77° – and returned by the west side of Cornwallis Island. Sir John Franklin commanding the Expedition. *All well*. Party consisting of 2 officers and 6 Men left the Ships on Monday 24th. May 1847.[18]

Both the entries on these forms are in Fitzjames' hand, written on board *Erebus* before the party left (probably to complete a North West Passage by passing down the west coast of King William Island, thus linking James Ross's Victory Point and Dease and Simpson's Cape Herschel.) Dr Cyriax remarks that both these records contain the same mistakes: the date of the wintering on Beechey Island is given as 1846-47 and its longitude is incorrect.

The second record, which was eventually given to Lady Franklin and is now at Cambridge, lay undisturbed in its tin cylinder, solder unbroken, in the cairn at Gore Point (McClintock's subsequent place-name) until Hobson found it.

The other more historic record (now at Greenwich) was almost certainly deposited in 1847 by Graham Gore in James Ross' cairn at Point Victory (Ross' furthest, as we have seen), but removed by Lieutenant John Irving and brought to Captain Crozier in April 1848, at what Crozier thought was Victory Point after the ships had been abandoned, still beset in Victoria Channel. The record was then placed in a new cairn, after Fitzjames had added the following words:

> (25th April)1848 H.M.Ship(s) Terror and Erebus were deserted on the 22nd April, 5 leagues NNW of this (hav)ing been beset since 12th Septr. 1846. The Officers and Crews consisting of 105 souls, under the command (of Cap)tain F.R.M. Crozier landed here – in Lat 69 °37′42″ Long 98 °41′. (This p)aper was found by Lt. Irving under the cairn supposed to have been built by Sir James Ross in 1831, 4 miles to the Northward – where it had been deposited by the late Commander Gore in June 1847. Sir James Ross' pillar has not however been found, and the paper has been transferred to this position which is that in which Sir J Ross' pillar was erected – Sir John Franklin died on the 11th of June 1847 and the total loss by deaths in the Expedition has been to this date 9 Officers and 15 Men.
>
> James Fitzjames, Captain H M S Erebus
> F.R.M. Crozier Captain and Senior Offr.

and start on tomorrow 26th for Backs Fish River.[19]

These records, and particularly the second with its added inscription, comprise the only written evidence as to the proceedings of the *Erebus* and *Terror*, after departing from Beechey Island, before and after wintering there in 1845-46. As Captain Penny maintained, they did indeed sail up Wellington Channel, but turned south in latitude 77°N to reach Barrow Strait again, through an unknown channel to the west of Cornwallis Island, which was subsequently called Crozier Strait and for whose existence the two records found in 1859, constituted the sole evidence for nearly ninety years. After being freed from the ice in the summer of 1846, the ships must have sailed south from Peel Sound, into what McClintock named Franklin Strait, where they encountered the polar, oceanic or palaeocrystic ice from the central polar basin scouring, churning, groaning and forcing its way down what was later called M'Clintock Channel. Franklin may have considered proceeding (if the ice conditions allowed) down the east coast of King William Island, but it was not then known that a strait existed there. McClintock in his *Voyage of the* 'Fox' writes of this route as the only navigable North West Passage and one which he would have taken, had not Bellot Strait been blocked at its western end. Collinson, as we have seen, offered to take a steamer beyond the *Enterprise's* eastern turning point. Roald Amundsen was to pass this way in the *Gjoa* early in the twentieth century.

Franklin's ships must have found open water during the summer of 1846; they were beset, however, that September and still beset in May 1847 to the northwest of Cape Felix, the most northerly point of King William Island. All was well and Sir John Franklin was still in command when Lieutenant Graham Gore, Des

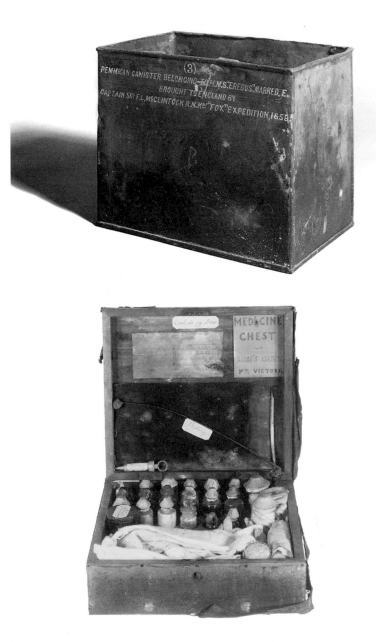

Top: One of the numerous relics of the Franklin expedition brought back from King William Island by Captain McClintock. Like those found by Dr Rae and later by Lieutenant Schwatka, it was labelled for display in the former Royal Naval Museum, Greenwich. (NMM, D1394)

Above: Medicine chest abandoned by the Franklin expedition at Crozier's landing place on the west coast of King William Island in 1848. Like most of the other relics, it is now in the National Maritime Museum, Greenwich. (NMM, A4910)

Voeux and party travelled across the sea ice and along the coast to James Ross's Point Victory, where the record now at Greenwich was deposited the following month. It is probable that they reached Cape Herschel on the south coast of the island and thus connected a North West Passage. McClintock was disappointed, at Cape Herschel, to find no record deposited by them in the once 'ponderous cairn' built by Dease and Simpson, which had been largely dismantled by the Eskimos when he examined it in May 1859.

The *Erebus* and *Terror* never escaped the grip of the ice in Victoria Strait, slowly drifting with it southwards until in April 1848, after the death of Sir John Franklin the previous June, Captain Crozier ordered their abandonment, three long years after the expedition's departure from England. We know nothing of Franklin's death in a vast Arctic wilderness. When McClintock brought the last records to his widow in 1859 she must have been thankful that he did not take part in the ultimate tragedy.

Hobson's journey resulted in the discovery of these last records, which had fortunately lain undisturbed by the Eskimos since their deposit. The same can be said of the numerous relics which he and McClintock found, despite the snow, on the shores of King William Island. No doubt bearing in mind the importance of leaving a record at some recognised spot, Captain Crozier (by then in command of the expedition) landed at what he thought was James Ross's Point Victory, but which in reality was almost certainly a few miles south of it.[20] Here, in Hobson's words, 'they seem to have had a regular overhaul and got rid of all that was deemed superfluous', since a 'vast number of things lay strewn about this cairn . . .' before setting out southwards for the mainland and Back's Great Fish River.[21]

*   *   *

Meanwhile, the early part of Captain McClintock's journey of May 1859 proved less fruitful. Petersen and he interviewed, or attempted to interview, two groups of Eskimos, one very friendly, the other very frightened, but both having wood, and the first group silver plate, from the Franklin Expedition. McClintock's search of Montreal Island, in the estuary of Back's Great Fish River, proved fruitless and he was disappointed to meet few natives during his whole journey. His party crossed over to the southern shore of King William Island and marched westwards towards Cape Herschel, along the route which the retreating parties from the *Erebus* and *Terror* must have followed. On 25 May a bleached human skeleton, face downward, was found partly covered by snow on a gravel ridge, probably a steward (from his uniform), who may have died of exhaustion in his sleep. 'It was a melancholy truth', remarked McClintock, 'that the old woman spoke when she said "they fell down and died as they walked along" '. Only part of the skull appeared above the snow and one of his men, thinking it was a stone, rested his shovel against it, but drew back in horror when the hollow sound revealed its true nature. These remains may have been those of Thomas Armitage, Gunroom Steward of the *Terror* and friend of Harry Peglar, whose papers he carried.[22] McClintock thought that the snow may have concealed other skeletons.

Disappointed to find no record at Cape Herschel, McClintock continued further west along the more exposed coast, where he found Hobson's cairn containing news of his discovery of 'THE RECORD, so ardently sought for' ... but no sign of a wreck, nor of natives. Of the record, McClintock commented, 'So sad a tale was never told in fewer words'. He found the simplicity of the message 'deeply touching', as indeed it is, when one thinks of the doubtless scurvy-ridden remaining '105 souls', their provisions nearly exhausted, landing on that barren shore, Fitzjames having to thaw the ink before putting pen to paper. We do not know why so high a proportion of officers had died – nine by comparison with fifteen of the men.

On 29 May 1859, McClintock's party reached the western headland of King William Island, which he named after Captain Crozier, finding few living creatures and scanty traces of the Eskimos along the ridged low limestone shore, bordered by many heavy floes amid broken pack ice, making a forbidding prospect to seaward. Next day, they camped beside the large boat discovered by Hobson almost invisible in the snow, on his return journey. 'In her', Hobson wrote, 'we found a vast quantity of clothing, the remains of two men, two double guns, one barrel of each loaded and capped, placed ready to the hands of those who probably laid down to sleep and never awoke'. He added, 'We should never have found this boat had not two awning stanchions been left shipped'.[23] McClintock's party were 'transfixed with awe' at the sight of the skeletons. The tattered clothing in the boat showed no marks of ownership. The boat measured 28 feet long and 7 feet 3 inches wide. It had been built 'with a view to lightness and light draught of water', wrote McClintock, 'and evidently with the utmost care for the ascent of the Great Fish River'. It weighed about 750lbs, he thought, but was mounted on a massive sledge, constructed of two thick oak planks, over 23 feet long, weighing at least 650 pounds. Boat and sledge together would have made a heavy load for seven strong healthy men.

Besides the great quantity of clothing in the boat, there was an astonishing variety of articles (including two rolls of sheet lead), which the 'modern sledge traveller in these regions', wrote McClintock, would consider a useless accumulation of dead weight, likely to cripple the sledge crews. In the after part of the boat were twenty-six silver spoons and forks, eight bearing Franklin's crest and the remainder those of officers of both ships. There were no iron spoons, usually used by the men, which implied, he thought, that the silver had been issued to the crew, as the only means of saving it. There were also several watches and pocket chronometers. The only food was a small amount of tea and nearly 40lbs of chocolate, plus an empty tin of pemmican and some tobacco.

McClintock was puzzled that only two skeletons were found of the twenty or thirty who must have been attached to the boat. He was even more surprised to find the boat pointing back towards Point Victory, his own destination. He concluded that this boat was 'returning to the ships', then 60 miles away, to obtain more provisions. He also concluded that the main party, making for Back's Great Fish River (one of whom was the steward whose skeleton lay 70 miles away in the other direction) had left the boat party to fetch more supplies, while they themselves proceeded southwards for the mainland. McClintock observed that we do not know whether they reached the ships, but that the Eskimos reported only one body aboard the vessel when it drifted on shore.

Still travelling northwards up the gloomy and desolate snow-clad west coast of King William Island, McClintock's party reached Crozier's landing place, his so-called 'Point Victory' on 2 June. Before arriving there, McClintock drove round an inlet off Back Bay by dog-sledge and named it after Captain Collinson. At Crozier's landing place, where the more historic record found by Hobson had been deposited, there was a huge heap of clothing, four feet high, but none of it marked. Around the cairn numerous articles were strewn, including four heavy sets of boats' cooking stoves, pick-axes, brass curtain rods (perhaps intended as gifts for the Eskimos), shovels, a dip-circle, a sextant and a small medicine chest made of mahogany, which has been described in detail.[24]

'These abandoned superfluities', wrote McClintock, 'afford the saddest and most convincing proof that here – on this spot – our doomed and scurvy-stricken countrymen calmly prepared themselves to struggle manfully for life'. Be that as it may, it is puzzling that so many heavy and obviously useless items were ever taken ashore. Had discipline broken down and allowed a free for all? The alternative to landing would have been to remain in the ships, (unless they were badly damaged by the pressure of the heavy ice,) and to rely on their drifting the remaining 60 miles in the coming summer to reach Queen Maud Gulf and the American mainland. However, there was probably little food left on board, since the expedition was provisioned for three years only, but sadly there were twenty-four fewer mouths to feed.

Sherard Osborn pointed out that no preserved meat tins were found on the trail of Franklin's crews, not even at Cape Felix in 1847. This would imply that these so-called 'fresh meat' provisions had been exhausted or found unfit for consumption, and that therefore salt meat would have been the diet, resulting in 'certain death by scurvy'. Again, thought Osborn, the absence of a cache of provisions ashore, either salted or 'fresh', pointed to there being none at all left aboard ship and that the remaining food was carried on the sledges, in the hope that seals, salmon and deer could be shot further south. The 'Investigators' had found plenty of game near the Bay of Mercy on Banks Island. In contrast, the west coast of King William Island is virtually barren of animal life and unfrequented, therefore, by the Eskimos. In addition, the ships were firmly beset in heavy ice, 15 or more miles from the shore.[25] One wonders what were Crozier's reasons for choosing to retreat up the Great Fish River rather than making for Barrow Strait and, why he kept the party together, rather than dividing it, as McClure had planned to do. Perhaps they were all so broken in health that he realised only a very few, if any, would live to tell the tale. Perhaps he wanted to complete the last link in the North West Passage, even though this could only be

'The North-West Passage. "It might be done and England should do it." ' by Millais, 1874. The old sea captain shares with his daughter his chart, journal and memories of his Arctic voyages. The painting sums up the mood of nostalgia and aspiration with which the public of the time identified. (Tate Gallery, London 1999)

done with the loss of all their lives. Perhaps he thought that since the river had been descended by a search party, when plans were made to find the Rosses, that one might come that way for them too. He may also have believed that the provisions on Fury Beach would be exhausted by then.

As McClintock travelled on, the higher temperatures of mid June caused the snow to melt on top of the ice, so that sledging became a great labour for men and dogs. Not far from the ship, the sledges had to be left, the tired and sore-footed dogs preferring to stay behind. On 19 June 1859, after scrambling over hills and through snow valleys, the party sighted 'our poor dear lonely little "Fox" ', after an absence of seventy-eight days. Hobson had arrived nearly a week earlier, unable to walk or stand on his own, being so badly afflicted with scurvy that his men had hurried back with him on the sledge. The expedition had already suffered the deaths of Scott and George Brand, the engineer. Dr Walker told McClintock of a third death, during his absence, that of Thomas Blackwell, ship's steward.

*   *   *

Allen Young was still out, having departed on 7 April with a sledge-party of four men, and another sledge drawn by six dogs, driven by Samuel Emanuel, one of the two Greenlanders. Wishing to extend his journey, Young sent back all but George Hobday, whom McClintock described as a 'fine young man-of-war's man' of few words. After some weeks travelling and surveying the southern half of Prince of Wales Island, as far as Osborn's earlier turning point, Young attempted to cross what was later called M'Clintock Channel, unable to see more than a 100 yards ahead, because of the massive hummocks and deep chasms. He struggled for 14 miles, but then gave up, to travel southwards along the coast, marvelling at the heavy ice in the Channel, 'which ploughed up the shallow bottom to form ridges, furrows and shingle patches'. He concluded that any ship beset there would be in grave danger.[26]

After a brief return to the ship for medical aid, Young set off on a second journey to complete his part of the search, during which he finished the survey of both shores of Franklin Strait in dreary weather and through deep sludge and melt water. McClintock became anxious for Young's return and set off to meet him on 25 June. He found his own dogs lying quietly beside the sledges left on the return from King William Island. They had existed on some pemmican, blubber, leather straps and a specimen gull. He reflected that the Eskimo dogs have a hard life, even Petersen 'who is generally kind and humane' believing that they had little or no feeling. McClintock gave his dogs a good feed and with them proceeded to Pemmican Rock, where he met Young, who was returning after a depressing journey during which no trace of Franklin had been found though he had explored altogether 380 miles, an important geographical achievement. Once reunited, on board the *Fox* a great feast (including pickled whaleskin, said to be an anti-scorbutic) assuaged their sledging appetites. Young had felt that their division into separate parties at the beginning of the season was like the 'breaking-up of a happy family', so that he must have taken a particular pleasure in their reunion. The *Fox* entered Blackwall docks, London, at the end of her homeward voyage on 23 September 1859. The fate of Franklin had at long last been ascertained and some 800 miles of new coastline had been surveyed.

McClintock received a knighthood from Queen Victoria, while Hobson was immediately promoted. Parliament later voted £5000 to the officers and men of the *Fox* and the Royal Geographical Society, whose President Sir Roderick Impey Murchison had been prominent in his support for the expedition, awarded its Patron's Gold Medal to McClintock. At a time when there were no women Fellows, it awarded its Founder's Gold Medal to Lady Franklin. The citation began, 'Desirous of commemorating in an especial manner the Arctic researches of our associate the late Sir John Franklin, and of testifying to the fact that his Expedition was the first to discover a North-West Passage . . .' It praised her own 'noble and self-sacrificing perseverance', but those first lines recognised the accomplishment of all she had striven for.[27]

CHAPTER 16

The Last Searches

It has been described how Captain C F Hall discovered the relics of Frobisher's expedition of the 1570s when he was searching for survivors and records of Franklin's. In 1860, at the age of thirty-eight, he had abandoned his engraving business and his own newspaper in the booming industrial and commercial city of Cincinnati to travel to the Arctic, having interested Henry Grinnell and other prominent Americans, and gained the practical help of the whalers. He appears to have had an almost religious calling to rescue any survivors, despite the conclusions of the McClintock expedition that there were none.

Hall's second attempt (1864-69) resulted in finding none either, nor of any of the records that he believed (through an Eskimo report) were buried in a vault on King William Island. He spent four winters at Repulse Bay (Dr Rae's earlier wintering place), living with the Eskimos. He never truly mastered the language and relied on his two faithful Inuit friends Ebierbing ('Eskimo Joe') and his wife Tookoolitoo ('Hannah'). Sadly, the couple were to lose two infants during their association with Hall. He met a number of Eskimos who had recollections of the white men's visits to their land, but unfortunately for Hall these related almost certainly to Parry's wintering near Fury and Hecla Strait in 1822-23, to Dr Rae's expedition in 1847 across the Melville Peninsula, to Sir John Ross in the *Victory*, 1829-33 and only in part to Franklin.

However, he did make a valuable contribution to the history of the lost expedition by recording the Eskimos' reminiscences, and by recovering various relics in their possession. R J Cyriax highlights the descriptions of the tent at Terror Bay, the meeting with white men on King William Island, the accounts of the deaths at Starvation Cove on the North American mainland, of the abandoned ship at O'Reilly Island (west of the Adelaide Peninsula) and of the tragic retreat towards the Great Fish River.[1] Hall did not live to write a narrative of his second expedition, during which he was only able to spend a week on the south coast of King William Island. However, from his manuscripts Professor J E Nourse compiled the *Narrative of the second Arctic Expedition made by C.F. Hall*, published in Washington, 1879.

Hall had written of his mission, 'What burned within my soul like a living fire all the time was the full faith that I should find some survivors of Sir John's memorable Expedition living among the natives, and that I would be the instrument in the hand of heaven, of their salvation'.[2] He was fortunate in having the company on King William Island of the Inuk who had told Rae about the tragedy, Innookpoozheejook, but only for a week. His Eskimo companions would not stay longer. A skeleton was found on 12 May 1869 at a place (near Piffer River) where the wind had cleared the snow away and Hall brought the bones and skull back to the United States. The skeleton is believed to be that of Lieutenant H T D Le Vesconte of HMS *Erebus*. It was later interred at Greenwich.[3] His biographer concluded:

> For a week Hall wandered the dreary southeast coast of King William Island, a forlorn and discouraged man. At several places where the Eskimos said they had seen relics or bodies, he held ceremonies and built little monuments on the deep snow. It was all he could do. This was the conclusion of the great quest to which he had dedicated ten years of his life – a caretaking for the unfound dead.[4]

Schwatka's Search for Franklin Relics and Records 1878-1880

In contrast to McClintock and Hobson's search in deep snow along the coast of King William Island, and that of C F Hall, the visit of Lieutenant Frederick Schwatka of the US Army took place in the summer of 1879, when the land was largely bare. However, by then the Eskimos had themselves visited the west coast and taken away much that was useful from among the items abandoned by the crews of the *Erebus* and *Terror*. Schwatka was accompanied by Lieutenant Colonel W H Gilder, Harry (Heinrich) Klutschak and Frank Melms. The expedition originated in a whaler's report that a cairn containing books and other Franklin material was known to the Eskimos. This proved to have no foundation once the party had landed from a whaling vessel at Chesterfield Inlet, northwest Hudson Bay in 1878.

Instead of returning disappointed to the United States, Schwatka decided to winter among the native people and then to travel to King William Island for a summer search. Fourteen Eskimos accompanied the party on 1 April 1879 when they set off to make the overland crossing, with three sledges drawn by over forty dogs, relatively few provisions, but a large quantity of arms and ammunition. One of the Eskimos was Ebierbing, 'Eskimo Joe'.[5] They reached King William Island on 5 June 1879, having discovered a route via the Lorillard and Hayes rivers. More relics and skeletons of the lost expedition were found, and Eskimo reports recorded, leading to the belief that the Todd Islands, rather than Montreal Island, were where a number of the last survivors had died. Others had reached what Schwatka called Starvation Cove to the west of Richardson Point on the mainland, where a box of records in a boat appeared to have been opened and dispersed by the Eskimos. R J Cyriax has suggested that the footprints of white men, seen by the Eskimos near here may have belonged to the last survivors – those who returned to the ships, one of which may have sunk off O'Reilly Island, and in which a body was found.[6]

A skeleton, discovered by Schwatka's party at Crozier's encampment, was believed from a prize medal found beside the grave to be that of Lieutenant John

Irving of *Terror*. It was eventually buried in Dean Cemetery, Edinburgh. Both McClintock and Cyriax concluded that since Irving fetched the record from Ross's cairn at the true Point Victory, after the ships were abandoned, he was unlikely to have died and been more likely to have been one of a group returning to them later in the year.[7]

McClintock prefaces the later editions of his *Voyage of the Fox* with accounts of Hall's and Schwatka's expeditions, on which he made informed comments. 'Undoubtedly the most arduous part of Schwatka's brilliant achievement was his return march, during the winter 1879-80', he wrote. Schwatka's sledge journey lasting nearly twelve months covered 2,709 geographical miles (3,124 statute miles), the longest ever made at that time. Like Rae to an extent, and Captain Hall, the party adopted the Eskimo way of life and was able to find sufficient deer and other animal food to live on. Colonel Gilder, who represented the *New York Times*, wrote the expedition narrative on its return. Schwatka's own short account was not published until 1965. Klutschak's narrative appeared in Vienna in 1881 and has been recently translated.[8] Schwatka himself, at a dinner given in his honour by the American Geographical Society, which had sponsored the expedition, in October 1880 briefly summed up its progress and results. His main point was that the destruction of the Franklin records had been established 'beyond all reasonable doubt'. Combined with the death of the party and the burial of the dead, he considered the 'Franklin problem' to have been setttled 'in all its important aspects'.[9] In a report to the Royal Geographical Society, its Hon Secretary praised the remarkable achievement of Lieutenant Schwatka during a journey 'without parallel' in some respects. He concluded by saying that Englishmen, reading the heroic story of the fate of Franklin 'generation after generation' would at the same time, 'always cherish a feeling of gratitude for the kindly deed of the brave Americans, who tenderly collected and buried some of the bones of our heroes – a task which, we well know, entailed no small amount of peril and hardship'.[10]

The fate of Franklin has continued to intrigue and inspire not only readers, but explorers, up to the present day.[11] In 1993 the late Barry Ranford, discovered the remains of what he believed to be a second boat, not the one found and described by McClintock but perhaps that located by Schwatka, whose stem is in the National Maritime Museum. The previous year, he had come across what appears to have been a new site on a small island across the mud flats in Erebus Bay. Here eleven individuals had died. A comb, a pipe and a boot sole ringed by nails (to provide a grip on the ice) were revealed by an archaeological dig in 1993. Laboratory analysis of the bones appears to provide evidence of cannibalism, and of high lead content.[12] These were returned to the site in 1994.

The fate of the *Erebus* and *Terror* has also continued to fascinate people. Cyriax concluded that one sank off O'Reilly Island and the other in deep water. In the 1920s, the theory that two ships seen on an iceberg in April 1851 may have been Franklin's was revived by Lieutenant Commander R T Gould, who was on contract to the Admiralty Hydrographic Department as an historian from 1916 to 1927.[13] The little known Admiralty chart no. 5101, published in May 1927 and withdrawn about 1970, was compiled by Gould and a most interesting one it is. Entitled 'Chart showing the vicinity of King William Island, with the various positions in which relics of the Arctic Expedition under Sir John Franklin have been found', it distinguishes between the personal observations of British and American explorers and the Eskimo reports recorded by them. But a complete picture of what happened to Franklin, his ships and his men in those icy waters can never be painted.

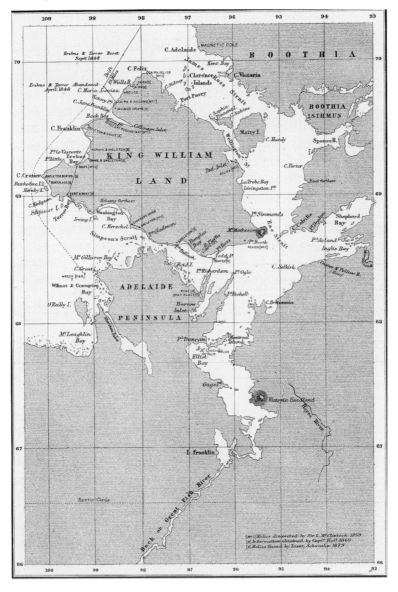

The line of retreat of the Franklin expedition. Published in 1880 (Author's collection)

CHAPTER 17

The Navigation of the North West Passage

By the end of the Franklin Search, all the Arctic waterways were known, revealing several possible North West Passages. The ice at the western end of Bellot Strait prevented the *Fox* from proceeding south down Franklin Strait, Ross Strait and Rae Strait to the mainland of North America. 'Perhaps some future voyager', McClintock wrote afterwards, 'profiting by the experience of Franklin, and the observations which my journey round King William's Island has enabled me to make, may succeed in carrying his ship through from sea to sea; at least he will be enabled to direct all his efforts in the true and only direction'.[1] That future voyager was Roald Amundsen, the Norwegian best known for his conquest of the South Pole in 1911, who earlier gained the distinction of being first to navigate the North West Passage.

Allen Young in the *Pandora* had made an attempt in 1875, but was stopped by ice in Peel Sound. He was diverted from a second attempt in 1876 by answering the Admiralty's request to deliver mails for the *Alert* and *Discovery* in Smith Sound. He did not try again. Had he done so, he might well have succeeded.[2]

Roald Amundsen and the Gjøa

Amundsen had already served as Mate during the Antarctic voyage of the *Belgica* at the turn of the century and so was experienced in ice navigation. Built on the Hardangerfjord, his small ship the *Gjøa* was a herring boat with sails and a small engine. Amundsen had strengthened her in Tromsø, although she had earlier sailed in the icy seas north of Norway. Inspired by his reading as a boy about Franklin and the North West Passage and by Nansen's voyage in the *Fram*, Amundsen was determined to become an explorer himself. His voyage in the *Gjøa* of 1903-07 aimed at navigating the Passage and at locating the North Magnetic Pole. Unlike Allen Young, Amundsen had few private means and much of his life seems to have been a struggle to raise money in order to fulfil his dreams. With six companions and six dogs, which had been brought back in the *Fram* by Otto Sverdrup in 1902, Amundsen, aged 29, departed from Christiania (Oslo) in June 1903, later acquiring more dogs in Greenland.

Their first landing in the Canadian Arctic was on Beechey Island, where Amundsen found the 'heaviness and sadness of death' hanging over the island. They inspected the ruins of Northumberland House Depot, the graves and the monuments. The magnetic observations pointed them to the southwest, rather than towards the abundant game of Melville Island. They took away some coal, shoe leather and an old anvil, which Amundsen's smith could not bear to leave behind.[3] The *Gjøa* sailed down Peel Sound, passing the western end of Bellot Strait on 28 August, everyone very cheerful because of their good progress and because food was ample. Helmer Hanssen, one of the crew, who later accompanied Amundsen to the South Pole, described life on board

> The days went quickly, with Amundsen as the hub about which everything turned. The discipline was instinctive. Nobody even thought of behaving familiarly towards Amundsen. He himself said often, that on board we must all be captains and all be crew . . . In the daily life there were no distinctions of rank, and yet no one was ever in doubt about who was in command on board.[4]

Amundsen's second-in-command was a Danish naval officer, Lieutenant Godfred Hansen, a man with a great sense of humour and a fund of funny stories. He had no experience of ice navigation, but he soon became 'as good an ice-man as any of us'.[5]

Escaping a fire in the engine room near the petrol tanks and a grounding on some skerries near Matty Island, the *Gjøa* found a land-locked harbour on the south coast of King William Island, which was also suitable for the magnetic work. Had the navigation of the Passage been their only aim, they would have pressed on. Here the observatories were built. The Norwegians seem to have got on well with the 'Inhabitants at the Magnetic Pole', as Amundsen called the Netsilik Eskimos, who are pictured in photographs and to whom he devoted a chapter of his book. However, since they were such a small party, the 'Kabloonans' took the precaution of demonstrating their power by blowing up an empty igloo at the end of a long fuse. Amundsen compared the Eskimos who had been in contact with civilisation with those who had not. After meeting the people of ten different tribes during the lengthy voyage, he became convinced that the isolated ones were 'the happiest, healthiest, most honourable and most contented among them'. Unless they were protected in future by law from 'contaminating influences', they would be ruined.

Amundsen made a journey towards the Magnetic North Pole in 1904. The 1905 sledging and survey party of two led by Lieutenant Hansen, with Peder Ristvedt, returned on 24 June, after eighty-four days' absence, during which they had explored what Amundsen called the only remaining uncharted portion of the archipelago, the west coast of McClintock Channel (the east coast of Victoria Island beyond Rae and Collinson's furthest.) They crossed the heavy ice of Victoria Strait with difficulty and named the islands at its southern end in honour of the Royal Geographical Society, which had subscribed to the expedition. Amundsen's 'Queen Maud's Sea', to the south of these islands, is now called Queen Maud Gulf. During the depot-laying trip of the previous year to

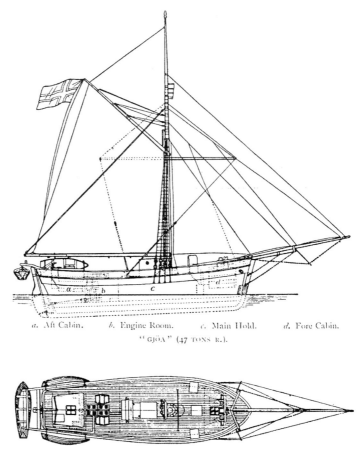

a. Aft Cabin.   *b.* Engine Room.   *c.* Main Hold.   *d.* Fore Cabin.

"GJÖA" (47 TONS R.).

DECK OF THE "GJÖA."

Amundsen's little *Gjøa*, the first vessel to navigate the North West passage from end to end, during his expedition from Norway, 1903-06. She is now preserved in Oslo. (from Amundsen's *Narrative*)

Cape Crozier (the western point of King William Island), the skulls and bones of two white men were found, scattered over the shore at Point Hall. Nearby was a stone on which Captain Hall had carved the words, 'Eternal Honour to the Discoverers of the North-West Passage'. The bones were collected and placed in a cairn, with Hall's inscription on the top. Hansen and Ristvedt's furthest north on Victoria Island in 1905 was named Cape Nansen, leaving some 100 miles still unsurveyed. They covered altogether 800 miles.[6] Musing on the journey, Hansen considered sledge travelling a free and manly life, despite its dangers and difficulties.

One makes acquaintance with hunger, cold, wet and fatigue. The fare is frugal. You have to say good-bye to cleanliness, when every drop of water has to be produced at the expense of the most precious of all your possessions, fuel. However, on you go and every mile covered seems another victory. And life: *La vie n'est pas un plaisir ni une douleur, mais une affaire grave, dont nous sommes chargée, et qu'il faut conduire et terminer à notre honneur.*[7]

Regrets mingled with joy in Amundsen's thoughts when the *Gjøa* departed from her anchorage at King William Island after so many months on 12 August 1905.

One of his regrets concerned the North Magnetic Pole, whose position had been determined in 1831 by James Clark Ross. Although Amundsen's observations proved that the Pole had moved northwards since then, subsequent calculations showed that he had failed to reach it during the sledge journey of April 1904. According to his biographer, this was 'a source of the deepest mortification' to Amundsen until the end of his days.[8] Before continuing with his narrative of the voyage, he paid a handsome tribute to Captain Collinson's navigation of HMS *Enterprise* in these waters, his survey being of great help to the Norwegians.

> Sir Richard Collinson appears to me to have been one of the most capable and enterprising sailors the world has ever produced. He guided his great, heavy vessel into waters that hardly afforded sufficient room for the tiny *Gjøa*. But, better still, he brought her safely home.

Collinson's reward for such heroism was but scant, considered Amundsen. In contrast to McClure who 'found a North West Passage which was not navigable, Collinson found one which was practicable although not suitable for ordinary navigation'. Amundsen praised Dr Rae's discovery of his strait and also remarked that he had not regretted taking McClintock's advice as to the achievement of the Passage by this route. As they passed Hall Point at sunset on their first day at sea again, the little *Gjøa* flew her colours in honour of her unfortunate predecessors of Franklin's last expedition. Bearing the responsibility of command on his shoulders, Amundsen found the navigation of the channels between the Arctic islands and the mainland so nerve-wracking that he could neither eat nor sleep. On 15 August 1905, he wrote, for example:

> From an even, sandy bottom, we came to a ragged stony one. We were in the midst of a most disconcerting chaos; sharp stones faced us on every side, low-lying rocks of all shapes, and we bungled through zig-zag, as if we were drunk. The lead flew up and down, down and up and the man at the helm had to pay very close attention and keep his eye on the look-out man who jumped about in the crow's next like a maniac, throwing his arms about for starboard and port respectively . . .

On 17 August 1905, they reached Cape Colborne, at the entrance to Cambridge Bay, where the *Enterprise* had wintered. Amundsen rejoiced on this 'significant day in the history of our expedition,' because the *Gjøa* had sailed through the 'hitherto unsolved link in the North West Passage'. He was relieved to know that ahead of them the waters had already been ploughed by a large vessel already. The chart even bore an occasional sounding. Collinson's descriptions proved helpful as the *Gjøa* passed through Dease Strait, Coronation Gulf and Dolphin and Union Strait in open water. On 26 August, they were abreast of Nelson

Head, the southern cape of Banks Island, in the sea area later named Amundsen Gulf on the Admiralty chart.

Next morning he was somewhat annoyed to be woken after his night on watch by Lieutenant Hansen rushing down into his cabin. However on his calling out, 'Vessel in sight, sir!' Tears came into Amundsen's eyes at these 'magical words', which heralded the *Charles Hanson*, a small two-masted schooner from San Francisco. 'The North West Passage had been accomplished – my dream from childhood', wrote Amundsen about that meeting. On going aboard, the four Norwegians found hardly enough room to cross the deck, while Eskimo women in red dresses mingled with negroes in variegated costumes, 'just as in a land of fable'. The negroes probably came from the Cape Verde Islands, off Africa, where whaling was indigenous.[9] Captain James McKenna, an old Arctic hand, welcomed Amundsen and his shipmates to a good dinner and produced some old newspapers, which to them were quite recent. Gifts of potatoes and onions were a special bounty.

Further west along the coast at Cape Sabine they landed and found great tree trunks and other driftwood, from which they picked out a piece to replace the *Gjøa*'s gaff. Flowers, tall grasses and shrubs and no doubt the smell of the earth made their walk inland like one through paradise, after so long in icy seas.

Further on they found that the shores of Franklin's 'Polar Sea' were no longer lonely: American whalers, rounding Point Barrow had invaded the western Arctic in the late nineteenth century, often using Herschel Island as a wintering place or harbour.[10] Russian America had become Alaska since its purchase by the United States in 1867. Gold had been found in the Yukon and elsewhere.

The *Gjøa* was stopped by ice near the mouth of the Mackenzie River. She wintered 1905-06 at King Point, where magnetic observations were continued, and where Wiik died, to be buried in the observatory he had built. Amundsen had meanwhile made an overland journey to Eagle City, Alaska, to send a telegram announcing his success and to collect the mail. He was away for five months.

After departing from King Point on 10 July 1906, the *Gjøa*'s engine proved of very great use through the ice-encumbered channels among the sandbanks off the coast between Herschel Island and Point Barrow. With a small crew, the work was often varied: Amundsen cites the cook, Lindstrom for instance, all in one evening taking the meteorological readings, making soundings, baking bread and attending to the engine. Fog, gales, heavy masses of drifting ice, shallow waters and the strong northeasterly current near Point Barrow made progress difficult along the coast to the west. In addition, the engine stopped suddenly and while the mainsail was being hoisted, the gaff broke again, though it was repaired. 'To manoeuvre a sailing ship in closely packed ice', Amundsen observed, 'requires many years' experience; anyone can make headway with a steamer'. After a struggle, the *Gjøa* rounded Point Barrow on 20 August. She passed through Bering Strait on 30 August, thus completing the first navigation of the North West Passage. After a great welcome in Nome, the *Gjøa* reached San Francisco on 19 October, where she remained until returned to Norway in 1972.

The *Arctic,* formerly *Gauss.* Commanded by Captain J-E Bernier, she made three voyages, during the early twentieth century to the Arctic Islands, mainly to confirm Canadian sovereignty. (Author's collection)

She can be seen, a tiny vessel, at the Sjøfartsmuseum in Oslo, not far from her far larger and even more celebrated neighbour, Nansen's *Fram.*

In February 1907, Amundsen lectured on the voyage to the Royal Geographical Society and the slides he must have used have since been published.[11] During the *Gjøa's* years in the Arctic, Norway had become independent of Sweden and Fridtjof Nansen, who had helped Amundsen a great deal, was Norwegian ambassador in London. Nansen spoke after the lecture and said:

> As Captain Amundsen has already pointed out himself, the fact that it has been possible for him to accomplish that great deed is due entirely to the work of British seamen . . . But a Norwegian has been the lucky man to finish this quest for the North-West Passage . . . I think we may say we belong to the same race, and . . . of these . . . gallant achievements we may say with Tennyson –
>
> > One equal temper of heroic hearts,
> > Made weak by time and fate, but strong in will,
> > To strive, to seek, to find, and not to yield.[12]

Joseph-Elzéar Bernier 1908 and 1910

Joseph-Elzéar Bernier was a very experienced sea captain, who was born on the south bank of the St Lawrence River, some 50 miles below Quebec City. He made a contribution towards the navigation of a more northerly North West Passage which is less hampered by shoals than the inner passage pioneered by McClintock, Collinson and Amundsen. In the D G S *Arctic* (formerly *Gauss*), which had been built on the lines of Nansen's *Fram* for the German Antarctic Expedition of 1901-03, he made three voyages to Melville Island, at the western end of what is now called Parry Channel. Their purpose was mainly to show the flag and to issue licences on behalf of the Canadian Government, to which Great Britain had ceded the Arctic archipelago in 1880. Numerous nineteenth-century cairns, memorials and depots were visited and restored. Documents were removed for the Public Archives of Canada and new ones deposited.

The *Arctic* only made a brief visit to Melville Island in August 1906, but during the outward voyage of 1908 she sailed some way into McClure Strait (Cape Providence) and wintered at Parry's Winter Harbour from August 1908 to mid-August 1909. In his autobiography, Bernier states that since no ice could be seen to the westward in late August 1908, had his instructions included making the North West Passage it could have been done. He considered the 'proper route' to accomplish this was down the west coast of Banks Island, ignoring Prince of Wales Strait. Only a month out from Quebec, Bernier thought the *Arctic* could have reached the Bering Sea or even Vancouver during the following month. Bernier also compared the ease with which his vessel had entered the harbour with the difficulty Parry had experienced 89 years before, when a two-mile channel had to be cut for the *Hecla* and *Griper* to reach safe winter quarters.[13] Two sledging journeys were made across McClure Strait to raise the flag on Victoria and on Banks Island. There was no trace of HMS *Investigator* at Mercy Bay. The caches and cairns, apart from several tons of coal and pieces of rope, sails and packaging, had gone. The three graves could not be found.[14]

Bernier's next Arctic commission of 1910-11 was to show the great difference that an open ice season (as in 1908-09) could make as far as the navigation of these icy seas was concerned. In 1910, he was given permission to attempt a North West Passage, after passing through Davis Strait, Baffin Bay, Lancaster Sound, Barrow Strait, Melville Sound and M'Clure Strait (ie Parry Channel.) On meeting an ice floe nearly 60 feet thick 'with hills on it as high as any berg' on 2 September 1910, when 30 miles south of Cape Providence, Melville Island, and 'at the furthest point in this direction of any vessel', the *Arctic* turned east, there being no prospect of making the North West Passage that year.

One of the monuments repaired by Captain Bernier during these Arctic patrols was that to Sir John Franklin and his crews on Beechey Island. Bernier was later rescued with his own crew from a sinking ship during an Atlantic convoy of the First World War 1914-18. Of these two matters, he wrote later,

While in England as a guest at a country house a lady rushed in, and much to my embarrassment threw her arms around my neck and kissed me. It turned out that she was a relative of Sir John Franklin and took this means of thanking me for putting the Franklin Monument in good repair. That adventure in the Atlantic and the reception by the impulsive lady ashore, I always regarded as my two most exciting adventures, one at sea and the other on land. I was then 64 years of age.[15]

St Roch 1940-42

The schooner *St Roch* (80 tons), now preserved near the Vancouver Maritime Museum, was constructed in 1928 at Burrards Shipyard, North Vancouver, for the Royal Canadian Mounted Police. She is 104 feet in length, with a beam of 25 feet, and built of thick timbers of Douglas fir, sheathed in iron bark and then fitted with a diesel engine of 150hp. Her crew of nine men were all RCMP constables and her duties were to patrol the Canadian Arctic, to convoy supplies to various police detachments along the coasts of the islands and mainland, to winter in remote areas, to maintain sensible game laws, and to transport Eskimo patients to hospital and children to school in Aklavik, south of the Mackenzie delta. One of her original crew was Henry Larsen, a Norwegian from the Oslofjord, who had taken Canadian nationality. He had already served in Norway as a young officer in sail and steam, and in addition had made his first visit to the Canadian North in the schooner *Maid of Orleans*, owned and skippered by Christian Klengenberg. During this voyage and the earlier ones in *St Roch*, Larsen got to know both Eskimos and whites and learnt how to travel by dog sledge and of course to navigate in ice. His autobiography makes most interesting reading.[16] It was, of course, a time of change even for the more isolated native people, and for all northerners, with radio and aircraft beginning to shorten both time and distance there.

Early in 1940, during the Second World War, Larsen was put in command of the *St Roch* to resupply the RCMP detachments in the western Arctic, keeping eighteen months' supplies for the ship then to proceed to Halifax, Nova Scotia – in other words to be the first vessel to attempt the North West Passage from the Pacific to the Atlantic. The Government had realised the importance, in wartime, of demonstrating Canadian sovereignty over the Arctic islands, in case of enemy intrusion into its vast territory of 500,000 square miles. The *St Roch* departed from Vancouver in June 1940, a year which proved a bad one for ice navigation and after rounding Point Barrow she proceeded as far as Cambridge Bay, Victoria Land. Unable to penetrate further east, she turned westwards and wintered in Walker Bay, Collinson's old winter quarters, from September 1940 until late July 1941. From there journeys were made to Banks Island, by dog sledge, to visit the Eskimos from the Mackenzie delta, who were trapping on the west coast, the island having been forbidden to white trappers. Larsen described his party's sledging methods, clothing and cooking in some detail. Often a sledge of 16 to 18 feet long carried 1,500 pounds, pulled by eleven dogs, which were fed

on dried fish and blubber or beef tallow, all cut up ready to swallow. Eskimo caribou skin clothing was worn, consisting of double outfits in really cold weather;
the inside garment had the fur next to the body and the outer one, the fur outside. Long butcher's knives were carried to make snow houses. Cooking was
done on a primus stove, while the food, made from ordinary supplies like beans
and bacon, was prepared beforehand, then frozen and broken up with an axe into
small chunks, placed in canvas bags.[17]

During the last sledge trip from Walker Bay, Larsen and 'Frenchy' Chartrand,
who sadly died of a heart attack later in the voyage, looked for possible anchor-
ages in Prince of Wales Strait. They found the Princess Royal Islands, McClure's
winter quarters in the *Investigator*, 1850-51, of great interest. 'How he had managed to hang on there in the strong current', wrote Larsen, 'without an engine,
was a mystery to me, but then McClure was one of the greatest Arctic navigators'.[18]

On leaving Walker Bay on 31 July 1941, the *St Roch* transported an injured
Eskimo boy to Tuktoyaktuk for medical attention and picked up supplies. The
vessel turned eastwards again on 8 August, reaching Cambridge Bay a week later.
She successfully navigated the shallow and shoaling waters of Simpson Strait and
after rounding the southeast point of King William Island proceeded northwards
through Rae Strait along the coast of Boothia. However, at Matty Island, where
Amundsen had nearly lost the *Gjøa*, they found solid ice stretching from shore
to shore. Northwesterly gales brought heavy floes crashing down from
M'Clintock Channel, while blinding snow made it impossible to see. The vessel
sheltered behind a small island not much bigger than herself. The anchors held
and she was saved from disaster. By 3 September, the *St Roch* had worked
through the heavy blue floes issuing from M'Clintock Channel and edged up to
Pasley Bay, where a sheltering inlet was shown on the Admiralty chart, first published in 1855. Here, on the west coast of Boothia, near the North Magnetic Pole,
after more hair-raising difficulties and dangers, the *St Roch* was 'jammed in close
to the beach' on 11 September 1941. All the ice in the bay then lay still, for nearly a whole year.[19]

During the winter, the RCMP constables made a number of patrols, mainly to
take a census of the scattered population. On the east coast of the Boothia
Peninsula, where the Rosses wintered from 1829 to 1832, Larsen found that the
older Eskimos had heard of this from their grandparents. The iron from the
Victory's engine and other equipment, put ashore by Sir John Ross, had proved
a gold mine to these people. From the light boiler plates they had made knives,
seal spears and blubber lamps. They believed the *Victory* herself must have sunk.
On Larsen's enquiring whether there were any guns from the ship, he was taken
to Victoria Harbour, where on the shore were lengths of cable, pieces of iron,
nuts and bolts, two ice anchors and other items. He was amazed to be shown a
'big beautiful bronze cannon of a wonderful blue-green colour after 110 years up
there'. It had not even been scratched. Weighing about 1000lbs, the cannon
could have been pulled on a sledge, but with the census work only half done, this

Boat left by Captain Kellett of HMS *Resolute* on Dealy Island in 1854, found by Captain Bernier in 1908, together with two of McClintock's sledges, graves and other relics and records, during the voyage of *Arctic*, 1908–09. (Bernier's *Report*)

was not feasible. Eventually, the cannon was transported 'Outside' to be displayed with other old guns at the headquarters of the Royal Canadian Mounted Police in Regina.

On 4 August 1942, the voyage continued, but the *St Roch* was nipped by the heavy ice from M'Clintock Channel and Franklin Strait, when only 15 miles beyond Pasley Bay. She drifted helplessly back and forth near where the *Erebus* and *Terror* had been beset in 1846, nearly a century earlier. The situation was so dangerous, that Larsen took emergency measures in case the *St Roch* had to be abandoned. However, in contrast to Franklin, they had the little diesel engine, which could be started at a moment's notice, ready to take advantage of any openings that appeared. Such a lead enabled them to work up to the Tasmania Islands, until they were abeam of Bellot Strait, which was entered on 29 August. It looked like a huge canyon, with its inaccessible cliffs rising steeply on either side. There was a tremendous current creating whirlpools, in which the ice floes spun round and round near the middle of the strait where the tides met. Heavy ice was stranded there against which the *St Roch* could easily have been crushed. Fortunately, she won through, helped perhaps by the prayers of Canon John Turner, those of Father Henri of Pelly Bay and by the hymn singing of the two passengers. These were a young Eskimo couple who stood on the fo'c'sle head, when the ice pressure was at its worst and it looked as if the *St Roch* might be crushed like a box of matches. Eventually, the vessel was released and arrived towards midnight at the eastern end of Bellot Strait, where a warm welcome and hot meal awaited them at the trading post of Fort Ross.

When the *St Roch* later entered Pond Inlet, on the east coast of Baffin Island, the whole population came aboard. Here spare Arctic gear was left ashore, as well as the dogs, of whom, wrote Larsen, 'one becomes as attached . . . as to one's fellow human beings'. The dogs set up a tremendous howl when they saw their ship leave without them. The *St Roch* eventually arrived in Halifax on 11 October 1942, the first vessel to complete the North West Passage from the Pacific to the Atlantic Ocean. Each member of the crew, including their former shipmate Albert Chartrand, was later awarded the Polar Medal by King George VI. A book giving an account of this voyage was published in Toronto at the end of the War.[20] In all the vicissitudes of the voyage, Sergeant Larsen had proved a worthy successor to his countryman, Roald Amundsen.

St Roch, East to West in one Season 1944

In the summer of 1943, the *St Roch* went on patrol to the eastern Arctic and returned to Halifax in the autumn. The bold decision was then made that she should attempt the northern deep water passage through Parry Channel to Melville Island and across M'Clure Strait to Banks Island. Staff Sergeant Henry Larsen was again in command. A new engine, twice as powerful as the old, had been installed, while a mizzen mast, on which a small riding or storm sail could be carried, had been added. Larsen had some difficulty finding a crew. This eventually included three regular police constables and Ole Andreassen, aged sixty-five, a Norwegian who like Larsen originally came from the Oslofjord and who had travelled with the well-known explorer, Vilhjalmur Stefansson, across part of the Beaufort Sea, during the Canadian Arctic Expedition of 1913-18. There was also great difficulty, in wartime, getting anything at all done in the way of preparations for the voyage.

The *St Roch* departed from Halifax on 22 July 1944. There was trouble with the new engine, but she arrived safely at Pond Inlet on 12 August to unload cargo and to take on other equipment, as well as an Eskimo hunter and his family (nine in all), who had seventeen dogs. At snow-covered Beechey Island, Larsen went straight away to see the Franklin memorial. At Northumberland House, he found only thousands of barrel staves, lumps of coal and a stone wall remaining and the keel, stem and planking of Sir John Ross' yacht *Mary*. After proceeding further west, they sighted Captain Kellett's cairn of 1853 from a distance with its barrels mounted on a spar at the summit of Dealy Island. The house walls, so carefully built of stone, still stood, but polar bears had picnicked on the contents of the depot for many years. However, a few square rock-hard biscuits, stamped with Queen Victoria's broad arrow, were extricated from the rusting iron tanks.

> Canned meats and vegetables, stacked up and covered with sod, formed part of one wall, and the centre of the building was a hodge-podge of broken barrels of flour, clothing, coal, rope, salt beef and broken hardwood pulleys for ships' blocks.[21]

Much was frozen in ice, 'but leather sea boots, broken barrels of chocolate, peas and beans and other items were spread around outside'. Larsen relates how they picked out a few good tins of Ox Cheek Soup made in 1850, by a manufacturer opposite East India House, London. Directions for opening read: 'Take a hammer and chisel and cut out one end while being careful not to let flakes of the paint which covers the cans get into the soup'. These and some tins of preserved

The *St. Roch* watering ship in the Canadian Arctic. Commanded by Sergeant Henry Larsen, R.C.M.P. and crewed by constables of the Royal Canadian Mounted Police, she made the first transit of the passage from the Pacific to the Atlantic Ocean in 1940-42 and the first transit in one season in 1944. She is preserved near Vancouver Maritime Museum. (Author's Collection)

carrots, as well as others marked 'Normandie Pippins' (small dried apples) were eventually handed over at RCMP headquarters for analysis. Larsen doubted whether modern tinned food would have lasted so long under similar conditions.

A number of cans from Dealy Island and some from Beechey Island were analysed and tested in 1945 by the Division of Chemistry of the Canadian Department of Agriculture. The contents of three out of four cans of Ox Cheek Soup (stew) were in excellent condition and were fed to rats for fourteen days, giving the same gains approximately as milk. No vitamin B1 was found, but it is interesting that there was a vitamin B2 content of three micrograms per gram. The mutton was also well preserved and fed to rats for fourteen days, giving normal gains in weight. The single can of carrots was badly corroded and the contents inedible. The two cans of sliced carrots were in poor condition and no analyses were made.[22] A full can of roast beef from Dealy Island is among the collections of the Royal Geographical Society. It weighs over four pounds.

On 28 August, in the continuing thick snowy weather, the *St Roch* made for Winter Harbour, Melville Island. Besides the inscription on Parry's rock commemorating the *Hecla* and *Griper*, Larsen found a large copper plate inscribed with the Union Flag and the Canadian coat of arms deposited by Captain Bernier, that 'doughty and great Canadian skipper', thirty-five years before. It recorded the Dominion's claim to the vast Arctic archipelago as far as the North Pole.

Soon the *St Roch* was sailing in waters never before traversed by any vessel – the eastern entrance to M'Clure Strait. Here, as might be expected, she met the heaviest ice of the voyage – 'gigantic floes of old blue ice from the Polar Sea itself', in Larsen's words.[23] Little by little, the *St Roch* edged southwards, sometimes secured to the gyrating ice floes and sometimes making headway between them. Fog, mist and heavy rain hampered progress, but on 31 August at noon, the weather brightened briefly and Larsen glimpsed the northern entrance to Prince of Wales Strait. This was where McClure in HMS *Investigator* and Collinson in HMS *Enterprise* had been prevented from proceeding further north into Melville Sound. The strait divides Banks Island from Victoria Island, with Russell Point on Banks Island and Peel Point on Victoria Island guarding its entrance.

The super tanker, *Manhattan* (150,000 tons displacement) was the first merchant ship to navigate the North West Passage in 1969. Modified at very considerable expense, she tested the economic feasibility of tanker traffic through ice-infested waters. (Photo C W M Swithinbank)

Larsen mistook Russell Point for Peel Point and the *St Roch* worked her way for 15 miles into Richard Collinson Inlet, where she might have been embayed like the *Investigator*, never to escape. However, once the error was detected, the vessel went about and before long was navigating Prince of Wales Strait, in sunshine and clear skies, and in almost open water. Soon she steamed at seven knots past the Princess Royal Islands, where McClure had wintered so long ago. A blinding snowstorm rising to a full gale made them thankful later to find refuge in the harbour at Tuktoyaktuk. Better weather enabled the *St Roch* to reach Herschel Island, where the Eskimo family was left with plentiful supplies. Despite difficult ice conditions, she rounded Point Barrow and passed on 27 September through Bering Strait. On 16 October 1944, the vessel docked in Vancouver at the end of a voyage of 7,295 nautical miles from Halifax in eighty-six days. This was the first transit of the North West Passage in one season.

*   *   *

Besides paying tribute to his crew at the end of the voyage, Larsen reflected on their predecessors in Arctic seas and with concern on the future of the Inuit. He remembered the long patrols of the Royal Canadian Mounted Police, making sledge journeys often surpassing those of explorers. In the future, icebreakers should be able to navigate the North West Passage, he thought, probably by the route taken by the *St Roch*. But the Arctic Sea would always be the Arctic – 'the main thing is', wrote Larsen in 1948, 'to watch the ice movements and be in the right spot at the right time'. He ended his account of the voyages of the *St Roch* through the elusive North West Passage with these lines:

> But getting back to the early explorers, when I reached places which had known the footsteps of such men as Sir Edward Parry, Sir John Ross, Captain Henry Kellett, Captain Francis L McClintock, Captain Robert McClure, Sir John Franklin and many others, I felt that I was on hallowed ground. I pictured them and their crews wintering in isolation and discomfort in crowded ships, optimistically waiting for spring and better ice conditions. Some of them perished, all risked death, to carry the proud flag of Britain into new territory. Sometimes during our passage I fancied I could see the tall majestic ships that had preceded us in most of these waters over a hundred years ago.[24]

END

NOTES

Chapter 1

1. James A Williamson, *The Cabot voyages and Bristol discovery under Henry VII* (Cambridge, 1962) and D B Quinn, ed, The Hakluyt handbook, 2 vols (London, 1974).
2. George Best, A true discourse of the late voyages of discoverie . . . (London, 1578). In Vilhjalmur Stefansson and Eloise McCaskill, eds, *The three voyages of Martin Frobisher*, Vol 1 (London, 1938) p46.
3. Christopher Hall, *The first voyage of M Martine Frobisher, to the Northwest* . . . In Stefansson and McCaskill, *The Three Voyages* . . . , Vol 1, p153.
4. C Hall, *The First Voyage* . . . , p153.
5. Michael Lok, 'Doynges of Captayne Furbusher', British Library, Lansdowne ms. 100/1, quoted in D D Hogarth *et al, Mines, minerals, metallurgy (Martin Frobisher's Northwest venture)*, Hull, Quebec, Canadian Museum of Civilisation, 1994, p30.
6. George Best, in Stefansson and McCaskill, *The Three Voyages* . . . , Vol 1, p68.
7. Dionyse Settle, *A true reporte of the late voyage into the West and Northwest Regions* . . . (London, 1577), in Stefansson and McCaskill, *The Three Voyages* . . . , Vol 2, p17.
8. George Best, *A true discourse* . . . , in Stefansson and McCaskill, *The three voyages* . . . , Vol 1, p123-9.
9. Dionyse Settle, *A true reporte* . . . , in Stefansson and McCaskill, *The Three Voyages* . . . , Vol 2, p19-22.
10. Paul Hulton and David B Quinn, *The American drawings of John White*, 2 vols (London, 1964).
11. N Cheshire *et al,* 'Frobisher's Eskimos in England', *Archivaria*, No 10, Summer 1980, p23-50; William C Sturtevant and David B Quinn, *This New Prey* . . . , in Christian F Feest, ed, *Indians and Europe* (Aachen, 1987) p61-140.
12. Thomas Ellis, *A True Report of the Third and Last Voyage into Meta Incognita* . . . (London, 1578), in Stefansson and McCaskill, *The Three Voyages* . . . , Vol 2, p38.
13. Charles Francis Hall, *Arctic Researches and Life Among the Esquimaux* (New York, 1865).
14. For an account of the three voyages and of the mining done see D D Hogarth *et al, Mines, minerals, metallurgy*. . . Likewise William W Fitzhugh and Jacqueline S Olin, *The Archeology of the Frobisher Voyages.* (Washington, D.C., 1993); T H B Symons and S Alsford, eds, *Meta Incognita, a Discourse for Discovery: Martin Frobisher's Arctic Voyages, 1576 to 1578*, Hull, Quebec, Canadian Museum of Civilisation, 1999, 2 vols. The maps are reproduced in Stefansson and McCaskill, *The Three Voyages* . . . , Vol 1, facing p13, and on p2 and p107.
15. Albert Hastings Markham, *The Voyages and Works of John Davis the Navigator* (London, 1880) pi.
16. Quoted in Clements R Markham, *A Life of John Davis, the Navigator* . . . (London, 1889), p14.
17. A H Markham, ed *The Voyages and Works of John Davis* . . . , p7.
18. A H Markham, *The Voyages and Works of John Davis* . . . , p8.
19. A H Markham, *The Voyages and Works of John Davis* . . . , p9.
20. A H Markham, *The Voyages and Works of John Davis* . . . , p9.
21. A H Markham, *The Voyages and Works of John Davis* . . . , p10.
22. A H Markham, *The Voyages and Works of John Davis* . . . , p12.
23. David B Quinn, *The Northwest Passage in Theory and Practice*. In John Logan Allen, ed, *North American Exploration Vol. 1, A New World Disclosed,* University of Nebraska Press, 1997, p321-3.
24. Stefansson and McCaskill, *The Three Voyages* . . . , Vol 1, p154.
25. Stefansson and McCaskill, *The Three Voyages* . . . , Vol 2, p39.
26. Selma Huxley Barkham, *Itasoa 3. Los Vascos en El Marco Atlantico Norte. Siglos xvi & xvii* (San Sebastian, 1987).
27. A H Markham, *The Voyages and Works of John Davis* . . . , p49-58.
28. Helen Wallis, 'England's Search for the Northern Passages', *Arctic* [Calgary], Vol 37, No 4, 1984, p466-7.
29. Quinn, *The Northwest Passage* . . . , p324.

Chapter 2

1. D B Quinn, *The Northwest Passage* . . . , p332.
2. C R Markham, ed, *The Voyages of William Baffin, 1612-1627* (London, 1881).
3. C R Markham, *The Voyages of William Baffin*, pxxxii.
4. C R Markham, *The Voyages of William Baffin*, pxxxii.
5. L E Pennington, ed, *The Purchas Handbook*. Vol 1 (London, 1997), p46.
6. One map was published in Sir John Barrow's Arctic voyages of 1818 and the other in the 1818 edition of Daines Barrington's *The possibility of approaching the North Pole,* where, however, there are references to Baffin's Bay as far as 72° in the appendix.
7. Quoted by C R Markham, *The Voyages of William Baffin*, plvii.
8. Quinn, *The Northwest Passage* . . . , p134.
9. C C A Gosch, *Danish Arctic Expeditions, 1605 to 1620. Book 2. The Expedition of Captain Jens Munk* . . . (London, 1897).
10. Quinn, *The Northwest Passage* . . . , p343.

Chapter 3

1. E E Rich, *Hudson's Bay Company, 1670-1870,* 2 vols, (London, 1958-9).
2. *A Brief History of the Hudson's Bay Company,* published by the Company c1980, p4.
3. Rich, *Hudson's Bay Company* . . . , Vol 1, p56.
4. Quoted by John Geiger and Owen Beattie in *Dead Silence: the Greatest Mystery in Arctic discovery* (London, 1993), p169.
5. Samuel Hearne, *Journey from Prince of Wales fort . . . to the Northern Ocean* . . . (London, 1795), pxxiv.
6. Hearne, *Journey* . . . pxxxi-xxxii.
7. Geiger and Beattie, *Dead Silence* . . . , pxii.
8. William Barr and Glyndwr Williams, eds, *Voyages to Hudson Bay in Search of a Northwest Passage, 1741-1747,* Vol 1 (London, 1994), p3.
9. Barr and Williams, *Voyages to Hudson Bay* . . . , Vol 1, p9.
10. Barr and Williams, *Voyages to Hudson Bay* . . . , Vol. 1, p104.
11. Middleton's Journal in Barr and Williams, *Voyages to Hudson Bay* . . . , Vol 1, p208.
12. Barr and Williams, *Voyages to Hudson Bay* . . . , Vol 2, (London, 1995), p209.

13. Barr and Williams, *Voyages to Hudson Bay . . .* , Vol 2, pxii.
14. Hearne, *Journey from Prince of Wales fort . . .* , p350-1.
15 Quoted in J C Beaglehole, *The Journals of Captain James Cook,* Vol 3, (London, 1967), pxxx. A half-hearted attempt to find the Passage via the Pacific had been made by Commodore John Byron in H M Ships *Dolphin* and *Tamar,* 1764-6. See Robert E Gallagher, ed, *Byron's Journal of his Circumnavigation, 1764-1766,* (London, 1964).
16. Glyndwr Williams, *Myth and Reality: James Cook and the Theoretical Geography of Northwest America,* in Robin Fisher and Hugh Johnston, eds, *Captain James Cook and his Times* (Vancouver, 1979), p79.
17. W Kaye Lamb, ed, *The Journals and Letters of Sir Alexander Mackenzie* (London, 1970), p16.
18. Letter from Sir Alexander Mackenzie to John Franklin, 21 May 1819, published in *Sir John Franklin's Journals and Correspondence . . . 1819-1822,* edited with an introduction by Richard C Davis (Toronto, 1995), p289-91.
19. W Kaye Lamb, ed Alexander Mackenzie, *Journals . . .* , p19.
20. George Vancouver, *A Voyage of Discovery to the North Pacific Ocean . . .* , edited by W Kaye Lamb, 4 vols (London, 1984).
21. Glyndwr Williams, *The British Search for the Northwest Passage in the Eighteenth Century* (London, 1962), p271.

Chapter 4
1. Christopher Lloyd, *Mr Barrow of the Admiralty* (London, 1970). For his role as the driving force behind African and Arctic exploration, see Fergus Fleming, *Barrow's Boys* (London, 1998).
2. Sir John Barrow, *An Auto-biographical Memoir . . . from Early Life to Advanced Age* (London,1847), p333.
3. Tom and Cordelia Stamp, *William Scoresby, Arctic Scientist* (Whitby, 1976), p65, p66.
4. Sir John Barrow, *A Chronological History of Voyages into the Arctic Regions* (London, 1818), p378-9.
5. F W Beechey, *A Voyage of Discovery Towards the North Pole* (London, 1843), p10.
6. Albert Hastings Markham, *Life of Sir John Franklin and the North-west Passage* (London, c1890).
7. *Quarterly Review,* October 1817.
8. John Ross, *A Voyage of Discovery . . . for the Purpose of Exploring Baffin's Bay . . .* (London,1818), p2.
Un-numbered quotations which follow are from this book
9. On the whalers of Davis Strait and beyond, see Gordon Jackson, *The British Whaling Trade* (London, 1978) and A G E Jones, *The Greenland and Davis Strait Trade, 1740-1865* (Bluntisham Books for the author, 1996).
10. Richard Vaughan, *Northwest Greenland: a history* (Orono, 1991), p98.
11. J C H King, 'A Preliminary Description of a Polar Eskimo Sledge Collected by Sir John Ross', *Inter-Nord,* No 16, 1982, p278-81.
12. RGS Archives, Library mss, William Harvey Hooper, Journal, 31 August 1818.
13. M J Ross, *Polar Pioneers: John Ross and James Clark Ross* (Montreal and Kingston, 1994), p49.
14. RGS Archives, Library mss, William Harvey Hooper, Journal, 1 September and 8 November 1818.

Chapter 5
1. Richard J Cyriax, *Sir John Franklin's Last Expedition* (London, 1939), p3-4. Reprinted 1997 by the Arctic Press.
2. RGS Archives, Library mss, William Harvey Hooper, Journal, 4 September 1819.
3. W E Parry, *Journal of a Voyage for the Discovery of a North-west Passage . . .* (London, 1821), p129.
4. *Sir John Franklin's Journals and Correspondence: the First Arctic Land Expedition 1819-1822,* edited with an introduction by Richard C Davis (Toronto, 1995), p279-89.
5. Instructions from Lord Bathurst, dated 29 April 1819, are given in *Sir John Franklin's Journals and Correspondence . . .* , p285-8.
6. All the un-numbered quotations in this chapter are from John Franklin's *Narrative of a Journey to the Shores of the Polar Sea in the Years 1819-20-21-22.* (London, 1823, reprinted 1970 by Hurtig).
7. Ann Savours, *The Voyages of the 'Discovery'* (London, 1992, 1994), p105-59.
8. For life at York Factory, see Michael Payne, *The Most Respectable Place in the Territory: everyday Life in Hudson's Bay Company Service, York Factory, 1788 to 1870* (Ottawa, 1989).
9. A H Markham, *Life of Sir John Franklin . . .* , p109.
10. A H Markham, *Life of Sir John Franklin . . .* , p116-17.
11. John Richardson, *Arctic Ordeal: the Journal of John Richardson . . . 1820-1822,* edited by C Stuart Houston (Montreal, 1984), p15.
12. Robert Hood, *To the Arctic by Canoe . . . the Journal and Paintings of Robert Hood,* edited by C Stuart Houston (Montreal, 1974), pxxxi-xxxii.
13. Robert Hood, *To the Arctic by Canoe . . .* and George Back, *Arctic Artist: the Journals and Paintings of George Back . . . 1819-1822,* edited by C Stuart Houston, commentary by I S MacLaren (Montreal, 1994).
14. Back, *Arctic Artist . . .* , p176-7.
15. Richardson, *Arctic Ordeal . . .* , p133.
16. Barbara Tomlinson, 'The Boots that Franklin Ate', *The Maritime Yearbook* (Greenwich) No 4, 1996/7, p29-31.
17. John Richardson, in Franklin's *Narrative,* 1824, p348. See also Richardson, *Arctic Ordeal . . .* , p148-61 for his Report.
18. Leslie H Neatby, *In Quest of the North West Passage* (London, 1958), p79.
19. *Sir John Franklin's Journals and Correspondence . . .* 1995, plxxxi.

Chapter 6
1. RGS Archives, classmark MUS/146, letter from Eleanor Anne Franklin to Betsey Franklin, Devonshire Street, London, 11 May 1824.
2. RGS Archives, classmark MUS/146, letter from Eleanor Anne Franklin to Betsey Franklin, 11 May 1824.
3. None of the engravings in Franklin's *Narrative* illustrates the 'walnut shell', but there is a watercolour in the NMM Greenwich. See Lindsey Macfarlane, 'Franklin's 'Walnut-Shell' ', *Polar Record,* Vol 24, 1988, p249-50.
4. John Franklin, *Narrative of a Second Expedition to the Shores of the Polar Sea* (London, 1828, reprinted by Hurtig, 1971), pxvi-xvii. Un-numbered quotations in this chapter are from this volume.
5. See *The Journals and Letters of Sir Alexander Mackenzie,* edited by W Kaye Lamb, Hakluyt Society, 1970, p201-3, which pages give the text of Mackenzie's journal for 14 July 1789.
6. National Maritime Museum, ms FRN/1, letter from John Franklin to his niece Miss Kay, Fort Franklin, Great Bear Lake, 8 November 1825.
7. RGS Archives, classmark MUS/146, letter from John Franklin to the Reverend T B Wright and his wife Henrietta, Fort Franklin, Great Bear Lake, 6 February 1826.
8. Robert E Johnson, *Sir John Richardson* (London, 1976),

p59-60; Franklin, 1828, p303-13.

9. Letter from John Franklin to Captain Wm Pryce Cumby, London, 23 November 1827, transcribed by Sonia S Bershad, *A Calendar of Letters and Documents in . . . the Arctic Institute of North America,* University of Calgary, 1980, p47.

10. Barbara Tomlinson, 'One Little Indian', *Signals: the Museum Newsletter,* 22 February 1995; National Maritime Museum, ms FRN/1, letter from John Franklin to Mary Anne Kay, Fort Franklin, 8 November 1825.

Chapter 7

1. William Edward Parry, introduction to his first Voyage, pii-iv. Un-numbered quotations in this section come from W E Parry, *Journal of a Second Voyage for the Discovery of a North-West Passage . . . 1821-22-23 . . .* (London, 1824).

2. Letter to his family from W E Parry, probably December 1820, cited in Ann Parry, *Parry of the Arctic* (London, 1963), p72.

3. G F Lyon, *Private Journal,* (London, 1824), p99.

4. W E Parry's ms journal, cited in A Parry, *Parry of the Arctic* (London, 1963), p77.

5. G F Lyon, *Private Journal,* p119-20.

6. RGS Archives, Library mss, William Harvey Hooper, journal 1821-3, Spring 1822.

7. Lyon, *Private Journal,* p145.

8. Lyon, *Private Journal,* p176-7.

9. Sir John Barrow, *Voyages of Discovery and Research Within the Arctic Regions from the Year 1818 to the Present Time* (London, 1846), p179.

10. See Michael T Bravo, 'The Accuracy of Ethno-science: a Study of Inuit Cartography and Cross-cultural Commensurability', *Manchester Papers in Social Anthropology,* No 2, 1996, which relates directly to Parry's second voyage. See also, G Malcolm Lewis, 'Maps, Mapmaking, and Map Use by Native North Americans', in David Woodward and G Malcolm Lewis, *The History of Cartography,* Vol 2, Book 3 (Chicago, 1998), p154-70., and on a related theme, John MacDonald, *The Arctic Sky: Inuit Astronomy, Star Lore and Legend* (Toronto, 1998).

11. Dr C W M Swithinbank, Personal communication, 1 August 1996.

12. W E Parry, letter to his brother Charles, cited in A Parry, *Parry of the Arctic,* p83.

13. Un-numbered quotations in this section are from W E Parry, *Journal of a Third Voyage for the Discovery of a North-West Passage* (London, 1826).

14. RGS Archives, Library mss, William Harvey Hooper, journal kept on Parry's third voyage.

15. RGS Archives, Library mss, Berkley Westropp, journal kept on Parry's third voyage.

16. Frederick William Beechey, *Narrative of a Voyage to the Pacific and Beering's Strait . . .* (new edition, 2 vols, London, 1831), Vol 1, pxv. Un-numbered quotations are from this work.

17. E H H Archibald, *Dictionary of Sea Painters,* (second edition, Woodbridge, Suffolk, 1989), p72.

18. George Peard, *To the Pacific and Arctic with Beechey: the Journal of Lieutenant George Peard of* HMS *Blossom 1825-1828,* edited by Barry M Gough (Cambridge, 1973), p20-2.

19. G F Lyon, *A Brief Narrative of an Unsuccessful Attempt to Reach Repulse Bay . . .* (London, 1825).

20. RGS Archives, 'The Voyage of the Griper', anonymous typed compilation based on Edward Nicholas Kendall's letter to his mother.

21. Ann Parry, *Parry of the Arctic,* p95.

22. Clements R Markham, *Arctic Navy List* (London, 1875, reprinted 1992), p30.

23. *A Peep at the Esquimaux, or, Scenes on the Ice, by a Lady* (London, 1825, reprinted Montreal, 1973).

Chapter 8

1. Scott Polar Research Institute, ms 248/35/7, Diary 4 February 1819, quoted in M J Ross, *Polar Pioneers,* p70.

2. Ross, *Polar Pioneers,* p119.

3. SPRI, ms 438/26/184, letter to his brother Charles, quoted by Ross in *Polar Pioneers,* p124.

4. Sir John Ross, *Narrative of a Second Voyage in Search of a North-West Passage . . .* (London, 1835) p10. Un-numbered quotations are from this book.

5. A W H Pearsall, 'Ships in the Arctic, 1600-1850', in Sylvie Devers, ed, *Pole Nord 1983/North Pole 1983 . . .* (Paris, 1987) p169-77.

6. Ross, *Polar Pioneers,* p131.

7. Quoted in Ross, *Polar Pioneers,* p131.

8. Ross, *Polar Pioneers,* p132.

9. George Back, *Narrative of the Arctic Land Expedition to the Mouth of the Great Fish River . . .* (London, 1836, reprinted Edmonton, 1970), p307.

10. Richard King, *Narrative of a Journey to the Shores of the Arctic Ocean* (London, 1836), Vol 1, p173.

11. Quoted in Ross, *Polar Pioneers,* p134-5.

12. Back, *Narrative of the Arctic Land Expedition . . . ,* p390, quoted in Ross, *Polar Pioneers,* p192.

13. King, *Narrative,* 1836, Vol 1, p296-7.

14. King, *Narrative,* Vol 1, p298.

15. Alan Cooke and Clive Holland, *The Exploration of Northern Canada . . .* (Toronto, 1978), p160.

16. John Murray Archives, quoted in Ross, *Polar Pioneers,* p193.

17. RGS Archives, R J Le M McClure, Private journal, HMS *Terror,* June 1836 to September 1837.

18. George Back, *Narrative of an Expedition in* HMS Terror *. . . 1836-7* (London, 1838), p408.

19. Cited by A W H Pearsall, 'Bomb Vessels', *Polar Record,* Vol 16, 1973, p787. For a wider, more detailed study, see Chris Ware, *The Bomb Vessel . . .* (London, 1994).

20. A W H Pearsall, 'Bomb vessels', p788.

Chapter 9

1. E E Rich, *Hudson's Bay Company, 1670-1870,* Vol 3 (New York, 1961), p489.

2. Rich, *Hudson's Bay Company,* Vol 3, p461.

3. Alexander Simpson, *The Life and Travels of Thomas Simpson, the Arctic Discoverer* (London, 1845), p51.

4. Alexander Simpson, *The Life and Travels . . . ,* p178.

5. Rich, *Hudson's Bay Company,* Vol 3, p648-9.

6. Alexander Simpson. 'Memoir of Thomas Simpson, A.M.' in Thomas Simpson's *Narrative,* pxviii and *The life and travels of Thomas Simpson,* p372-373.

7. Alexander Simpson, *The Life and Travels . . . ,* p18.

8. Thomas Simpson, *Narrative of the Discoveries on the North Coast of America, Effected by the Officers of the Hudson's Bay Company . . . 1836-39* (London, 1843), p3. Un-numbered quotations are from this book.

9. Alexander Simpson, *The Life and Travels . . . ,* p275-6.

10. Alexander Simpson, *The Life and Travels . . . ,* p257.

11. Alexander Simpson, *The Life and Travels . . . ,* p308.

12. Alexander Simpson, *The Life and Travels . . . ,* p340-1.

13. Alexander Simpson, *The Life and Travels . . . ,* p388-96.

14. L H Neatby, *Thomas Simpson,* in Richard C Davis, ed, *Lobsticks and Stone Cairns, Human Landmarks in the Arctic* (Calgary, 1996), p83.

Chapter 10

1. H D Traill, *The Life of Sir John Franklin,* RN, (London, 1896), p142-3.

2. Ann Savours and Anita McConnell, 'The history of the Rossbank Observatory, Tasmania', *Annals of Science,* Vol 39, 1982, p527-64 and Savours and McConnell, 'Return to Rossbank . . .', in Joan Kenworthy and Malcolm Walker, eds, *Colonial Observatories and Observations . . .* (Durham, 1997) p49-58.

3. See Kathleen FitzPatrick, *Sir John Franklin in Tasmania* (Melbourne, 1949).

4. John Barrow, *A Chronological History of Voyages into the Arctic Regions . . .* (London, 1818); *Voyages of Discovery and Research Within the Arctic Regions from . . . 1818 to the Present Time* (London, 1846).

5. Richard J Cyriax and J M Wordie, *Geographical Journal,* Vol 106, 1945, p173-4.

6. Cited in Cyriax, *Sir John Franklin's Last Expedition* (London, 1939, reprinted Plaistow, 1997).

7. *Quarterly Review,* Vol 18, 1817, p219-20.

8. Cited in Cyriax, *Sir John Franklin's Last Expedition,* p20.

9. Sir John Barrow, letter to Lord Haddington, 27 December 1844, quoted in Cyriax, *Sir John Franklin's Last Expedition,* p20-1.

10. Sir Clements Markham, *Antarctic Obsession . . .* (Harleston, Norfolk, 1986), p2.

11. Cited in Cyriax, *Sir John Franklin's Last Expedition,* p24-5.

12. Franklin, *Narrative of a Second Expedition . . . ,* p316-19.

13. Cited in Ross, *Polar Pioneers,* p275.

14. Undated letter from Lady Franklin to Sir James Clark Ross, cited in Ross, *Polar Pioneers,* p274-5.

15. Fitzjames' letters are in private hands, but some were published in the *Nautical Magazine* during the Franklin Search.

16. Cited in Ross, *Polar Pioneers,* p277.

17. Cyriax, *Sir John Franklin's Last Expedition,* p208-15.

18. Cyriax, *Sir John Franklin's Last Expedition,* p208-15.

19. Cited in M J T Lewis, *'Erebus'* and *'Terror', Journal of the Railway and Canal Historical Society,* Vol 17, No 4, 1971, p65.

20. Lewis, *'Erebus'* and *'Terror',* p66-7.

21. Lewis, *'Erebus'* and *'Terror',* p67.

22. Cyriax, *Sir John Franklin's Last Expedition,* p41.

23. Cyriax, *Sir John Franklin's Last Expedition,* p42.

24. See Douglas Wamsley and William Barr, 'Early photographers of the Arctic', *Polar Record,* Vol 32, No 183, 1996, p295-316.

25. *Journal of the Royal Geographical Society of London,* Vol 15, 1845, pxlvi, quoted in Cyriax, *Sir John Franklin's Last Expedition,* p56.

26. *Polar Record,* Vol 5, Nos 37/38, 1949, p349-50. Original then owned by P V W Gell, Franklin's descendant.

27. Quoted in Ross, *Polar Pioneers,* p284.

Chapter 11

1. Frances J Woodward, *Portrait of Jane* (London, 1951) p256.

2. Sir John Richardson, Arctic Searching Expedition . . . (New York, 1854), p32-3. Un-numbered quotations following, which relate to this expedition, are from this book.

3. Quoted in Robert E Johnson, Sir John Richardson (London, 1976), p78.

4. A G E Jones, 'Sir James Clark Ross and the Voyage of the Enterprise and Investigator, 1848-49', Geographical Journal, Vol 137, Part 2, June 1971, p165-79; Richard J Cyriax, 'Sir James Clark Ross and the Franklin Expedition', Polar Record, Vol 3, No 24, 1942, p528-40.

5. Ross, Polar Pioneers, p300. On King, see also Hugh N Wallace, The Navy, the Company and Richard King . . . (Montreal, 1980), p71-87.

6. Quoted by Ross, Polar Pioneers, p302.

7. See Trevor H Levere, *Science and the Canadian Arctic: a Century of Exploration, 1818-1918* (Cambridge, 1993).

8. Ross, *Polar Pioneers,* p309.

9. Quoted in Ross, *Polar Pioneers,* p313.

10. Quoted in F J Woodward, *Portrait of Jane,* p273.

11. F J Woodward, *Portrait of Jane,* p273.

12. Quoted in Ross, *Polar Pioneers,* p324.

13. F J Woodward, 'William Penny, 1809-92', *Polar Record,* Vol 6, No 46, 1953, p809-11; Clive R Holland, 'William Penny, 1809-92', *Polar Record,* Vol 15, No 94, 1970, p25-43.

14. Robert Randolph Carter, *Searching for the Franklin Expedition,* edited by Harold B Gill, jr and Joanne Young (Annapolis, 1998).

15. E K Kane, *The U S Grinnell Expedition in Search of Sir John Franklin* (New York, 1854), p25.

16. RGS Archives, CRM/3, Sir Clements Markham, private journal kept in HMS *Assistance.*

17. Elisha Kent Kane, *The US Grinnell Expedition in Search of Sir John Franklin: a Personal Narrative* (New York, 1854), p146.

18. Sherard Osborn, *Stray Leaves from an Arctic Journal* (New edition, London, 1865), p25.

19. British Library, Barrow Bequest, Add. mss. 35306, letter from Sherard Osborn to John Barrow, jr, Stromness, 11 May 1850.

20. Osborn, *Stray Leaves . . . ,* p25-6.

21. Richard Vaughan, *Northwest Greenland: a History* (Orono, 1991), p31.

22. Richard J Cyriax, 'Adam Beck and the Franklin Search', *Mariner's Mirror,* Vol 48, No 1, 1962, p37-51.

23. *Arctic Miscellanies: Souvenir of the Late Polar Search . . .* (second edition, London, 1852), p229.

24. Kane, *The US Grinnell Expedition . . . ,* p153.

25. National Maritime Museum, HSR/C/6, contemporary signed copy of Captain Ommanney's report to Captain Austin, from HMS *Assistance* off Griffith Island, 10 September 1850.

26. Kane, *The US Grinnell Expedition . . . ,* p162-3, plate facing p162. See Constance Martin, *James Hamilton, Arctic Watercolours* (Calgary, 1984).

27. Owen Beattie and John Geiger, *Frozen in Time: the Fate of the Franklin Expedition* (London, 1987), p164.

28. British Library, Barrow Bequest, Add. ms. 35306, section 4, E A Inglefield to John Barrow, 14 September 1852.

29. Cited in Beattie and Geiger, *Frozen in Time,* p118.

30. Kane, *The US Grinnell Expedition . . . ,* p164-5.

31. Kane, *The US Grinnell Expedition,* p165.

32. Richard J Cyriax, 'Sir John Franklin: a note on the absence of records on the shores past which he sailed during his last voyage', *Scottish Geographical Magazine,* Vol 75, No 1, 1959, p30-40.

33. British Library, Barrow Bequest, Add. ms. 35307.

34. Osborn, *Stray Leaves . . . ,* p88.

35. Trevor Harwood, 'Voyage Round Cornwallis Island, Northwest Territories 1950', *Polar Record,* Vol 6, No 46, 1953, p795.

36. Captain De Haven's report cited in Kane, *The US Grinnell Expedition . . . ,* p201.

37. Kane, *The US Grinnell Expedition . . . ,* p210-12.

38. R R Carter, *Searching . . . ,* p55.

39. Osborn, *Stray Leaves . . . ,* p96-7.

40. Osborn, *Stray Leaves . . . ,* p114-19.

41. *Arctic Miscellanies* (second edition, London, 1852), p320-8. See also C R Markham, 'On the origin and migrations of the Greenland Esquimaux'. Journal of the Royal Geographical Society, 1865, p1-16, map.
42. Osborn, *Stray Leaves . . .* , p121.
43. *Arctic Miscellanies*, p124-5.
44. RGS Archives, CRM/40, C Markham, 'Story of my Service'.
45. RGS Archives, CRM/40, C Markham, 'Story of my Service'.
46. RGS Archives, CRM/40, C Markham, 'Story of my Service'.
47. Osborn, *Stray Leaves . . .* , p91.
48. Richard J Cyriax, 'Arctic sledge travelling by officers of the Royal Navy, 1819-49', *Mariner's Mirror,* Vol 49, No 2, 1963, p127-42.
49. Clive Holland, *Arctic Exploration and Development . . . an Encyclopedia* (New York, 1994) p232.
50. Sir Clements Markham, *Life of Admiral Sir Leopold McClintock* (London, 1909) p123-5.
51. Holland, *Arctic Exploration . . .* , p232.
52. Sir Clements Markham, *McClintock,* p133.
53. Sir Clements Markham, *Franklin's Footsteps,* (London, 1853). In this are the words of the pantomime performed on board, *Zero or Harlequin Light.*
54. C Markham, *McClintock,* p134.
55. R A Goodsir, *An Arctic Voyage to Baffin's Bay and Lancaster Sound in Search of Friends with Sir John Franklin* (London, 1850, reprinted 1996).
56. Peter C Sutherland, *Journal of a Voyage in Baffin's Bay and Barrow Straits . . .* , 2 vols (London, 1852). Un-numbered quotations in this section are from this book.
57. Sutherland, *Journal of a Voyage in Baffin's Bay . . .* , Vol 1, p366, Vol 2, p235-6, p293, plate facing p237; 'The Esquimaux'. Journal of the Ethnological Society, Vol 4, 1856, p193-214.
58. Captain Penny's Report, in Sutherland, *Journal of a Voyage in Baffin's Bay . . .* , Vol 2, p160-3.
59. Sutherland, *Journal of a Voyage in Baffin's Bay . . .* , Vol 2, p100.
60. Captain Penny's Report, in Sutherland, *Journal of a Voyage in Baffin's Bay . . .* , Vol 2, p164 and Sir John Richardson's Report, in Sutherland, *Journal of a Voyage in Baffin's Bay . . .* , pcxxii-cxxx.
61. Trevor Harwood, 'Voyage Round Cornwallis Island', p794-6
62. British Library, Barrow Bequest, Add. mss 35306, note by John Barrow on Captain Penny's letter to him of 3 January 1852.
63. David Harrowfield, personal communication from the Canterbury Museum, Christchurch, 9 March 1976.
64. British Library, Barrow Bequest, Add. mss 35306, Penny to John Barrow, 7 October 1856.

Chapter 12
1. A G E Jones, 'Robert Shedden and the *Nancy Dawson'.* In *Polar portraits: collected papers* [of A G E Jones]. Whitby, 1992, p333-35. (Reprinted from *Mariner's Mirror,* Vol. 4, 1958).
2. Richard Collinson, *Journal of* HMS Enterprise . . . (London, 1880), p27-8.
3. For the Franklin Search in the Alaskan region, including five boat expeditions and the *Plover's* proceedings 1848-54, as well as an interesting account of the western Eskimos, see *The journal of Rochfort Maguire 1852-54,* edited by John Bockstoce, 2 vols (London, 1988); likewise H F Pullen, *The Pullen expedition in search of Sir John Franklin.* Toronto, 1979.

4. RGS Archives, AR176.
5. T B Collinson, Note 8, Separation of the Ships, in: R Collinson, *Journal of* HMS Enterprise . . . , p358-9.
6. Henry Piers, 'Journal 14 December 1849 to 31 March 1852', National Maritime Museum, Greenwich, MS JOD/102. Quoted in Ann Savours, 'The diary of Assistant Surgeon Henry Piers, HMS *Investigator,* 1850-54', *Journal of the Royal Naval Medical Service,* Vol 76, 1990, p3-38.
7. Henry Piers, 'Journal, 14 December 1849 to 31 March 1852, quoted by Ann Savours and Margaret Deacon, 'Nutritional Aspects of the British Arctic (Nares) Expedition of 1875-76 and its Predecessors', in James Watt *et al, Starving Sailors: the Influence of Nutrition upon Naval and Maritime History* (London, 1980), p131-62.
8. National Maritime Museum, classmark JOD/102, Henry Piers, journal.
9. RGS Archives, journal mss, copy sent by Sir George Back for publication in the *Geographical Journal,* having been read to the society on 14 November 1853 and published in an edited form in Vol. 54, 1854.
10. Sherard Osborn, *The Discovery of the North-West Passage by* HMS Investigator (second edition, London, 1857), p283-7.
11. Parliamentary papers, William T Domville, Journal, 10 March to 19 April 1853, p664-9.
12. Public Record Office, Adm 7, 198, 262-4.
13. British Library, Barrow Bequest, Add. mss 35307, Captain Henry Kellett, private letter dated 12 and 19 April 1853 from Dealy Island aboard HMS *Resolute* to John Barrow, at the Admiralty.
14. Alexander Armstrong, *A Personal Narrative of the Discovery of the North-West Passage . . .* (London, 1857), p561.
15. Alexander Armstrong, *A Personal Narrative,* p576-7.
16. Johann Miertsching, *Frozen Ships: the Arctic Diary of Johann Miertsching, 1850-1854,* translated and with an introduction and notes by L H Neatby (Toronto, 1967), p187-8.
17. Johann Miertsching, *Frozen Ships . . .* , footnote p201. See also L H Neatby, 'McClure and the Passage', *The Beaver,* Winter 1960, Outfit 73, p33-42.
18. Wynniatt was able to return to duty after a few months' leave: letter to the Archivist of the RGS among the McClure papers, 10 October 1990, from A G E Jones.
19. *Illustrated London News,* 28 October 1854.
20. British Library, Barrow Bequest, Add. mss 35308, letter dated 13 September 1850.
21. Richard Collinson, *Journal of* HMS Enterprise . . . *1850-55* (London, 1889), edited by Major General T B Collinson, p209-19.
22. Sir John Barrow, *Voyages of Discovery and Research within the Arctic Regions . . .* (London, 1846), p460.
23. T B Collinson, editorial note in R Collinson, *Journal of* HMS Enterprise, p233.
24. Sir John Richardson, *Arctic Searching Expedition* (New York, 1854), p306.
25. Quoted in *John Rae's Correspondence with the Hudson's Bay Company, on Arctic Exploration 1844-1855,* edited by E E Rich, assisted by A M Johnson, with an introduction by J M Wordie and R J Cyriax (London, 1953), p167.
26. Dr John Rae, report dated Fort Simpson, 27 September 1851, *John Rae's Correspondence with the Hudson's Bay Company . . .* , p197.
27. Cited in *John Rae's Correspondence . . .* , pxcv.
28. See Kenneth J Carpenter. *The history of scurvy and Vitamin C.* (Cambridge University Press, 1986). Also Robert E Feeney. *Polar journeys: the role of food and nutrition in early exploration.* (Fairbanks, University of

Alaska, 1997).

29. See A G E Jones, 'The Halkett Boat and Other Portable Boats', *Mariner's Mirror,* Vol 44, No 2, 1958, p154-8. One of these boats can be seen in the museum at Stromness, Orkney.

30. Rochfort Maguire, *Journal,* Vol 2, p429-32.

31. G H Richards, letter to the editor, in R Collinson, *Journal of* HMS Enterprise . . . , px-xi. Professor Neatby called him 'the invincible Collinson'.

32. British Library, Barrow Bequest, Add. mss 35308.

Chapter 13

1. William Barr, 'The Cold of Valparaiso . . .', *Polar Record,* Vol 34, No 190, 1998, p203-4,

2. Woodward, *Portrait of Jane,* p277.

3. William Kennedy, *A Short Narrative of the Second Voyage of the Prince Albert in Search of Sir John Franklin* (London, 1853), pix.

4. Barr, 'Valparaiso. . .', p205-10.

5. Cited in Frances Woodward, 'Joseph René Bellot', *Polar Record,* Vol 4, No 39, 1959, p398-407.

6. British Library, Barrow Bequest, Add. mss 35306, section 5, William Kennedy, undated letter.

7. National Maritime Museum, FRN/1, letter dated 4 July 1852.

8. Captain C R D Bethune, letter cited in Sir Archibald Day, *The Admiralty Hydrographic Service, 1795-1919* (London, 1967), p65.

9. G S Ritchie, *The Admiralty Chart: British Naval Hydrography in the Nineteenth Century* (London, 1967), p260, new edition 1995, p283.

10. Sir Edward Belcher, *The Last of the Arctic Voyages,* 2 vols (London, 1855). The artists were Belcher, W W May and G F M'Dougall.

11. National Maritime Museum, FRN/1, Sir Edward Belcher, letter to J W Croker, 4 July 1852.

12. Quotations from G H Richards, British Library, Barrow Bequest, Add. ms 35307, letter to John Barrow, July 1852.

13. Ritchie, *The Admiralty Chart . . .* (1995), p284.

14. The printed prayer is in British Library, Barrow Bequest, Add. ms 35307.

15. Woodward, *Portrait of Jane,* p283; 'Edward Augustus Inglefield, 1820-94', *Polar Record,* Vol 5, 1948, p189-92.

16. British Library, Barrow Bequest, Add. ms 35306, section 4, Edward Augustus Inglefield, Letter to John Barrow from Ponds Bay, 14 September 1852.

17. Quoted in the introduction to *Dr Kane's Voyage to the Polar Lands,* edited by Oscar M Villarejo (Philadelphia, 1965), p46.

18. Cited in Villarejo, *Dr Kane's Voyage . . . ,* p15.

19. Woodward, *Portrait of Jane,* p291.

20. Villarejo, *Dr Kane's Voyage,* p176.

21. Woodward, *Portrait of Jane,* p295-6.

22. British Library, Barrow Bequest, Add. ms 35305.

23. Emile Frédéric de Bray, *A Frenchman in Search of Franklin: de Bray's Arctic Journal, 1852-54,* translated and edited by William Barr (Toronto, 1992).

24. F L McClintock, 'Reminiscences of Arctic Ice-travel in search of Sir John Franklin and His Companions', *Journal of the Royal Dublin Society,* February 1857; 'On Arctic sledge Travelling', *Proceedings of the Royal Geographical Society,* Vol 19, 1875, p464-79, reprinted in the *Antarctic Manual* (London, 1901), p293-304.

25. Sir Clements Markham, *Life of Admiral Sir Leopold McClintock* (London, 1909), p169-70.

26. RGS Archives, CRM/40, Sir Clements Markham, 'Story of my service . . . from the point of view of a midshipman . . . in 1848 to 1854'.

27. RGS Archives, CRM/40, C Markham, 'Story of my service. . .'.

28. G F M'Dougall, *The Eventful Voyage of* HMS Resolute . . . (1857), p492-5.

29. Cited in M'Dougall, *The Eventful Voyage . . . ,* p298.

30. C Markham, *McClintock . . . ,* p172-3.

31. British Library, Barrow Bequest, Add. ms 35307, Sherard Osborn, letter dated 31 March 1853 to John Barrow.

32. British Library, Barrow Bequest, Add. ms 35307, Sherard Osborn, letter dated 20 July 1853 to John Barrow.

33. British Library, Barrow Bequest, Add. ms 35307, G H Richards, letter dated July and August 1853 to John Barrow.

34. British Library, Barrow Bequest, Add. ms 35307, G H Richards, letter to John Barrow, February and 3 March 1854.

35. E de Bray, *A Frenchman in Search of Franklin . . . ,* p135.

36. J E Bernier, *Report on the Dominion of Canada Government Expedition to the Arctic Islands and Hudson Strait on Board the D.G.S. 'Arctic'* (Ottawa, 1910).

37. M'Dougall, *The Eventful Voyage . . . ,* p328.

38. M'Dougall, *The Eventful Voyage . . . ,* p331-2.

39. M'Dougall, *The Eventful Voyage . . . ,* p334.

40. M'Dougall, *The Eventful Voyage . . . ,* p341.

41. Parliamentary Papers, Frederick J Krabbé, Proceedings . . . , in Further Papers Relative to the Recent Arctic Expeditions in Search of Sir John Franklin, p96-7.

42. Miertsching, *Frozen Ships . . . ,* p230.

43. Parliamentary Papers, Captain Kellett's orders, p690.

44. Parliamentary Papers, G F Mecham, Journal entry for 'Nineteenth journey', p694.

45. Parliamentary Papers, Mecham, p698.

46. Parliamentary Papers, Mecham, p699.

47. Parliamentary Papers, Captain Kellett's orders to Lieutenant Mecham, H.M. Ship *Resolute* in Barrow's Straits, 8 May 1854, p703.

48. Parliamentary Papers, Mecham, p702.

49. Clive Holland, *Encyclopedia,* p243.

50. British Library, Barrow Bequest, Add. ms 35307, Captain Henry Kellett, letter to John Barrow, 20 September 1854 written during the voyage home.

51. M'Dougall, *Resolute,* p389-91.

52. British Library, Barrow Bequest, Add. ms 35307, F L McClintock, letter to John Barrow, off Disco, Greenland, 8 September 1854. 'Dovekie' was the sailor's name for the Little Auk.

53. British Library, Barrow Bequest, Add. ms 35307, McClintock, letter to John Barrow, 8 September 1854.

54. British Library, Barrow Bequest, Add. ms 35307, Bedford Pim, letter to John Barrow, from Beechey Island, June 1854.

55. T B Collinson, editorial note, in R Collinson, *Journal of* HMS Enterprise . . . , p257.

56. M'Dougall, *Resolute,* p461-2.

57. British Library, Barrow Bequest, Add. ms 35308, Lady Franklin, letter to John Barrow, London, 10 January 1857.

58. M'Dougall, *Resolute,* 1857, p473-5.

59. Sydney Withington, *Two Dramatic Episodes of New England Whaling,* (Mystic, Conn, 1958).

Chapter 14

1. National Maritime Museum, AGC/5/27, John Hepburn, letter to Sir John Richardson from Milford Haven, 11 October 1854.

2. *John Rae's Correspondence with the Hudson's Bay Company on Arctic Exploration 1844-1855,* introduction by J M Wordie and R J Cyriax (London, 1953), plxxiv.

3. British Library, Barrow Bequest, Add. mss 35308, Dr John Rae, letter to John Barrow, from Sault Ste. Marie, Lake Superior, 9 May 1853.
4. R L Richards, *Dr John Rae* (Whitby, 1985), p94-5.
5. Parliamentary Papers, Dr John Rae, report dated 1 September 1854 at York Factory, Hudson Bay to the Hudson's Bay Company in London, p835-45.
6. Francis Herbert, 'A cartobibliography . . . of the Arrowsmith/Stanford North Pole map, 1818-1937'. Bulletin of the Association of Canadian Map Libraries, No. 62. 1987.
7. Richards, *Rae . . .* , p98 and note.
8. Quotations from Parliamentary Papers, p831; the list of articles and sketches on p832-3.
9. Parliamentary papers, p833-4.
10. *John's Rae's Correspondence with the Hudson's Bay Company . . .* , plxxxi.
11. *Household Words,* No 246, 9 December 1854, p392.
12. *Household Words,* No 248, 23 December 1854, p233-5 and No 249, 30 December 1854, p457-9.
13. British Library, Barrow Bequest, Add. ms 35308, letter to John Barrow, 28 December 1854.
14. Parliamentary Papers, p845. *See Illustrated London News,* 4 November 1854.
15. Parliamentary Papers, Admiralty to Alexander Barclay, Hudson Bay House, London, 27 October 1854, p846-7.
16. Alan Cooke and Clive Holland, *The Exploration of Northern Canada* (Toronto, 1978).
17. James Anderson, letter to Sir George Simpson, 17 September 1855, *Royal Geographical Society Journal,* Vol 26, 1856, p18.
18. Their statements and numerous other documents relating to the 1855 expedition appear in William Barr, ed, *The Land Arctic Searching Expedition: James Anderson's and James Stewart's Search for Franklin via the Back River, 1855* (London, 1999).
19. Neville W Poulsom, *The White Ribbon* (London, 1968).
20. *Arctic Dispatches* (London, 1853) p31-40.
21. *Arctic Dispatches* (London 1853) p38.
22. J Sainthill, *Suggestions for a Medal to Record the Discovery of the Passage by the North Pole* (Cork, 1856), reprinted from *Numismatic Crumbs* (London 1855).

Chapter 15
1. A G E Jones, 'Admiral Sir Leopold McClintock: a Different View', *Fram: the Journal of Polar Studies,* Vol 2, Part 1, 1985, p291.
2. Quotations from Lady Franklin's letter, from 60 Pall Mall, 25 February 1857 to Richard Monckton Milnes, bound up in a volume in the library of Lord Crewe, bought by Maggs Bros (London) prior to 1959.
3. National Maritime Museum, MCL/18, McClintock's diary.
4. Angus B Erskine and Kjell-G Kjaer, 'The Arctic Ship Fox', *Polar Record,* Vol 33, No 185, 1997, p123-32.
5. Jones, 'Admiral Sir Leopold McClintock. . .', *Fram,* Vol 2, Part 1, 1985, p290-325.
6. British Library, Barrow Bequest, Add. mss 35309, Sir Robert McClure, letter from Singapore dated 29 May 1859 to John Barrow.
7. William Scoresby, jr, *The Franklin Expedition, or Considerations on Measures for the Discovery and Relief of our Absent Adventurers in the Arctic Regions* (London, 1850), p50-2.
8. Sir Leopold McClintock, *The Voyage of the 'Fox' in the Arctic Seas . . .* (London, 1859), p6. Un-numbered quotations are from this, or from the 1908 edition.
9. National Maritime Museum, SHP/12, William R

Hobson, letter dated 17 February [1860?] from 9 Westbourne St Hyde Park to his brother-in-law, Philip Ruffle Sharpe.
10. National Maritime Museum, MCL/18, McClintock's diary, 4 December 1857.
11. 'The Search for Sir John Franklin', from the private journal of an officer of the 'Fox', *Cornhill Magazine,* Vol 1, 1860, p160.
12. National Maritime Museum, MCL/18, McClintock's diary.
13. McClintock, Fox . . . , p121-32; William Scoresby, *Franklin's Expedition,* p56-79.
14. National Maritime Museum, MCL/18, McClintock's diary, entry for 16 July 1858 off Cape Warrender.
15. William Hobson, letter to Philip R Sharpe.
16. Carl Petersen, *Den sidste Franklin - Expedition med 'Fox', Capt. M'Clintock* (København, 1860).
17. William R Hobson, letter to Philip R Sharpe.
18. National Maritime Museum, HSR/2/6 and Scott Polar Research Institute 54/20/1, cited in R J Cyriax, 'The Two Franklin Expedition Records Found on King William Island', *Mariner's Mirror,* Vol 44, No 3, 1958, p179-89.
19. Transcriptions in Cyriax, 'The Two Franklin Expedition Records . . .', p179-89.
20. R J Cyriax, 'The Position of Victory Point, King William Island', *Polar Record,* Vol 6, No 44, 1952, p496-507.
21. W R Hobson, letter to Philip R Sharpe.
22. R J Cyriax and A G E Jones, 'The Papers in the Possession of Harry Peglar, Captain of the Foretop, HMS *Terror,* 1845', *Mariner's Mirror,* Vol 40, No 3, 1954, p186-95.
23. W R Hobson, letter to Philip R Sharpe.
24. R J Cyriax, 'A Historic Medicine Chest', *Canadian Medical Association Journal,* Vol 57, 1947, p295-300.
25. Sherard Osborn, 'The Career, Last Voyage and Fate of Captain Sir John Franklin', in *Stray Leaves from an Arctic journal,* (new edition, Edinburgh, 1865), p331-3.
26. A G E Jones, 'Allen Young and the Voyage of the 'Fox' ', *Fram,* Vol 2, Part 1, 1985, p337-8.
27. Woodward, *Portrait of Jane,* p304.

Chapter 16
1. R J Cyriax, 'Captain Hall and the So-called Survivors of the Franklin Expedition', *Polar Record,* Vol 4, No 287, 1944, p170-85; Cyriax, 'The Unsolved Problem of the Franklin Expedition Records Supposedly Buried on King William Island', *Mariner's Mirror,* Vol 55, No 1, 1969, p23 32.
2. Quoted in Paul Fenimore Cooper, *Island of the Lost* (London, 1961), p203.
3. Ann Savours, 'Franklin Memorial at the Royal Naval College, Greenwich', *Mariner's Mirror,* Vol 72, No 4, 1986, p480-1.
4. Chauncey C Loomis, *Weird and Tragic Shores: the Story of Charles Francis Hall, Explorer* (London, 1972), p224.
5. Heinrich Klutschak, *Overland to Starvation Cove . . . ,* translated and edited by William Barr (Toronto, 1987), p14.
6. R J Cyriax, *Sir John Franklin's Last Expedition,* p184-85, 190-91.
7. R J Cyriax, *Sir John Franklin's Last Expedition,* p178-79; Ralph Lloyd-Jones, 'An Evangelical Christian on Franklin's Last Expedition: Lieutenant John Irving of HMS *Terror*', *Polar Record,* Vol 33, No 187, 1997 p327-32; McClintock, *The Voyage of the Fox* (6th edition, 1908) p[64-65].
8. W H Gilder, *Schwatka's Search . . .* (New York, 1881); Frederick Schwatka, *The Long Arctic Search,* edited by Edouard A Stackpole (Mystic, Conn, 1965); Heinrich

Klutschak, *Overland to Starvation Cove,* translated and edited by William Barr (Toronto 1987).

9. Frederick Schwatka, *The Long Arctic Search,* p116.

10. Clements Markham, 'Expedition of Lieutenant Schwatka to King William Land', *Proceedings of the Royal Geographical Society,* 1880, p657-62, map facing p720.

11. William Barr, postscript to *Overland to Starvation Cove,* p207-19, in which post-Schwatka expeditions are summarised. See also Cyriax, *Sir John Franklin's Last expedition, passim; David Woodman, Unravelling the Franklin Mystery: Inuit Testimony* (Montreal, 1991); Owen Beattie and John Geiger, *Frozen in Time* (London, 1987).

12. Anne Keenleyside *et al,* 'The Final Days of the Franklin Expedition: New Skeletal Evidence', *Arctic,* Vol 50, No 1, 1997, p36-46; Barry Ranford, 'In Franklin's Footsteps', *Equinox* (Toronto), No 69, June 1993, p46-53; B Ranford, 'Bones of Contention', *Equinox,* No 74, Spring 1994, p69-87; B Ranford, 'More Pieces of the Franklin Puzzle', *Up Here,* July/August 1995, p37-9; Margaret Bertulli. NgLj-2, A Franklin site on Erebus Bay, King William Island: field work in 1993. Unpublished report. (Prince of Wales Northern Heritage Centre, Yellowknife, 1995). Patricia D Sutherland, ed, *The Franklin Era in Canadian Arctic History, 1845-1859* (Ottawa, 1995).

13. R T Gould, *Oddities* (London, 1928) p79.

Chapter 17

1. McClintock, *The Voyage of the Fox* (1908), p239.

2. R J Cyriax and J M Wordie, 'Centenary of the Sailing of Sir John Franklin with the *Erebus* and *Terror*', *Geographical Journal,* Vol 106, Nos 5, 6, 1945, p169-97.

3. Roald Amundsen, *The North West Passage,* Vol 1 (London, 1908), p1-54.

4. Helmer Hanssen, *Voyages of a Modern Viking* (London, 1936), p16.

5. Hanssen, *Voyages,* p16-17.

6. Godfred Hansen, 'Towards King Haakon VII's Land', in Roald Amundsen, *NW Passage,* Vol 2, p296-364.

7. Hansen, in Amundsen, *NW Passage,* Vol 2, p362-3.

8. R Huntford, *Scott and Amundsen* (London, 1979), p104.

9. C E Whittaker, *Arctic Eskimo* (London, 1937), p234.

10. John Bockstoce, *Whales, Ice and Men: the History of Whaling in the Western Arctic* (Seattle, 1986).

11. Roland Huntford, ed, *The Amundsen Photographs* (New York, 1987).

12. Cited in Roland Huntford, *Scott and Amundsen* (1979), p114.

13. J E Bernier, *Master Mariner and Arctic Explorer: a Narrative of Sixty Years at Sea from the Logs and Yarns of Captain J E Bernier* (Ottawa, 1939), p328-9.

14. J E Bernier, *Report on the Dominion of Canada Government Expedition to the Arctic Islands and Hudson Strait* (Ottawa, 1910), p161, 176.

15. Bernier, *Master Mariner . . . ,* p372.

16. Henry Larsen, *The Big Ship, an Autobiography . . .* (Toronto, 1967).

17. Henry Larsen, *The North-West Passage 1940-1942 and 1944 . . .* (Vancouver, 1954), p19-21.

18. Larsen, *The Big Ship,* p148-9.

19. Larsen, *The NW Passage,* p23.

20. G J Tranter, *Plowing the Arctic . . .* (Toronto, 1945).

21. Larsen, *The Big Ship,* p186-7.

22. Ann Savours and Margaret Deacon, 'Nutritional Aspects of the British Arctic (Nares) Expedition . . .', p161, note 19.

23. Larsen, *The Big Ship,* p189.

24. Larsen, *The NW Passage,* p51.

Transits of the North West Passage, 1906–1900

Compiled by the late Captain Thomas C Pullen and Charles Swithinbank.
Copyright Scott Polar Research Institute; abstracted from *Polar Record; Vol 27, No 163, 1991.*

Year	Ship	Commander	Flag	Notes
1906	*Gjøa*	R Amundsen	Norway	47-ton Norwegian herring boat, 13hp engine: wintered 1903 at Gjoa Haven, King William I; 1904 at King Point, Yukon Territory.
1942	*St Roch*	H A Larsen	Canada	80-ton, 30m, Royal Canadian Mounted Police auxiliary schooner. Wintered 1940 in Walker Bay, Victoria I; 1941 in Pasley Bay, Boothia Peninsula.
1944	*St Roch*	H A Larsen	Canada	See above: first transit in one season.
1954	HMCS *Labrador*	O C S Robertson	Canada	First warship and icebreaker to complete passage, also first continuous circumnavigation of North America.
1957	USCGC *Storis*	H L Wood	USA	Light icebreaker travelling with *Spar* and *Bramble* (below). First squadron, first US ships to make passage.
1957	USCGC *Spar*	C V Crewing	USA	Buoy tender travelling with *Storis* (above) and *Bramble* (below).
1957	USCGC *Bramble*	H H Carter	USA	Buoy tender travelling with *Storis* and *Spar* (above).
1960	USS *Seadragon*	G P Steele	USA	First transit by submarine.
1962	USS *Skate*	J Skoog	USA	First submerged eastward passage.
1967	CCGS *John A Macdonald*	P M Fournier	Canada	First transit by CCG icebreaker, circumnavigated North America.
1969	USCGC *Northwind*	J D McCann	USA	USCG icebreaker.
1969	SS *Manhattan*	R A Steward	USA	Icebreaking tanker making first commercial transit. Draft 17m, length 306m, displacement 155,000 tons.
1969	CCGS *John A Macdonald*	P M Fournier	Canada	Accompanied SS *Manhattan* (*above*).

Year	Ship	Commander	Flag	Notes
1969	SS *Manhattan*	R A Steward	USA	Carried symbolic cargo of one barrel of Prudhoe Bay crude oil.
1969	CCGS *John A Macdonald*	P M Fournier	Canada	Accompanied SS *Manhattan* (above).
1969	USCGC *Northwind*	J D McCann	USA	USCG icebreaker.
1969	USCGC *Staten Island*	E F Walsh	USA	Accompanied SS *Manhattan* (above).
1970	CSS *Hudson*	D W Butler	Canada	Oceanographic research ship: first to circumnavigate the Americas.
1970	CSS *Baffin*	P M Brick	Canada	Hydrographic survey ship.
1975	CCGS *Skidegate*	P Kalis	Canada	Small buoy tender and training ship.
1975	*Pandora II*	R Dickinson	Canada	58m hydrographic research ship. First transit via Hudson Strait.
1975	MV *Theta*	K Maro	Canada	Converted sealer.
1976	CCS *J E Bernier*	F Chouinard	Canada	Icebreaking buoy tender.
1977	*Williwaw*	Willy de Roos	Holland	13m ketch, first yacht, first single-handed passage.
1978	*J E Bernier II*	R Bouvier	Canada	Ketch: wintered 1976 in Resolute Bay; 1977 at Tuktoyaktuk.
1978	CCGS *Pierre Radisson*	P M R Toomey	Canada	Icebreaker on maiden voyage.
1979	CCGS *Louis S St Laurent*	G Burdock	Canada	Canadian icebreaker.
1980	CCGS *J E Bernier*	E Chasse	Canada	Icebreaking buoy tender.
1980	*Pandora II*	R Jones	Canada	58m hydrographic research ship.
1981	CCS *Hudson*	F Mauger	Canada	Oceanographic research ship.
1982	*Mermaid*	K Horie	Japan	Sloop: wintered 1979 and 1980 at Resolute Bay; 1981 at Tuktoyaktuk.
1983	MV *Arctic Shiko*	J Dool	Canada	69m tug and supply ship.
1983	MV *Polar Circle*	J A Strand	Canada	Survey ship.
1984	MV *Lindblad Explorer*	H Nilsson	Bahamas	First passenger ship.
1985	USCGC *Polar Sea*	J T Howell	USA	USCG icebreaker.
1985	MV *World Discoverer*	H Aye	Liberia	First eastward transit by passenger ship.
1988	*Belvedere*	J Bockstoce	USA	18m motor sailer, first US yacht and the first yacht to make passage eastward. Wintered 1983-87 at Tuktoyaktuk.
1988	*Vagabond II*	W Jacobson	Canada	Yacht: wintered 1985 at Tuktoyaktuk; 1986-87 in Gjoa Haven.

Year	Ship	Commander	Flag	Notes
1988	CCGS *Henry A Larsen*	S Gomes	Canada	Icebreaker on maiden voyage.
1988	MV *Society Explorer*	H Aye	Bahamas	Former *Lindblad Explorer* (above): first passenger ship to transit in both directions.
1988	MV *Canmar Explorer II*	Various	Canada	Drillship escorted to Beaufort Sea 1976, completed passage 12 years later.
1988	CCGS *Martha L Black*	R Mellis	Canada	Icebreaking buoy tender.
1988	USCGC *Polar Star*	P R Taylor	USA	Icebreaker: blocked by ice off Alaska; had to circumnavigate North America.
1989	USCGC *Polar Star*	R Hammond	USA	Circumnavigated North America.
1989	*Mabel E Holland*	D S Cowper	Britain	22-ton, 13m lifeboat: wintered 1986-87 at Fort Ross; 1988 at Inuvik. First single-handed circumnavigation of North America
1989	*Northanger*	R Thomas	Britain	13m ketch: wintered 1988 at Inuvik.
1989	MV *Arctic Nanabush*	S Wiseman	Canada	Supply ship.
1989	MV *Arctic Nanook*	S Wiseman	Canada	Tug. Wiseman made the passage twice in one season (above).
1990	USCGC *Polar Sea*	R McClelan	USA	Accompanied part of the way by icebreaker CCGS *Pierre Radisson*.
1990	MV *Ikaluk*	R Cormier	Canada	Entered the passage in 1983, worked in Beaufort Sea until 1990.

APPENDIX II

Relics of Sir John Franklin's last expedition at the National Maritime Museum, Greenwich

The largest part of the National Maritime Museum's polar collection consists of the relics of Franklin's last expedition. They are strange, fragmentary things – gloves, battered tins, pieces of soap, watch backs – and just one document, the famous printed form with its message noting the death of Franklin, the abandonment of the ships and the decision to head for the Back River. The sad trail of objects, littering the bleak corners of the icy archipelago, assumed enormous importance to those searching for the expedition as well as the public at home.

Objects were either found directly by the search expeditions, such as the gloves found by Sherard Osborn at Beechey Island, which had been left out to dry in 1846. Other objects were traded from the Eskimos. A major breakthrough was Dr Rae's recovery of expedition material from the Eskimos at Repulse Bay in 1854. McClintock tracked the missing expedition up the west coast of King William Island, finding a trail of bodies and discarded possessions.

The finds made their way to the National Maritime Museum by various routes. The Rae collection, for instance, was handed over to the Admiralty by the Hudson's Bay Company, who in turn presented it to Greenwich Hospital for display in the Painted Hall. It is still on loan from Greenwich Hospital. Some came from the Royal United Services Institution, but the bulk came from the former Royal Naval Museum at Greenwich.

The relics at the Museum were catalogued by Barbara Tomlinson and they are arranged by place of discovery. The prefix AAA to all the catalogue numbers has been omitted in this appendix.

BEECHEY ISLAND

William Penny Search Expedition 1850-1 Brigs *Lady Franklin* **and** *Sophia*
2026 Wooden direction post
2037 Fragment of sailcloth

Search Expedition 1850-1
2027 Glazed and painted china ashtray

Ommanney Search Expedition, HMS *Assistance*
2031 Wine bottle

CAPE RILEY, BEECHEY ISLAND

2028 Mounted clay pipe, found 23 Aug 1850 at Cape Riley

Inglefield Search Expedition 1852
2029 Limestone hone
2030 Goldner meat tin
2032 Metal canteen
2033 Meat tin
2034 Goldner tin
2038 Goldner soup tin
2039 Metal canteen

Belcher Search Expedition 1852-4
2035 Two cotton gloves, found by Lt Sherard Osborne

Also found at Beechey Island
2036 Meat sample from Beechey Island tin
2267 Ball of wool
2269 Part of a woollen stocking

Collinson Search Expedition 1850–55

CAMBRIDGE BAY, VICTORIA ISLAND, OCTOBER 1852

2085 Adze head (ex RUSI 395)

Rae Expedition 1853–4

OBTAINED FROM THE INUIT AT PELLY BAY, 24 APRIL 1854?
(Greenwich Hospital Collection)

2082 Gold lace cap band. Caribou skin added by the Inuit

REPULSE BAY 26 MAY–4 AUG 1854

2041 Fragment of shirt with initials of Charles Frederick de Voeux
2042 Three brass buttons (Commissioned Naval Officers, Military & Civil Branch 1843–91). Maker: P & S Firmin, London
2043 Fragment of a gold watch chain
2044 Fragment of a gold watch chain
2045 Seaman's certificate case. Owner: William Fowler (HMS *Erebus*)
2046 Seaman's certificate case. Owner: William Mark (HMS *Erebus*)
2047 Bone-handled knife inscribed with initials of Cornelius Hickey (HMS *Terror*). Maker: Millikin, London
2048 Horn-handled penknife
2050 Cook's knife, with wooden handle. Maker: Young
2051 Ulu (blade only). Maker: R Timmings & Sons
2052 Silver pocket chronometer (works missing). Made in London 1809–10
2053 Four plain brass buttons
2054 Ebony box
2055 Two pages of 'The Students Manual'.
2056 Brass pocket compass
2057 Round brass lid
2058 Brass cogged watch wheel
2059 Part of draw tube of telescope
2060 Silver pencil case

2061 Knife blade with part of horn handle. Maker: Wigfall & Co
2062 Table knife converted to a snow knife by the Inuit. Maker: Wigfall & Co (blade)
2063 Shell gimlet
2064 Bradawl
2065 Brass match box
2066 Brass object glass cover
2067 Fragment of a silver watch case. Maker: W J of Chester
2068 Fragment of a silver watch case
2069 Fragment of a silver watch case. Maker: Thomas & Joseph Guest? ca.1808–9
2070 Fragment of a silver watch case
2071 Fragment of a silver watch case. Maker: R Peppin, London
2072 Fragment of a silver watch case. Maker: Jos Hardy, London 1824–5
2073 Fragment of a silver watch case. Maker SB
2074 Fragment of a silver watch case. Made in London 1844–5
2075 Gold plate from the interior of a watch
2076 Fragment of a gold watch case, engine-turned surface. Maker: WR 1843–4
2077 Fragment of a gold watch case: Owner: James Reid (Icemaster HMS *Erebus*)
2078 Fragment of a silver pencil case
2079 Badge of a Knight Commander of the Royal Hanovarian Guelphic Order. Gold and enamel. Presented to Sir John Franklin 23 Jan 1836.
2080 Fragment of a gold watch case. Maker: SC, Sheffield
2081 Silver disc inscribed 'Sir John Franklin KCB'.

PELLY/REPULSE BAYS

2180 Silver table fork. Owner: Thomas Henry Dundas Le Vesconte. Maker: M

West, Dublin 1834-5

2049 Silver table fork. Owner: Lt Robert Orme Sargent. Maker: Thomas Northcote, London 1792

2293, 2379 Two silver table forks. Owner: Sir John Franklin. Maker: George Adams, London 1844-. 2379 inscribed 'WR' (William Rhodes, HMS *Terror*)

2380 Silver dessert fork. Owner: Sir John Franklin. Maker: George Adams, London 1844-5

2387 Silver table spoon. Owner: Sir John Franklin. Maker: George Adams, London 1844-5

2388 Silver tea spoon. Owner: Sir John Franklin. Maker: George Adams, London 1844-5

2381 Silver table fork. Owner: H D S Goodsir (Assistant Surgeon, HMS *Erebus*). Maker: William Marshall, Edinburgh

2382 Silver table fork. Owner Alexander MacDonald (Asssistant Surgeon, HMS *Terror*). Maker: 'BD' (Benjamin Davis or Benjamin Dexter), London 1831-2

2383 Silver table fork. Owner: Gillies Alexander Macbean (2nd Master, HMS *Terror*). Maker: William Trayes, London 1837-8

2384 Silver table fork. Owner: Lt John Irving (HMS *Terror*). Maker: George Ferris, Exeter 1824

2385 Silver table spoon. Owner: Capt F R M Crozier (HMS *Terror*). Maker: Josiah Low, Dublin 1839-40

2386 Silver table spoon. Owner: Lt James Walter Fairholme (HMS *Erebus*). Maker: William Eaton?, London 1842 (inscribed 'CH')

2389 Silver dessert spoon. Owner: John Smart Peddie (Surgeon, HMS *Terror*). Maker: Robert Walliss, London 1844-5

2390 Silver dessert spoon. Owner: Lt Graham Gore (HMS *Erebus*). Maker: John Harris IV, London 1824-5

2391 Silver table fork. Maker: George

Ferris, Exeter 1818

2472 Silver table spoon 'FJSP' on back of handle

2473 Silver table spoon. Maker: Thomas Barker, London 1805

3273-5 Three silver table forks. Owner: Lt Thomas Henry Dundas Le Vesconte. Maker: M West, Dublin 1834

3276 Silver table fork. Owner: Lt James Walter Fairholme. Made in Edinburgh 1812-13

Anderson Search Expedition

MONTREAL ISLAND 31 JULY 1855?

2083 Boat sheet hook (ex RUSI 397)

2084 Part of a telescope. Brass ring from object glass (ex RUSI 398)

2086 Piece of rope (according to RN Museum 1913 Catalogue see NMM 20/3 found by McClintock)

McClintock Search Expedition 1857-9
(Ex Royal Naval Museum, Greenwich)

BOUGHT FROM THE BOOTHIAN INUIT AT THE MAGNETIC POLE, MARCH–APRIL 1859

2090 Two plain brass buttons

2091 Brass RN button. Maker: Firmin & Sons (Commissioned Officers, Military and Civil Branch 1843-91)

2092 Brass RN button (see above). Maker: Thomas H Hasle?

2093 Brass RN button (see above). Maker: Turner & Sons

2094 Fragment of embossed brass plate

2095 File blade

2096 File blade, bone handle is Inuit replacement

2097-2100 Four snow knives. Made by Inuit from salvaged material

2101 Knife. Made by Inuit from salvaged material. Maker of blade: Millikin, London

2102 Knife. Made by Inuit from salvaged material

2103 Knife. Made by Inuit from salvaged material. British maker: Turner, Yeominster
2104 Knife. Made by Inuit from salvaged material.
2105-7 Three bows. Made by Inuit from salvaged wood
2108-10 Three arrows, with copper heads. Made by Inuit from salvaged material
2474 Silver dessert spoon. Owner: Lt Thomas Henry Dundas Le Vesconte (HMS *Erebus* 1826). Maker: John James Whiting, London 1837
2475 Silver table fork. Owner Alexander Macdonald (Asssistant Surgeon, HMS *Terror*). Maker: 'BD' (Benjamin Davis or Benjamin Dexter), London 1831-2
2476 Silver table spoon. Owner: Lt Edward Couch (HMS *Erebus*). Maker: Isaac Parkin, Exeter 1831
2477 Silver table fork. Owner: Sir John Franklin. Maker: George Adams, London 1844-5
2478 Silver table spoon. Owner: Alexander Macdonald (Assistant Surgeon, HMS *Terror*). Maker: William Chawner II?, London 1819

DESERTED SNOW HUTS, CAPE NORTON, KING WILLIAM ISLAND MARCH–APRIL 1859

2112 Piece of wood with deposits of tar

BOUGHT FROM INUIT, CAPE NORTON, KING WILLIAM ISLAND, 7 MAY 1859

2111 Bone handle of a knife with a broken steel razor inserted
2479 Silver table spoon. Owner: Sir John Franklin. Maker: George Adams?, London 1844-5
2480 Silver table fork. Owner: Sir John Franklin. Maker: George Adams, London 1844-5
2481 Silver tea spoon. Owner: Lt James Walter Fairholme. Maker: John & Henry Lias, London 1842

2482 Silver tea spoon. Owner: Alexander Macdonald (Assistant Surgeon, HMS *Terror*). Maker: Randall Chatterton, London 1844-5

MONTREAL ISLAND 16 MAY 1859

2087 Three pieces of iron
2088 Six pieces of copper
2089 Part of a meat tin

CAPE HERSCHEL 25 MAY 1859

(found with skeleton presumed to be that of Harry Peglar, HMS *Terror*)

2113 Clothes brush
2114 Leather wallet containing newspaper cuttings and notes
2115 Pocket comb
2116 Knotted neckerchief
2117 Fragments of waistcoat (now reduced to powder)
2118 Two silk-covered buttons
2119 Fragment of cotton shirt

NORTHERN CAIRN CAMP SITE, CAPE FELIX, KING WILLIAM ISLAND, 25 MAY 1859

(Found by Lt W R Hobson at an abandoned camp site)

2120 Cork bung of a water keg
2121 Shako Plate (Royal Marine's cap badge)
2122 Screw plug for powder keg
2123 Three wire cartridges
2124 Eleven musket balls
2125 Part of a pair of steel-rimmed spectacles made into snow goggles
2126 Part of a wool glove
2127 Portable stove
2128 Fragments of a wool naval ensign
2129-30 Two pike heads
2131 Tea canister
2132-5 Four packets of needles. Maker: F Barnes & Co, London
2133-8 Pork bones
2139 Plain brass button

2140 Lid of a powder case
2141 Two sextant eyepieces
2142 Six brimstone matches
2256 Iron fitting
2263-5 Three fragments of a china tea cup
2357 Iron plug with broad arrow

 EREBUS BAY, KING WILLIAM ISLAND MAY 1859
(Found in an abandoned boat)

2143 Three metal stanchions
2144 Fragment of canvas weather cloth
2145 Shot charger
2146 Roll of waxed twine
2147-8 Two elm tingles for repairing the boat
2149 Wooden button
2150 Port-fire (device for firing a rocket)
2151 Shot contained in three fingers of a kid glove
2152 Fragment of a New Testament
2153 Cover of Book of Common Prayer
2154 Book 'The Vicar of Wakefield'
2155 Government paper
2156 Fragment of a grass cigar case
2157 Silk neckerchief printed with seaweed pattern
2158 Silk neckerchief printed with anthemion pattern
2159 Cotton neckerchief printed with spots and diamond pattern
2160 Cotton neckerchief printed with spots and diamond pattern
2161 Sewing kit (housewife)
2162 Four fragments of scented soap
2163-4 Two pairs of snow goggles
2165 Fishing line wound on leather holder
2166 Sailmaker's palm
2167 Knife sheath
2168 Pocket water flask
2169-70 Two shot flasks
2171 Sword belt spring hook
2172 Sword belt spring

2173 Gold lace sewn into circular band
2174 Gold cord
2175 Two packets of ammunition cartridges
2176 Cherry wood pipe stem
2177 Clasp knife
2178 Spectacle lenses
2179 Tweezers for collecting natural history specimens
2181 Beaded purse
2182 Sealing wax
2183 Cork stopper of drinking flask
2184 Brass vesta case (match box)
2185 Telescope eyepiece
2186 Tin
2187 94 Brass percussion caps. Flanged type-79, Smith patent type-4, small sporting type-11
2188 Fragment of a pocket watch. Maker: J Cox Savory, London
2189 Fragment of a pocket watch. Made in London
2190 Fragment of a silver watch case. Maker: Joseph Taylor, London
2191 Fragment of a silver watch case. Made in London ca.1842-3
2192 Fragment of a silver watch case.
2193 Book 'Christian Melodies'. Owner: Lt Graham Gore, HMS *Erebus*
2194 Wooden paddle
2195 Spectacles with tinted lenses in a case
2196 Pemmican tin
2197 Glass seal with masonic device
2198 Sheet block and hook
2199 Book 'A Manual of Private Devotions' by Charles James Blomfield, published by B Fellows
2200 Oak chock
2201 Table knife
2202 Pocket chronometer issued to HMS *Erebus*. Maker: J R Arnold, London
2203 Pocket chronometer issued to HMS *Terror*. Maker: Parkinson & Frodsham
2204 Pencil case

2205 Stoppered bottle containing a white powder
2206 Stoppered bottle containing a brownish residue
2207 Table knife with initials WR (William Reed, HMS *Erebus* or William Rhodes, HMS *Terror*)
2208 Brass pocket compass
2209 Leather boot lace
2210 A Bible
2211 The New Testament in French
2212 Prayer book
2213-4 Two copper nails
2215 Rivet and washer
2216 Sewing scissors
2217 Cobbler's awl
2218-9 Two shell gimlets
2220 Bristles (possibly used for mending boots)
2483-5 Three silver tea spoons. Owner: Sir John Franklin. Maker: George Adams, London 1844-5
2486-7 Two dessert spoons. Owner: Sir John Franklin. Maker: George Adams, London 1844-5 (2486 scratched with initials IW, 2487 scratched with initials TT – Thomas Terry or T Tadman)
2488 Silver table spoon. Owner: Thomas Henry Dundas Le Vesconte. Maker: John & Henry Lias, London 1844
2489 Silver tea spoon. Owner: Capt F R M Crozier. Maker: Josiah Low, Dublin 1838-9
2490 Silver dessert fork. Owner: Lt E Couch (HMS *Erebus*). Maker 'RE', London 1826-7
2491 Silver dessert spoon. Owner: Lt E Couch (HMS *Erebus*). Maker JH, London 1815?
2492 Silver fork. Maker: William Esterbrook?, London 1844
2493-4 Two silver tea spoons. Maker: William Esterbrook?, London 1844
2495 Silver table spoon. Owner: Frederick J Hornby (HMS *Terror*). Maker

IL, Exeter 1833
2496 Silver dessert fork. Owner: Lt Robert Thomas (HMS *Terror*). Maker: Charles Shipway, London 1844
2497 Silver dessert fork. Owner: Lt Graham Gore (HMS *Erebus*). Maker JR, Exeter 1831-2
2498 Silver table spoon. Owner: H D S Goodsir (Assistant Surgeon, HMS *Erebus*). Made in Edinburgh 1814-5
2499 Silver dessert spoon. Owner: Lt George Henry Hodgson (HMS *Terror*). Maker: Charles Davy, London 1817-18
2500 Silver table spoon. Owner Lt George Henry Hodgson (HMS *Terror*). Makers: William Eley and William Fearn, London 1807
2501 Silver table spoon. Owner: Lt Robert Orme Sargent (HMS *Erebus*). Makers: Matthew Boulton and John Fothergill, Birmingham 1773
2502 Silver table fork. Owner: Lt Robert Orme Sargent (HMS *Erebus*). Maker: Thomas Northcote, London 1792
2503 Silver table spoon. Owner: Stephen Samuel Stanley (Surgeon HMS *Erebus*). Maker: William Eaton?, London 1837
2504 Silver table fork. Owner: John Smart Peddie (Surgeon HMS *Terror*). Maker: Robert Walliss, London 1844
2505 Silver table spoon. Owner: Lt John Irving (HMS *Terror*). Maker: Hester Bateman, London 1788
2506 Silver tea spoon. Owner: Alexander Macdonald (Assistant Surgeon, HMS *Terror*). Maker: Randall Chatterton, London 1844

ROSS CAIRN, POINT VICTORY, KING WILLIAM ISLAND, 2 JUNE 1859

2221, 2231 Two copper spindles
2222 Flint and steel (found by William Jones, the dog driver of Hobson's party)
2223 Dip circle. Maker: Robinson,

London (2376 the case for the instrument)
2224 Medicine chest (see 'A Historic Medicine Chest', A J Cyriax, *Canadian Medical Journal* 57, p295-300)
2225 Carpenter's rule
2226 Gun-cleaning rod
2227 Two pieces of a telescope draw tube
2228 Two pieces of a curtain rod
2229 A record tin
2230 Double sextant. Maker: E & E Emanuel. Engraved with name 'Frederick Hornby RN' (stolen)

Hall Search Expedition 1864-9
(Royal Naval Museum, Greenwich)

OBTAINED FROM THE INUIT NEAR POINT BOOTH, 1869

2232 Copper strip marked with broad arrow (possibly from Ross expedition 1829-33)

OBTAINED FROM THE INUIT AT SHEPHERDS BAY, 17 MAY 1869

2233 Mahogany chronometer box

OBTAINED FROM THE INUIT AT PELLY BAY, 12 JULY 1869

2234 Table knife (handle marked DN)
2235 Tin match box. Maker: J Hynam, London
2236 Sledge runner made from file
2237 Knife blade made from a saw
2333 Brass and wood box lid

Schwatka Search Expedition 1878-9
(Royal Naval Museum, Greenwich)

IRVING BAY, KING WILLIAM ISLAND
(In grave of Lt John Irving)

2238 Four fragments of a wool overcoat
2239 Two brass RN buttons
2240 Fragments of velvet
2241 Fragment of canvas

2242-3 Two fragments of navy sail canvas

NORTHERN CAIRN, CAPE FELIX, 3 JULY 1879

2244 Fragment of a seaman's bag
2245 Fragment of sail canvas
2266 Fragment of glazed and painted earthenware
2262 Thirteen fragments of clay pipes
2268 Top of a tin of Edward's Preserved Potato
2270 Fragment of a glass bottle. Maker: Powell & Co, Bristol
2351-3 Three pairs of scissors

ROSS CAIRN, POINT VICTORY, KING WILLIAM ISLAND, 11 JULY 1879

2246 Brass surgeon's tourniquet (Petit type). Maker: Millikin, London
2247 Oak block
2248 Four wooden buttons
2249 Five buckles
2250 Four wooden buttons
2251 Two horn buttons
2252 Two shell buttons
2253 Button (linen-covered iron ring)
2254 Brass button
2255 Fragment of a wooden box
2257 Part of a shovel
2259 Five bone buttons
2260 Clothes brush. Owner: Henry Wilkes (Royal Marines)
2261 Sledge harness marked 'T11' (HMS *Terror*)
2330 Telescope draw tube

CAPE MARIA LOUISA
(Inuit Cache)

2040 Three cut-down soup tins used as beakers, one may be a billy can
2258 Hip flask
2271 Wood and metal canteen
2272 Oak staves from a canteen
2273 Axe head with sawn-off shaft
2274-5 Two Goldner food cans
2276 Goldner soup can

2277 Tin flask
2278 Oak staves of a vinegar keg. Maker:
J Bagnall & Sons
2279 Copper plate

EREBUS BAY, KING WILLIAM ISLAND
(Found in an abandoned boat)

2280 Sheet lead
2281 Rope
2282 Keel of boat, with piece of
keel-stem and keelson attached. Marked
'XXIV [24 foot] W [Woolwich] CON
[contract] N61 Apr 184.'
2283 Two sledge runners (sledge under
the boat)
2284-5 Two bone combs
2286 Canvas bag of shot
2294 Two wire cartridges
2295 Lead musket ball
2349-50 Two wooden toggles
2374 Rope grommet
2597-8 Shot wrapped in paper
2319-21 Three boat's thimbles

WASHINGTON BAY, KING WILLIAM ISLAND

2306 Two fragments of the blade of an
oar

ADELAIDE PENINSULA

2302-4 Three fish hooks made from
expedition copper found in possession of
Inuit (RUSI 401)

STARVATION COVE, ADELAIDE
PENINSULAR

2296 Leather sea boot
2297 Foot part of boot
2300 Part of a mast hoop
2301 Yard hoop, marked with broad
arrow
2305 Heel of shoe
2307 Medal, launch of SS *Great Britain*
1843
2308 Part of sea boot

HAYES RIVER, MAY 1879

(Found in possession of Inuit)

2298 Seal spear? Made of salvaged copper
2331 Telescope eye piece cap
2332 Telescope, object glass cap

SHERMAN INLET, ADELAIDE PENINSULAR
(Found in possession of Inuit)

2299 Part of a block

Burwash Expedition 1926
(Ex Royal Naval Museum, Greenwich)

2309 Saw made from cask hoop
2310 Four fragments of fabric
2311 Part of a lantern?
2312 Fragment of wood
2313 Stone knife with wooden handle
2314-5 Two wooden bowls
2316 Leather fragment
2317 Leather fragment

Unprovenanced
(ex Royal Naval Museum)

2318 Timber fragment
2328 Dried meat
2334 Part of belaying pin
2335 Part of pocket compass. Maker:
Robinson, London
2336-8 Three dowels
2346 Axe handle
2354 Tin cylindar of shot
2375 Gun tampion
3948-9 Parts of snow goggles

(RUSI 405)

3953-4 Two hammers made from the
bones of polar bears?

(unknown origin)

2322 Horn whip handle, William Forder
2323 Iron chest handle
2324 Goldner soup can
2325 Shackle eyebolt?
2326 Ivory bottle top?
2327 Brass RN button. Maker: Boggett &
Reynolds, London

2329 Fragment of a block sheave

2339-43 Five bolts? With notches in the sides

2344 Record tin?

2345 Cap of record tin?

2348 Pen knife

2355 Two bone buttons

Unidentified objects

2356, 2358-2373, 2377-78, 3951

Gloves discovered by Sherard Osborn on Beechey Island in 1850.
(NMM. A6169)

Index

Page numbers in italic refer to illustrations